Coping with Calamity

Contemporary Chinese Studies

This series provides new scholarship and perspectives on modern and contemporary China, including China's contested borderlands and minority peoples; ongoing social, cultural, and political changes; and the varied histories that animate China today.

A list of titles in this series appears at the end of this book.

Coping with Calamity

Environmental Change and Peasant Response in Central China, 1736–1949

Jiayan Zhang

University of Hawai'i Press

HONOLULU

Printed in paperback in 2015 in the United States of America by
University of Hawai'i Press
2840 Kolowalu Street
Honolulu, HI 96822
www.uhpress.hawaii.edu

20 19 18 17 16 15   6 5 4 3 2 1

First published in Canada by
UBC Press
The University of British Columbia
2029 West Mall
Vancouver, BC V6T 1Z2
www.ubcpress.ca

Financial support from the Chiang Ching-kuo Foundation and Kennesaw State University is greatly appreciated.

Library of Congress Cataloging-in-Publication Data

Zhang, Jiayan, author.
Coping with calamity : environmental change and peasant response in rural China, 1736–1949 / Jiayan Zhang.
    pages cm
First published in Canada by UBC Press.
Includes bibliographical references and index.
ISBN 978-0-8248-4104-1 (pbk. : alk. paper)
1. Jianghan Region (China)—Environmental conditions—History.   2. Jianghan Region (China)—Economic conditions.   3. Floodplain management—China—Jianghan Region—History.   4. Agriculture—China—Jianghan Region—History.   5. Dikes (Engineering)—China—Jianghan Region—History.   6. Peasants—China—Jianghan Region—Economic conditions.   I. Title.
    DS793.H75Z468 2015
    333.709512'12—dc23

                                                                                    2014024569

University of Hawai'i Press books are printed on acid-free paper and meet the guidelines for permanence and durability of the Council on Library Resources.

Printed by Sheridan Books, Inc.

For my family.

Contents

Illustrations

Map

Figure

Acknowledgments

I owe my greatest intellectual debt and deepest thanks to Philip Huang and Kathryn Bernhardt for their guidance, motivation, support, and encouragement in the long and arduous process of writing and revision. Without their invaluable advice and insightful criticism, this book would not have taken its present form. Professor Huang tirelessly answered my countless questions. I am extremely lucky to have had him as my advisor. Ivan Berend, the late Kenneth Sokoloff, and particularly Yunxiang Yan, also generously offered advice and encouragement. They deserve my profound thanks.

   I would also like to express my gratitude to, among others, Norm Apter, Brian Demare, Thomas Dubois, Danny Hsu, Margaret Kuo, Fangchun Li, Jennifer Neighbours, Huey Bin Teng, Elizabeth VanderVen, Liu Yang, and particularly Lisa Tran, for their critiques of, and help with language in, draft chapters; to Joseph Esherick, and Mingfang Xia for their comments and help on draft chapters and chapter articles; and to Mark Elvin for the informal yet stimulating critique and suggestions he offered on several occasions. My special thanks go to Christopher Isset, who not only reviewed multiple draft chapters as well as the entire manuscript but also offered detailed comments and incisive critiques; and to Richard Gunde, who graciously offered his excellent editorial help to polish the revised manuscript and turn it into a book. All remaining errors are mine.

   I also want to take this opportunity to thank my colleagues in the Department of History and Philosophy at Kennesaw State University for their hospitality and support, particularly Tom Keene, who read an early version of the manuscript and provided practical suggestions. At UBC press, I want to thank Emily Andrew, my editor, for her enthusiasm, patience, encouragement, and help; and Megan Brand, for her guidance on style and related matters. I am also grateful to all three readers for their astute commentary, pointed critique, and useful suggestions; their comments and suggestions helped me sharpen some of my arguments and clarify the whole presentation.

For financial support, I would like to thank the Department of History, the Center for Chinese Studies, and the Institute of Asian Studies at UCLA for their funding support of my research. A Chiang Ching-kuo Foundation for International Scholarly Exchange (Junior Scholar Grants) and an Incentive Funding Awards for Scholarship of Kennesaw State University made it possible for me to focus on writing and to return to China to collect additional research materials in 2008. The Department of History and Philosophy at Kennesaw State University also supported two of my research trips to the Harvard-Yenching Library and two research trips to the UCLA East Asia Library. Other than these two libraries, over the long period of writing and revising, I also visited the Hoover Library of Stanford University, Nanjing Library, Shanghai Library, the National Library of China, Hubei Library, the Hubei Provincial Archives, and many other such institutions. I thank the staff in all these libraries and archives for their help. At this financially difficult time, the Chiang Ching-kuo Foundation, the Dean's Office of the College of Humanities and Social Sciences of Kennesaw State University, and the Office of the Vice-President for Research of Kennesaw State University provided a publication subvention. I sincerely appreciate their generosity.

Some of the materials in this book were published as articles in *Modern China* (32 [1]: 2006), *Late Imperial China* (27 [1]: 2006), *Chinese Historical Review* (16 [2]: 2009), and *Zhongguo jingjishi yanjiu* (1: 2011). I thank the publishers for permitting me to include them in this book.

Finally, I also want to thank my parents and siblings, who always supported me and helped me when I needed it; and my wife, Ningxia, whose unfailing emotional support made the lonely process of writing and revising more bearable.

Coping with Calamity

Introduction

An Environmental Approach

Rural China has undergone tremendous changes since the inception of economic reform in the late 1970s, evident in the remarkable growth of the non-agricultural sector and peasant income, the increasing use of modern scientific technologies (involving changes in crop varieties, the application of chemical fertilizers and pesticides, mechanization and electrification, etc.), the escalation of land productivity (higher yields), and the rapid expansion of rural industrialization and the urban employment of peasants *(nongmin gong)*. All these changes, however, have taken place at the cost of the rural environment, as seen in deforestation and desertification, the degradation of the quality of farmland, the depletion of underground aquifers, and environmental pollution. Some of these changes have become so serious that some villagers have deserted their land or left their communities for good. Since China is still home to about 900 million peasants (by registration), knowledge of the Chinese rural economy, rural environmental change, and peasant economic behaviour is essential to understanding how the country is being transformed.

In the past six decades, however, Chinese studies of pre-1949 rural China have been dominated by the class-relations (or class-struggle) paradigm, which was orthodoxy from the 1950s to 1970s, and by the market school, which has become ascendant since the early 1980s. According to the class-relations paradigm, which is based on Marxism and views the traditional rural economy as a feudal economy consisting mainly of an exploiting class (landlords and rich peasants) and an exploited class (peasants and agricultural labourers), China's countryside was filled with peasants driven to rebellion by oppression and exploitation. According to the market school, which is based on Adam Smith's classical notion of economics (division of labour and specialization) and elaborated by Theodore Schultz as a rational peasant theory in which peasants search for maximum profit in response to market incentives and opportunities (Schultz 1964; Smith 1976, 1:7-16), Chinese peasants have always been rational investors motivated by market incentives and profits. The first interpretation was obviously influenced by the revolutionary ideology of the Chinese Communist Party (CCP), and the second was shaped by the politics and economics of the post-Mao era. Although Chinese history contains both peasant rebellions and vigorous rural commercialization, the rebellious and profit-seeking constituted only a small proportion of all peasants: most were ordinary cultivators trying their best to adapt to the natural environment in order to survive.

Yet earlier Chinese-language studies on environmental change (mostly carried out by scientists or historical geographers) focused solely on alterations in the physical environment, including hydrological change affecting the Yellow River (Tan 1962), climate change in Chinese history (Zhu 1972), historical changes in the landscape, historical changes in the distribution of animals and vegetation, and historical changes in the agro-economic environment (e.g., Chen, Wang, and Yu 1989; Wu 1992; Wen 1995). Environmental history as a subject of study only appeared in China in the 1990s. Since then, some scholars have studied the relationship between economic development and ecological change in Southwest China and the relationship between the natural environment and social control in the Yangzi delta (Lan 1992; Feng 2002). Others have examined historical changes in the Chinese diet and in diseases (e.g., Wang 2000; Cao and Li 2006; Zhou 2007), which also can be considered a part of environmental history. And there is a new and vigorous trend among Chinese scholars today of grappling with the role of the environment in the large historical context of socio-economic changes.[1]

In Western-language studies of pre-1949 rural China and Chinese peasants, attention to environmental change emerged fairly early. Philip Huang, for example, devotes a separate chapter to the subject in each of his two books on rural China (Huang 1985, 53-66; Huang 1990, 21-43). He believes that, although studies of court politics, gentry ideology, and urban development may be able to ignore ecological relationships, "a rural social history needs to begin with a consideration of the interrelationships between the natural environment and the sociopolitical economy" (Huang 1985, 53). Huang's studies, of course, cannot be simply classified as environmental history, but they illustrate the growing tendency among Western scholars to consider the role of the environment in rural studies as well as in the socio-economic history of China in general. Elizabeth Perry (1980), for example, points out that the rise of the Red Spear Association in northern Anhui had close relations with the decay and uncertainty of local ecology. Joseph Esherick (1987), in another instance, argues that it was the ecological deterioration in North China that contributed to the economic decline of that area in the Ming-Qing era and planted the seeds for the Boxer Uprising. Others have examined various topics – such as water control, the state-peasant relationship, and land reclamation under different environmental settings – in Hunan, the Lower Yangzi region, and the Xiang Lake region of Zhejiang (Perdue 1987; Schoppa 1989; Osborne 1994). However, as in Lingnan, they all "experienced similar problems of land shortage, deforestation, upland erosion, and lowland flooding" in the eighteenth to nineteenth centuries (Marks 1998, 342).

This trend has become even clearer in studies influenced by theories of sustainable development, environmental protection, and economic globalization (Elvin 1993, 2004; Marks 1998; Mazumdar 1998; Isett 2007; Muscolino 2009). Some researchers have even taken the environment (ecology) to be the primary determinant of economic development. Both Kenneth Pomeranz and John Richards, for example, view the environment as a biological variable affecting the traditional Chinese rural economy. According to them, the environmental (ecological) crisis in late nineteenth-century China was a resource or energy crisis. More precisely, it was a crisis precipitated by a shortage of wood (as fuel and as a building material): for example, the peasants of Huang-Yun (on the North China Plain) had a difficult time finding the materials necessary to build dikes and dug out virtually the last blade of grass to fuel their cook stoves (Pomeranz 1993, 120-52), and China as a whole lacked wood for both industrial use and daily consumption (Richards 2003, 112-47).

Recently, proponents of economic globalization have focused their research on comparisons of Western Europe and East Asia – especially, England and the Yangzi delta (Wong 1997; Frank 1998; Pomeranz 2000; Marks 2002). From a Eurasian comparative perspective, Pomeranz constructs an argument that makes ecology a key factor in the development of the early modern economy of England. Agricultural products (particularly cotton) from the North American colonies, which eased the "ecological" pressure on England, and the easy accessibility of coal, he believes, were ecological advantages that were crucial in promoting England's modern economic growth and contributing to its divergence from an economic pattern like that found in the Yangzi delta (Pomeranz 2000).

To be sure, scholars who emphasize the role of the environment in their research by no means rely on a single approach. Some try to understand changes in the Chinese society and economy by adding the environment to a number of other factors being considered (Li 2007), while others make the environment the centrepiece of their research. But few examine the link between the environment and socio-economic change from the viewpoint of peasants or agricultural production. In studying the development of a pre-industrial rural economy, however, and especially of traditional agriculture, the natural environment cannot be treated simply as a biological variable or an independent physical entity: the changes it undergoes cannot be separated from related socio-economic structures and human activities, particularly peasant activities.

In this book, I explore the central role of the interactive relationship between environmental changes and peasant responses to these changes in rural China, and I investigate how this relationship unfolded during the Qing and the Republican periods. The focus of my investigation is the Jianghan Plain, a typical alluvial plain (about the size of the Netherlands) in the Hubei basin, Central China. In the Qing dynasty (1644-1911) and the Republic of China (1912-49), dikes were a necessary and crucial means of protecting farmland from annual high water. As the population grew – which it did throughout these centuries – more and more lakefront wasteland was reclaimed, and more and more dikes were built. But the dike building could not keep up with the incessant demand for more land, with the result that water calamities became increasingly frequent and the local environment suffered greater and greater alteration. In fact, ironically, the dike building itself contributed to the assault on the environment. Environmental change, in turn, influenced peasant behaviour by forcing them to adapt their agricultural practices to their altered environment and, thereby, played a decisive role in the formation and transformation of the local economy and society.

I therefore propose an environmental approach that takes into account not only environmental change and population increase but also state policies, community action, market forces, and peasant behaviour; that considers the interactive relationship between environment and human action and takes into account human-environment interaction not only synchronically but also diachronically, addressing dynamic change over time. I pay special attention to peasant behaviour but by no means suggest that peasants are responsible for all environmental change; rather, I emphasize how they contributed to it, how they reacted to the changed and changing environment, and, finally, how those changes, in turn, influenced their behaviour.

The Jianghan Plain

The environmental history of China is still an understudied field, but an increasing number of scholars are working on it. In his newest book, Robert Marks (2012) provides a comprehensive survey of Chinese history from an environmental perspective – based mostly on English-language scholarship.

For the purpose of this book, I want to particularly mention three Chinese anthologies.

Examining climate, land reclamation, disease, and government responses to, and elite attitudes towards, environmental changes in areas as diverse as South China, the Yangzi River valley, Tibet, and Taiwan, a group of (mostly Western) scholars has contributed to an anthology that comprehensively surveys Chinese environmental history (Liu and Elvin 1995).[2] As the title of the book – *Sediments of Time: Environment and Society in Chinese History* – suggests, the essays place the environment within a large social context in order to examine the interaction of human social systems and the natural world. In another anthology, specifically focusing on the role of natural disasters in North China, the Yangzi delta, and the middle Yangzi valley, a second group of scholars (all but one Chinese) focuses on Chinese environmental history, similarly putting natural disasters into their social context (Fudan daxue lishi dili yanjiu zhongxin 2001). A third anthology also examines environmental change in Chinese history from a broad social perspective – it actually has a title very similar to that of the Liu and Elvin volume – *Zhongguo lishi shang de huanjing yu shehui (Environment and Society in Chinese History)* (Wang 2007). The method applied in these three anthologies is very close to my environmental approach, but none of these works offers systematic research or a focused historical investigation into a particular area with sustained attention to peasant responses to the environment. Given the great diversity of the Chinese natural environment and its related socio-economic conditions, such systematic elaboration, based on a detailed examination of a particular area in a specific historical period, is necessary in order to gain an understanding of the interaction of human society with the natural world.

The Jianghan Plain, an area with severe hydraulic problems, is one of the best sites for exploring such interactive relationships. First, because of the plain's geographical position in the middle Yangzi River valley and its "opening" in late imperial times, studying it involves topics such as immigration; the growth of grain and non-grain cash crops; the enclosure of *yuan* (land encircled by dikes [see the definition and description in Chapter 1]);[3] the trade in grains, cotton, and cotton cloth; fisheries; environmental change; and damage caused by water calamities.

Second, compared to the North China Plain and the Yangzi delta, the relatively "late" development of the Jianghan Plain allows us to see some clear historical continuities into the present. Many characteristics of earlier periods – such as the water-rich environment, the importance of both paddy fields and dry land, the conflict between water and humans, and the importance of the dike systems – remain relevant today. Thus, studying the agrarian history of the Jianghan Plain during the Qing and the Republic from an environmental approach can help us to understand its present rural economy. Furthermore, although the Jianghan Plain is one of the most important agricultural areas of China, its historical development has received far less academic attention than has that of the Yangzi delta and the North China Plain.

Up to now, Chinese and Western scholarship on rural China has dealt primarily with the North China Plain and the Yangzi delta. That is understandable because of the richness of the sources available on those areas, from a range of gazetteers (down even to the town level in the Yangzi delta) and archival records of everyday village disputes (e.g., the Huailu Archives) to modern anthropological surveys (such as the Mantetsu [The South Manchuria Railway Company] surveys of the 1930s).[4] In recent decades, the Pearl River delta and the larger Lingnan region has also attracted increasing academic attention among scholars. But, geographically speaking, the North China Plain, the Yangzi delta, and the Pearl River delta constitute only a small part of China, and other regions contain completely different ecosystems. One part of China cannot be taken as representative of the whole country.[5] To take an environmental approach to the differences in the traditional rural economy in various areas and to the changes that have occurred, we must understand the regional environments and the interactive relationships between socio-economic conditions and the environments within those regions.

For the sake of convenience, researchers on China usually focus on one or two provinces. But provinces are administrative creations, encompassing multiple ecosystems; thus, a province-wide study may conceal important environmental differences between, say, plains and mountains. For example, the population-to-cultivated-land ratios in both the plain and mountainous areas of Huguang (Hunan Province and Hubei Province) apparently declined in late imperial times. But that decline was expressed and experienced in very different ways in those two areas (Gong 1993a, 1993c; Zhang Jianmin 1994) and would have had different meanings for the plain and mountain residents because of their different levels of agricultural production and living standards. Anyone who has visited the remote mountains of western Hunan and western Hubei is aware of the harsh environment and poverty that the local people still face. For those mountain peasants, whose staple foods are corn (maize) and potatoes, the plain peasants, whose staple food is rice, appear to be living in paradise, while peasants on the plain are eager to leave what they consider their poor and backward area and move to towns, cities, and coastal areas. Even the plain itself has diverse natural environments – dryland areas, paddy field areas, lake areas, and hilly land – whose differences are reflected in the varied levels and modes of agricultural production, living standards, and social organization of the local people. I make frequent reference to such differences throughout this study.

I also have some personal reasons for choosing the Jianghan Plain as the site of a case study, all connected with my own experiences. In this context, the "personal" is also the academic, for researchers working in regional or local studies should have some practical understanding of the area on which they focus. Since I was born in a village in the Jianghan Plain and was educated there (from elementary school to college) and have visited almost every county in the area, I am familiar with its physical environment and rural society. Moreover, I sometimes worked on farms on the plain, from the time I was in the third grade until after I finished graduate school (from the early 1970s to the early 1990s); thus, I have first-hand knowledge of agricultural production in this area. And because I was trained in agronomy in college and worked after graduation with peasants for three years as a local agro-technician, I understand agriculture and peasants from a technical as well as a practical angle, a combination that is particularly helpful in an environment-based research project that incorporates geography, climatology, agronomy, and epidemiology. My personal experience and technical training always warn me to draw arguments *from* empirical evidence, not to impose arguments on it.

Research in the Jianghan Plain

In comparison to the voluminous literature on the North China Plain and the Yangzi delta, scholarship on the middle Yangzi River valley, especially the Jianghan Plain, is relatively sparse. The methods of production and the life-styles of the people in this "marshy kingdom" still remain mostly unknown. Some works in Chinese, such as publications that appeared during the Republic by Zhong Xin (1936) and Sun Fushi (1939), address the middle Yangzi River plain from the angle of hydraulic technology. But these writings deal briefly and simply with water control for the entire Yangzi River valley, devoting just a few pages to the Jianghan Plain. Nevertheless, their making water control in this area a subject of analysis is a significant achievement since the altered relation between rivers and lakes and the growth of the dike systems are the most important environmental changes of the Jianghan Plain in the past several centuries.

Japanese scholars have long researched and published numerous works on water control in Chinese history,[6] but few have shown interest in Central

China. An exception is Morita Akira, whose comprehensive study of water conservancy in the middle Yangzi River plain in the Qing examines the development of the dike systems and irrigation in Hunan and Hubei (Morita 1960, 1974). The most notable of the few existing English-language publications that deal specifically with hydraulic issues in the Jianghan Plain during the Qing are those by Liu Ts'ui-jung (1970) and Pierre-Etienne Will (1985). Liu's study, based on a reading of one part of a late Qing gazetteer, offers a general description of dike construction in Jingzhou (which lies in the Jianghan Plain), in which she makes it clear that, in the late Qing, dike management was supervised by local officials but carried out by the local people. Will (1985) discusses the role of the state apparatus in construction and in administrating hydraulic installations in the Hubei basin (i.e., the Jianghan Plain) during the Qing. He argues that, in the early Qing, the state still functioned as a mediator in local conflicts over water control; however, in the middle and late Qing, as environmental degradation caused by flooding increased, and as the conflicts between the state and local society grew, the state was overcome by these difficulties and finally withdrew from water control.

These pioneering studies have contributed a great deal to our understanding of dike management in the Jianghan Plain. However, they do not cover broader socio-economic issues that relate to the dike systems in the Jianghan Plain, such as migration, agricultural growth, rural commercialization, and environmental change.

Since the 1980s, historians in China have begun to extensively explore the development of the Jianghan Plain in the Ming-Qing period. Their research is based on more detailed, first-hand source materials and covers a wide range of subjects overlooked by non-Chinese scholarship. The various topics they study include the relationships between the dike systems and frequent inundation, between land reclamation and agricultural growth, and between population pressure and environmental deterioration.

According to these scholars, the broad "opening" of the Jianghan Plain began in the Ming and was primarily characterized by the construction of dikes to reclaim wasteland from lakefronts and marshes, which subsequently led to increased production of cotton and, especially, rice. As early as the late Ming (the mid-sixteenth century), the Jianghan Plain had become a new centre of rice production. Together with the Lake Dongting Plain (which surrounds Lake Dongting *[Dongting hu]*, China's second largest freshwater lake), it replaced the Yangzi delta as the most important rice exporter during the early Qing. In the late Qing, however, the economic situation of Hubei Plain declined. Instead of being a rice exporter, it became a rice importer; it no longer absorbed immigrants but generated emigrants. This dramatic change was precipitated by population increase and frequent floods (or breaks in the dike systems). According to these Chinese scholars, the major reasons for the frequent inundation include soil erosion on the upstream mountains, which caused silt to build up in the middle Yangzi River valley and the lower Han River valley; the never-ending enclosure of *yuan* in the Jianghan Plain, which shrank the flood discharge area; and the incompetence of the Qing government with regard to dike management (viz., corruption and lack of cooperation). The first two reasons were, in one way or another, consequences of population pressure (e.g., Zhang Jianmin 1984, 1987a, 1999; Tan 1985; Zhang Guoxiong 1989, 1994a, 1995; Zhang Jiayan 1992b; Peng and Zhang 1993; Mei, Zhang, and Yan 1995; Gong 1996; Yang and Chen 2008; Yin 2008).

Although their studies point out how over-reclamation, which led to environmental deterioration and eventually to economic decline under population pressure, affected the Jianghan economy, they emphasize changes in the physical environment and its impact on agriculture. In so doing, they pay little attention to some important interactive relationships between human beings and the environment. For example, their simplified model largely overlooks the relationships between the state and local society, environment and management, environmental change and market change, peasant choices under changing environmental and market conditions, and the effects of all these relationships on the rural economy and society. They also do not sufficiently consider tenancy relationships and fisheries, two topics that are important to understanding the rural economy of the Jianghan Plain. Moreover, they do not pay sufficient attention to the behaviour of the peasants themselves, although, as I demonstrate, the response of the peasants to socio-economic and environmental change is a key factor in the socio-economic-cum-environmental relationship.[7] Finally, and perhaps most important, because they mostly focus on the Jianghan Plain or Hunan-Hubei area, their scholarship does not make clear the significance of the history of this region to understanding the history of rural China generally. In this book, I explore each of these subjects.

A Larger Context

The Jianghan Plain, located in the middle of the Yangzi River valley, is a part of the Hunan-Hubei Plain. Another important part of the Hunan-Hubei Plain is the Lake Dongting Plain. Peter Perdue's research on Hunan is by far the most comprehensive to date. His is also so far the only study in English of the socio-economic changes in Hunan in the Ming-Qing era. Emphasizing state-peasant relations, Perdue (1987) discusses the processes involved in population growth, the increased area covered by *yuan,* agricultural growth, and environmental deterioration in Hunan, particularly in the Lake Dongting Plain, from the mid-Ming to the mid-nineteenth century.

Although all of these processes also occurred in the Jianghan Plain during the same time, and both plains are located in the middle Yangzi River valley, they have some major differences. The primary dikes in the Lake Dongting area are *yuan* dikes, while both *yuan* dikes and river dikes are important in the Jianghan area; the "opening" of the Lake Dongting Plain came later than that of the Jianghan Plain, with a new tide of reclamation occurring as late as the early twentieth century; and the major crop in the Lake Dongting area is rice, while both rice and dryland crops are important in the Jianghan Plain.

There are also some differences between Perdue's research and mine. First, Perdue's research covers the whole of Hunan Province, including not only the Lake Dongting Plain but also some mountainous areas, while my research covers the Jianghan Plain and only occasionally refers to the surrounding mountainous regions. Second, in terms of time, his research encompasses the mid-Ming to the middle of the nineteenth century, while my research ranges from the early eighteenth century to 1949, particularly the late Qing and the Republican eras, when the area suffered the most frequent water calamities and the environment was largely unstable. Third, he focuses on the state's role in the development of agriculture, while I focus on the peasant response to a changing and vulnerable environment.

Like Perdue, Kenneth Pomeranz, in his research on the Huang-Yun area (a part of the North China Plain), examines the role played by the state in the development of agriculture. According to Pomeranz, the late Qing government intentionally "abandoned" Huang-Yun by shifting its focus from inland areas to coastal areas. The result was the decline of Huang-Yun since the withdrawal of government support (hence no more material support from the outside) had a negative impact on the local economy, such as a lack of fuel, the disrepair of water-control projects (particularly the Grand Canal dike), the deterioration of soil quality (because of a lack of fertilizers), and the reduction of agricultural productivity (Pomeranz 1993). In his research, Pomeranz intentionally focuses on the activities of the elite, while in my research, I concentrate on the activities of peasants.

Although Perdue argues that population growth and commercialization gradually transformed Hunan from an inland frontier into an agricultural core region of the empire in the Ming-Qing era, and Pomeranz explains how Huang-Yun changed from an economic core to an economic hinterland (or from a key area to a periphery) from the 1850s to the 1930s, both highlight the role of state and water-control projects in the traditional Chinese economy.

State and water-control projects played a very important role in the traditional Chinese economy and, indeed, in Chinese history as a whole. Chi Ch'ao-ting (1963 [1936]), for example, explores the importance of water-control projects (particularly irrigation and flood control projects built and maintained by the state) in the formation of key economic areas in different dynasties as well as how the control of these areas became the foundation for the unification of China. According to Dwight Perkins (1969), however, from 1368 to 1968, the return on investment in water-control projects such as irrigation and drainage was low.

Mark Elvin takes a different approach to the analysis of water-control projects in Chinese history. With an eye to environmental change and sustainable development, he argues that the traditional Chinese economy, from the first millennium BCE to the present, has undergone, as his title puts it, "three thousand years of unsustainable growth." As evidence, he points mainly to the harm done to the environment by mountain reclamation and forest clearance under population pressure, and the high cost of maintaining water-control projects, throughout Chinese history, particularly in the past several centuries (Elvin 1993). Elvin is right to point out that people had to carefully maintain water-control projects year after year at a considerable cost in both time and money. But if growth was unsustainable, how could it continue for three thousand years?

To state the obvious, China's history is long and its land is extensive. Undoubtedly, the reclamation of mountains and hillsides has done great harm to the environment throughout Chinese history, as Elvin argues, yet other truths need to be remembered: water-control projects in the mountains differed substantially from those in the plains, those in South China differed from those in North China, and, moreover, throughout Chinese history such projects undeniably contributed enormously to the economy (see, e.g., *Zhongguo shuili shigao* 3 1989; Yao 1987; Vermeer 1988; Wang and Zhang 1990). Given the importance of water-control projects – particularly the myriad dikes – in the Jianghan Plain in the past several centuries, the rise or fall of its economy has been directly related to the continued protection (or its lack) of the dike systems. Examining the story of the Jianghan Plain since the Qing dynasty thus provides a good means of testing the arguments of both Perkins and Elvin.

In discussing water control in Chinese history, we should not ignore Karl Wittfogel and his theory of oriental despotism. According to Wittfogel, water conservancy in ancient China was the main origin of so-called oriental despotism as agriculture relied on large-scale works that were maintained by a despotic and centralized bureaucratic system (Wittfogel 1957). Chinese agrarian historian Wang Yuhu (1981), however, argues that we should not ignore the differences between state-managed water conservancy projects (such as river management and large-scale irrigation works) and household-level irrigation works (such as irrigation channels, ponds, and weirs) and that a nationwide irrigation network never existed in China. In the Jianghan area, as we will see, the central government did not get involved in the management of most major dikes.

The Jianghan experience has additional significance in helping us understand the general history of China. A recent study, for example, argues that the best weather conditions in history in the middle and lower Yellow River valley contributed to the prosperity of the local Neolithic culture and eventually, late in the third millennium BCE, to the establishment of the first dynasty in Chinese history, the Xia (Wang Xingguang 2004). From the Later Han to the late Tang, when nomadic people controlled the middle reaches of the Yellow River and turned farmland into pasture, the Yellow River valley enjoyed a relatively stable period without suffering from frequent inundations; however, after the end of the Tang dynasty (618-907), these inundations returned once Han peasants resettled in the area and again began to farm it (Tan 1962). Similarly, according to Lan Yong (2001), the introduction and spread of New World crops in Southwest China, in many respects a notable achievement, in fact contributed to the region's environmental degeneration and "structural poverty."

The environment, needless to say, shapes how peasants engage in agriculture. In the frequently flooded regions of North China, for example, fear of flooding such as had been experienced in the past dissuaded some peasants living along the Yellow River in Chang'an in the Republic from applying fertilizer to their land (Xia 2000, 219-20). In the Jianghan Plain in the mid-nineteenth century, one break of the Han River dike was not blocked owing to a war, and it continued to overflow other places for eight years. As a result, the residents of Mianyang (now released from possible inundation) did not raise their dikes as they should have done (*Xiangdi cheng'an* 1969, 2: 20ab). Such choices had nothing to do with class exploitation and price fluctuations but, instead, represent some of the simplest forms of environmental adaptation.

Thus the Jianghan experience can also help us to understand some larger and more general questions regarding the history of rural China, particularly when we compare it with the North China Plain and the Yangzi delta. Because of China's range of natural conditions and the different agricultural systems that they support, Chinese traditional agriculture is usually divided into two general patterns: the northern pattern, which focuses on dryland farming (in recent centuries, more accurately, wheat-maize farming), and the southern pattern, which focuses on paddy field farming (mainly rice cultivation). This distinction has fundamentally shaped our understanding of the Chinese rural economy. Scholars, particularly Western scholars, have tended to focus on the rural economy of the North China Plain, which is representative of the northern pattern, and the Yangzi delta, which is representative of the southern pattern. In fact, most influential English-language studies on the Chinese rural economy thus far have drawn their conclusions from investigations of these two areas. And they have dominated the Western image of rural China.

Of course, the North China Plain pattern and the Yangzi delta pattern are not the only two forms of rural economy in China. The rural economies of Northeast China, Northwest China, Southwest China, Central China, and South China (or Lingnan) all have their own distinctive characteristics. In this study, undertaken from an environmental perspective, I present a different pattern – the Jianghan pattern. In some respects, the Jianghan pattern has much in common with the North China Plain pattern and the Yangzi delta pattern, but in many others it diverged from them during the Qing and the Republic.

From an environmental perspective, the Jianghan experience can also, in many ways, help us to understand China's environmental history. As Robert Marks (2012, 332-37) highlights in his recent book, land utilization, climatic change, water control, deforestation and land reclamation, the simplification of ecosystems, and agricultural sustainability are some of the main themes in China's environmental history. Throughout this book, I show that the Jianghan experience touches on almost all of these topics.

A study of the environmental history of the Jianghan Plain can tell us not only how environmental conditions in this region have changed over the past three centuries but also how the state, rural communities, and peasants have responded to those changes. It can reveal the relationships between the state and local society, between population growth and environmental change, between environmental disaster and environmental management, and between environmental change and economic change. In short, such a study can tell us about the interrelationships among population increase, economic growth, environmental change, state policies, community action, and peasant behaviour. Uncovering these interrelationships, I believe, will contribute to our understanding of environmental change in China and China's rural history and, indeed, to a more comprehensive interpretation of the history of China in general.

Source Materials and Research Structure

I draw on three basic sets of sources. First are local gazetteers, both the traditional gazetteers compiled in the Qing and the Republic and the new gazetteers compiled after 1949. The traditional gazetteers hold rich local economic information on late imperial times that cannot be obtained anywhere else. In the absence of agricultural treatises and farming diaries, they are the most accessible sources for analyzing the rural economy. In addition, since the 1980s thousands of volumes of newly compiled gazetteers have been published in China, but previous researchers have rarely used them systematically. The Chinese government, at different levels, expended much time and effort to compile these gazetteers; thus, their data are relatively comprehensive and undoubtedly useful. To be sure, they contain obvious ideological biases, but the basic economic information in which I am interested (such as cropping patterns, number of *yuan*, and the water-to-land ratio) is rarely affected by ideology. In fact, I find that the new gazetteers quote many pre-1949 surveys, though the data are presented differently.

My second set of source materials are the memorials written by high-ranking officials in charge of Hubei Province and reports written by local officials in charge of counties (or prefectures or departments) during the Qing (all translations from these memorials are my own). Because they wrote these memorials to report what they saw to the emperor, they by and large avoided exaggerations or omissions (such problems can be found by double-checking different memorials written by two or more officials who had different opinions on the same issue) and, therefore, should be reasonably accurate. Some of those that focused on water control offer a highly detailed description of selected cases as writing such memorials required on-the-spot personal investigation. Many of these famous memorials and reports referring to specific cases that occurred along the Han River valley were selected and compiled by local officials in *Records on the Han River Dikes (Xiangdi cheng'an)*. Memorials about other cases along both the Yangzi River and the Han River were collected in a series entitled *The Golden Guidance of Inland Navigation (Xu xingshui jinjian, Zai xu xingshui jinjian),* and more regular memorials regarding water calamities were collected in a huge volume of archival data entitled *Archival Materials on Flooding and Waterlogging of the Yangzi River and the International Rivers in Southwestern China in the Qing Dynasty (Qingdai Changjiang liuyu xi'nan guoji heliu honglao dang'an shiliao).* Although these memorials contain many vivid descriptions of how the local people made their decisions as their environmental situation changed,[8] most have been neglected in past studies of the Jianghan Plain.

The third set of source materials I use consists of modern surveys. Research on the Ming-Qing agrarian economy of the Jianghan Plain is facilitated, in part, by its late "opening" in the Ming-Qing era. Since the Jianghan Plain lacks detailed modern anthropological surveys like those undertaken by Mantetsu on the Yangzi delta and the North China Plain, I instead rely on county-based Republican surveys. The detailed contemporary surveys in agriculture, geography, water control, and demography also offer a baseline that aids in tracing the historical development of the Jianghan Plain before 1949.[9] In addition to this, I used some archival materials of the Republican era and the early stage of the People's Republic of China (PRC), which have only recently caught the attention of researchers.

Before writing this book, I had already published a series of empirical studies (in Chinese) on the agrarian history of the Jianghan Plain in the Ming-Qing era, in which I argue that immigrants played an important role in the population increase and that they were also the primary reclaimers of land from lakesides and marshes. Such reclamation was the main means by which cultivated land in the Jianghan Plain was increased. Furthermore, as the area of land under cultivation – primarily rice – increased, as one would expect, total output also increased, making it possible for the Jianghan Plain to become an important exporter of rice. An increase in grain production was clearly paralleled by an expansion in the cultivation of non-grain cash crops such as cotton. As the production of rice and cotton grew and greater volumes were exported, trade in local commodities developed and rural towns flourished. But, unlike the Yangzi delta, the Jianghan Plain did not undergo a transformation from a rice-centred rural economy into one focused on cotton production and the domestic textile industry (Zhang Jiayan 1991, 1992a, 1992b, 1995, 1996). This book goes further than those preliminary discussions of the rural economy, examining environmental change, dike systems, agricultural production, the structure of the rural economy, tenancy relationships, fisheries, the characteristics of a water-rich society, and, particularly, peasant responses in order to elaborate the interactive relationships between environment and people in the Jianghan Plain in the Qing and the Republic.

The rest of the book is divided into seven chapters, plus a conclusion. Chapter 1 outlines the environment of the Jianghan Plain and the tremendous changes it underwent in the course of history, particularly from the Ming dynasty onward. The most important changes include alterations in the relationship between rivers and lakes, the proliferation of dikes, and the increasing number of water calamities.

Chapter 2 discusses water calamities and the dike systems. It examines the relationship between frequent inundation and dike management in the Jianghan Plain and pays particular attention to the local people, who were in fact responsible for the maintenance of most dikes. It shows how the worsening conditions of the dike systems in the Jianghan Plain led to more conflicts (and less cooperation) over water control, and it demonstrates how these conflicts contributed to the frequency and severity of water calamities.

Chapter 3 looks at the relationship of the dike systems and the rural economy in the Jianghan Plain. On the one hand, dikes were the basic means of protecting the local economy; on the other hand, their extensive construction had side effects that harmed local agriculture, and the local people had to spend huge amounts of time, capital, and materials to maintain them. Drawing on post-1949 data, I offer a contemporary interpretation of the heavy monetary burden of dike fees in the Qing and the Republic, explaining how and why such fees were imposed and their effect on the local economy and on the question of whether or not agriculture in the Jianghan Plain was sustainable.

Chapter 4 investigates the diverse crop choice in an unstable environment. By analyzing both the biological features of the varieties of crop planted and the characteristics of cropping systems in the Jianghan Plain since the Qing, I examine how the important consideration of environmental adaptability shaped peasant choices. I also explore villagers' reactions to the environmental changes caused by frequent flooding and extensive dike construction in the Jianghan Plain – specifically, how they contended with the worsening problem of waterlogging. I argue that, under these circumstances, environmental factors outweighed market factors in influencing economic change and peasant responses.

Chapter 5 demonstrates the ways in which the unstable environment had a direct and important effect on how the relations of agricultural production – particularly land distribution and tenancy relationships – were formed and evolved in the Jianghan Plain in the Qing and the Republic. I conclude that the relations of agricultural production were not simply "feudal" and therefore expressed in the form of class exploitation. In other words, landlord-tenant relations were not simply shaped by economic factors; rather, they were very much shaped by the local environment.

Chapter 6 considers the relative importance of fisheries in the rural economy of the Jianghan Plain. I show that fishing was in fact more important than the domestic cotton textile industry in the non-farming production of rural households living along rivers and near lakes, and I point out how the structure of the rural economy of the Jianghan Plain differed from that of traditional China. I also discuss why and how some peasants were involved in fishing, and how their lifestyle differed from that of other peasants.

Chapter 7 explores the impact of frequent water calamities on local society and economy, the cultivation of famine-relief crops and the growth/collection of aquatic products as substitute foods, the daily life of the local people in a "marshy kingdom," and the deterioration of human relations and the socio-political features of *yuan*. During the long-term struggle against water and for land reclamation, the Jianghan people constantly adapted to and modified their environment and, finally, formed a unique dike-*yuan* society. Almost every aspect of their daily life was affected by their water-rich environment and the dike systems.

Though all these chapters, with the exception of Chapter 1, can be read as self-contained essays, they also fall into three thematic clusters: environment and management (Chapters 2 and 3); peasant economic choice within a changing environment (Chapter 4); and tenancy, fisheries, and socio-economic life in a water-rich environment (Chapters 5, 6, and 7). Overall, I argue for the importance of examining the changes in interactive relationships between human beings and the natural world.

1 Changes in the Environment of the Jianghan Plain

The natural environment in which people live can hardly be described as "natural": our environment is at least partly human-made. This is especially true for the Jianghan Plain. In the past few centuries, in addition to farming, the primary human activity in the Jianghan Plain has been dike construction and *yuan* enclosure, both of which have fundamentally changed the plain's original physical environment (particularly the water system) and have had a wide and profound impact on agricultural production and on the lives of the local people. This chapter gives an overview of the physical environment of the Jianghan Plain and some of the major changes it underwent in the course of history, particularly in the past four centuries, and the effects of such changes on the local economy and society.

Physiographic Features of the Jianghan Plain

The Jianghan Plain, as noted in the Introduction, is located in the middle Yangzi River valley in the central basin of Hubei Province. It lies between the Yangzi River (*Changjiang, Jiang* for short) and its largest tributary, the Han River (*Hanshui* or *Hanjiang, Han* for short), which joins the Yangzi in Hankou.

Historically speaking, the Jianghan Plain *(Jianghan pingyuan)* roughly encompasses what, in the late Qing, were the prefectures of Jingzhou (excluding Yidu),[1] Hanyang (excluding Huangpi), and Anlu; the department of Jingmen (excluding Yuan'an); the counties of Yunmeng and Yingcheng in the prefecture of De'an, and the county of Jiangxia in the prefecture of Wuchang. Throughout, the names of all counties, departments, and prefectures are those used during the Qing and the Republic (except for Honghu, which was established as a county in 1951; and Jiangxia County, which was renamed Wuchang County in 1912) as they have been frequently changed since 1949. It covers about 45,865 square kilometres (reckoned according to the area of each county given in the *Hubei sheng ditu ce* 2000 [1998]) (Map 1).

In terms of climate, the Jianghan Plain belongs to the north subtropical zone. It is warm and moist, and rich in water and sunlight. The annual average temperature of Jingzhou District,[2] for example, ranged from 15.9 to 16.6

Map 1

The Jianghan Plain of Hubei, c. 1820

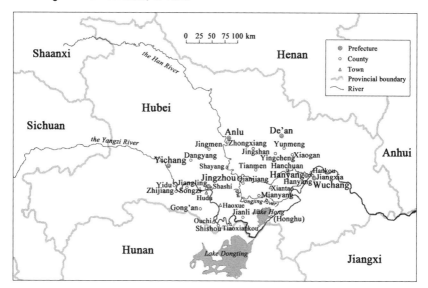

Source: Tan 1996 [1987], 35-36.

degrees Centigrade (60.62 to 61.88 degrees Fahrenheit), high in the summer and low in the winter, in the late twentieth century. The frost-free period ranges from 245 to 265 days, with two thousand hours of sunshine per year on average. The average annual rainfall ranges from eleven hundred to thirteen hundred millimetres (19.4 to 51.2 inches), and 70 percent of the rainfall comes during the main crop-growing period (April to September). This kind of climate is favourable for the growth of rice and cotton, the two major crops in the Jianghan Plain (Wang 1989, 18; *Hubei sheng zhi dili* 1997, 1151).

According to modern research, in the long process of geological change there was a slowly counter-directional movement between the continual rise of the periphery of the Jianghan Plain and a large-scale descent of its centre, and a concomitant emergence of a slightly north-to-south slope. As a result, the plain slopes from northwest to southeast, with an altitude of thirty-five metres (1 metre = 3.28 feet) or so in the northwest and fewer than twenty-five metres in the southeast (*Hubei sheng zhi dili* 1997, 278, 1149).

Thousands of years ago, the Jianghan Plain was a famous, huge marsh known as the Yunmeng Marsh *(Yunmeng ze),* but it gradually shrank as the Yangzi and the Han Rivers deposited silt in it that formed innumerable islands of various sizes. Before the Song dynasty (960-1279), the marsh had been replaced by a fluvial area studded with lots of lakes and small marshes.

Figure 1

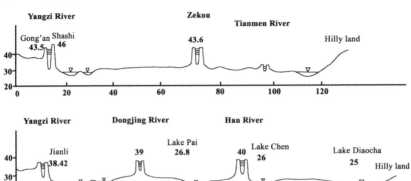

Typical topographical cross-section of the Jianghan Plain

Source: Hubei nongye dili 1980: 80 [Distance: Kilometres, altitude: metres].

Hence the Jianghan Plain is formed by the alluvial soils of the Yangzi and the Han Rivers as well as by the sludge of the lakes (*Jingjiang dadi zhi* 1989, 15-16; *Hubei sheng zhi dili* 1997, 278).

With long-term silting, the land along the rivers gradually ascended and formed four long but narrow depressions between the Yangzi River, the Han River and some of their tributaries (*Hubei sheng zhi dili* 1997, 1150). The triangular area between these two rivers – that is, the so called four-lake area – is particularly low: in the 1970s, 80 percent of its land was six to ten metres lower than the water level of the surrounding rivers (*Hubei nongye dili* 1980, 53). Thus, in Jingzhou District in the 1980s, about two-thirds of the population lived below the water level during the annual high-water seasons (usually from June to September) (Figure 1) (*Jingzhou diqu zhi* 1996, 123).

Such an uneven landscape affected the cropping pattern in Jingzhou. In the 1980s, there were about 5.5 million *mu* (1 *mu* = one-sixth of an acre, or 667 square metres) of relatively high land along the banks of the Yangzi River, the Han River, and the Dongjing River (a tributary of the Han River and the third largest river in the Jianghan Plain since the late Qing). This is dry land and good for dryland crops such as cotton. There were about 5 million *mu* of low-lying wet flatland in the depressions located between the rivers. The majority of this land is good for rice production and was devoted to paddy fields. There were 13 million *mu* of middle flatland between the highland and the depressions. This land is easily drained and irrigated and is good for both rice and dryland crops. There were also about 1.67 million *mu* of river beach located outside the major dikes and suitable for growth of dryland crops (Wang 1989, 4-5).[3] The majority of arable land in the Jianghan Plain consists of alluvial soil high in natural fertility and rich in effective nutrients, while the land reclaimed from the lakefront wasteland has a thick layer of topsoil with high fertility (*Hubei nongye dili* 1980, 22-24, 81-82).

It was the long-term silting up of fluvial soil in the course of the history of the Jianghan Plain that led to the formation of its basic physiographic features. And it was this relatively rich fluvial soil that provided the foundation for an environment conducive to farming.

Changing River-Lake Relationship

Historical Geography of the Water System in the Jianghan Plain

In ancient times, there was no clear dividing line between rivers and lakes in the Jianghan Plain. From about the time of the Spring and Autumn Period (770-476 BCE) to the Western Han (206 BCE-24 CE), the inland delta enlarged and the lakes shrank due to the long-term deposit of river silt. Rivers and lakes in the Jianghan Plain began to separate from each other, and the main course of the Jing River formed. The Jing River *(Jingjiang)* is the name of one section of the Yangzi (in the Jianghan Plain) from Zhicheng to Chengling ji (roughly from Zhijiang to lower Jianli on Map 1). Some tributary rivers also appeared in this period. Some of them converged into the Yangzi, while others converged into the Han and then converged into the Yangzi. The result was a pattern of netlike waterways in the Jianghan Plain. The climate during the period from the first century to the sixth century became cooler. This was favourable for land reclamation, and the size of lakes in the Jianghan Plain shrank further. The climate turned warmer during the period from the Sui (581-618) to the Southern Song (1127-1279), and the water volume of the Yangzi River increased. Though the lakes to the north of the Jing River were reduced in size, those to its south grew larger. Lake Dongting became larger and the so-called "800 *li* wide Dongting" (1 *li* = 0.5 km) was mentioned in Tang dynasty poems. There were many branch waterways that connected rivers and lakes in the Jianghan Plain, and, as late as the Song dynasty, the Jing River still had many outlets that discharged high water. From the Southern Song to the late Qing the course of the Yangzi and the Han Rivers changed due to the closing of many outlets, the reclamation of lakefront land, and dike construction. First, many river branches (outlets) – essentially, all but some of the larger ones – of both the Yangzi and the Han Rivers vanished.

By the end of the Qing, only four southward outlets remained. Second, the riverbeds narrowed and meandered and an increasing number of sandbars in the middle of the riverbeds merged and became larger (Zhongguo kexueyuan dili yanjiusuo et al. 1985, 64-68).

Although in general the course of the Yangzi River is much more stable than that of the Yellow River, it changed from time to time. Even more unstable was the course of the Jing River. Nowadays the Jing River course is 349 kilometres long, but it is only 182.1 kilometres or so as the crow flies. The meander of the river course of the lower Jing River is even bigger than that of the upper Jing River: it is 240 kilometres long but only eighty kilometres as the crow flies. This earned the Jing River the title of "nine-meanders-ileum" (*jiu qu hui chang*). On average, the width of the lower Jing River course is only one thousand metres. This is not good for the flow of seasonal high water and causes swings in the river's course. Historical records show that, during the past two centuries, the range of the swings of the Jing River course could be up to thirty kilometres. Changes in the course of the Jing River occurred even more frequently after 1860 (*Hubei sheng zhi dili* 1997, 519-21; *Jingjiang dadi zhi* 1989, 17-26). These changes in the course of the Jing River, plus human activities (reclamation and enclosure), brought a great geographical change to the Jianghan Plain: the water system became extremely disordered. Though the size of the lakes in the Jianghan Plain shrank, their number increased (Guan 1983, 35).

Despite the extensive dike system, before 1949, the rivers – the Yangzi, the Han, and the Dongjing – and the lakes in the Jianghan Plain were not completely separated from each other. Thus, in the high-water seasons, it was easy for river water to flow back into the lakes. This destroyed many dikes and *yuan*, particularly in the lower Han River valley. The free connection of rivers and lakes also had a great impact on the rise and fall of the water level of lakes. Before the 1950s, the water level of Jianghan's lakes was mainly determined by the water level of the Yangzi and the Han Rivers, varying by one to two metres over the year (by three to four or more metres for medium-sized and large lakes) (*Hubei sheng zhi dili* 1997, 588-89). The size of a lake therefore could vary dramatically in different years. The size of Lake Hong, for example, was only six to seven hundred square kilometres in normal years, but it was seven thousand or more square kilometres in 1954 (Hua 1974, 14). Once the water level of lakes rose, the surrounding *yuan* would be inundated. Thus, the river dikes did not necessarily protect the lakeside *yuan* from annual high water. Although the *yuan* dikes could usually (although not always) defend against annual high water outside their boundaries, they could not protect the land within *yuan* from the rising lake water, particularly where the water could not easily drain. Moreover, most *yuan* dikes could not protect *yuan* from floods caused by a rupture of river dikes. According to a source from the 1990s, during the annual high-water seasons, three-quarters of the farmland of Jingzhou District lay below the river's water level and therefore was directly or indirectly affected by seasonal high water (*Jingzhou diqu zhi* 1996, 123).

Such long-term changes paralleled the constant rise of the high water level of the Jing River. In the past five thousand years the level of the Jing River has risen 13.6 metres. From Neolithic times to the Han dynasty, the rise was smooth and slow, at only 0.0087 centimetres per year on average. From the Han to the Song, it also rose slowly, at an annual rate of 0.164 centimetres. After the Song-Yuan transition in the late thirteenth century, however, it rose very dramatically, at an annual rate of 1.39 centimetres. Though the reasons for this were related to such natural factors as the deposit of river silt, the most important reason had to do with human activity, particularly dike construction and *yuan* enclosure. After the final formation of four southward outlets on the Jing River in the late Qing the shrinkage of Lake Dongting became one of the primary reasons for the rise of the high water level of the Jing River (Zhou 1986).

Relationship between the Jing River and Lake Dongting
Although the Jianghan Plain once contained a vast body of water, the existence of the reputedly gigantic Yunmeng Marsh, which was said to have spread across the Jing River and to have included both the lakes in the Jianghan Plain and Lake Dongting, is debatable. Some believe that that kind of giant lake had already vanished before recorded history and, thus, that the Yunmeng Marsh was no more than an intermittent phenomenon created by the Jianghan lakes connecting with each other during the floods (Hua 1974, 12-14). The notion of a huge marsh only became popular in the Ming-Qing period, and it referred to the lakes in the Jianghan Plain (or perhaps only to some of them). Most lakes in what is today Hubei were formed after the Song dynasty and had nothing to do with the ancient Yunmeng Marsh (*Hubei sheng zhi dili* 1997, 584-85; *Hubei shuili zhi* 2000, 134).[4]

The final formation of the four southward outlets along the Jing River (developed out of a combination of natural and human action) had a great effect on the relationship of the Jing River and Lake Dongting. It affected not only the course of the Jing River but also the silting up of Lake Dongting. Particularly after the formation of Ouchi outlet (Ouchi *kou*) in the 1850s and Songzi outlet (Songzi *kou*) in the 1870s, about three-quarters of the silt carried by the Yangzi River water was deposited in Lake Dongting. This caused the lake to shrink with unprecedented speed. An underwater delta in the northwest part of Lake Dongting soon rose above the water and became available for reclamation. Indeed, this land was reclaimed, resulting in hundreds of *yuan* along Lake Dongting (Changjiang liuyu guihua bangongshi 1979, 142-43; *Jingjiang dadi zhi* 1989, 41; *Hubei sheng zhi shuili* 1995, 29-30). The formation of four southward outlets for discharging floodwater from the Jing River and the increasing reclamation dramatically shrank the surface of Lake Dongting: from about 6,000 km^2 in 1825, to 5,400 km^2 in 1896, 4,700 km^2 in 1932, 4,350 km^2 in 1949, 2,691 km^2 in 1983, and 2,625 km^2 in 1995 (*Jingjiang dadi zhi* 1989, 42; *Jingjiang fenhong gongcheng zhi* 2000, 32). In the end, the Jing River lost its natural flood diversion area, and the relationship between the Jing River and Lake Dongting became even more complicated.

This had a great effect on the local environment and society in the middle Yangzi valley. Both the Jianghan Plain and the Lake Dongting Plain are *yuan*-rich plains that relied heavily on dike protection. The high water period of the Yangzi River (August to September) and Lake Dongting (May to July) usually did not coincide, but once they did, the local dikes became threatened. The people of Hubei accused the people of Hunan of causing the threat and condemned them for not taking action to resolve it. The people of Hunan levelled exactly the same charge against the people of Hubei. Hubei residents wanted Hunan people to dredge Lake Dongting and blamed them for enclosing too much *yuan* around the lake; Hunan residents wanted Hubei people to dredge the Jing River and blamed them for building too many dikes and sluice gates along the river (*Hubei sheng zhi shuili* 1995, 31).

Mediating this dispute was difficult. In any case, in the end, those who insisted on sacrificing the interests of Hunanese to promote the interests of the people of Hubei won, and thus the four southward outlets on the Jing River remained as its main flood diversion exits.[5] This largely reduced the threat of the high water of the Jing River discharging onto the Jianghan Plain, but it caused more silt to be deposited on the south side of the Jing River. Some Hunanese were actually happy to have more land to reclaim. Even the people of the counties in the Jianghan Plain that lay on the south side of the Jing River (i.e., Songzi, Gong'an, and Shishou) got an opportunity to enclose more *yuan* (Mei, Zhang, and Yan 1995, 125-31). Songzi, for example, grew by hundreds of thousands of *mu* of farmland from the 1870s to the 1930s. The increase of farmland even surpassed the increase of population (*Songzi xian zhi* 1982 [1937], 217), a very rare phenomenon in the Jianghan area in late imperial times. One century later, in the 1980s, the ground on the southern side of the Jing River was about five metres higher than on its northern side, and, at times of high water, the water level of the Jing River was ten to fourteen metres higher than the ground on its northern banks (*Jingjiang dadi zhi* 1989, 14). This, in fact, put the Jianghan Plain at even greater risk.

Han River Valley

After the Han River flows through the mountains of northern Hubei and enters the Jianghan Plain, its course becomes wider and changes more frequently. The modern course of the lower reaches of the river (from Zhongxiang to Hankou) formed around the end of the Ming dynasty (Lu and Pan 2004, 46-75). When the water level of the Han River is low, the width of its course ranges from three to four hundred metres in the dry season but expands to over eight to ten kilometres in the high-water seasons (*Hubei sheng zhi dili* 1997, 314). On the other hand, the river course of the Han narrows as it flows down from its middle valley to its lower valley through the Jianghan Plain. The distance between the dikes on both sides of the Han River can be as wide as 4.5 kilometres where it enters the Jianghan Plain and as narrow as four hundred metres in the very centre of the Jianghan Plain (*Jingzhou diqu zhi* 1996, 73).

For this reason, in its lower valley the Han River failed to carry the huge volume of high water that came from its upper reaches, and thus the dikes were breached, particularly when they were poorly managed. Due mainly to this kind of over-flooding after a rupture of the dike and the silt deposit that followed, the natural levee along the Han River gradually ascended. Relatively speaking, the plain along the Han River valley got lower and lower: the farther one travelled from the river, the lower the ground became. The lowest place was at the foot of the nearby hills that surround the Jianghan Plain (*Hubei sheng zhi dili* 1997, 314; see also Figure 1).

The Dongjing River, a tributary of the Han River, flows across the centre of the Jianghan Plain and converges with the Yangzi River. In the Ming, it lacked a fixed riverbed and, in 1573, even separated into two branches: the east branch was called the Dongjing River.[6] Because there were no dikes along its lower reaches, these two branches connected with other tributaries of the Han River. Whenever the water of the Han River rose, the Dongjing River and other nearby rivers and lakes would become connected. The very centre of the Jianghan Plain was thus turned into a vast body of water, a situation that changed only after 1949 by virtue of the extensive water-control projects that finally constrained the Dongjing River to a single river course with two continuous dikes on either side (*Dongjinghe difang zhi* 1994, 1-4).

In the long run, the rivers and lakes of the Jianghan Plain gradually changed from being free to connect with each other to being separate from each other.

The course of each river became one single river course; however, as this happened, riverbeds and water levels were getting higher and higher, and the diversion of annual high water became more and more difficult. The water system also changed from running naturally in early imperial times, to running in an extremely disordered pattern in late imperial times, to running in a largely controlled pattern after 1949.

Dike Systems and Their Changes

Both the Yangzi and the Han Rivers have three *xun* (high-water seasons). These are known as *taohuaxun* (peach blossom high water), from March to April; *xiaxun* (summer high water), from May to August; and *qiuxun* (autumn high water), from September to November. The peach blossom high water is not very serious, but the autumn and, particularly, the summer high water were dangerous (Song 1989, 251). In the late Qing, however, the autumn high water created even more problems than did the summer high water because it was slower to recede than the latter, whose quicker disappearance allowed time to replant (Zhang Jiayan 1993).

These regular annual high water periods, the physiographical conditions, and the complex river-lake relationship in the Jianghan Plain made the dike systems there crucial for relatively stable farming. Dikes began to be constructed in the Jianghan Plain as early as in the Spring and Autumn Period (*Jingjiang dadi zhi* 1989, 55), but they became especially widespread in late imperial times. They ranged in size from the major levees along the Yangzi and the Han Rivers and their major tributaries to the minor dikes that protected the myriad *yuan*.

Liu Ts'ui-jung (1970) describes all the dikes along the Yangzi and its tributaries as the main dikes, the so-called moon-like dikes (or moon-shape dikes, dikes built on the interior side of an important river dike in order to support it) as a kind of secondary dike, and the dikes that surrounded *yuan* as *yuan* dikes. As the name suggests, a moon-shape dike usually curves like a crescent moon. Pierre-Etienne Will (1985, 298) calls dikes along rivers "long dikes" and dikes that enclose *yuan* "circular dikes," respectively. I prefer to label them "major dikes" and "minor dikes," or "river dikes" and "*yuan* dikes" (although some *yuan* dikes also functioned as river dikes, particularly in the lower reaches of the Han River).

Major, or River, Dikes

The major, or river, dikes include dikes along the Yangzi River, the Han River, the Dongjing River and many of their small tributaries, and moon-shape dikes that supported some important sections of river dikes, which protected against the seasonal high waters of these rivers. These dikes were constructed alongside rivers but not at the river's edge (except for some short sections). They were usually built of earth, reinforced with stone in some important sections, and contained sluice gates for flood diversion and for irrigation.

The most important of such dikes is the Jingjiang Great Dike, or the Jing River Great Dike (*Jingjiang dadi* – it was called the Wancheng dike [*Wancheng di*] before its name was changed in 1918), which is located on the northern bank of the Jing River in Jiangling (in Jianli since 1954), and which protects a large part of the Jianghan Plain. It is claimed that this dike is the second most important dike in Republican China (the most important being the Yellow River dike) (*Jingjiang di zhi* 1937, 4: 28). Although human activities in the region can be traced back to the Neolithic age (Hubei sheng Jingzhou bowuguan 1999), the dike was first built in the Eastern Jin dynasty (317-420) and was extended in the Song and the Ming and became an uninterrupted dike in 1650, after the last northern outlet of the Jing River was closed. The dike was made higher and wider in the Qing dynasty, with a length of 124 kilometres. It was finally extended to Jianli in 1954, at a total length of 182.35 kilometres. In terms of size, its typical cross-section in 1685 was 11.2 metres wide at the top and 48 metres wide at the bottom, and its height was 5.12 metres. By 1733, these dimensions had grown to 12.8, 51.2, and 5.44 metres, respectively; by 1788, they ranged from 19.2 to 25.6 metres, 48 to 54.4 metres, and 4.8 to 7.36 metres. In the Qing, the Jingjiang Great Dike was supported by moon-shaped dikes in thirty-five locations, for a total of 23,013.6 metres (*Jingjiang dadi zhi* 1989, 55-60, 101-2). A Western traveller at the end of the nineteenth century described the dike around Shashi as "averaging 150 feet in width at the bottom, and twenty-five at the top, twenty feet high on the river side, and forty on the land side" (Bishop 1899, 85). After more reconstruction, by 1949 it was 4 to 8 metres wide at the top and 12 to 16 metres high (*Jingjiang dadi zhi* 1989, 60).

The dikes along the Han River in the Jianghan Plain were first built in the Five Dynasties (907-960) by a local governor to protect his fief (Will 1985, 300n7). They were greatly extended in the Ming and gradually united in the Qing and the Republic (Lu and Pan 2004, 217-315). The length of the dikes along the Han River was 620 kilometres in the Republic (Changjiang liuyu guihua bangongshi 1979, 500). In 1985, the dike on the west bank of the Han River was 368.49 kilometres in length and on the east bank it was 358.44 kilometres, for a total of 726.93 kilometres (*Hubei sheng zhi shuili* 1995, 223).[7]

The first part of the Dongjing River dike was possibly built in the late Yuan along the river's upper reaches. In the late Qing, some of the *yuan* along this river were gradually merged and their dikes linked together (partly to function as river dikes). After the closing of some outlets of the Dongjing River in the late Qing and the Republic, part of the dikes on both sides were joined, with a total length of 272 kilometres on both sides together (by 1949). An on-the-spot survey in 1950 revealed that these dikes were usually 2 to 3 metres wide at the top, 4 to 5 metres high on the land side, and 2 to 3 metres high on the river side. Before 1949, however, there was no uninterrupted dike on this river's lower valley, where floods were an almost annual occurrence (*Dongjinghe difang zhi* 1994, 71-79).[8] The dikes were finally connected into an uninterrupted dike and linked with the Yangzi River dike and the Han River dike in 1955 (*Jingzhou diqu zhi* 1996, 74).

Thus the rivers in the Jianghan Plain were gradually restrained between long dikes. In the long fight against floods, the dikes on both sides of the Jing River and the Han River kept being raised, and at the same time the riverbeds were raised by the deposit of silt carried by the rivers. Though the silt load of the Jing River was far less than that of the Yellow River, it was still large due to the huge volume of water carried by that river. As for the Han River, in the 1960s, the average silt content of its water was 4.3 times that of the Jing River; the silt content of the middle and lower Han River has been dramatically reduced since the construction of the Danjiangkou reservoir in 1968 (*Jingzhou diqu zhi* 1996, 73-74; *Hubei sheng zhi dili* 1997, 528, 539). As a result, the riverbed and the area adjacent to the river got higher and higher. Thus, in the Jianghan Plain, the new dike was higher than the old dike, and the dike along the river was higher than the inland dike. In the end, the high water level of the Jing River and the Han River was higher than the ground inside the dikes. In other words, both the Yangzi (where it flows through Jingzhou) and the Han became above-ground rivers (see Figure 1).[9] Therefore, once there was a dike rupture, a disastrous flood would immediately follow. Furthermore, it became difficult to drain logged water inside the *yuan*. Some *yuan*, such as the Diaocha *yuan* in Hanchuan (see Chapter 4), the Zhengzhu *yuan* (and six or more other *yuan*) in Honghu, and a former market town in Songzi turned back into lakes (*Honghu xian zhi* 1992, 59; *Songzi xian zhi* 1982 [1937], 85). Though there were such land-to-lake switches, in the long run, more and more lakes vanished due to over-reclamation. This tendency accelerated in the Republic and the People's Republic of China.

Minor, or *Yuan,* Dikes

Aside from the major, or river, dikes, the Jianghan Plain in the Qing and the Republic also had numerous *yuan* dikes, which encircled some existing land and the land enclosed from lakeshore or riverside. Also built of earth, these were usually smaller than river dikes. The dikes of the fifty-six *yuan* in Xiaogan County in the early Qing, for example, were about five *chi* (1 Qing *chi* = 32 centimetres) wide at the top and ten *chi* high (*Hanyang fu zhi* 1747, 15: 24b), and the dike of Diaocha *yuan* in Hanchuan in the mid-eighteenth century was about two to five *chi* wide at the top and three to six *chi* high (*Xu xingshui jinjian* 1937, 3585), while the height of *yuan* dikes in Dangyang in the twentieth century ranged from two to three metres (*Dangyang xian zhi* 1992, 244).

Some *yuan* were encircled by a single dike, but others shared part of their dikes. In places that lacked river dikes, many *yuan* dikes were sometimes linked together and functioned as river dikes as well or eventually turned into river dikes (*Jianli difang zhi* 1991, 72, 80). In other places, the only function of some *yuan* dikes was to protect the *yuan* from floodwater once the river dike had broken (*Dangyang xian zhi* 1992, 244). Thus different *yuan* faced different problems. The residents of the *yuan* that were close to rivers sometimes had to protect their *yuan* from overflowing river water and outlets that had been deliberately opened by others; at the same time, the *yuan* that were close to lakes suffered from inundation and waterlogging (*Hanchuan xian zhi* 1873, juan shou: 13b-14a). In any case, in view of the physical features and the river-lake relationship in the Jianghan Plain, it is easy to understand that the *yuan* dikes were as important as the river dikes in protecting against annual high water.

The area surrounded by *yuan* dikes is called *yuan* (or *wei* in some places, in which case the dike surrounding it is called a *wei* dike). *Yuan* first appeared in the Hubei-Hunan basin in the Song-Yuan period (960-1368) and became widespread in the Ming-Qing period (1368-1911) (Yao 1987, 374-75; Zhang 1989). A typical *yuan* was high on its perimeter and low in the middle. Packed among rivers and lakes, their high density gave them the appearance of a honeycomb (*Hanchuan xian zhi* 1873, juan shou: 12b-13a; *Jianli xian zhi* 1994, 51). Thus the farming area in the Jianghan Plain in general, or in an individual *yuan* in particular, extended from a high position to a low position. The density of population was parallel: dense in high places and less dense in low places (*Gong'an xian zhi* 1990, 68).

According to their legal status in the Qing, there were three kinds of *yuan*: (1) official *yuan* (*guanyuan*), (2) people's *yuan* (or civilian *yuan*, communal *yuan*, *minyuan*), and (3) private *yuan* (*siyuan*, which were illegal). The difference lay mainly in their source of funding. Those built with funds from the government were official *yuan;* they were considered legal and were registered with the government. Those built by the local people's funds were people's *yuan;* they were also legal but were not reported to the government.

The private *yuan* were illegal; they were mostly built outside the major dikes and were not supposed to exist and did not appear on the land tax registers (Zhang 1989; Wang and Zhang 1990, 381; Peng and Zhang 1993, 209-10).[10]

Broadly speaking, almost all of the cultivated land inside the major dike systems could be classified as *yuan,* as in Jingzhou where it was reported that "the locals build dikes around the land to protect against floods; these are called *yuan*" (*Jingzhou fu zhi* 1880, 20: 1a). From the perspective of hydraulic engineering, any *yuan* should include a *yuan* dike, a sluice (on the *yuan* dike), and canals (within *yuan,* which functioned as a drainage and irrigation system) (Wang and Zhang 1990, 381). Mei Li and her colleagues define *yuan* land as "a kind of high yield water-conservancy-land encircled by dikes and containing drainage and irrigation works. Dikes, sluice gates, and canals are essential parts of the *yuan* in the area" (Mei, Zhang, and Yan 1995, 91). This description applies only to relatively large *yuan;* small *yuan* that had only about one hundred or fewer *mu* of land did not necessarily meet all these criteria.

The length of dikes, the number of sluice gates, and the scale of canals all varied according to the size of the *yuan.* At the small end of the scale, some *yuan* had fewer than one hundred *mu* of land – some *yuan*-like enclosures even had only a few *mu* of land. At the other end of the scale, some had more than 100,000 *mu* (*Hanchuan xian zhi* 1873, 9: 7a-33b; *Jianli xian zhi* 1959, 109-19). Some large *yuan* contained many small *yuan.* Baiju *yuan* in Jiangling, for example, contained thirteen small *yuan,* and, moreover, there were partition dikes among small *yuan.* These partition dikes were intended to protect *yuan* land from the floodwater of lakes inside the *yuan* and/or to protect other small *yuan* in case one small *yuan* was flooded (Mei, Zhang, and Yan 1995, 89). Tongcheng *yuan* in Mianyang even contained seventy-two officially registered *yuan* with 206,593 *mu* of land in total and had a circumference of two hundred *li* (Shuili dianlibu shuiguan si kejisi, shuili shuidian kexue yanjiuyuan [hereafter Shuili dianlibu] 1991, 460). Not every *yuan* contained a lake, but some *yuan,* particularly large ones, may have contained one or more lakes. Xinxing *yuan* in Jianli, for example, contained 73,800 *mu* of farmland with nine lakes and thirteen deep pools (Xu and Yang 1989, 72).

When no more *yuan* could be easily reclaimed inside the major dikes, the Jianghan people started to reclaim river beaches or sandbars outside the major dikes, or islets located in the middle of the river course. Locally called *tan yuan* ([river] beach *yuan*) or *zhou yuan* (sand-bar *yuan* [Ni 1885 [1876], 8: 1b-7a]), these *yuan* (which were illegal private *yuan*) began to be built at the end of the Ming and in the early Qing and became widespread in the middle and late Qing. By the time of the reign of Daoguang (1821-50), almost every section of the Jing River had islets, and almost every islet had *yuan* inside it (Mei, Zhang, and Yan 1995, 120, 200). In the Republic, such *yuan* along the Jing River covered more than a million *mu* (*Jingjiang di zhi* 1937, 4: 10).

Enlargement of the Dike Systems

Although some old dikes fell into disuse when waterways changed course, the overall trend was an increase in the length of dikes. The length of dikes in the early Qing is unclear, but by the reign of Daoguang, the total length of all the major dikes combined in the Jianghan Plain was about 1,500 kilometres. The length of river dikes in the Jianghan Plain was 4,214.1 km by 1985, including 1,557 km of major dikes along the Yangzi River, 726.9 km of major dikes along the Han River, 492 km of important branch dikes, and 1,438.2 km of regular branch (small tributary) dikes. In addition, there were 2,836.2 km of people's dikes. Taken together, in the 1980s they protected about 30 million *mu* of farmland and 25 million people (*Hubei sheng zhi shuili* 1995, 5-6, 204).

Although there was a general tendency for dikes to be lengthened, the major (or river) dikes and the minor (or *yuan*) dikes were, in fact, different in this respect. In the long run, the length of both river dikes and *yuan* dikes had increased before 1949. For the river dikes, the increase can be seen in the construction of the Han River dikes that occurred beginning in the early Qing and the Dongjing River dikes since the late Qing. For the *yuan* dikes, more and more *yuan* were enclosed in the late Qing and the Republic, and their dikes were subsequently lengthened. But, after 1949, the overall length of river dikes increased by virtue of the extensive construction of new dikes, while the *yuan* dikes got shorter and shorter due mainly to a change in their function. Many *yuan* dikes were no longer necessary for protecting *yuan* from seasonal high water since high water had now been blocked by major dikes. Some *yuan* dikes thus were replaced by channel dikes (i.e., dikes along drainage and irrigation channels) (*Jianli difang zhi* 1991, 52).

Generally speaking, therefore, from the early Qing to the Republic, more and more dikes were built in the Jianghan Plain, and they were made higher and longer. But after 1949, the river dikes were increased in length while *yuan* dikes were decreased.

Immigration, Land Reclamation, and Environmental Deterioration

Immigration

Economic growth in the Jianghan Plain in the Ming-Qing era was due mainly to extensive reclamation of *yuan*. In this process, immigrants played a major

Table 1a

The time of arrival of immigrants to the Jianghan Plain (based on 108 genealogies)

Arrival time	(dynasty)	Number of genealogies
Song	(960-1279)	7
Yuan	(1279-1368)	15
Ming	(1368-1644)	64
Qing	(1644-1911)	4
Unknown		18

Table 1b

The native provinces of immigrants to the Jianghan Plain

Native provinces	Number of genealogies
Jiangxi	78
Anhui	8
Shandong	4
Shaanxi	3
Jiangsu	3
Shanxi	2
Hunan	2
Henan	1
Hebei	1
Inner Mongolia	1
Neighboring counties	3
Unknown	2

Sources: Zhang Guoxiong (1995, 265-73). The Jianghan Plain in the above table includes Jiangxia, Jiangling, Mianyang, Jianli, Xiaogan, Hanyang, Yunmeng, Yingcheng, Hanchuan, Tianmen, Qianjiang, Jingmen, Shishou, Gong'an, Zhijiang, and Jingshan, which is slightly different from the area of the Jianghan Plain in the original data.

role. Thus, the changes in the rural economy in the Jianghan Plain after the Ming were closely related to immigration and emigration. According to the available local genealogies, the high tide of immigration to the Jianghan Plain lasted through four dynasties, with most immigrants coming from ten different provinces (Table 1a and Table 1b).

The data in Table 1a and Table 1b are in a sense limited since they are taken from the relatively small number (108) of extant genealogies and so do not reflect the process of immigration in all its detail. Nonetheless, some general tendencies can be seen from this sample. First, the time of arrival was long, but it was concentrated during the Ming. Second, although the immigrants hailed from different provinces, more than 70 percent of them came from Jiangxi Province. Given the social disorder in the Ming-Qing transition, there was another high tide of immigration in the early Qing that is not reflected in Table 1a (Zhang Guoxiong 1995, 18).

The people who moved into the Jianghan Plain included war refugees, small merchants, artisans, and retired officials (Rowe 1990, 53-65; Zhang 1992a). But, generally speaking, most of those who migrated to the Huguang area, including the Jianghan Plain, were "economic immigrants," particularly agricultural producers (Zhang Guoxiong 1995, 85-98). The most important reasons for moving to the Jianghan Plain included the attraction of its large amount of reclaimable lakefront wasteland and the state's policy of encouraging reclamation (e.g., through a light tax levy or a tax exemption during the early stages of reclamation). Thus many *yuan* were reclaimed with the coming of immigrants (Zhang Guoxiong 1989; Zhang Jiayan 1992a, 1992b).

The long-term result of this influx of immigrants, together with the natural increase of both the immigrants and the original inhabitants, was steady population growth. By the Qing, the Jianghan Plain was the most populous area of Hubei. There were only 19.1 people per square kilometre in 1578 in the Jianghan Plain; by 1820, that density had ballooned to 247.7 people per square kilometre – an almost thirteenfold increase (Zhang Guoxiong 1995, 158-59).

Land Reclamation

Rapid population growth resulting from migration forced the local peasants to reclaim more land. They had no choice in this as they relied on land for everything – food, clothes, and their very livelihood. Thus it was impossible for people to leave any arable land uncultivated. They even tried their best to reclaim poor mountain land and lakeside wasteland (*Shishou xian zhi* 1866, 3: 12ab, 16a). The enclosure of *yuan* reached its first heyday in the mid-Ming. In the early Qing, following the postwar recovery of the rural economy, the number of *yuan* returned to that of the late Ming. *Yuan* enclosure had a second heyday in the mid-Qing, but the result was over-reclamation, which led to more frequent water calamities in the late Qing (Zhang 1989; Song 1989). Subsequent to and because of this, every year in the late Qing, 20 to 40 percent of all *yuan* in the Jianghan Plain lost part of their harvest or had no harvest at all (Mei, Zhang, and Yan 1995, 213). Many *yuan* turned back into lakes (*Honghu xian zhi* 1992, 59). Frequent water calamities and unstable *yuan* enclosures were also common in the Republic. In the long run, more and more *yuan* were enclosed until early in the PRC, when newly built large-scale water-control projects reduced the traditional function of *yuan* dikes.

Many *yuan* dikes were demolished and the number of *yuan* was reduced (see, e.g., *Xiaogan xian jian zhi* 1959, 41-42; *Jianli difang zhi* 1991, 71, 80).

There are several ways of enclosing *yuan,* all of which shrink the flood diversion areas in one way or another. The first way involves blocking small tributaries and enclosing the former river course as farmland. Over the course of the Qing, for example, seventeen small tributaries were blocked or silted up in Hanchuan and eight in Qianjiang due to reclamation (Peng and Zhang 1993, 256-57). Though the local people thereby found a new source of income, the enclosures actually posed an even greater threat to river dikes (since all high water was now contained within river dikes) and contributed to their frequent breach. The blockage of the small tributaries also made it difficult to drain water that accumulated inside *yuan,* wreaking havoc on the water systems inside the *yuan* and exacerbating waterlogging.[11]

A second means of creating *yuan* involved enclosing lakefront land. This, of course, shrank the size of the lake. Ultimately, many lakes completely vanished as they were turned into *yuan.* For example, gazetteers record that six lakes in Qianjiang, twenty-four in Hanchuan, and fourteen in Tianmen officially vanished over the course of the Qing (Peng and Zhang 1993, 256-57). Here "officially" means they were recorded in gazetteers. The number of (vanished but) unrecorded lakes may have surpassed those that were recorded. People who enclosed *yuan* from lakesides assured themselves of a food supply, but such enclosure greatly diminished the flood diversion areas. It also posed a great threat to the dike systems (both river dikes and *yuan* dikes) and, indeed, contributed to more frequent inundation. Thus, what may have been beneficial from the perspective of individual peasant households was harmful from the perspective of local society as a whole. As one local resident said in the early Qing, one family might benefit from a dike built along the lake, but many other families would suffer from it (*Tianmen xian zhi* 1765, 6: 4b).

A third way of creating *yuan* involved enclosing land between major river dikes and the river course. The *yuan* so enclosed were usually illicit. The Qing government had repeatedly issued orders forbidding illicit *yuan,* but to no avail. The dikes in these *yuan* could protect the nearby major dike in years when the high water reached a normal level for the area. But they would undermine the integrity of the major dikes if the high water was unusually high because they blocked the water course and thus increased the likelihood that water would breach the nearby river dike (*Jingjiang dadi zhi* 1989, 84).

A fourth way of creating *yuan* was to enclose sandbars and islets in the middle of both the Yangzi River and the Han River course. By the early nineteenth century, many islets in the middle of the Han River and its river beaches in the Jianghan area were reclaimed and brought under the plough, and even villages were built on this reclaimed land (Wang 1832, 1: 11b). This kind of land seemed well suited for cotton production. The gazetteer for Zhijiang, for example, states: "The islets are particularly good for the production of cotton" (*Zhijiang xian zhi* 1866, 7: 7b). The same was true in the Lake Dongting Plain, where "much of the newly silted sand-bar land around the lake was cleared for cotton, not grain" (Perdue 1987, 247). But this kind of *yuan* also blocked the watercourse and thus posed a threat to river dikes.

According to a late Qing gazetteer, there were 138 sandbars or islets (in the course of the Yangzi River) in Jingzhou alone – 24 in Jiangling, 5 in Gong'an, 36 in Shishou, 50 in Jianli, 6 in Songzi, and 17 in Zhijiang (*Jingzhou fu zhi* 1880, 19: 2a-27a). These reclaimable sandbars or islets were most attractive to the local people. For example, even though the government permanently prohibited reclamation of the Jiaojin islet after an inundation in 1788, someone was "illegally" farming on it thirty years later (Shuili dianlibu 1991, 628).

For those peasants who enclosed *yuan* in any of these four ways, the results seemed beneficial: they got food, cotton, and many other products, and the land supported more people. But for the Jianghan area as a whole, this simply served to exacerbate the pressure on the local hydrology. As more and more *yuan* were enclosed, the flood diversion areas shrank, increasing the pressure on the overall dike system and causing more frequent breaks and worse floods. Even when the dikes held, waterlogging became worse. In the end, the result was detrimental to the Jianghan area as a whole.

Early in the nineteenth century, immigration to the Jianghan Plain almost stopped; instead, more people were emigrating out. In the middle of the nineteenth century, flood refugees from Mianyang and Jianli frequently went to Hunan to borrow grains, and many of them stayed there. They moved to the Lake Dongting Plain to reclaim newly silted lakefront land (Perdue 1987, 95; Zhang Guoxiong 1995, 233). Some Jianghan residents even went abroad in order to survive. For instance, Tianmen, although an inland county, is famous for its large population of overseas Chinese, many of whom fled to Russia and elsewhere in Europe as well as to Southeast Asia in the late nineteenth century and the early twentieth century due to frequent flooding at home (*Tianmen xian zhi* 1989, 74; Zhang Guoxiong 1995, 162; Lu 2005). Population growth and increasing water calamities together turned the Jianghan Plain from an immigration absorber to an emigration contributor.

In the neighbouring upstream mountains located along Hubei's borders with the provinces of Sichuan and Shaanxi, particularly northwest Hubei, "some two million fugitives" had assembled by the mid-Ming (Leong 1997, 163). Immigrants rushed into this area again in the mid-Qing and set off

another high tide of "opening" mountain land. This reclamation partly reduced the population pressure in their native places (including the Jianghan
Plain), but the method they applied – that is, shifting cultivation (Rawski
1975) – just brought more environmental pressures to the lower reaches of
the Han River.

   From an individual perspective, in bringing hill and mountain land under
cultivation, peasants found another resource to support themselves, at least
temporarily. But this also caused large-scale hillside erosion. In the end, the
topsoil from the mountains flowed down with rainwater to the lower reaches
of the Han River (as well as to the middle reaches of the Yangzi River) and was
deposited there as silt. This raised the riverbed of the Han River and increased
the frequency of dike breaks and added to the problem of waterlogging in its
lower basin. The removal of natural ground cover to make way for agriculture
also caused quick and heavy flooding since it removed natural barriers that
had caught rainwater and slowed its movement. Consequently, faster and
stronger floods broke the downstream river dikes and caused dangerous
inundation. Topsoil erosion also increased the already high silt content of
the Han River. The erosion and silting of sand in the lower reaches of the Han
River formed many sandbars and islets, giving the local people the opportunity to enclose the land so formed. But this further constricted the river course,
and again it was detrimental to the Jianghan area as a whole.

Environmental Deterioration

Under population pressure, some of the Jianghan people either moved to
upstream mountains to reclaim mountain land or continued to move to even
lower places to enclose more lakefront wasteland. Both of these actions increased farmland but also caused environmental deterioration.

   Contemporaries recognized this clearly. In numerous memorials, many
Qing officials had unequivocally reported that the frequent water calamities
of the Hubei basin were directly related to the over-reclamation of both
lakefront wasteland in the basin and neighbouring upstream mountains.
In 1831, Lu Kun, the governor general of Hunan-Hubei, wrote one of the
most detailed memorials, clearly recognizing the interrelation of population
pressure, mountain reclamation, and environmental deterioration in the
Jianghan Plain. As he put it:

> The prefectures of Jingzhou, Anlu, and Hanyang are bothered by water calam-
> ities every year. They can be inundated not only by heavy floodwater, but also
> by normal seasonal high water. I sent [someone] to go along the Yangzi and
> the Han Rivers to examine whether waterways were blocked or open, to collect

local information, and to seek causes. They found that in earlier times, the river was wide and the tributaries were deep, the high water was easily taken in and discharged, and [therefore] the counties along these rivers suffered from few water calamities. Recently, more and more people have reclaimed land in the upstream mountains in Shaanxi, and earth and stone have been loosened and flow down with water. [In the lower reaches] the water slows down and the sand deposits; therefore there are many sand islets in the main course of rivers. In addition, the locals build more and more *yuan* dikes for their own benefit and thus block the waterways. The former branches and outlets that discharged high water in Jiangling, Gong'an, and Jianli along the Yangzi River, in Mianyang, Hanchuan and Hanyang between the Yangzi and the Han Rivers, and in Zhongxiang, Jingshan, Qianjiang, Tianmen, and Jingmen along the Han River have all been blocked recently. [In the end] whenever there is heavy rain, the water rises, the water in the upper reaches pours down [as] from the roof, and the residents of the lower reaches worry that the water will flow back. This causes frequent inundation. The dikes built by the local people are usually thin, and one break leads to more ruptures. Once land has been inundated, the water has nowhere to go since the rivers are higher than the *yuan*. Grain land in hundreds of *yuan* thus becomes inundated. The sluices in Jianli in Futian si, Menglanyuan, and Luoshanyao, and in Mianyang in Xindi, which were built in 1809, once worked well and drained trapped water effectively. Recently, however, they have been damaged and now fail to drain water successfully. The sluices in Menglanyuan and Luoshanyao also do not drain water well because the beach outside the sluices has been silted up. Therefore the counties along the Yangzi and the Han Rivers suffer water calamities every year. (Shuili dianlibu 1991, 728-29)

Lu summarized at least three major results of over-reclamation. First, it greatly reduced the water-holding capability of the banks of various rivers and tributaries and caused more frequent flooding in the mountains, and it also increased the pressure of storage and discharge of seasonal high water in the middle Yangzi River valley. Second, the eroded sand and earth deposited in the riverbeds of the Han River and the Jing River raised their water levels and increased the pressure of seasonal high water on their dikes. Third, the increased deposit of sediments stimulated the local people to enclose even more *yuan,* and this further shrank the flood diversion area. All of this increased not only the danger of dike ruptures but also the likelihood of water calamities.

Thus, although the enclosure of *yuan* along lakefronts created more farm-land and partly reduced population pressure in the Jianghan Plain, this, along with the land reclamation in nearby mountains, also degraded the local environment and caused more frequent water calamities.

Water Calamities: Formation and Distribution

Formation of Water Calamities

Both natural factors and human factors contributed to the formation of water calamities. But in the main it was the latter that was responsible for the frequent water calamities that contributed to the instability of the Jianghan Plain in the Qing and the Republic. In fact, the Jianghan Plain had the least stable environment in the Yangzi River valley. From the nineteenth century onward, there were more water calamities in the Han River valley than in the Yangzi River valley, and waterlogging became more serious than floods. These water calamities resulted in unstable harvests and inflicted heavy damage on the local society and economy.

The Jianghan Plain has to take a huge amount of water from outside due to its low elevation and its position in the middle Yangzi River valley and the lower reaches of the Han River. It was found in the last half of the twentieth century that more than 96 percent of the Jing River's high water comes from the upper reaches of the Yangzi River (between the cities of Yibing and Yichang),[12] while only a small part comes from the Qing River (Qingjiang) and the Juzhang River (Juzhanghe) in Hubei Province (*Jingjiang dadi zhi* 1989, 50-51). The Han River's high water also mainly comes from this river's upper reaches. The huge amount of high water, however, only provides potential conditions for water calamities, it does not necessarily cause them.

A possible natural cause of water calamities is the uneven distribution of rainfall. Modern records show that rainfall in the Jianghan Plain (a subtropic monsoon area) is extremely unevenly distributed within the year. The majority of the annual rainfall is concentrated in the summer and autumn high-water seasons (the rainfall from April to August in Hankou accounts for two-thirds of annual rainfall [*Hubei sheng zhi shuili* 1995, 2]) and readily leads to floods. Historically, rainfall also varied largely from year to year in Jingzhou, with the highest summer rainfall being seven times the lowest (*Jingzhou diqu zhi* 1996, 65). Based on the historical records of solar activities, however, it was found that the change and uneven distribution of rainfall had contributed to water calamities in the mid-Qing but was not sufficient to cause more frequent water calamities in the late Qing (Qiao 1963; Mei, Zhang, and Yan 1995, 198). To find the causes of water calamities we have to look to human activity, mainly dike construction and *yuan* enclosure in the Jianghan Plain and land reclamation in the neighbouring upstream mountains.

Distribution of Water Calamities in the Jianghan Plain

Although various sources differ on the frequency of water calamities, they all show that they increased over time. One source indicates that water calamities (i.e., one-quarter of the whole area suffered from floods and/or waterlogging) in the Jianghan Plain increased from once every 3.2 years in the reign of Kangxi (1662-1722) to once every 2.7 years in the reign of Qianlong (1736-95) and to once every 1.5 years in the reign of Daoguang (1821-50) (Song 1989, 250). Another source indicates that water calamities (in either the Yangzi River valley and the Han River valley together or in one of them alone) in the Jianghan Plain occurred every 2.3 years in the Qing and every 1.7 years in the Republic (Table 2).

Although the criterion for determining "water calamities" in Table 2 is unclear, it is still apparent that there was a growing number of them from the early Qing to the Republic. This was the general situation with water calamities in the whole Jianghan Plain. But, as discussed above, the dike systems, waterways, silt load of the Yangzi and the Han Rivers, and dike management were all different. If taken separately, we find that the frequency of water calamities along these two rivers also differed. Indeed, it even varied along the same river: in Hubei in the Qing and the Republic, the frequency of water calamities in the Han River valley was much higher than in the Yangzi River valley; in the Yangzi River valley (of Hubei), water calamities often occurred in its middle section (i.e., along the Jing River); in the Han River valley, water calamities tended to occur in its lower section (*Hubei sheng zhi dili* 1997, 1188-92). In other words, water calamities along both rivers were concentrated in the Jianghan Plain.

This trend relates to the disorder of the waterways in the lower Han River valley. As discussed above, the formation of Ouchi *kou* in the 1850s and

Table 2

The frequency of water calamities in the Jianghan Plain from 221 BCE to 1949

Period	Number of years	Incidence	Frequency (years/incidence)
221 BCE–618	839	51	16.5
618-907	289	14	20.6
907-1279	372	50	7.4
1271-1368	97	25	3.9
1368-1644	276	61	4.5
1644-1911	267	115	2.3
1911-49	38	22	1.7

Source: Hubei sheng zhi shuili (1995, 212). Frequency is calculated by the author.

Songzi *kou* in the 1870s mitigated the threat of high water to the Yangzi River dikes. But the Han River lacked such outlets, while its high silt content contributed to the rise of its river course. Also, its wide-to-narrow river course and weak dikes, and increasing conflicts over control of those dikes, all jeopardized the Han River dikes and caused more water calamities.

Sources do not distinguish between water calamities caused by major rivers and those caused by tributaries. But a 1745 memorial already reported that "the damage caused by the break of tributary [dikes] is equal to the damage caused by the major river [dikes]" (Shuili dianlibu 1991, 266). In fact, in the late Qing, the damage caused by water calamities related to branches or tributaries was more serious than that related to major rivers. Nor does the source for Table 2 distinguish between the two main types of water calamities: flooding and waterlogging. In the late Qing, however, waterlogging caused more serious damage than did flooding. Thus, a consideration of water calamities in the Jianghan Plain in the late Qing should focus on the Han River valley, the tributaries, and waterlogging (Zhang Jiayan 1993).

Distribution of Water Calamities in the Yangzi River Valley

The increase in the number and frequency of water calamities in the Han River valley undermined the environmental stability of the whole Jianghan Plain. In the early Qing, in its water-control projects the state paid much attention to the Yangzi delta; there were many memorials regarding this subject. But the memorials of the middle and late Qing regarding water calamities of the Yangzi River mostly referred to the middle Yangzi, particularly the Jianghan area. This implies that the water calamities in this area were more frequent or the damage more severe. According to the statistics contained in collected memorials on flooding and waterlogging in the Yangzi River valley from 1736 to 1911, water calamities in the Jianghan Plain were more frequent than in any area of the Yangzi River valley (Table 3). Wang Baixin, a local elite famous for his opinions on water control, actually stated in 1840 that Hubei suffered more water calamities than any other provinces, and water calamities in Hubei mostly occurred in the Jianghan area (Yu 1999 [1840], Wang's preface).

The impact of water calamities depended on the economic importance of the region involved. A big inundation in a non-populated area of virgin land would obviously not be worthy of much note. But the economic importance of the Jianghan Plain in late imperial China could not compete with that of the Yangzi delta. Thus the logical reason for the large number of memorials regarding the Jianghan Plain is that the flooding and waterlogging there were particularly frequent and the subsequent calamities were more severe.

Table 3

Number of years with water calamities in the Yangzi River valley as reported in memorials, 1736-1911

The Jianghan Plain				The Lake Dongting Plain		The Yangzi delta			
The Han River valley		The Yangzi River valley							
N	County	N	County	N	County	N	County	N	County
105	Mianyang	105	Jiangling	96	Lizhou	61	Jiaxing	22	Wuxi
102	Tianmen	94	Jianli	86	Wuling	43	Jiashan	21	Yixing
101	Qianjiang	77	Jiangxia	85	Anxiang	43	Pinghu	17	Fengxian
99	Hanchuan	73	Gong'an	80	Huarong	40	Huating	16	Nanhui
91	Jingmen	59	Shishou	80	Longyang	37	Wuxian	15	Shanghai
81	Hanyang	55	Songzi	77	Yuanjiang	32	Changshu	13	Jinkui
69	Zhongxiang	51	Zhijiang	66	Xiangyin	32	Wujin	13	Jiading
63	Jingshan	10	Dangyang	61	Baling	27	Baoshan	10	Chuansha
54	Xiaogan			60	Yiyang	26	Qingpu		
52	Yingcheng			52	Linxiang	24	Jiangyin		
38	Yunmeng					24	Kunshan		

Note: In the original source, the counties of Jingmen and Mianyang were included in the Yangzi River area, but I put them in the Han River area. This is because the flooding of the Han River had a more important impact on Mianyang and because the Han River runs through Jingmen but the Yangzi River does not.

Source: Shuili dianlibu (1991, 20-21). N stands for times (number of years of water calamities).
   According to the original table, each year counts as one time. Even though there may have been more than one memorial reporting water calamities in that year, it only counts as one time.

Although the officials who wrote the memorials might not have thought the damage was serious (Zhang Jiayan 1993), the places that they most often mentioned in these memorials did indeed have frequent floods. Tianmen, for example, appears 102 times in Table 3 and had suffered water calamities seventy-seven times from 1821 to 1949 due to breaks in the Han River dike (*Tianmen xian zhi* 1989, 126).

   This comparison also reveals that the river system of the middle Yangzi River valley had become far less stable than that of the lower Yangzi River valley. Since the mid-Qing, the environmental stability of the Jianghan Plain was much lower than that of the Lake Dongting Plain. In the Jianghan Plain, the counties along the Yangzi River had a more stable environment than did the counties along the Han River. As Table 3 shows, all the counties that had over one hundred water calamities were located in the Han River valley. Although Jiangling was a Yangzi county, it was also inundated by the Han River. As for Mianyang, a department located between the Yangzi and the

Han Rivers, the inundation of either river caused damage, and the latter inundated it almost every year in the late Qing. Thus, Jiangling and Mianyang had the greatest number of water calamities. In the Republic, water calamities were still one of the most common forms of natural disaster in almost all the counties of the Jianghan area, particularly in the lower Han River valley (*Hubei xianzheng gaikuang* 1934, 12; LS 31-4-2007).[13]

As an alluvial plain studded with lakes and criss-crossed by rivers and waterways, the Jianghan Plain acquired its basic physical features through the long-term deposit of natural silt, while the rich fluvial soil laid the foundation for generally productive farming. In the course of history, however, the changes of river courses and their relationships with lakes constantly reshaped the local environment. The most important human-made factors were land reclamation in neighbouring upstream mountains and dike building and *yuan* enclosure in the Jianghan Plain. After the mid-Qing, with the increase in the area enclosed within the *yuan,* the lake surfaces were reduced and the drainage of water inside *yuan* became more difficult.

Land reclamation of neighbouring upstream mountains, dike building, and *yuan* enclosure in the Jianghan Plain alleviated population pressure but accelerated environmental degeneration. In other words, from a hydraulic perspective, particular individuals may have benefited from the reclamation but, at the same time, it caused long-term environmental degradation and economic uncertainty in the region as a whole. Thus, although the frequent water calamities in the Jianghan Plain were due partly to natural factors, the human-made factors were the major causes. In the Qing, water calamities steadily increased in frequency, and the damage caused by waterlogging or floodwater from tributaries became more serious than the damage caused by flooding of major rivers.

2 Water Calamities and the Management of the Dike Systems

The relationship between the state and water control has long been an important topic in Chinese studies. In the 1950s, Karl Wittfogel's theory of "oriental despotism," which claimed that China's "despotism" was rooted in water-control projects (Wittfogel 1957), was very influential, though now it convinces no one (Elvin 1975, 82; Perdue 1987, 2-7). Based on a case involving the so-called Fankou Dam controversy (1876-83), William Rowe argued that Chinese politics was really a pluralist system that was "almost precisely the opposite of ... despotism" (Rowe 1988, 354). Indeed, most scholars, especially in China and Japan, tend to lay the blame for water calamities at the doorstep of the Qing government. The government, they argue, was incompetent in managing water control and, in fact, in the end it abandoned such efforts. This interpretation dominates recent scholarship on the middle Yangzi River valley – mainly the Jianghan Plain and the Lake Dongting Plain – an area plagued with hydraulic problems since late imperial times (particularly in the late Qing). In the view of these scholars, water-control projects (mainly in the form of dike systems) fell into a cycle that roughly paralleled the dynastic cycle. In the early period of a dynasty, the state encouraged reclamation, and water-control projects worked well, but widespread dike building and *yuan* enclosure also caused an increase of water calamities (floods, waterlogging, and the like). With the decline of the dynasty, the state's ability to solve hydraulic problems weakened, water-control systems fell into disrepair, and the economy declined. A new cycle began with the establishment of a new dynasty (Morita 1974; Will 1985; Perdue 1987; Peng and Zhang 1993; Mei, Zhang, and Yan 1995; Zhang Jiayan 1997).

Morita Akira was the first to advance this critical view of the Qing authorities. Drawing on his comprehensive studies of the development of dike systems and irrigation in both Hunan and Hubei – including the formation, size, role, and management of dikes and the relationship between state power and dikes (particularly in the management of the Wancheng dike and the Han River dikes in Hubei) – he argues that, in the late nineteenth century, the Qing government's control of water conservancy weakened (Morita 1974,

21-138). Although he cites many original Chinese sources that touch on almost every aspect of dike management, he does not provide a deep analysis of them (at least according to Elvin [1975]), nor does he make clear the great difference between official dikes *(guangong/guandi)* and people's dikes, or communal dikes *(min'gong/mindi)*.[1] Government and the local people always played different roles in dike management, and, in the late Qing, the government became more involved in dike management, though this did not lead to greater effectiveness.

In one of the few existing English-language publications, Liu Ts'ui-jung (1970) offers a general description of dike building in Jingzhou. She makes it clear that, in the late Qing, dike management was supervised by local officials but carried out by the local people, though she does not explore the relationship between the dike systems and frequent inundation. Pierre-Etienne Will (1985) focuses on the role of the state apparatus in constructing and administering hydraulic installations in the Hubei basin but discusses neither *yamen* runners (when considering government personnel) nor the role of the peasants (when examining dike management).

Chinese researchers have studied wider subjects and contributed more penetrating analyses, particularly on the relationship between the dike systems and frequent inundation. The major reasons for frequent inundation, according to them, include the over-reclamation of upstream mountains, which caused eroded silt to build up in the middle Yangzi River valley and the lower Han River valley; the never-ending dike building and construction of *yuan* in the Jianghan Plain, which shrank the flood diversion area; the blockage of outlets of the Yangzi and the Han Rivers, which created problems for flood diversion; and the incompetence of the Qing government with regard to dike management (particularly due to its corruption and its lack of cooperation and coordination). The first two reasons for frequent inundation concern, in one way or another, population pressure (Zhang Jianmin 1984, 1987a, 1999; Tan Zuogang 1985; Zhang Guoxiong 1989, 1994a, 1995; Peng and Zhang 1993; Zhang Jiayan 1992b, 1997; Mei, Zhang, and Yan 1995; Gong 1996).

These general reasons for inundation are persuasive but require closer scrutiny. Consider the following facts: the population in the Jianghan Plain more than doubled in the last half of the twentieth century. Moreover, silting and enclosure during this period were even more extensive than during the late Qing: measured by surface area, more than half of Jianghan's lakes were transformed into land. Yet there has been no serious inundation or catastrophic break in the major dikes in the Jianghan Plain since 1955. Taken together, these circumstances suggest that, although the silting up of the riverbeds and the enclosure of the flood diversion areas contributed significantly to frequent inundations in the Jianghan Plain in the late Qing and the Republic, in the long run, their role might be less important than poor dike management (which certainly is not the *only* factor). As the local people say, the frequent dike ruptures (and floods) "though attributed to nature, are actually human-made" (Hu 1999 [1838], 157). A 1937 Songzi county gazetteer makes it even clearer that human beings (through their lack of planning, mismanagement of dikes, etc.) were entirely responsible for the damage caused by floodwater (*Songzi xian zhi* 1982 [1937], 73).

Without question, in both the Qing and the Republic, no leading local official wanted the dike systems under his jurisdiction to decline. In theory, officials sought to do whatever was needed to protect dikes, and, at times, their management was indeed effective.[2] But why, from the mid-Qing onward, despite the involvement of more people in dike management, did dike ruptures and inundation increase – with the Han River valley being inundated and *yuan* dikes rupturing with greater and greater frequency? Were the Yangzi River dikes and the Han River dikes managed differently? What were the differences between the management of river dikes and the management of *yuan* dikes? And how did these managerial differences contribute to the frequency of dike ruptures in the Jianghan Plain in the Qing and the Republic?

Unlike the Yellow River dike systems and the Grand Canal, which were directly controlled and managed by the central government, during the Qing most of the dikes in the Jianghan Plain did not fall into the category of "government works" *(guangong)*.[3] It is therefore not enough to simply attribute all problems to some presumed mismanagement by a powerful but corrupt Qing government – particularly the central government – as Chinese scholars have tended to do. As we will see, although, in theory, officials should have been responsible for all dikes, and the local government (i.e., at the level of the prefecture *[fu]* or lower) did in fact manage parts of the dikes, most dikes were managed by the local people – that is, by individuals outside the government. It is thus crucial to analyze the responsibility and authority of all of the different parties, including the different levels of government, the rural gentry, and the villagers, with an emphasis on the local people. Yet past scholarship has generally overlooked the important role played by the local people in managing dikes in the Jianghan Plain.[4]

In an attempt to rectify this situation, this chapter focuses on the role different parties played in dike management, particularly regarding the mobilization and organization of the local people in the construction, repair, and maintenance of the dike systems in the Jianghan Plain in the Qing and the Republic. Dike management entailed both conflict and cooperation. Perhaps more than anything else, problems with dike management led to frequent inundation. Understanding the role different parties played in dike management in the Jianghan Plain can contribute not only to our knowledge of the social and environmental history of the province of Hubei but also to our knowledge of Chinese rural society in general (not to mention the role of the state in local society).

Roles Different Parties Played in the Management of Dike Systems

Philip Huang (1985, 219) describes rural China's political system in late imperial times as a triangular relationship between the state, the gentry, and the village, as opposed to a dualistic structure consisting of the state and the gentry. In fact, this three-way relationship was reflected in dike management in the Jianghan Plain. Dike work in the Jianghan Plain during the Qing dynasty can be divided into three types, depending on funding sources and the people or institutions responsible. In the first type, the government was in charge of collecting funds and managing dike work *(guan zheng guan xiu)* (this usually applied to very important sections of the major dikes). In the second type, the government was in charge of collecting funds but only supervised the dike work, while non-government personnel actually performed it *(guan zheng min xiu/guan du min xiu)* (this usually applied to other dikes along the Yangzi and the Han Rivers and their major tributaries). In the third type, government personnel were involved neither in collecting funds nor in dike work *(min zheng min xiu)* (this usually applied to minor or *yuan* dikes or to repairing minor damage to major dikes). In all three of these types, *guan* refers to the government and its personnel, and *min* refers to the rural gentry and common villagers. The following sections discuss their different roles in dike management.

Role of Government Personnel

Water control, particularly ensuring the integrity of the dike systems, was of utmost importance to local government officials.[5] Not surprisingly, then, an early Qing official thought that the magistrates of the counties (and departments) located in the Han River valley should devote 60 to 70 percent of their energy *(jingshen)* to dike affairs *(Mu ling shu* 1990 [1848], 9a: 41a). In 1859, the prefect of Anlu said that, "in the counties of Zhongxiang, Jingshan, Tianmen, and Qianjiang, dike work is the most important of [administrative] affairs" *(Jingshan xian zhi* 1882, 4: 6a). The same was true in the Yangzi River valley. For example, a prefect of Jingzhou, in the late nineteenth century, went even further than the prefect of Anlu, declaring: "In my prefecture, since the annual repair [of dikes] is closely related to the people's welfare, it is really the number one priority in governing" (Ni 1885[1876], 6, jingfei I: 5b). The compiler of a late Qing gazetteer of Gong'an County also mentioned that dike affairs were the number one priority in governing (*Gong'an xian zhi* 1874, 3: 37a). Dealing with dike affairs was considered even more important than maintaining social order and tax collection, two traditional responsibilities of local officials (Ch'u 1988 [1962], 15-16). In fact, the security of the dikes was a prerequisite for timely tax collection and a stable social order as, in cases of inundation, it would be difficult if not impossible to collect taxes on time. Furthermore, frequent inundation would engender disputes over water control.

According to Qing regulations, if a dike was not built solidly enough to resist inundation, the officials responsible for that dike would be punished. After 1788, the officials in charge of repairs to the Wancheng dike (and repair projects for any important dike that cost more than five hundred taels) were asked to send a report to the Board of Works (*Gongbu* – a central government ministry in charge of engineering projects, water control, and transportation, etc.) and had to guarantee the integrity of the dike for a period of ten years *(baogu shinian)*. If the dike held during this period, the responsible official would be rewarded with a promotion; if the target dike broke within this period, he would have to pay part or even all of the cost of rebuilding it.[6] He would also lose his position, or, depending on the seriousness of the inundation, even be imprisoned, or beheaded (*Zai xu xingshui jinjian* 1970 [1942], 486). Clearly, the purpose of punishment was to force the responsible officials to pay close attention to the dikes under their purview. After 1840, the government also required that any government-involved dike work, regardless of whether it involved building a new dike or repairing an existing dike, be good for three to ten years.[7] After 1883, ensuring the integrity of dikes became a mandatory official duty for local officials. This duty was considered such an essential and routine part of their job that they would not be rewarded for simply doing it (*Zai xu xingshui jinjian* 1970 [1942], 509).

Ideally, the local officials of the Jianghan Plain should have been responsible for the construction and maintenance of all dikes under their jurisdiction in order to ensure their integrity. But, in fact, they only assumed responsibility for the major dikes under their jurisdiction, and, on different dikes or dike sections the institutions and people responsible also differed. In 1674, the Kangxi emperor issued an edict assigning some officials the special task of taking charge of the dike systems in the Jianghan Plain; all of them (except for the prefect of Hanyang) were low-level officials (i.e., below the level of

Table 4

Titles of officials responsible for dike construction and maintenance

Administrative level	Places	Official titles
Prefecture (*fu*)	Hanyang	Prefect (*zhifu*)
	Wuchang, Jingzhou, Anlu, De'an	Sub-prefect (*tongzhi*)
Department (*zhou*)	Mianyang, Jingmen	First-class assistant department magistrate (*zhoutong*)
County (*xian*)	Jiangxia, Zhongxiang, Jingshan, Tianmen, Jiangling, Gong'an, Shishou, Jianli	Assistant county magistrate (*xiancheng*)
	Qianjiang	Second deputy magistrate (*zhubu*)
	Hanyang, Hanchuan, Dangyang, Yunmeng, Yingcheng, Xiaogan, Songzi	District police chief (*dianshi*)

Source: *Qing huidian shili* (1991 [1899], 931: 688).

prefect and county magistrate) (see Table 4).[8] Their responsibilities included leading the local people in controlling high water during the summer-autumn season and rebuilding or repairing dikes during the winter-spring season (*Qing huidian shili* 1991 [1899], 931: 688).

After a terrible flood in 1788, the ranks of officials responsible for certain dikes were raised. The official responsible for the Wancheng dike, the most important dike of all in the Jianghan Plain, for example, was changed from the county magistrate of Jiangling to a higher-rank official, the sub-prefect in charge of water conservancy in Jingzhou (*Jingzhou shuili tongzhi*). At the same time, the emperor ordered the governor general of Huguang and the governor of Hubei to go to Jingzhou in person each year, in turn, to supervise high water control during the high-water seasons. If they were too busy to go, they were to direct the circuit intendant (*daoyuan*) or prefect to serve as their representative. After 1832, the Jingzhou prefect assumed direct responsibility for the Wancheng dike because the *Jingzhou shuili tongzhi* was not of a sufficiently high rank to marshal the necessary financial resources for dike work and to supervise other local officials (Liu 1970; *Jingjiang dadi zhi* 1989, 217).

Because major dikes – particularly those along the Han River – may have crossed several counties, responsibility for managing them was divided up among the various county magistrates: each magistrate was responsible for dikes within his county. Important dikes that were located within one county could be divided into different sections and managed by different officials. For instance, the Wancheng dike was divided into three sections after 1788, with different subcounty officials assuming responsibility for each section.[9]

Moreover, after 1788, a small number of troops (*Jingzhou shuishi ying,* the marine battalion in Jingzhou) were assigned the job of taking care of the most vital part of the Wancheng dike. Almost a century later, in 1869, this job was taken over by the marine battalion of the Yangzi River *(Changjiang shuishi ying).* After 1876, the marine battalion was abolished and replaced by a dike protection battalion *(difang ying),* which recruited new members from among local peasants (Liu 1970).

The military was involved in the management not only of the Wancheng dike but also of other dikes. There were many *wei* (grain transport stations) in the Jianghan Plain, which were also responsible for dikes known as *jundi* (military dikes, or army dikes). Because the people responsible were too busy dealing with the business of tribute grain to be sent to the imperial court in the autumn, they had no time to repair the dikes under their juris- diction. Sometimes they postponed dike repair at will, thus weakening the dikes. Military dikes were usually located along rivers and were important, so in 1828 the emperor ordered them to be directly managed by the relevant local government (*Zai xu xingshui jinjian* 1970 [1942], 76).

In addition to their direct management, the military was also involved in other dike affairs. An 1883 report on dike repairs, for example, was co- reported by a military officer and the magistrate of Tianmen. This report mentioned that some soldiers (led by local officials) supervised labourers, while, if necessary, others were ordered to help the labourers actually build the dikes. The military officer who wrote this report also functioned as a major supervisor (*Zai xu xingshui jinjian* 1970 [1942], 481-82). Many times, military forces were engaged in suppressing conflicts arising from disputes over control of the dike systems (*Zai xu xingshui jinjian* 1970 [1942], 471; *Hubei sheng zhi shuili* 1995, 10). The involvement of the military in dike management not only reduced the cost of management in some situations but also demonstrated the Qing government's increasing concern with it.

Role of the Local People

Officials functioned as leaders or supervisors of dike work, while the local people contributed almost all of the physical labour.[10] By "the local people" I mean two general groups: (1) the gentry, who functioned as sub-leaders, and (2) the common villagers, who undertook the actual labour. The maintenance of the dike systems actually included two jobs: high water control and annual repairs. The purpose of high-water control was to prevent the dikes from rupturing during the high water seasons in summer and autumn. The responsible parties were to patrol the dikes day and night in order to find and remedy any dangerous conditions. The task of annual repairs included repairing broken dikes, building up the height of the old dikes, strengthening the weak parts of existing dikes, and constructing new dikes. This work usually took place in the dry season – that is, winter and spring. Beginning in the late Qing, the annual repairs became more important than high water control as they could prevent emergencies (Shu 1896, 6: 4b).

The earliest organization for high water control and annual repairs in Jingzhou was established in 1560 by the prefect Zhao Xian under the name *dijiafa* (the dike tithing system, or the system of dike headmen). According to this system, every one thousand *zhang* (1 Qing *zhang* = 3.2 metres) of dike had a *dilao* (dike elder), every five hundred *zhang* had a *dizhang* (dike administrator), and every one hundred *zhang* had a *dijia* (head of the dike) and ten *fu* (labourers) (*Songzi xian zhi* 1869, 4: 9a). After 1788, the Wancheng dike was divided into sixty-seven sections (five hundred *zhang* per section). Each section had one *dizhang*, five *dijia*, and twenty-five *fu*, all of whom lived close to the dike and were appointed for one year, during which time they were exempted from miscellaneous corvée (*Jingjiang dadi zhi* 1989, 264).

In the Qing there was a great variety of such organizations in different counties and/or *yuan*. In general, however, these organizations can be categorized into two types: those responsible for the major dikes and those responsible for the minor dikes. Their responsibilities may have overlapped, and not every *yuan* had these two organizations at the same time. The organization responsible for the major dikes usually consisted of a head and a few assistants. The head was known by various titles, including *ditou* (dike head); *weizhang* (*wei* chief); *dilao, dizhang, celao* (an elder in charge of records); and *zongwei* (*wei* general, or head of dike affairs). He could be a relatively well-off member of the rural gentry or a common villager, and he was either chosen by his peers or assumed the position in turn. The assistants were known by such titles as *dijia, weijia* (*wei* head, or secondary head, of dike), and *weilao* (*wei* elder). Assistants tended to be less well-to-do members of the rural gentry or common villagers; they usually served by rotation. Under them were specially assigned common villagers such as *fu, youfu* (roving labourers) and *yanfu* (smoke labourers) (*Zai xu xingshui jinjian* 1970 [1942], 6; *Qianjiang xian zhi* 1879 10: 35b; *Zhijiang xian zhi* 1866, 3: 2b; *Songzi xian zhi* 1869, 4: 9a).[11] These different titles suggest that not every village household was involved in this organization at the same time. The organization for major dikes usually undertook both high water control and annual repairs. In some counties, such as Songzi, the organization for annual repairs was separate from the organization for high water control; however, as in other counties, it also consisted of heads, assistants, and some assigned labourers.[12]

The organization responsible for *yuan* dikes consisted of a head, his assistants, and the rest of the common villagers in related villages or *yuan* or lineages. The heads were called *yuanzong* or *yuanzhang* (*yuan* chiefs) and *weizhang* or *weitou* (*wei* heads). Heads were either relatively rich gentry or were "chosen" by their peers. In any case, they usually came from a powerful lineage in the community, and it is likely that the position of head was passed down through lineages. In some places the local people took these positions in turn or were assigned to them according to the amount of land they owned. The assistants were known by such titles as *weijia, yuanfu* (*yuan* labourers), *yuetou* (head labourers), *futou* (labourer heads), and *weiyue/weiyi* (*wei* labourers). They may have been gentry or common villagers, and they served in turn or were assigned by the head. Each assistant was in charge of several individual households (Hu 1999 [1838], 184; *Xiangdi cheng'an* 1969, 1: 250a; *Jiangling xian zhi* 1794, 8: 10b; *Mianyang xian zhi* 1989, 147; Peng and Zhang 1993, 207). In some places, once a dike was under threat, the local people were called up by the striking of a gong and, led by *yuanzhang* (and *futou*), headed to the dike (*Mianyang xian zhi* 1989, 147).

Qing dike management organizations continued into the early Republic but with some changes. In the 1920s and 1930s, as a part of the nation-building movement, the government shifted its water-control emphasis from old traditions to new technology, thus the formation of some modern hydraulic government departments (Pietz 2002). Water conservancy commissions or bureaus for repair and high water control were established at the county level to take care of official dikes and important people's dikes. Above the county level, some special organizations, such as the Bureau of Dike Work on the Jing River *(Jingjiang digong ju)* and the Bureau of Engineering Work on the Yangzi and the Han Rivers *(Jianghan gongcheng ju),* were established to take care of individual dikes. Each organization had full-time clerks. *Yuan* dikes, however, continued to be managed by local villagers and headed by (elected) local gentry or better-off residents (LS 31-4-1405; LS 36-2-15; SZ 113-2-11; *Jiangling difang zhi* 1984, 71; *Jianli difang zhi* 1991, 298-99).

Although it is unclear how many of these gentry were resident or absentee, it is certain that they had as strong and direct an authority over village affairs as the gentry-landlords in the North China Plain and that they were even more powerful than their Yangzi delta counterparts. The local strongmen in the rural North China Plain had no interest in the position of *xiangbao* head but, rather, preferred to control the *xiangbao* from behind the scenes (Huang 1985, 227-28), while the gentry-landlords in the Yangzi delta usually lived in market towns and kept their distance from daily village affairs.

In general, in the Jianghan Plain in the Qing and the Republic, the involvement of officials in charge of and responsible for the management of major dikes increased. On the other hand, the local people remained in charge of the management of minor, or *yuan*, dikes. Local management organizations varied somewhat from county to county and *yuan* to *yuan*, but, in general, the gentry played a leading role in these organizations.

Source of Funds for the Management of Dike Systems

In addition to the different responsibilities of government personnel and the local people in dike management, there were also differences in how funds for dike work were raised. These funds included money from the government and/or money that was raised by officials as well as money collected from local residents, mostly villagers.

Although during the Qing most of the major dikes in the Jianghan Plain, even the all-important Wancheng dike, never belonged to the category of "government work,"[13] under special conditions (such as catastrophic flooding and the resulting lean harvests), the government did allocate money to rebuild or repair dikes in the areas affected. The largest sum of government funds used on the dikes in the Jianghan Plain was allocated in 1788, when a destructive flood inundated Jingzhou City. Two million taels of silver were allocated to rebuild the Wancheng dike that year (Liu 1970).

But this kind of ad hoc funding from the state treasury was rare, and local officials therefore had to raise dike funds themselves, via any available means, particularly in the middle and late Qing. The sources of these funds included money from interest on special funds that had been set up to pay for annual repairs; donations from, or fines paid by, officials; and various kinds of loans. Most of these loans had to be paid back by the local people – the repayment period could be as long as eight years (*Zai xu xingshui jinjian* 1970 [1942], 63) – and some of these loans could be in kind (e.g., in grain rather than in cash) (*Xu xingshui jinjian* 1937, 3576).

Beginning in the reign of Daoguang, borrowing money from the government to fund dike work became increasingly common.[14] These funds fell into different categories, including money borrowed from the commercial tax *(huoli)*, customs duty *(yangshui)*, salt tax *(yanli)*, land-and-labour-service tax *(diding[yin])*, and commercial transit tax *(lijin)* (*Zai xu xingshui jinjian* 1970 [1942], 316-17, 359-60). Since the *lijin* was originally levied for the purpose of funding military expenditures, using it for dike work comprised one of the most significant changes in the source of funding for such work (Peng and Zhang 1993, 218). The government also collected special taxes, such as a boat tax *(chuanjuan/chuanli)*, for dike work;[15] it sometimes even sent troops to worksites in order to save money (*Zai xu xingshui jinjian* 1970 [1942], 517). All this demonstrates the government's deepening involvement in dike management.

Donations (or contributions) were another source of dike funds. An 1827 case reveals that officials were asked to "donate" – that is, they were forced to contribute rather than doing so of their own accord. The memorial explains that one reason for the shortage of money for dike projects was that "donations" from officials were not deducted (from their salary) on time. In order to raise more funds for dike projects, voluntary donations from officials were always encouraged. For example, in 1889, an official of Hanyang was permitted to "build a memorial archway for his parents" since he had donated to dike building (*Zai xu xingshui jinjian* 1970 [1942], 63, 546).

After a flood, the late Qing government (as well as the Republican government) used relief funds to hire the local people to repair dikes (*yi gong dai zhen* – providing work as a form of relief). In the Jianghan Plain, both the incidences of relief and the area covered by it increased in the late Qing (Mei, Zhang, and Yan 1995, 207-8). Although, with regard to these relief funds, no single expenditure exceeded 2 million taels, the types of official funding for dike repairs increased in the late nineteenth century, as did resorting to such funds.

The most important source of local funds was the "earth fee" *(tufei)*. In theory, anyone who had farmland protected by a dike had to pay the earth fee (temple land, school land, and charitable land were excepted) (Shu 1896, 6: 30b). According to the specific situation of different counties, the earth fee could be collected annually, or it could be collected only once and the interest it earned used to fund future annual repairs, or it could be collected only if and when there was a dike rupture.

The personnel and organizations responsible for the collection of the earth fee varied considerably from place to place and changed over time. In Jiangling, for example, as early as 1801 two (government-run) *tuju* (earth bureaus) were set up in Shashi and Haoxue to collect the earth fee. After the responsibility for the Wancheng dike was shifted to the prefect of Jingzhou in 1832, more *tuju* were set up in both city and countryside. The people responsible for the collection of dike fees included *jingshu* (accountants or clerks), *dongshi* (dike managers), and *gunshou* (heads of payment) (Ni 1885 [1876], 6, jingfei I: 2b-5a). The reason for the establishment of *tuju* in Jianli, however, was different. In Jianli, the earth fee was collected by the *dilao* long before 1835; however, if the *dilao* (or *dongshi*, dike managers) failed to collect the earth fee on time, they had to pay it themselves. This bankrupted many *dilao* and made it hard to fill the position. Thus, in 1835 a *tuju* was established to collect the earth fee. The head of the *tuju* was known as the *jushou* (bureau head); the people who took the *tuquan* (earth tickets) and collected the earth fee were known as *tuzhang* (collectors of the earth fee) (*Jianli xian zhi* 1872, 3: 10b-11a).[16]

These earth fees usually went towards the cost of maintaining river dikes. Of course, the fees for maintaining *yuan* dikes were also born by the local people. These included the money for annual repairs and high water control and for the construction of new dikes. The levy for annual repairs and high water control was usually prorated by the people of one *yuan* or of a neighbouring *yuan* that benefited from the same *yuan* dike (*Hubei An Xiang Yun dao shuili ji'an, II:* 2b). As for the money used for new dike construction, a late Qing report warned that "if any person in a *yuan* who does not abide by the law and collects a fee in the name of private dike construction will be punished for disobeying an imperial decree" (Ni 1885 [1876], 8: 21b). Here the dikes in question were illegal (*si*, or private) *yuan* dikes. This implies that the money for the construction of new *yuan* dikes was also prorated by the local people.

Only those who lived within a *yuan* were required to contribute their share of labour and money to *yuan* dike works. But the local people did not, or could not, always pay the earth fee on time, especially in post-flood years or years of lean harvests. Thus, in Songzi, there were agents in each township who "urged" the villagers to pay. These agents, who were called *cuifu* (fee expediters/prompters), delivered an earth bill (*tudan*, which contained a list of payers) to the *danshou* (head of the bill), the first person (or perhaps the richest person or the person who paid the largest amount of the fee) on the list. The *danshou* was made responsible for collecting the earth fee from each individual household *(sanhu)* on his "bill" (*Songzi xian zhi* 1869, 4: 12b).

In Tianmen, the local people were not required to pay the earth fee each year. Instead, if a dike was threatened or required important repairs, the responsible official (*yinguan*, "seal-holding official") would select some members of the gentry in the *yuan* and organize a bureau to collect the earth fee and assign labourers according to the amount of land each owned or worked. If the money collected and labourers recruited were insufficient, neighbouring *yuan* that benefited from the *yuan* in question were to pay their share. After that, if the money and labour were still insufficient, the local government would provide support. The bureau that handled this would be abolished after the work was completed (*Xiangdi cheng'an* 1969, 1: 250ab).[17]

In addition to the earth fee, the local people – including gentry, merchants, and peasants – also donated to some small dike projects. This included individual donations and collective donations (whereby everyone in a village or a *yuan* contributed a share). The gentry usually acted either as the single donor of a special dike work or as the initiator of a donation for a *yuan* dike (*Xiakou xian zhi* 1920, 5: 10ab; Wang Pingsheng 2004, 52-54).[18] Some of the many market towns located along the banks of the Yangzi and the Han Rivers required merchants to share in funding the dike work (especially in case of an emergency) under the title of commercial tax, groceries tax, and rent. For example, merchants of Shashi were frequently called on by the local officials to contribute money to local dike work (Liu 1970, 11). In 1880, in the town of Yuekou in Tianmen County, merchants who dealt in daily necessities were required to contribute one *wen* (copper cash) from each *chuan* (string of copper cash) they traded, and merchants who sold medicine were required to contribute two *wen* (*Xiangdi cheng'an* 1969, 1: 250b). The major responsibility of merchants of this county during the Qing dynasty regarding dikes was to make contributions (*Tianmen shuili zhi* 1999, 271).

Just as the organization of dike management underwent changes in the Republic, so too did the source of dike fees. After 1920, the salt tax was partly used for dike work (*Jingjiang dadi zhi* 1989, 276); after 1926, all imports and exports of Hunan, Hubei, and Jiangxi were charged a 1 percent special tax to be used to maintain Hubei's dikes (LS 31-4-58). In the 1930s, Hubei began to collect a dike tax in all dike-related counties. The revenue from this tax was delivered to the provincial government to be used on major dikes along the Yangzi and Han Rivers. But the Dongjing River dike was still a people's dike, and the fees for people's dikes and *yuan* dikes were still collected from the local people in the area who benefited from the dike involved, according to the amount of land owned (He 1984, 53; *Jianli difang zhi* 1991, 356-57). Although in theory everyone should have paid a share of dike fees, in fact it appears it was the poor peasants who bore the largest share of this burden (*Honghu xian zhi* 1992, 101; *Hangyang xian zhi chugao* 1960, 34), just as in the late Qing (see Chapter 3).

During the Qing, therefore, the dike fees in the Jianghan Plain came from both the government and local society.[19] Both the amount and type of funds from the government increased in the late Qing, though many of the funds had to be paid back later by the local people. In the Republic, except for some major dikes that depended on the new dike tax, the construction and maintenance of most dikes still depended on funds collected from the local inhabitants.

Cooperation and Conflict in the Management of Dike Systems

No matter who the people responsible were, or where the dike fees came from, the task of dike work was usually carried out within a particular unit, such as a prefecture, a department, a county, or a *yuan* (which might comprise one or more villages). Dike projects can be divided into two kinds according to the number of administrative units involved: (1) single construction, which involved only one unit, and (2) co-construction, which involved two or more units. The latter can be further divided into co-construction but single repair, and co-construction and co-repair.

Necessary Cooperation

Because most of the major dikes along the Yangzi River were located in Jingzhou Prefecture, naturally the construction and repair of major dikes were usually carried out within this prefecture. Each county of Jingzhou was responsible for its own dikes; some counties cooperated with one another to construct or repair the dikes located along county boundaries. The prefecture of Jingzhou also cooperated with neighbouring prefectures on some special dike projects (*Dangyang xian zhi* 1866, 3: 6a-7b; *Zai xu xingshui jinjian* 1970 [1942], 282-83, 362-64).

In these kinds of cooperative efforts, the units involved were responsible for their agreed-on share. For instance, in Qianjiang County, during the early Qing, five jurisdictions contributed the necessary personnel for a cooperative project to build two dike sections along the Han River: the counties of Qianjiang (45 percent), Jingmen (15 percent), Jiangling (17 percent), Jianli (17 percent), and Jingwei (a grain transport station in Jingzhou) (6 percent) (*Qianjiang xian zhi* 1879 10: 38a).

This cooperative project reveals some differences between the Yangzi River dikes and the Han River dikes. The Wancheng dike along the Yangzi River, for example, was managed by one county; in contrast, there were five prefectures, two *zhou* (departments), and three *wei* (grain transport stations) involved in the management of the Han River dike. In addition to this, there were some other differences in the Han River dike itself. First, the riverbed of the Han River easily silted up due to the river's high sand content. Thus the job of raising the Han River dikes had to keep up with the rise of the riverbed. Second, the course of the Han River grew increasingly narrow from Zhongxiang (where it was a couple of thousand metres wide) to Hankou (where it was fewer than a thousand metres wide), and this placed greater pressure on the lower valley dikes. Third, the earth along the Han River contained a high ratio of sand, making it hard to build sturdy dikes. Fourth, unlike the Yangzi River dikes, the Han River dike was thin and low and was poorly maintained (*Zai xu xingshui jinjian* 1970 [1942], 182; Zeng 1898, 3b). Thus inundation occurred easily in the Han River valley and conflicts were much more common within its lower basin. If the dike in an upstream county broke, it may have caused little damage to that county, but it could wreak havoc in the downstream counties (due to their lower terrain).

Lower versus Upper Reaches

For the reasons given in the preceding section, the management of the Han River dikes was not the responsibility of any one county. For example, as early as in the Ming, the downstream counties had to share the responsibility for providing the funds and labour necessary for the upkeep of the upstream dikes in Zhongxiang. In 1663, the responsibility for these dikes was prorated as follows: Zhongxiang 40 percent, Jingshan 25 percent, Tianmen 25 percent, Qianjiang 3 percent, Jingzhou you wei and Anlu wei 4 percent (together), and Wuchang wei 3 percent (*Zhongxiang xian zhi* 1937, 3: 15b). In the 1680s, however, Wang Youdan, once the magistrate of Qianjiang, angered by the extortion of *yamen* clerks from Jingmen during their co-construction of a dike project, successfully petitioned the Board of Works to ban dike co-construction (*Zhongxiang xian zhi* 1795, 4: 2a; *Qianjiang xian zhi* 1879, 10: 47b-51a).[20] After that, each county or department had to assume responsibility for the rebuilding or repairing of its own dikes. As the magistrate of Tianmen said in 1818, the residents of his county "prefered to suffer natural disasters rather than suffer human-made calamities" *(ning shou tianzai, bu shou renhai)* (*Xiangdi cheng'an* 1969, 1: 56b).

Later, however, the rise of the Han riverbed and the blockage of its tributaries made inundation more frequent and the damage more severe. During the first stage of the Taiping Rebellion (1850-64), lower valley counties such as Tianmen agreed to co-repair the upstream dikes on one condition: they would never again be asked to help. The Zhongxiang dike broke in 1852 and, due to the war, remained unrepaired for six years. When the war ended, the residents of the lower valley, particularly Tianmen, were eager to repair the broken dike. They were even willing to offer a very small amount of their relief money – ten plus *wen* of money and a pinch of husked rice per person – to repair Zhongxiang's dike in order to prevent it from breaking so frequently in the future (*Xiangdi cheng'an* 1969, 1: 119a-124a, 163a-164a). By the end of the nineteenth century, inundation was so frequent and the damage so severe that the lower valley counties wanted to provide their share, but

Table 5

A brief history of repairs of the Han River dike in Zhongxiang

Year of break	Method of repair	Year of break	Method of repair
1658	Co-repair with seven units	1836	Responsible officials' fine, donations
1662	Co-repair with seven units	1840	Government funding
1676	Co-repair with seven units	1841	Loan
1691	Co-repair with seven units	1852	Did not repair
1706	Repaired by local labourers	1858	Boat tax, officials' donations,
1724	Repaired by local labourers		co-repair with three counties
1728	Government funding	1861	Co-repair with four countries
1740	Repaired by local labourers	1863	Co-repair with four countries
1779	Repaired by local labourers	1867	Magistrate-raised funds
1781	Repaired by local labourers	1869	Loan, government funding
1794	Government funding	1875	Magistrate-raised funds
1826	Government funding	1878	Magistrate-raised funds
1832	Magistrate-raised funds	1880	Magistrate-raised funds
1835	Government funding	1889	Government funding

Source: *Zhongxiang xian zhi* (1937, 3: 19a-21a).

they were unable to do so. At that time, repairs of the damaged dikes depended on emergency support from the government (if available) or on funds raised by the magistrate (Table 5).

The Han River dikes in Zhongxiang were of great importance to the counties on the lower reaches, but the people of Zhongxiang thought that the dikes "had one hundred disadvantages but no single advantage" for their county (*Zhongxiang xian zhi* 1937, 3: 14b). Because the interests of the different parties varied, conflicts over dike affairs became more common than cooperation. Furthermore, these conflicts usually occurred in zero-sum conditions. For example, the opening of a silted upstream tributary as an outlet may have been good for nearby residents (whose burden of coping with high water would have been lightened) but it would have been a catastrophe for downstream residents (who would suffer horrendous inundation). The latter would be absolutely against reopening the silted tributary to serve as an outlet. Given the management structure, conflicts were unavoidable.

One Bank versus the Other

Conflicts occurred not only between people on the upper reaches and those on the lower reaches but also between people on different sides of the same section of the river. Regardless of which section of the Han River in the

Jianghan Plain one considers, if the dike on one side were to break, the integrity of the dike on the opposite side would automatically be guaranteed. During the post-flood season, the people who lived on the unbroken side would oppose repairing the broken dike on the opposite side for the simple reason that the broken side now served as an outlet, assuring that the dike on their side would not break any time soon.

For this reason, the people on the northern bank of the Han River and the people on its southern bank sued each other and fought over the opening/blockage of the Zekou (*Ze* outlet) for seven decades (1844 to 1913) (*Dongjinghe difang zhi* 1994, 2). Before this, the local people were said to have been cautious and kind (*Xiangdi cheng'an* 1969, 2: 36a), but during these seven decades they became "cunning" and violent (*Xiangdi cheng'an* 1969; *Da zekou cheng'an* 2004). In the late Qing, other court battles were waged in, for instance, Penggong *yuan* and Qishier *yuan*, which were situated along the boundary of Tianmen, Mianyang, and Hanchuan (*Hubei sheng zhi shuili* 1995, 8). More frequently, the local people would fight each other directly in order to find a solution: sometimes they even used real weapons, including firearms (see Chapter 7). In all of these conflicts, the local gentry played an important role: they were leaders of feuding militia, composers of appeals to the upper levels of government, and negotiators among different parties.

Local Governments versus Central Government

Conflict also occurred between local governments and the central government. Few magistrates dared to act openly against the interests of their assigned counties, even if it meant going against the wishes of upper-level jurisdictions. Their attitude towards the banning of private *yuan* provides a good example. Despite always prohibited (Shuili dianlibu 1991, 298), year after year more and more private *yuan* were enclosed.[21] One of the main reasons for this involved local government support. From the point of view of the central and provincial governments, private *yuan* were not supposed to exist; but from the point of view of the local government, private *yuan* were a source of tax revenue (Ni 1885 [1876], juanmo: 8b; Tan 1985). Thus, magistrates were reluctant to prohibit them. During the reign of Daoguang, there were so many private *yuan* that the emperor ended up tacitly consenting to the status quo. In 1833, he did not ask local officials to destroy the existing private *yuan* but only to prohibit the opening of new ones (*Zai xu xingshui jinjian* 1970 [1942], 101-2).

In 1867, the magistrate of Shishou even helped the local people build a "private" *yuan.* He turned a deaf ear to the banning of private *yuan* and, instead, led the local people in reinforcing some private *yuan* that should not have been built, recording them in the new gazetteer to ensure their legal status (*Zai xu xingshui jinjian* 1970 [1942], 321). The Republican government, like its imperial predecessor, issued orders banning private *yuan* (*Jingjiang di zhi* 1937, 4: 6), which of course meant that the enclosure of private *yuan* was still a problem in the Republic.

Officials versus Villagers

There was much conflict between officials and villagers. In some cases, on their own initiative angry residents went to a certain dike section to block an outlet that had been opened by the state (*Da zekou cheng'an* 2004). In other cases, once local officials got involved, the villagers would express their grievances to those officials who stood on the opposite side or who failed to do their job, both literally and figuratively. Thus, in 1876, some villagers of Jianli, in the belief that the prefect of Jingzhou opposed the blocking of an outlet, attacked him as he went to investigate the situation (*Zai xu xingshui jinjian* 1970 [1942], 388-89).

When it came to dike management, unlike peasants who rebelled against exorbitant taxes and levies, these villagers struggled simply to protect their livelihood and to resist officials who had different views or who did not do their job. In 1877, some Tianmen peasants, angered at being overcharged for dike fees and having the clerk and runners of the Dike Bureau of Yuekou force them to pay, openly destroyed the bureau (*Tianmen shuili zhi* 1999, 331). In 1881, some residents of Qianjiang, led by "wicked" gentry of Mianyang, even dared to resist troops that had been sent to ban their illegal dam building in Zekou (Shuili dianlibu 1991, 988). In 1910, an expectant county magistrate was sent to supervise the emergency repair of a *yuan* dike in Mianyang. Unfortunately, this weak *yuan* dike broke and inundated some other *yuan* in Hanchuan. Victims were angered and condemned the incompetence of this expectant county magistrate. The poor man was so desperate that he jumped into the water in an attempt to commit suicide. People around immediately saved him (*Zai xu xingshui jinjian* 1970 [1942], 659).

Villagers versus Villagers

Even within the same *yuan*, people's attitudes towards working on the dikes differed, depending on the distance between their property and the dikes. Those who lived in high places and far from the dikes were reluctant to go to work on the *yuan* dikes and also often refused to pay their share of the earth fee.[22] But those who lived near the *yuan* dikes usually had neither sufficient money nor labour power to ensure, on their own, that they were maintained in good condition. Moreover, some local powerful individuals refused to work on the dikes, preferring to pay their tenants to take their place (*Jiangling xian zhi* 1794, 8: 10b). Because of the lack of cooperation on dike repairs and high water control, some *yuan* in Qianjiang, Mianyang, and Tianmen in the Qing simply separated into two or three smaller individual *yuan* (Peng and Zhang 1993, 211).

Thus, although the gentry played an important role in dike management, conflicts and lack of cooperation among the local people led to the unavoidable deterioration of their dikes. The conflicts over dikes continued in the Republic. A survey conducted in Gong'an County contains a detailed description of such conflicts:

> The territory of Gong'an is low, and the dikes are essential to the life of the residents. There are about 80 *yuan,* large and small. There is no unified method of apportioning earth and fees – each *yuan* decides on that. Although the managers of *yuan* dikes are chosen by the villagers in the *yuan,* almost all of [the managers] are despotic gentry and rich households. Although the apportionment of the earth fee must be approved by the *yuan* assembly, this is only a formality. Although the controller *(jiancha)* has cleared the account [of the earth fee], it is usual to give inflated figures in the report and to squander the funds. Therefore, the files of the disputes regarding dike affairs each winter stand in piles many feet high and there are countless lawsuits – no magistrate has a solution. Because the size of the various *yuan* differs, the number of households of each *yuan* differs too; the fertility of *yuan* land varies; some dike projects are easy while others are difficult; and the work required varies year by year. Thus it is exceptionally difficult to [find] a unified [way of apportioning] the earth fee. This is the first reason. According to local customs regarding *yuan,* the earth fee is usually collected after the autumn harvest, while all dike projects are carried out early in the spring. The funds needed for these projects are paid in advance by managers and rich households in the *yuan,* and therefore no households other than those of despotic gentry and rich families can assume the position of managers. The spring dike projects could not be carried out if the system of managers were abolished. This is the second reason. Due to these two factors, the burden of the earth fee will not be apportioned equally until it is unified; the corrupt practices of the system of managers cannot be reduced unless the system itself is abolished. But in practice it is difficult to unify the earth fee and to abolish the system of managers. That is why the [problem of] dike-related disputes has not been thoroughly resolved. (*Hubei xianzheng gaikuang* 1934, 1004)

In 1947, in Hanchuan County, it was found that each individual *yuan* was only responsible for its own dikes and rarely cooperated with neighbouring *yuan* to protect against high water (LS 31-4-1531).

From the Qing to the Republic, there appears to have been a growing number of conflicts over the Jianghan Plain dikes. These conflicts were caused by the changing and unstable environment and, in turn, further damaged the environment. Clearly, if these conflicts were intelligently settled, both parties benefited; however, if they were not, the result was often not only wrangling but also never-ending inundation. Neither party would benefit and local society and the state would suffer as well.

Decline of the Management of Dike Systems

The increasing conflict over the dike systems partly reflected the serious problems with dike management, which became increasingly ineffective during the Qing and the Republic. By the mid-Qing, with the expansion of the dike systems, especially with the increasing enclosure of *yuan,* most of the tributaries of the Yangzi and the Han Rivers, and many lakes between these two rivers, had become silted up. Furthermore, islets and shoals became densely distributed outside the river dikes. Both officials and the local people knew where the former flood diversion areas were, but they were unable to restore them because many of these areas had already been turned into villages and farmland (*Zhongxiang xian zhi* 1937, 3: 13a).

It is true that the shrinking of the flood diversion areas and the increasing disorder of waterways did contribute to frequent inundation, but one should not downplay the importance of the dike management in dike safety. Studies have found that, in the late Qing, solar activities became weaker and annual rainfall decreased, which were favourable for the reduction of inundations. But, by contrast, inundations in the Jianghan Plain in this period became more and more frequent (Qiao 1963; Mei, Zhang, and Yan 1995, 202). That means frequent inundation might not have been eliminated but could have been reduced. Thus, in the long run, aside from the increasing disorder of waterways, a more important major cause of the more frequent inundation was the decline in the effectiveness of dike management, including the increase in various conflicts over water control.

As indicated earlier, most of the major dikes along the Yangzi and Han Rivers in the Jianghan Plain were people's dikes. These can be traced back to the early Qing. In a 1715 edict, the Kangxi emperor argues: "The Yangzi River does not change its course [as the Yellow River course does], so [the central government] has handed it over to local governments to take care of it" (*Qing huidian shili* 1991 [1899], 931: 688-89). In a 1727 edict, the Yongzheng emperor allowed the river dikes of Jingzhou – including the Wancheng dike – to remain as people's dikes. He thought that if these dikes were made imperial dikes *(qindi),* either the local people would not take the necessary measures to maintain them once they had problems or they would relax their vigilance and rely on the central government to maintain them. Therefore, he decided that, although the government would sometimes finance these dikes, their classification as people's dikes would not be changed (*Jingzhou fu zhi* 1880, 17: 1ab). These decisions placed government personnel in a supervisory role in dike management, while the local people had to bear the burden of providing both funds and labour. This also shows that, from the view of the central government, the river dikes in the Jianghan area were far less important than was the Yellow River dike. Although the Wancheng dike was nominally made an official dike after 1788, it in fact remained a non-government work since the fees for its annual repair still came from the local society.

The Jing River (a section of the Yangzi River in Jingzhou) was very unstable; therefore, the central government should have paid more attention to the care of its dike, as it did for the Yellow River dike and the Grand Canal. This, of course, is not to argue that if the major dikes in the Jianghan Plain had been directly controlled by the central government they would have been more effective since, after all, the management of the Yellow River dike, which was under the control of the central government, was still problematic and ineffective in the Qing (Dodgen 1991). River administration alone should not bear all the blame (Finnane 1984). However, according to Pomeranz (1993), the withdrawal of government involvement in the management of the Grand Canal in the Huang-Yun area made matters even more problematic. In other words, we must make a distinction between the role of central government and the role of local government in dike management.

When the government funded a dike project, the officials in charge of that project usually asked for more money than was really needed, and they pocketed the difference. A report delivered to the Board of Works in 1780 stated that the total expenditure for repairs on the dikes of Hubei amounted to 78,500 taels. Later it was discovered that the figure had been inflated by 19,600 taels. This so enraged the Qianlong emperor that he confiscated the difference and used it to fund future dike work (*Xu xingshui jinjian* 1937, 3599-3600). In the edict dealing with this report, the emperor said that it would have been "reasonable" if the total had been inflated by "only" a couple of thousand taels. He was angered not over the fact that the report was distorted but, rather, over the extraordinary amount that was siphoned off. This suggests that, at that time, "false reports" and the corruption of government personnel was widespread and tolerated even by the emperor. Similar corruption could be found in the management of the Yellow River dikes in Huang-Yun in the Qing (Pomeranz 1993, 193-201).

By the late Qing, corruption had become a widespread and stubborn disease among officialdom,[23] and dike management was hardly immune from this malady. Lin Zexu had found that, in some large counties in the Jianghan Plain, there were thousands of "fraudulent/pretend *yamen* runners" – similar to unregistered *yamen* runners *(baiyi)* – who collected fraudulent taxes and fees from villagers (*Zai xu xingshui jinjian* 1970 [1942], 179), and many of these (pretend) *yamen* runners worked on dike affairs. Actually, a special class that depended on the dike fees for survival gradually emerged from among administrative personnel. For instance, in Mianyang, "in each *yuan* ... there are several kinds of persons who specialize in embezzling dike fees. They are called *jushen* (bureau gentry). There are no less than seven or eight thousands of them in the whole department, and all of them are connected with the city and collude with each other" (Li 1957, 935). The clerks and runners of the Bureau of Dikes *(diju)* in the three counties of Tianmen, Jingshan, and Qianjiang in the 1870s completely controlled the collection of dike fees and frequently overcharged and extorted money from villagers (*Zai xu xingshui jinjian* 1970 [1942], 487). It was said that in Jiangling in the late Qing, being an accountant or clerk for a dike bureau "had almost become a hereditary position. [They] smoked foreign cigarettes, made friends and enriched their family [with embezzled dike fees], [and they were] accustomed to taking [money] from the treasury and enjoying themselves" (Ni 1885 [1876], 6, jingfei I: 13b). It must have been remarkably easy for dike bureau staff to embezzle dike fees.

Some capable and honest high-ranking officials such as Lin Zexu attempted to ban *yamen* runners from involvement in collecting the earth fee, and the local people were asked to carefully select fair-minded local gentry to collect and manage the earth fee (Lin 1935, 106). While the ideal candidates for *yuanzhang* (responsible for flood control) should be experienced, upright, and well-off (Hu 1999 [1838], 199), unfortunately, some of the gentry were as dishonest as the *yamen* runners. Sometimes they overcharged the earth fee or cooperated with *yamen* runners in delaying the completion of dike projects. In fact, as early as 1819, the magistrate of Tianmen once banned the gentry members of every *yuan* from being *weizhang* (Wang 1832, 2: 62a). In 1858, the magistrate of Jiangling even refused to rely on the local gentry or *yamen* runners to collect the earth fee and, instead, sent his relatives and personal secretaries *(muyou)* to deal with the collection (*Zai xu xingshui jinjian* 1970 [1942], 266). Later, the prefect of Jingzhou found that the corruption of the gentry exceeded even that of the *yamen* runners, and the corruption of the *yamen* runners exceeded even that of local officials (Ni 1885 [1876], 6, jingfei I: 1b). According to Bradly Reed (2000), however, the corruption of *yamen* runners was usually exaggerated: many fees collected by the *yamen* runners were an inseparable part of the government's income to maintain the daily operation of county *yamen* and were not "corrupted" by the *yamen* runners.

In most cases, therefore, the involvement of government personnel was unavoidable, no matter how the dike fees were collected or used. Thus, it was difficult to curb corrupt practices such as inflating reports *(fumao)*, jerry-building *(toujian)*, extorting *(xusuo)*, and proxy remittance in tax payment *(baolan)* (Wang 1832, 1: 12b-13a). Whenever a new regulation was issued, the people responsible would, as a rule, begin work promptly, but that soon changed. Even capable and honest officials could not do everything themselves and had to assign some *yamen* runners as their representatives. After 1788, the governor, prefects, and even the magistrates sometimes sent assistants to supervise dike work (particularly high water control). These representatives, however, needed transportation and meal allowances as well as money to cover the costs involved in investigating, checking, and supervising dike work (*Zai xu xingshui jinjian* 1970 [1942], 795). This actually increased the burden of the earth fee and the chances of corruption. Counties along the lower Han River had some special petty officials *(xunyuan)* in charge of dike work; they might actually go to the dike, but paid no attention to repair work after receiving bribes (called *guili* [customary fees]) from *ditou* and *weizhang,* and they, too, neglected the rise or fall of high water and did not supervise the local people in patrolling the dikes during high-water seasons (*Zai xu xingshui jinjian* 1970 [1942], 6). Thus, a regulation of dike maintenance during the reign of Daoguang suggested appointing first-term officials and upright and honest local gentry to deal with dike affairs (*Jianli difang zhi* 1991, 200). Even funds collected from the local people were subject to speculation. It was found in late Qing Jiangling that the *yamen* runners who were in charge of collecting the earth fees pocketed 70 percent of what they collected and only 10 percent of the local people had not paid (Ni 1885 [1876], 6, jingfei I: 6b). When one *futou* got a sum of the earth fee funds for dike work, more than twenty charges had been illegally deducted from that fund (Ni 1885 [1876], 6, jingfei II: 2b-3a).

In theory, the fact that so many institutions and officials were involved in dike management might have been an indication that the dike systems were receiving careful attention. But in practice, as we have seen, things often went awry. All of the expenditures on dike management, including the cost of people who worked in the dike bureau and the *shoushi* (dike manager, or chief manager) who supervised dike works, and the salaries of the special petty officials or clerks in charge of dike work who were sent out by the dike bureau, were directly taken from the dike fees (*Jingshan xian zhi* 1882, 4: 17a). Thus, the greater the number of people who were involved in dike management, the greater the expenditure on management.[24] And the establishment of new organizations for management in fact offered more chances for more people to embezzle dike fees. As a result, the money that could have been used on the dikes was significantly reduced. It was said that, in some *yuan* of Hanchuan in the late Qing, less than half of the dike fees was actually spent on the dikes (*Hanchuan xian zhi* 1873, 9: 29b). And, in late Qing Mianyang, only 20 to 30 percent of the earth fees were used on dike projects (Peng and Zhang 1993, 237).[25] Thus, even though we should not assume that all officials were corrupt, as the Qing official Wang Fengsheng (1832, 1: 12b-13a) asserted, a mere handful of honest officials could not change long-standing corrupt practices. In the Republic, even official reports revealed that, at most, only 60 percent or so of the dike taxes collected from dike-related counties was used on dike work, and 30 percent or so was spent on other uses (*Gailiang digong yijian shu* n.d., attached table).

The management of *yuan* dikes, as we have noted, was also subject to problems. In Jiangling, for example, the post of head of the *yuan* was usually passed down through a single lineage. Over time, work on the dike became more and more careless and both powerful households and households that lived far from the *yuan* dike became reluctant to help repair and maintain it. The result was increasingly frequent floods. However, in contrast, in Baiju *yuan* and Hulu *yuan,* the people cooperated effectively in managing their *yuan* dike: the rich contributed money and the poor contributed labour. Thus, even in the massive flood of 1788, the dikes in these two *yuan* did not break (Ni 1885 [1876], zhiyu: 2b). This is a positive example that demonstrates, again, the relationship between *yuan* dike security and management.[26] In Jianli, there were three different organizations responsible for annual repair, high water control, and dike fee collection, respectively, but most of them declined or were abolished in the late Qing (*Jianli xian zhi* 1872, 3: 10b-11a).

Compared to government-managed dike work, work run by the local people had some intrinsic weaknesses. First, because no responsible officials were involved, there was no guarantee of quality. Second, since there was no requirement for a "safety period," if any section of these dikes broke, no one could be held responsible. Third, work on these dikes usually was not reported to the Board of Works, making it difficult for the government to assess the dike's actual condition in case of a break. For instance, it was found that official dikes were usually more solidly built than people's dikes, most of which were short, thin, and easily broken. Thus ruptures usually occurred on dikes run by the local people (albeit supervised by government personnel) (*Xiangdi cheng'an* 1969, 2: 5b; *Zai xu xingshui jinjian* 1970 [1942], 125). Furthermore, there were differences in the people's attitudes towards major dikes and minor dikes (*yuan* dikes). It seems they tended to pay less attention to the major dikes than they did to the minor ones. This may be because the minor dikes directly protected their land and property (or perhaps just because they were more likely to break). This despite the fact that, if a major dike broke, it was hard to ensure the integrity of the *yuan* dikes.

One of the most common problems in dike work was jerry-building. This included using inferior material such as sand instead of soil, reducing the time spent on ramming the earth, scraping the ground of the old dike and falsely claiming it as a new one, and removing the earth at the foot of the old dike and falsely claiming an increase in height (Wang 1832, 1: 13a; *Zai xu xingshui jinjian* 1970 [1942], 124; Hu 1999 [1838], 170-72). Thus, the height, length, and volume of (official) dikes were not up to standard: frequently this resulted in inundation due to water overflowing the undersize dikes. Moreover, the dimensions of each section of a dike (i.e., length, width, and height) were not very clear, and it was easy to falsify them when a break occurred. Therefore, although there was a very strict requirement that a dike be secure for a certain period, this was often a mere formality, and most dike ruptures were caused by over-flooding (Wang 1832, 1: 13ab, 15b). At any rate, only government-funded dikes were subject to this requirement.[27] In some particularly vulnerable sections of official dikes, stone was dumped into the water to protect the walls. But, very commonly, the amount of stone was less than what had been requested: "The amount of stone is less than half due to corruption among the stone boat [personnel]" (Yu 1999 [1840], 138). Similarly, in the late Qing in the Han River valley, although people knew the inappropriateness of the construction method known as *jin bao yin* (earth wraps sand) – building dikes with a core of sand covered with soil – that inferior technique continued to be used.[28]

As a result, inundation in the Jianghan Plain became more frequent in the middle and late Qing. The Wancheng dike, for instance, broke on average every 5.1 years in the reign of Kangxi (1662-1722) but every 2.5 years in the reign of Daoguang (1821-50). Only the formation of two new southward outlets after that reduced the frequency of its rupture (1851-1908) (Table 6).[29] In the whole Jianghan Plain, water calamities occurred on average every two

Table 6

The frequency of breaks on the Wancheng dike in the Qing dynasty

Periods	1644-61	1662-1772	1723-35	1736-95	1796-1820	1821-50	1851-61	1862-74	1875-1908
Number of years	18	61	13	60	25	30	11	13	33
Breaks	4	12	2	6	5	18	3	2	3
Frequency*	4.5	5.1	6.5	10	5	2.5	3.61	6.5	11

Note:

* Frequency refers to average number of years between breaks.

Source: Jingjiang dadi zhi (1989, 69-74). Frequency is calculated by the author.

Table 7

The frequency of water calamities in the Jianghan Plain in the Qing dynasty

Periods	1644-61	1662-1772	1723-35	1736-95	1796-1820	1821-50	1851-61	1862-74	1875-1908	1909-11
Number of years	18	61	13	60	25	30	11	13	33	3
Times*	6	21	4	21	3	22	7	12	19	2
Frequency**	3	2.9	3.3	2.8	8.3	1.3	1.5	1	1.7	1.5
Counties***	7.1	6.8	7.7	7.4	6.5	7.8	11.1	7	NA	NA

Notes:

* Times refers to the number of years that had water calamities.

** Frequency refers to average number of years between each occurrence.

*** Counties refers to the average number of counties that suffered from water calamities.

Source: Zhang (1994a, 143, Table 3).

to three years in the early and mid-Qing, and increased to every one to two years in the late Qing (Table 7).

The situation of dike management in the Republic was even worse. In the early Republic, even the *dilao* who were responsible for the daily maintenance of the Jingjiang Great Dike were driven off, and the local people were reluctant to take responsibility since now the dike belonged to the category of government dikes (this is exactly what the Yongzheng emperor had worried about two hundred years earlier). Furthermore, the people who were responsible for the collection of dike fees and the people who were in charge of dike work hardly cooperated at all. People were outraged that the dikes were even more poorly managed than they had been in the late Qing (*Jingjiang di zhi* 1937, 2: 67, 4: 20). In the 1930s, the engineers and technicians responsible for the annual repair of major, government-managed dikes and the local officials who were responsible for high water control generally did not cooperate effectively: the engineers had no authority to recruit peasants even in emergency situations, while the local officials had no authority over dike projects and had no idea whether projects were solid or not (*Hubei sheng zhi shuili* 1995, 22). There were some temporary official organizations responsible for high water control in summer, but nobody was in charge of daily maintenance after that. Therefore, the neglect of daily maintenance was the main reason for frequent dike ruptures (*Gailiang digong yijian shu* n.d., 4). When the record-high floodwater of 1935 broke a major dike in Jiangling, the magistrate of this county could not even find the file for this dike, thinking it belonged to another county, while the person who was sent by the Bureau of Dike Work on the Jing River (*Jingjiang digong ju*) to supervise the work on the Jingjiang Great Dike ran away when he realized its disastrous state (*Jiangling difang zhi* 1984, 16).

And very often dike fees were diverted to other uses (such as paying the local warlords' troops), or were used as administrative fees by the local government, or were stolen by responsible parties, or were embezzled by managers to buy opium, or were used to buy inferior materials (such as reeds) in place of standard materials (such as stone) for dike construction and repair (LS 1-5-644; LS 1-5-781; LS 19-8-55 [1]; He 1984, 59; Ao 1990, 10; *Jianli difang zhi* 1991, 358). A Republican report judged the dike fees as one of the major origins of official corruption in Hubei (*Gailiang digong yijian shu* n.d., 1). In the Republic there was a saying: "[The money] a county magistrate [can embezzle] in ten years doesn't compare with [what] a water official [can embezzle] in one year" (*Wuhan difang zhi* 1986, 96). After dike ruptures occurred, it was not uncommon for dike managers or responsible officials to be charged with dereliction of duty (LS 1-3-566; LS 1-4-452; LS 1-5-607; LS 1-5-838).

Another problem in the Republic concerned the fact that dikes were sometimes used as defence works, particularly by the Japanese invading army, which seriously damaged them in many places (*Jiangling difang zhi* 1984, 34-35).

Regarding people's dikes, it appears that it was landowners who had to bear the burden of dike fees. However, in practice, landlords passed the fees on to their tenants, or the fees were apportioned among the local people according to the number of members in each household (*Honghu xian zhi* 1992, 101). Moreover, landlords usually supervised dike work. At the same time, it was not unusual for the local government to extort extra money from the villagers in the name of dike fees (*Hanyang xian zhi chugao* 1960, 34). Besides, it seems it is very difficult for neighbouring *yuans* to cooperate with each other in order to control water (LS 31-4-1404; LS 31-4-1531).

In the end, then, an increase in the number of institutions and personnel responsible for dike management in the late Qing did not reduce the frequency of inundation but, paradoxically, contributed to the declining effectiveness of dike management. This was due to a lack of cooperation among the various parties and to institutional corruption. In the Republic, the separation of the responsibilities of high water control and annual repair only increased the difficulty of cooperation, thus making things even worse.

Conclusion

Although the increasing frequency of water calamities in the Jianghan Plain in the Qing and the Republic could be attributed to the over-reclamation of upstream mountains, which caused eroded silt to raise riverbeds in the lower reaches, and to the over-enclosure of *yuan*, which shrank flood diversion areas, a more important reason was the mismanagement of the dike systems, particularly when this occurred simultaneously with environmental deterioration and financial difficulties.

Over the course of the Qing and the Republic, the deteriorating environment in the Jianghan Plain led more to conflict than to cooperation in dike management. Problems grew even bigger and became harder to solve. Both the government and the local people had to pay more attention to, and expend more funds and personnel on, high-water control and annual repairs. In the long run, the Qing government became more deeply involved in dike management. Even in the late Qing, when the government was faced with a financial crisis, it increased, albeit reluctantly, its involvement in dike management. In fact, in the Jianghan Plain dike management became the major administrative task of magistrates and prefects. The Republican government even established special institutions to manage some major dikes that were more advanced (at least in their organization) than late Qing institutions.

Despite the proliferation of dike-management institutions and the increasing number of personnel assigned to dike management, state involvement in dike systems remained insufficient. First, the Qing central government refused to take full responsibility for the major dikes in the Jianghan Plain; it usually only provided financial aid in cases of emergency. For this reason, blaming the Qing state for its incompetence with regard to water control does not provide the full picture as the central state, in fact, left dike management to local government and the local people. Second, in addition to widespread (and well-known) corruption in dike management throughout the Qing and the Republic, local governments in the Qing did not cooperate well – either with each other or with the local people – regarding dike management (particularly for the Han River dikes), and technical offices set up to manage dikes in the Republic failed to cooperate with local governments. Although the state promulgated regulations to guide dike management, they generally did not work well. And third, although the number of institutions and personnel responsible for dike management increased until the late Qing, the overall effectiveness of government management did not increase; rather, money was wasted on a top-heavy, inefficient, and corrupt bureaucracy. In the Republic, the separation of technological organization from the administrative system made the upkeep of dikes even more difficult.

Of course, the officials responsible for dike management, especially the magistrates and prefects, did not want the dike systems to decline and, indeed, did what they could to avoid dike ruptures. But they were constrained in what they could do because of their limited power and because of inherent institutional corruption. Although dike management was theoretically their most important duty, it was only one among many of their official duties. Inevitably, officials had to rely on their assistants to deal with many things. However, if they relied on their clerks or the *yamen* runners, these petty officials were more than likely to engage in corruption and extortion, paying insufficient attention to the quality of dike work. If they relied on the local gentry, some of them were also likely to engage in corruption and extortion. It was hard for all of them to be just and upright all the time. Non-governmental organizations, under the leadership of the local gentry, were only sometimes effective in managing dikes (particularly *yuan* dikes). Overall, in both the Qing and the Republic, dike breaks were rarely caused by massive floods but, rather, by poor repairs, poor cooperation, and mismanagement.

The local gentry played a unique and crucial role in dike management through the Qing and the Republic. They were the bridges between the state and rural society; they held most of the *yuanzhang* and *weizhang* positions due to their economic power and social status; and they were usually the initiators and the primary funders of dike fee contributions. They collected and managed the dike fees, led and supervised dike work, mediated dike-related conflicts, reported the local people's opinions to the government, and commanded the local people in fights with opposing interests. Under these circumstances, it is safe to conclude that the fortunes of any rural community in the Jianghan Plain partly depended on the conscientiousness of its local gentry.

All this should lead us to reconsider the role of the state in rural China. According to Michael Mann (1984), traditional Chinese society was characterized by a high degree of despotic power but a low degree of infrastructural power; that is, traditional China had a very high level of centralized state power but the state's control of local society was relatively weak. Before 1949, the Chinese government mainly relied on informal officials and the gentry to control rural society. This kind of indirect infrastructural power was usually effective in dealing with many things, such as the collection of taxes and the mediation of civil disputes (Hsiao 1960; Ch'u 1988 [1962], 168-92). But it was ineffective in dealing with conflicts and problems over water control, such as those in the Jianghan Plain in the Qing and the Republic. To resolve these kinds of conflicts and problems, a high degree of infrastructural power was required, and this the pre-1949 Chinese state did not provide.[30]

3 The Dike Systems and the Jianghan Economy

The relationship between water calamities and the dike systems has been a major subject in recent Chinese scholarship on the Jianghan Plain, but almost all such scholarship focuses on the impact of dike-related floods on the local society and economy. Other than looking at some random examples, these studies rarely provide any systematic quantitative analysis of such topics as the economic benefits or the monetary cost of dike building and maintenance, or the monetary burden of the capital and labour that the local people spent on dike affairs in the Jianghan Plain in the Qing and the Republic, or the negative effects of the dike systems on local agriculture.

It is well known that water-control projects played a very important role in the development of the traditional Chinese economy. The economic historian Chi Ch'ao-ting (1963 [1936]) went so far as to argue that, during different periods in Chinese history, key economic areas were distinguished and defined by their varied styles of water-control projects. In seeking to highlight the key importance of water control in the traditional economy, Chi made his case in the broadest terms. Thus, although he discussed a great number of large water-control projects, he did not examine them in detail or provide even rough estimates of their returns on investment.

Using statistics relating to water-control projects recorded in traditional gazetteers, Dwight Perkins (1969, 60-70) analyzes the efficiency of water-control projects in China from 1368 to 1968 and argues that their return on investment, particularly in the case of agricultural water conservancy projects, tended to be very low. Some of these projects – especially irrigation projects in the North China Plain – could not usually be sustained for long. Thus, in the 1960s, the CCP shifted to emphasizing such low-cost projects as rural electrification and pumping stations.

Mark Elvin (1993), who looks at water-control projects from the perspective of environmental change and sustainable development, argues that the traditional Chinese economy underwent "three thousand years of unsustainable growth" due mainly to the negative environmental effects of the reclamation of mountains, the clearance of forests, and the high cost of maintaining water-control projects. Elvin's evidence is convincing: unquestionably, environmental change has been driven largely by human activities (undertaken mostly for survival), and, over the long term, the reclamation of upstream mountains and hills has caused serious hydrological problems for downstream plains. Elvin's paradoxical title "three thousand years" was intentionally chosen to stimulate a new way of thinking and to emphasize that everything, including water-control projects, has both advantages and disadvantages (Bao 2004a). Elvin's real subject is the side effects of the development of the traditional economy throughout China's long history.

While Perkins analyzed the rate of return to investment in water-control projects, and Elvin the impact of water-control projects on economic development, both reached the same negative conclusion. In Elvin's view, while they may have kept people alive for three thousand years, these projects were environmentally unsustainable. Both Perkins and Elvin looked at long-term changes across the whole of China; however, due to China's widely varied topography, there were great regional differences among the country's water-control projects.

Over the past several centuries, the rural economy of the Jianghan Plain grew or declined in response to environmental change. The present chapter, then, discusses the effects of the dike systems – the major water-control projects in the Jianghan Plain – on the local economy. In doing so, it analyzes those crucial topics that have been ignored by Chinese scholars and addresses the question of whether Jianghan agriculture, which took place within a deteriorating environment, was sustainable or unsustainable.

Role of Dike Systems in the Rural Economy of the Jianghan Plain

If we take the Jianghan Plain as a whole, we see that more than two-thirds of its land consists of *yuan* land or other land that, in one way or another, is protected by *yuan* dikes (Zhang Jiayan 2001, 137). If one adds to that the land beyond *yuan* dikes but inside river dikes, it becomes clear that Jianghan society was indeed a dike-protected society. Thus, it is not at all surprising that the compilers of many traditional county gazetteers emphasize that the people of their counties or of the lake areas of their counties "depend on dikes [to protect] their lives" *(yi di wei ming)* (*Jingshan xian zhi* 1882, 4: 17a; *Hanchuan tuji zhengshi* 1895, 3: 26a). Republican surveys also indicate as much. A survey of Mianyang, for instance, contends that "the people depend on dikes to live" (*Hubei xianzheng gaikuang* 1934, 815). Such a conclusion seems almost self-evident when one considers how many people, and how much farmland, were protected by dikes. For instance, in Hanyang County in the 1930s more than 90 percent of the population and more than 85 percent of the farmland were protected by dike systems (*Hanyang xian* 1938, 2). This was more or less the situation throughout the Jianghan Plain, and there was no fundamental change in it during the Republic. One Republican survey records that, in Gong'an, all taxes and the people's livelihood relied on the protection afforded by every single *yuan* dike (*Hubei xianzheng gaikuang* 1934, 1001); another contemporary gazetteer, that of Zhongxiang County, states that here "people cannot survive without [the protection of] the dikes, and officials cannot govern without [the protection of] the dikes" (*Zhongxiang shuili zhi* 1998, 63). All these are clear about the decisive role of the dike systems in the local rural economy. Even the popular saying "If Hunan and Hubei have a good year, the entire empire will be fed" reflects the centrality of *yuan* production (Mei, Zhang, and Yan 1995, 179-82).

The protection afforded by the dikes was crucial not only to the economy of the Jianghan Plain but also to the economy of all of Hubei Province and, indeed, to all of Central China as well. A late Qing source indicates that "[the people who] manage Hubei's revenue must take the harness of the Yangzi River and the Han River as their primary administrative duty. If the Yangzi River and the Han River are safe and the dikes are solid, local production will be abundant, the people's livelihood will be accomplished, and the national tax will be paid in full" (Hu 1999 [1838], 157). Another source indicates that the maintenance of the Wancheng dike was the most important administrative duty in Hubei (Ni 1885 [1876], Weng's introduction).

The crucial importance of dikes in the local society and economy is attested to by Qing officials of the Jianghan Plain who argued that dike work was one of the most important administrative duties for local officials. A Qing regulation on dike management made it clear that harnessing a river was equal to leading an army: it likened dikes to the wall that protects a city, and dike protectors to soldiers (*Songzi xian zhi* 1869, 4: 16b). In the Republic, dike-related affairs were still regarded as one of the principal routine duties of the provincial government of Hubei (*Gailiang digong yijian shu* n.d., 1).

In this regard, officials mainly talked about river dikes. In 1948, the magistrate of Hanchuan argued that the management of dikes – including *yuan* dikes – was the first priority in governing (LS 31-4-60b). In fact, the *yuan* dikes, which were usually managed by the local people, were of equal if not more importance than river dikes. It was the land protected by *yuan* dikes that made them of central importance to the local economy. The large amount of reclaimable *yuan* land was one of the major reasons the Jianghan Plain could accept hundreds of thousands of immigrants in the Ming-Qing era.

Table 8a

Tax (amount of husked rice) on different kinds of land in Jianli

Grade of paddy fields	Inside *yuan*	Outside *yuan*	Outside dike	Grade of dry land	Inside *yuan*	Outside *yuan*	Outside dike
Upper	2.76	2.57	1.80	Upper	2.15	1.85, 0.56 (barley)	3 (barley), 0.47 (wheat)
%*	100.00	93.12	65.22	%	100.00	86.05	
Middle	2.45	2.20	1.15	Middle	2.00	1 (wheat)	1.80 (barley)
%	100.00	89.80	46.94	Lower	1.30	3 (barley) 0.47 (wheat)	1.20 (barley)
Lower	1.60	1.30	0.45	Lower ponds	1.60	1.30	0.45
%	100.00	81.25	28.13	%	100.00	81.25	28.13

Note: Unit: *sheng/mu*

They came to reclaim *yuan* land not only because it could grow rice and other grain crops to meet their need for food (as well as many kinds of non-grain cash crops) but also because the land within *yuan* had a relatively high yield.

As discussed in Chapter 1, in the Jianghan Plain *yuan* were usually located in lake areas. The majority of *yuan* land consists of alluvial soil rich in organic materials and mineral nutrients. It has high natural fertility and a good texture, and it can be easily ploughed. *Yuan* reclaimed from lakefront wasteland have a thick layer of topsoil with high fertility: the content of organic materials is one or two times that of regular soil, and the content of nitrogen, phosphorus, and potassium – three key nutrient elements required by all crops – is also high (*Hubei nongye dili* 1980, 81-82). Thus, the yield of crops grown in *yuan* is usually higher than the yield of the same crops grown on other kinds of farmland. It follows that the land tax – which was usually based on yield within an area – levied on *yuan* land in the Qing was the highest levied on any kind of farmland. This was made very clear in the 1872 gazetteer of Jianli (see Tables 8a and 8b).

There were three kinds of land subject to tax in Jianli County: (1) farmland located inside *yuan* that was protected by both river dikes and *yuan* dikes; (2) farmland located outside *yuan* but still protected by river dikes; and (3) farmland protected by neither major dikes nor *yuan* dikes (e.g., beach land) (see Table 8a). The tax on upper-grade paddy fields inside *yuan* was

Table 8b

The distribution of different kinds of land in Jianli**

Paddy fields			Dry land			Ponds	
Inside *yuan*	Upper-grade	387,137.2	Inside *yuan*	Upper-grade	317,403.8	Low-grade ponds inside *yuan*	194.9
	Middle-grade	2,877.9		Middle-grade	2,200.9		
	Lower-grade	41,946.1		Lower-grade	13,625.5		
	Total	431,961.2		Total	333,230.2		
Outside *yuan*	Upper-grade	14,690.8	Outside *yuan*	Upper-grade	73,675.9	Low-grade ponds outside *yuan*	131.8
	Middle-grade	1,581.5		Middle-grade	6,702.2		
	Lower-grade	8,328.3		Lower-grade	47,436.4		
Outside dikes	Upper-grade	192.0	Outside dikes	Upper-grade	36,411.4	Low-grade ponds outside dikes	211.9
	Middle-grade	32.5		Middle-grade	5,565.6		
	Lower-grade	1,871.7		Lower-grade	24,250.8		
Total paddy fields		458,658.0	Total dry land		527,272.5	Total ponds	538.6
% of paddy fields inside *yuan*		94.2	% of dry land inside *yuan*		63.2		
Total upper-grade paddy fields		402,020.0	Total upper-grade dry land		427,491.1		
% of upper-grade paddy fields inside *yuan*		96.3	% of upper-grade dry land inside *yuan*		74.3		

Notes: Unit: *mu*. 1 *sheng* (0.22 gallon) = 1/100 *shi*. For husked rice, 1 Qing *shi* = 1.035 *shi shi* = 161.46 *shi jin* (1 *shi shi* = 156 *shi jin* [Xu (1983, 344)]), or 177.61 lb.
*   Land inside *yuan* is taken to be 100 as the basis for figuring the percentage of other kinds of land.
** Statistics and percentages are based on original data but have been rounded off.
Source: Jianli xian zhi (1872, 4: 2b-5a).

2.76 *sheng* and on upper-grade paddy fields outside *yuan* it was 2.57 *sheng*. But the tax on upper-grade paddy fields outside dikes was only 1.8 *sheng*, or only 65.22 percent of the tax on upper-grade paddy fields inside *yuan*. The difference in tax on lower-grade land was even greater. The tax on lower-grade paddy fields outside dikes was only 28.13 percent of the tax on lower-grade paddy fields inside *yuan*.

More than 90 percent of Jianli's paddy fields (and almost all of its upper-grade paddy fields) were located inside *yuan* (see Table 8b). Obviously, both river dikes and *yuan* dikes were crucially important for protecting paddy fields. As for dry land, more than 60 percent (and 74.3 percent of upper-grade dry land) was located inside *yuan*. Hence it is definitely not an exaggeration to say that almost all land tax revenue in this county depended on *yuan* land. The locals' needs were also inseparable from *yuan* land. It was said that, since the early Qing, Hanchuan, a county on the lower reaches of the Han River, also "relied on the dikes [that protect] *yuan* to pay the tax and to meet people's consumption needs" (*Hanyang fu zhi* 1747, 15: 27a). Even Jiangling, a county in which a large part of the land was protected by the Jingjiang Great Dike, still possessed about 179 *yuan,* from which more than half of Jiangling's tax came (*Jiangling xian zhi* 1876, 8: 2a, 32a).

In a word, the dike systems (if they worked effectively) protected farmland from annual high water and thus ensured a relatively stable harvest, while the quality of farmland inside *yuan* was usually high, resulting in a high yield. In the Jianghan Plain, the dike systems as a whole were the mainstay of the rural economy and the safeguard of the local people's livelihood.

Negative Effects of Dike Systems on Local Agriculture

The dike systems were intended to protect farmland from high water and to ensure stable farming, and the enclosure of *yuan* aimed at increasing cultivated land. While this contributed to the growth of the local economy in the Jianghan Plain, extensive dike construction and the inundation caused by dike ruptures could also have a decidedly negative impact on agricultural production. Some of the most obvious negative effects are discussed below.

Occupying Farmland

Farmland lost to dikes mainly included two kinds: (1) farmland directly occupied by dikes (and related water-control projects) and (2) farmland covered by sands deposited by floodwater. The land occupied by dikes and their safety zones was considerable. According to Qing regulations, the width of the safety zone of major dikes from the bottom of the dike to either side was supposed to be twenty *gong* (1 gong = 1.67 metres) (Wang 1832, 2: 59b), or about 33.4 metres. It is not clear how much of those lands were official land, private land, or wasteland.[1] But it is certain that some was farmland and was individually owned. As a late Qing source indicates: "If the land that will be used for [water-control] work is private land, to be fair, [the builder] should give a sum of money to the owner in order for him to buy another piece of land"

(*Xiangdi cheng'an* 1969, 2: 8b). A late Qing gazetteer states that the area of land occupied by dikes and abandoned because of dike construction (topsoil was removed to make dikes) in Mianyang was 82,223 *mu* in total. The same gazetteer records that paddy fields and dry land in this department amounted to 1,852,742 *mu* in total (*Mianyang zhou zhi* 1894, 4: 5ab, 41a). In other words, farmland occupied by dikes and dike-related abandoned land in this department accounted for about 4.4 percent of its total registered farmland.

A rough estimate of the amount of land occupied by dikes and their safety zones in the Jianghan Plain can be derived from some contemporary statistics. According to newly compiled gazetteers, the acreage under dikes and dike bases in Jianli in 1959 was seventy square kilometres, which accounted for 2.4 percent of that county's territory (2915.1 km²), or 4.5 percent of its cultivated land (1571.5 km²) (*Jianli xian zhi* 1959, 16). The major dikes in Hanchuan in the 1980s occupied 50,187.7 *mu,* which accounted for 2.01 percent of that county's territory (*Hanchuan xian zhi* 1992, 94). At the same time, there were 855,016 *mu* covered by dikes and dike bases in Jingzhou, which accounted for 1.98 percent of its territory, or about 3 percent of its cultivated land (Wang 1989, 10). The dikes of Jingzhou District in the early 1990s stretched for 5,062.48 kilometres, which was 2.2 times the length in 1949 (2,296.4 kilometres in total) (*Jingzhou diqu zhi* 1996, 123-25). If we assume that the acreage of land covered by one kilometre of dike in the 1980s was the same as in 1949, then Jingzhou District would have had 388,000 *mu* of farmland covered by dikes in 1949.[2] Adding to this the farmland covered by dikes in Dangyang, Zhijiang, Hanchuan, Xiaogan, Yunmeng, Yingcheng, Hanyang, and Jiangxia, which lay outside the boundaries of Jingzhou District, the total land under dikes in the Jianghan Plain in or before 1949 would have been over 500,000 *mu*. That is equivalent to the acreage of one hundred mid-sized *yuan* (five thousand *mu* each on average) or 250 small *yuan* (two thousand *mu* each on average) – or equivalent to half of the cultivated land of a small county in the late twentieth century (Shishou, for instance, had 1.1 million *mu* of cultivated land in the 1980s [Wang 1989, 11]).

The floodwater that rushed in from broken dikes also destroyed some farmland or blanketed extensive tracts of it with sand. Though it is unclear how much farmland was destroyed by inundation and was covered by sand over the years, it could, in some cases, be up to hundreds of thousands of *mu*. In 1935, for example, the Han River dike broke in Shizikou (in Zhongxiang County) and, since it was difficult to rebuild, a second dike (*yao di,* distant dike), with a length of eighteen *li,* was built behind the old dike. The farmland between the old and new dikes, 200,000 *mu* in total, was thus turned into wasteland (until 1968, when it was re-reclaimed). That same year, a break in the Luojiatan dike on the south bank of the Yangzi River (in Jiangling County) left thousands of *mu* of sand-covered land that still existed half a century later (*Hubei sheng zhi shuili* 1995, 218-19). In the Qing dynasty, the land from which water failed to drain, or that was covered by sand, was exempt from the land tax (Shu 1896, 6: 30b; *Mianyang zhou zhi* 1894, 4: 41a). Thus, the Qing government recognized this kind of loss of farmland, though in doing so it lost tax revenue.

Removing Topsoil

The regular annual repair of dikes did not require much soil, but rebuilding or blocking a burst dike, and constructing new dikes (including moon-shaped dikes) needed a large amount of earth. According to Qing regulations, labourers should have brought earth from twenty *gong* away from the dike for annual repairs and 20 *zhang* away for blockages. They were to take earth from the river beach or from the inner side of dikes only if no earth was available outside them (Hu 1999 [1838], 186). In practice, however, they usually took earth from as near the dike as possible, and, in most cases, they just took earth from the inner side of dikes (Yu 1999 [1838], 104; *Gailiang digong yijian shu* n.d., 4). They did this for their convenience: they had to carry most of the earth on their shoulders (only in a few cases were boats used to ship earth from afar).[3] But, according to a Republican regulation, if earth were to be taken from the inner side of dikes, labourers were not to dig the land deeply: they were only allowed to take topsoil to a depth of 0.5 metres (*Jianli difang zhi* 1991, 201). If they dug too deeply into the land that was close to the dike, the abandoned deep hollows would be a threat to the dike in the next high-water season (*Hanchuan xian zhi* 1873, 9: 2b; *Gailiang digong yijian shu* n.d., 4). Thus, every year some fertile farmland lost its topsoil and, in the process, the land near dikes was slightly lowered, leaving a peculiar landscape that is common in the Jianghan Plain.[4]

How much topsoil was removed for dike-related projects? It is estimated that the major dikes in the reign of Daoguang (1821-50) were about fifteen hundred kilometres in length. There were 7,050.4 kilometres of dikes (major and minor) in the Jianghan area (which is geographically larger than the Jianghan Plain of this research) in 1985, and, from 1950 to 1985, the amount of earth used on regular repairs was 1.35 billion cubic metres (*Hubei sheng zhi shuili* 1995, 204). That is to say, 5.32 cubic metres of earth was used per metre of dike per year. Thus fifteen hundred kilometres of dikes would need 7.98 million cubic metres of earth per year. If only half of that earth were taken from the land on the inner side near the dike to a depth of 0.5 metres, then about 11,964 *mu* of land would have lost its topsoil.[5] At the same time, the Wancheng dike had been raised several metres higher than what it was in the early Qing; in the process, a huge amount of earth would have been used.[6] In other words, the amount of 7.98 million cubic metres was very low, and so was the amount of 11,964 *mu*. If we include the numerous *yuan* dikes, the amount of topsoil that was removed for dike projects would be even larger.[7] If peasants were still farming those lands (which they usually were), they had to apply large amounts of fertilizer to recover the soil's fertility, otherwise, the yield would be very low.

Reducing Land Quality

With its topsoil removed, the land of course became infertile. These lands were usually dry land. For paddy fields, the problem was an increase in "cold [water] soaked fields" (*lengjin tian,* in local terminology) due to waterlogging. Even in the early Qing, one Hanchuan gazetteer recorded only 24,154 *mu* of upper-grade paddy field in the entire county, with 44,460 *mu* of middle-grade and 87,491 *mu* of lower-grade paddy field. At the same time, this county had about 102,101 or more *mu* of wasteland, consisting of submerged or abandoned land. The low percentage of upper-grade land in this county was probably related to dike construction: even if the water level of rivers outside *yuan* did not rise and each *yuan* was safe, rainwater was occasionally excessive, leading to logged water that was hard to drain, and some unavoidable inundation (*Hanyang fu zhi* 1747, 15: 16a-17b, 24: 1a-2a). A late Qing magistrate made it clear that, since the Han riverbed had become higher than the surrounding ground in Hanchuan, the level of the river water had risen and, with it, the level of underground water, which exacerbated the problem of waterlogging. It was also found that one *yuan* in this county, even if the dike was solid, could have only half a normal harvest (even in a good year) due to its low-lying location and waterlogging (*Hanchuan xian zhi* 1873, 9: 31a, 10: 7b). Which is to say that, in some cases, dike construction could reduce the quality of neighbouring lands. For the same reason, in the 1980s, about one-third of the cultivated land in the Jianghan Plain belonged to this category of low-quality land (*Hubei sheng zhi dili* 1997, 826).

Consuming Labour Power

In the Jianghan Plain, each year many personnel had to be devoted to dike maintenance. This had yet another major negative effect on local farming, particularly during the period of high water control. Since the annual repairs were usually undertaken in winter and spring or during off-seasons, this did not draw labour away from farming,[8] at least not significantly. But the peak of seasonal high water control (June to September) was also the busiest farming season. Moreover, the labourers who engaged in high water control, particularly in emergency work, were usually adult males and were also the main labour force for farming. Thus, high water control definitely hindered normal farming. The heavier the task of high water control, the bigger the impediment it presented.

In sum, the construction of dikes and related projects occupied a great deal of farmland, removed a large amount of topsoil, and reduced the quality of some farmland. Moreover, the large amount of labour needed in the high water-control season conflicted with the demands of regular farming. All of these conditions were obviously unfavourable for local agriculture.

Monetary Burden of Capital and Labour Spent on Dike Work

Although the dike systems occupied some farmland and involved the removal of some topsoil for annual repairs, no official in the Qing or the Republic clearly recognized this as a serious problem. Apparently, because far more farmland was created by the never-ending building of *yuan* enclosures than was lost to dike construction and repair, the negative effects of the dike systems on local agriculture were not dramatic enough to catch officials' attention. What they were most concerned about – and what they criticized the most – was the monetary burden of dike work.

This was also a burden the local people found hard to bear. The heaviest was the earth fee. Due to different dike sizes, the rate of the earth fee, in terms of either earth or cash, varied from county to county, from place to place within one county, and from one time to another. In Qianjiang in the early Qing, for example, landowners were levied twenty-one *wen* (copper cash) per *mu* of cultivated land for the earth fee (*Qianjiang xian zhi* 1879, 10: 65a). Since almost everywhere the earth fee was levied according to the acreage of cultivated land,[9] the size of a plot had a close relationship to the amount of earth fee it bore. In some places in Tianmen and Mianyang in the early eighteenth century, the length of dike that a certain plot of land was responsible for was to be clearly stated on all land sale contracts (*Hubei An Xiang Yun dao shuili ji'an* n.d., II: 2b-3a).

The earth fee could be paid either in the form of an amount of earth (responsible people went to the dike to pile up the earth) or in the form of cash (which was used to hire labourers to do the work). In terms of earth, the amount of the earth fee in Jiangling in 1833 was about 0.62 *fang* (1 fang = 3.28 cubic metres) of earth per *mu* of lake land, and 0.21 *fang* of earth per *mu* of mountain land (Shu 1896, 6: 13b-14a).[10] In Jianli in the late Qing, the total annual earth fee collected for the river dike was about 60,000 *chuan* (strings of copper cash), and the amount of earth used for annual repair was about 600,000 *fang* (*Jianli difang zhi* 1991, 356). According to a contemporary gazetteer, in the reign of Tongzhi (1862-74), Jianli had 976,091.6 *mu* of registered farmland (*Jianli xian zhi* 1872, 4: 5a); thus, landowners were responsible for 0.62 *fang* of earth per *mu* of farmland, the same as in Jiangling. In 1938 in Mianyang, however, under the jurisdiction of five bureaus of the Repair and Flood Control of the Commission of the Dongjing River Dike *(Dongjinghe difang weiyuanhui xiufangchu)*, the earth fee was levied at a rate of 1.35 to 3.7 *fang* of earth per *mu* of cultivated land, a rate that remained unchanged in the following decade (*Dongjinghe difang zhi* 1994, 306). This was much higher than the rate in Jiangling and Jianli in the late Qing, probably because this area of Mianyang suffered more frequent floods, the dikes were weaker, and the taxes in the Republic were generally higher than the taxes in the Qing.

In addition to the earth fee, local residents had to pay many surcharges related to dike affairs. For example, the local officials responsible for the dike systems, particularly county and prefectural magistrates, did not always supervise dike work in person as was required but, instead, sent *yamen* clerks as their representatives. In the early Qing, except for an informal subsidy provided by the local government, these agents did not get any additional payment for this job. By the late Qing, however, such subsidies had gradually been changed into a formal expense (Hu 1999 [1838], 173), and some counties included these expenses in their budgets (*Jingshan xian zhi* 1882, 4: 17a). In 1884 Tianmen, for instance, this expenditure was tied to tax revenue: forty *wen* was taken from each silver tael of tax as a payment for transportation (*Xiangdi cheng'an* 1969, 1: 250b-251a). In some places this kind of expense was officially and directly taken from the earth fee. This was the case, for example, in Songzi, where the general supervisor *(zongjian)* in charge of the management of *yuan* dikes also received a handsome income in the name of *fumafei* (transportation expenses) (*Songzi xian zhi* 1869, 4: 12b). At the end of the nineteenth century, in Jiangling even the salary of the *difang ying* (dike protection battalion) was shifted onto the earth fee (at a cost of seven thousand *fang* of earth) (Shu 1896, 6: 2a). This, in turn, increased the amount of the earth fee that the locals had to pay.

In the late Qing, with the increase in the frequency of water calamities, the earth fee was increased and numerous surcharges were tacked on to it. What was worse, in many places, most of the burden was borne by the poor. The rich and powerful tended to evade fees by concealing the amount of farmland they owned or by colluding with *yamen* clerks (Ni 1885 [1876], juanmo: 7b; *Jingshan xian zhi* 1882, 4: 17b). The burden of the earth fee became so heavy that some people either changed their occupation or moved out. It was said that, in Jingzhou in the mid-nineteenth century, more than half of the people who lived on the south bank of the Yangzi River changed from being farmers to being petty traders or fishers, or they simply fled.[11]

The situation of those who lived on the north side of the Yangzi River was no better. For instance, as early as the late seventeenth century, when winter came some residents of Qianjiang were forced to sell their land at low prices to buy a so-called labourer label *(fuqian)* at a high price *(guimai fuqian jianmai tian)* *(Qianjiang xian zhi* 1879, 10: 54a).[12] In the mid-eighteenth century, it was found that the income from one *mu* of farmland was less than the dike fee of one *zhang* of dike: consequently, there were cases in which residents did not even want to bother to repair ruptured dikes (Chen Zhenhan et al. 1989, 2: 408). In late Qing Jiangling, in some places, the dike fee was increased to more than three times the regular land tax (Peng and Zhang 1993, 264). One magistrate of this county complained that it was the heavy burden of the dike fees that made the common people *(baixing)* of Jiangling poor and that accounted for the fact that the county lacked rich people *(Jiangling xian zhi* 1876, 8: 57b). At the end of the Qing and into the early Republic, even in Zhongxiang, a county without many dikes, the dike fee for one *mu* of cultivated land was twice as much as the regular land tax *(Zhongxiang xian zhi* 1937, 3: 30a).

In addition to the burden of the earth fee, the local peasants had to spend a great deal of time on dike affairs. For example, the annual regular labour needed to repair Jiangxia's twenty-two *li* of the Yangzi River dike amounted to 140,000 labourer-days *(Jiangxia xian zhi* 1869, 2: 41a), and in Jingshan, which had about ninety *li* of the Han River dike, annual maintenance and repairs consumed 220,000 labourer-days *(Jingshan xian zhi* 1882, 4: 2a-3a). More labour was needed to block dike breaks. In Shishou, a total of 169,980 labourer-days were consumed in rebuilding a 580 *zhang* section of a *yuan* dike that broke in 1655 *(Shishou xian zhi* 1866, 1: 40a). For new construction, even more labour was needed. In Qianjiang in the early Qing, for example, the construction of two short dike sections – one 459 *gong* and the other 333 *gong* in length – took, respectively, 226,160 and 106,414 labourer-days *(Qianjiang xian zhi* 1879, 10: 38a).

Clearly, the labour demanded by dike-related projects was huge. According to statistics from Shishou, from 1950 to 1985, 168 million standard labourer-days were spent on its 440.37 kilometres of dikes *(Shishou xian zhi* 1990, 129) – about eleven thousand standard labourer-days per kilometre of dike per year. In the 1970s, in the area along the Yangzi River from Shashi to Wuhan, the annual labour spent on high water control and dike repairs consumed about a quarter of its major labour power (Yuan 1978, 5). According to another statistic, about 800 million labourer-days (or 19 million labourer-days per year) had been used on dike works in Jingzhou District from 1949 to 1990 (*Jingzhou diqu zhi* 1996, 124). Certainly, the amount of labour expended in dike works in the Qing and the Republic could not compare to what was spent after 1949. Of course, before 1949, almost all work was done by hand, so it is no surprise that a single dike project could easily require more than 100,000 labourer-days.

Some people who lived within *yuan* had to take care not only of the river dikes but also of the *yuan* dikes. In Hanchuan in the late Qing and the Republic, some *yuan* had two, three, or even four sides that faced the water. The dikes were so long that the residents were hard pressed to deal with water control in the annual high-water seasons (*Hanchuan xian zhi* 1992, 148). In the late Qing, dike work consumed more and more labour. In some *yuan,* the majority of residents who benefited from dikes had to spend more than half of each year on dike works: annual repairs usually lasted for about four months (in winter-spring) and high water control lasted another three months (in summer-autumn) (Zhang Jianmin 2001, 377). This six-month period should be understood as a generalization as not every labourer had to spend such a long time on dike work every year.

Other than some official dike work that was paid for by the government and undertaken by hired labourers, the work on people's dikes and *yuan* dikes was usually funded by the local people and the work was apportioned among them. In most cases the labour/time they spent on dike work was not compensated.[13] In addition, they also needed to provide their own food and bedding as well as bring their own tools; in some cases villagers had to work on dikes far from their homes and had to sleep outside (*Jingshan xian zhi* 1673, 3: 40ab; *Jiangxia xian zhi* 1869, 2: 41a-42a). They contributed their labour and suffered from cold and hunger; some even gave their lives (*Qianjiang xian zhi* 1879, 10: 48b).

All of this was, needless to say, a real hardship. The local people not only suffered from the various fees for dike work but also worried about the burden of such work that would follow inundation. The residents of Jiangling who bore the earth fee and provided labour "thought working on dikes was a perilous undertaking" *(shi zhudi wei weitu)* (*Qing jingshi wenbian* 1992 [1889], 117: 14b, 17b). And the residents of Qianjiang also reportedly worried about the heavy burden of dike work (*Qianjiang xian zhi* 1879, 10: 54a).

In the reign of Qianlong (1736-95), some even thought that the dike systems had turned out to be a handicap. As a high ranking official comments:

Hubei once was a land of plenty and was [one of] the richest [provinces] under heaven. The saying goes that "if Hunan-Hubei has a good harvest, the entire empire will be fed." It has two harvests within one year, which even the Yangzi delta relies on. Now if it suffers even the slightest from water calamities and drought, [the government] has no solution, and thus the result is that the people cannot avoid falling into poverty. Although this cannot be attributed entirely to the handicap of the river dikes, [it is because of the dikes] that every year [the locals] not only suffer from too many surcharges [for dike maintenance and repair] but also worry about how uncertain inundation puts their lives in jeopardy. Thus, are the river dikes not a handicap? (Yu 1999 [1840], 104)

Although the author may have exaggerated the richness of Hubei and the popularity of annual double cropping,[14] it is true that the local people were suffering from dike-related surcharges and unpredictable inundation. In fact, the rural economy along the lower reaches of the Han River had already been seriously affected by the frequent water calamities associated with the dike systems. Fan Zhongying, the magistrate of Hanchuan, who presumably knew the local situation well, describes his county:

The county of Hanchuan is located along the lower reaches of the Han River. Its territory is low ... In rainy years, the water of the Yangzi River rises, and the Han River water rises too. The water of the Yangzi River and the Han River flows back and inundates places that are not protected by dikes. Even *yuan* that are protected by dikes find it difficult to drain the water that accumulates inside the *yuan*. And thus the harvest usually is poor because of waterlogging. The water level of the Han River will go down only after the water level of the Yangzi River goes down. [The locals] can replant grain only after the water level of the Han River is lower than the level of logged water. If the summer high water rises early, there is no hope for an autumn harvest. If the autumn high water subsides late, there is no hope for a harvest of spring *mai*[15] ... [The locals] have to spend money on high water control when the summer and autumn high water comes, and [they also] have to spend money on dike construction in the winter and spring dry season. In general, the land within *yuan* could have one harvest of *mai* per year, but it is hard to say whether there will be an autumn harvest or not. Even the harvest of *mai* is uncertain in land outside *yuan*. One *mu* yields only 3 *shi*.[16] Everything – including seed, labour, high water control, dike construction, house building, and living – relies on the harvest, and the taxes and fees rely on it too. Thus the financial situation of the local people is poor. This is the hardship they face. (*Hanchuan xian zhi* 1873, 10: 7a-8b)[17]

This was the situation in the reign of Jiaqing (1796-1820). It got even worse in the reign of Daoguang (1821-50). Wang Baixin, a very influential figure in dike affairs at that time, went so far as to suggest that dike ruptures should be left untouched rather than repaired. He thought that the local residents had fallen into an endless cycle of building dikes and then repairing dike ruptures and thus suffered doubly. He argues as follows:

> If by luck there is no dike rupture, the income from farming leaves nothing after the payment of rent and taxes, clothes and food, weddings and funerals, and rites, plus the cost of the repair and the management of dikes. If unfortunately there is a dike rupture, the farmland and houses will be inundated, and families will be destroyed. The dike breaks this year, and [the locals] repair it next year. The building and breaking form an endless circle. (Cited in Song 1954, 62)

Whether or not it was possible in practice to leave dike ruptures unrepaired, Wang's concern for the locals' suffering from dike affairs is credible. After the Taiping Rebellion, it was particularly difficult to collect dike fees from villagers (Ni 1885 [1876], 6: 8b-11b).

Under these circumstances, it was not easy to motivate the common people to work on dike projects. In Xiaogan, a county without many dikes, in the late Qing and the Republic, the local officials usually had to force the local peasants to build dikes, and they punished those who refused to follow their orders. In households that were too poor to pay the assigned dike fee, even children aged twelve or thirteen had to go to work on dike projects. Dike building demanded such heavy labour that some of these people were seriously hurt when carrying loads of earth and remained disabled for the rest of their lives (*Xiaogan shi zhi* 1992, 840). Consequently, in the eyes of at least some officials, the great amount of capital and labour that the local peasants invested in the dike systems in the late Qing had become a drag on the local economy – "water benefit" *(shuili)* had become "water harm" *(shuihai)*.

A Contemporary Interpretation of the Burden of Dike Fees

The above discussion only provides a very rough picture of the burden of dike fees. A quantitative analysis should give us a more precise picture. For example, how much of the gross income from agriculture in the Jianghan Plain went to dike fees? What proportion of the local people's total taxes went to dike fees? If the dike systems had really become a severe handicap to the growth of the local economy, as some Qing officials believed, then how do we understand the large amount of money and time the local people spent on dikes? Because of the limitations of the source materials, it is very difficult to address these questions with pre-1949 data. But dike-related source materials after 1949 can help us to interpret the past.

As discussed earlier, the Jingjiang Great Dike is the most important dike in the Jianghan Plain. From 1950 to 1985, the PRC governments (at both provincial and national levels) spent 240.37 million yuan RMB *(ren min bi)* on regular annual repairs to the Jingjiang Great Dike and 6.29 million RMB on high water control along the dike, for a total of 246.66 million RMB (*Jingjiang dadi zhi* 1989, 280-81). In other words, on average, the yearly expenditure on regular annual repairs and high water control was 6.68 million RMB and 0.18 million RMB, respectively, for a total of 6.86 million RMB.[18] Regular annual repairs accounted for about 97 percent of the entire investment in dike work, with the remaining 3 percent being spent on high water control.

What proportion of the gross income from local agriculture did this investment represent? According to official statistics, on average, the yearly agricultural gross income of Jingzhou District in 1978, 1980, 1984, and 1985 was 3,709.1 million RMB (*Jingzhou diqu zhi* 1996, 116). That is to say, the investment in the maintenance of the Jingjiang Great Dike in this district accounted for only 0.19 percent (6.86/3,709.1 = 0.19 percent) of the gross income from local agriculture – a figure almost too small to count.[19]

The annual average investment, however, may conceal variations from year to year. Let us choose one year for discussion. In the original sources, the expenditure on dike work in 1980 was one of the highest during the period between 1950 and 1985, while the gross income from agriculture in Jingzhou District in that year was the lowest among the years of 1978, 1980, 1984, and 1985. In 1980, the investment in regular annual repairs and high water control was 12.88 million RMB and 0.71 million RMB, respectively, for a total of 13.59 million RMB (*Jingjiang dadi zhi* 1989, 280-81). In the same year, the agricultural gross income of Jingzhou District was 2,409.31 million RMB (*Jingzhou diqu zhi* 1996, 116). In other words, the investment in the Jingjiang Great Dike in Jingzhou in 1980 accounted for only 0.56 percent (13.59/2,409.31 = 0.56 percent) of that year's agricultural gross income. Again, this percentage is very low.

Although the Jingjiang Great Dike is important, in terms of length it is only a very small part of the dike systems of the Jianghan Plain. We must look at the investment in other dikes as well. From 1949 to 1990, the provincial and central governments invested about 870 million RMB, and the local governments invested about 30 million RMB, for repairs, reinforcement, and maintenance of 5,062.48 kilometres of dikes and related flood diversion projects in Jingzhou District (*Jingzhou diqu zhi* 1996, 124-25). That makes 900 million RMB in total, or 21.43 million RMB per year.[20] This investment accounted for 0.58 percent (21.43/3,709.1 = 0.58 percent) of the average annual gross income from agriculture in Jingzhou District. This ratio is still very low.

One may argue that the ratio of investment to annual gross income from agriculture cannot represent the real ratio between investment (by the central government) and output. So let us look at the ratio of investment (in dikes) to tax revenue. From 1949 to 1993, Jingzhou District paid 6,884.6 million RMB in industrial-commercial taxes and 2,896.84 million RMB in agricultural taxes (*Jingzhou diqu zhi* 1996, 441), for a total of 9,781.44 million RMB, or 217.37 million RMB per year. Thus the annual investment in dikes accounted for about 9.9 percent (21.43/217.37 = 9.9 percent) of all taxes collected from Jingzhou District. Agricultural tax revenue alone was 64.37 million RMB per year. Thus, the expenditures on dikes accounted for 33.3 percent (21.43/64.37 = 33.3 percent), or one-third of the agricultural taxes collected in Jingzhou.

The provincial and central governments also had to invest in many other sectors, of course. Therefore, whether it was one-tenth or one-third of annual revenue, as a single item, expenditures of the provincial and central governments on the dike systems of the Jianghan Plain were substantial. Even though the provincial and central governments' incomes (tax revenues) were much greater than their expenditures on dikes in Jingzhou District, they simply returned some taxes for the purpose of repairing and maintaining the dikes. In other words, the people of Jingzhou District did not get extra money from the state for their dike works as what they received was far less than what they had paid in taxes.

All of this demonstrates that, first, during the rule of the CCP (until the mid-1980s), in theory, expenditures on the dike systems in the Jianghan Plain were not an unbearable financial burden on the local peasants.[21] Second, the low ratio of expenditures on dikes to total income is evidence that the economic benefits of the former were great. Moreover, the CCP actually launched many large water-control projects in the 1960s and 1970s that laid the foundation for the growth of Chinese agriculture since the 1980s. In fact, a new gazetteer of Xiaogan District concludes that water-control projects in this area from 1949 to 1989 yielded benefits *(xiaoyi)* (5.1 billion RMB) that were about seven times the initial investment (711 million RMB) (*Xiaogan diqu shuili zhi* 1996, 71-73). Another new gazetteer, that of Zhongxiang, even claims that, in that county, from 1949 to 1995, the benefits or income (8.37 billion RMB) from water control were 49.2 times the amount invested (170 million

RMB) (*Zhongxiang shuili zhi* 1998, 6). Taking Hubei as a whole, a crew of about one thousand people, after a year's work, calculated that water-control projects in the first forty years of the PRC returned net benefits that were fifteen times the investment (*Hubei shuili zhi* 2000, 22-23).

How does this help us to interpret the monetary burden of dike fees in the Qing? It can be seen that, in the PRC, the majority of the expenditures on major dikes came from the provincial and central governments. In the Qing, on the other hand, most of the dike fee was borne by the local people, and, in addition, they had to pay the land tax. In general, since each county or *yuan* was responsible for its own dikes, there were significant regional differences in the dike fee burden: the more dikes a county/*yuan* had, the more dike fees the local residents had to pay. For example, as discussed earlier, the earth fee was twice the amount of the land tax in Zhongxiang and three (or even six) times the land tax in Jiangling. According to Wang Yeh-chien (1973, 128), the land tax at the very end of the Qing only accounted for 2 to 4 percent of the whole harvest – except in the Yangzi delta, where it may have been as high as 8 to 10 percent. If the earth fee were three times the ordinary land tax, then the earth fee in Jiangling would have accounted for 6 to 12 percent of the whole harvest. Including the land tax, during the Qing dynasty the tax burden in total ranged from 8 to 16 percent of the whole harvest. In comparison, in the PRC, the agricultural tax rate in Jingzhou District was about 11 to 15 percent of all farming income in 1952-60, 5.43 to 7.47 percent in 1961-71, 3.86 to 6.53 percent in 1972-82, and less than 2 percent after 1992 (*Jingzhou diqu zhi* 1996, 435-36).[22] The rate of agricultural taxation in the PRC was getting lower and lower.[23] It is clear that, in theory, the burden of the earth fee and the land tax in Jiangling in the Qing was similar to that of the agricultural tax in 1952-60, although it was certainly higher than the agricultural tax after 1960. Nonetheless, it is conceivable that a tax rate of 16 percent of the whole harvest was not unbearably high for the local peasants.

Our calculation so far has not taken into account the cost of labour. This is because in the Qing and the Republic, only some of those who were involved in the regular annual repairs (and sometimes in high water control) of government works or official dikes received a subsidy; those who worked on either the annual repair or high water control of non-official dikes and *yuan* dikes usually did so without compensation. This remained almost the same in the PRC, except that those who were involved in building new dikes and annual repairs received a subsidy (e.g., *Xiaogan diqu shuili zhi* 1996, 70-71), while those who provided labour for high water control were usually uncompensated. Since it came from the state, some of the subsidy has already been included in the above calculation. Governments at the county level and below bore responsibility for local dikes (in Zhijiang, for instance, from 1949 to 1985, about half of the expenditure on water control came from governments at the county level and below [*Zhijiang xian zhi* 1990, 163]), and the peasants also had to provide for free many basic materials for high water control, such as rice straw and tools (*Jingjiang dadi zhi* 1989, 220, 277-78). The cost of such items is not included in my estimation/calculation.[24]

Obviously, calculating the return on the investment in the dike systems is very complicated. It is true that some Qing officials and scholars believed the dike systems were a drag on the local economy, but it is also possible that some of them may have exaggerated the burden of the dike fees. For example, the magistrate of Hanchuan might have used this as an excuse for his county's being in arrears with regard to tax collection. To build his case against the repair of dikes, Wang Baixin focused on the endless cycle of rupture and repair. But his suggested solution was impractical: it would have been impossible not to have dikes in this area because everything (except fishing) would have disappeared without their protection.

Furthermore, it is also possible that those who were not responsible for the major dikes got a higher rate of return than those who were responsible. For example, the Jingjiang Great Dike protected a large part of the Jianghan Plain, but only the residents of Jiangling were responsible for it; moreover, in Jiangling the earth fee for this dike was mostly borne only by the residents who lived on the north bank of the Yangzi River. If we take 4 percent of the harvest as the land tax rate in the Qing (the upper limit of Wang Yeh-chien's estimate), then those who had to pay an earth fee at a rate three times the land tax ended up paying 12 percent of the entire harvest for the earth fee and 4 percent for the land tax. That is to say, an owner-peasant household (the most common type) had to pay about one-sixth of its whole harvest in land tax and dike fees. A tenant household paid about 40 percent of its harvest as rent and 12 percent as dike fees (which were theoretically paid by the landowner but were quite often shifted to the tenant), making the combined cost equivalent to about 52 percent of the harvest. If one includes various surcharges – which probably even exceeded the regular tax[25] – it is very possible that a peasant would be left with little or nothing. And, of course, the situation would be even worse in years of poor harvest. If the dike fees were five or six times the land tax, a peasant household would definitely have nothing left of the harvest. We can understand why the compilers of one Jiangling gazetteer attributed the poverty of the Jiangling people to the dike fees (*Jiangling xian zhi* 1876, 8: 57b). We can also understand why, during years of hardship, some villagers along the Han River valley had to "sell their clothes and properties, or hire themselves out, go into a trade, or even sell their wives and sons" to pay the dike fees (*Xiangdi cheng'an* 1969, 1: 135b). This might also be one of the major reasons Qing officials, such as the magistrate of Hanchuan, worried about the hardship (which was undeniable) facing the local people.

Finally, it is not unusual that dike fees were unequally – or inequitably – distributed between the rich and the poor. In Jiangling in the late Qing, for example, it was usually the common villagers who paid the shared dike fee on time. By contrast, gentry families quite often deliberately refused to pay (Shu 1896, 6: 33b). The same was true in Jingshan: it was usually the common villagers, not the powerful families, who paid their dike fees (*Jingshan xian zhi* 1882, 4: 17b). In the Republic, although the dike tax was to have been paid by the owners of farmland, in some places it was the tenants who were responsible for it (*Honghu xian zhi* 1992, 101). In Hanyang, for example, it was the peasants who shouldered the heavy burden of dike fees, while the landlords paid nothing (*Hanyang xian zhi chuogao* 1960, 34).[26] In Jiangling, large landowners underreported the amount of land they owned and thus shifted the burden of dike fees to the poor, who paid more than they should have (*Hubei xianzheng gaikuang* 1934, 905). In Honghu, one poor peasant who was unable to pay the heavy dike fees even lost his land to the "evil" gentry (*Honghu xian zhi* 1963, 413).

To sum up, my interpretation of the burden of the dike fees in the Jianghan Plain in the Qing and the Republic is as follows. First, in the Jianghan Plain before 1949, the peasants had to bear the majority of the dike fee, and they had to pay the land tax as well. The dike fees varied substantially from region to region and were distributed unevenly between the rich (who paid less) and the poor (who paid more). In contrast, in the PRC, the state was responsible for the majority of the cost of maintaining and repairing the major dikes (excluding the cost of labour and some materials), while local peasants paid only the agricultural tax and were responsible for *yuan* dikes. And there was no significant individual inequity (within a certain area) when it came to building and maintaining major dikes. Second, there were frequent dike ruptures in the Qing, which not only increased the amount of the dike fees (which were needed to deal with emergencies) but also dealt a devastating blow to the local economy by reducing the capability of the peasants to bear the dike fee.[27] Again in contrast, in the PRC, the Jianghan Plain has not suffered any large-scale inundation since 1954.[28] Third, although the peasants of the Jianghan Plain in the Qing paid a large sum in dike fees, some or even most of which did not go to maintaining the dikes but, instead, was embezzled by *yamen* clerks and/or local gentry who collected them and/or supervised the dike works (see Chapter 2). In other words, it is not because of the dikes themselves that the dike fees were so heavy but because of the mismanagement and corruption in the administration of dike affairs – a serious problem in the Qing and the Republic. As a native of Hanchuan in the Qing said, the local people built dikes in order to protect themselves against water, but the dikes also caused malpractice (*Hanchuan xian zhi* 1873, 9: 21a). The real burden of the dike fees was due mainly to frequent ruptures, to regional and individual differences in the amount of the fee, to numerous surcharges, to widespread corruption in dike management, and to a lack of unified state investment.

Sustainable Agriculture versus Unsustainable Agriculture

How, in the long run, are we to evaluate the role of the dike systems in the local economy? Was the rural economy in the Jianghan Plain since the early Qing unsustainable?

As we have noted, according to Mark Elvin (1993), the negative effects of mountain reclamation and forest clearance under population pressure on the environment and, subsequently, the high cost of the maintenance of water-control projects made growth in the traditional Chinese economy unsustainable. Though Elvin does not define his notion of unsustainable growth or development, presumably he is referring to an economy whose expected growth has been slowed or even halted or reversed because of a degraded environment. Moreover, this slowdown, stagnation, or decline is irreversible. According to the World Commission on Environment and Development (1987, 43): "Sustainable development is development that meets the needs of the present without compromising the ability of future generations to meet their own needs." Since agriculture was the major sector of the rural economy in the Jianghan Plain in the Qing and the Republic, I now examine its sustainability.

Theoretically, the financial cost of maintaining the dike systems in the Jianghan Plain in the PRC seems not to have been too high. But in the Qing, considering regional differences and individual inequity in the payment of dike fees, frequent dike ruptures, and surcharges, the cost may have been devastating for many people.

Researchers have deplored the environmental degradation of the Jianghan Plain in the late Qing and the Republic. It is true that both the extensive enclosure of *yuan* (which disordered the natural waterways) and the over-reclamation of neighbouring upstream mountains (which changed the original environment) contributed to this kind of environmental degradation. The process of land opening, however, has always involved destroying old environments and creating new ones. If no people come to live and farm an area, there will be no environmental degradation in that area. Such reasoning led scholars in the Republic to argue: "If there had been no inundation since very ancient times due to very careful protection, then the Yunmeng marsh would still be a marsh, and there would not be a great expanse of fertile land" (Song 1954, 75). One hydrological expert thought this sort of passive reasoning, which called only for the return of farmland to the lakes, was akin to giving up eating for fear of choking (Sun 1939, 72-73).

In some ways, the frequent floods benefited agriculture. For example, the silt they deposited created new land and enriched soil fertility. The whole Jianghan Plain was, for the most part, an alluvial plain.[29] In addition to filling up low places and forming new land, the floodwater left a thin layer of sludge on any land over which it flowed.[30] Due to the rich quality of the sludge carried by the Han River, people who lived along this river sometimes hoped for a slight inundation, particularly in the fifth lunar month, because it would bring with it a lot of fertile sludge. According to one saying: "The fifth lunar month's [high water is] gold, the sixth lunar month's [high water is] silver, the seventh lunar month's [high water is] copper, and the eighth lunar month's [high water is] iron" (*wujin liuyin qitong batie*). This layer of fertile sludge enriched the soil and reportedly led, in the following year, to harvests that were much larger than those on average land (*Zai xu xingshui jinjian* 1970 [1942], 201; Song 1954, 75; Xia 2000, 59). The compilers of one Zhongxiang gazetteer – who opposed the building of dikes in this county (see Chapter 2) – said that, if there were no dikes in this county, the sludge deposited by floodwater after a slight inundation would heighten low-lying land and turn infertile land into fertile land (*Zhongxiang xian zhi* 1937, 3: 30a).

This function of sludge was nothing new in Chinese history. Chi Ch'ao-ting lists a number of examples of how people had used sludge in the North China Plain. He even argues that the frequent replenishment of sludge was one of the reasons the fertility of Chinese farmland did not decline over time, even though mineral fertilizers were not applied (Chi 1963 [1936], 19-20, 24).[31] I do not rate sludge so highly, and the positive effects of inundations on land productivity could not outweigh the negative effects. However, such things as the beneficial effects of sludge remind us that, in evaluating whether or not the traditional Chinese economy was sustainable, we must consider not only the environmental problem of mountain reclamation but also the use of farmland in the plain area. To judge whether the traditional Chinese economy was sustainable, we must first judge whether the traditional Chinese use of farmland was sustainable. Hence, we must investigate land productivity, a subject Elvin did not explore in depth. Inasmuch as the most important sector of the traditional Chinese economy was agriculture, the stability of soil fertility was central to the question of economic sustainability.

American agriculturist H.F. King (1911), who visited East Asia in the beginning of the twentieth century, praised the traditional agriculture of East Asian countries, particularly China, for maintaining soil fertility for four thousand years through the application of organic fertilizers. Elvin (1993, 46) mentions King at the end of his lengthy article in order to warn against romanticizing traditional Chinese agriculture and once again emphasizes that, due to environmental deterioration as a result of population pressure, the traditional Chinese economy was "not indefinitely sustainable."

Probably because he is attempting to stimulate a fundamental rethinking of long-established assumptions (Bao 2004a), Elvin focuses almost exclusively on the environmental problems caused by mountain reclamation and on the difficulty of maintaining water-control projects; he only mentions agriculture in passing and does not delve into the details of the traditional use of farmland in plains or the maintenance of soil fertility. Examining precisely those issues in the Yangzi delta, E.C. Ellis and Wang Siming (1997) argue that the local peasants used all available organic materials as fertilizers, applied different fertilizers to different crops at different times, and carefully managed their farms by using different cropping systems. As a result, traditional agriculture in the Lake Tai region in the Yangzi delta, from about 1000 to the 1950s, generated high productivity and supported a high density and stable agricultural population without degrading soil resources. This is a perfect example of sustainable agriculture. Indeed, Chinese scholars in general view agriculture in traditional China as "ecologically reasonable and sustainable" (Luo and Han 1990, 299). Chinese agrarian historians in particular proudly proclaim that traditional agriculture in China has a history of maintaining soil fertility that stretches back thousands of years (e.g., Liang Jiamian 1989).

Of course, the fertility of the soil of the Jianghan Plain was not replenished by sludge alone but also by the conscious and careful intervention of cultivators. The local peasants maintained soil fertility (and consequently land productivity) principally by the use of suitable cropping systems and the application of various organic fertilizers. The major cropping system in the Jianghan Plain was a single cropping system. In winter, most cultivated land was either left fallow in order to restore soil fertility or was covered with green manure. In addition to green manure, almost all of the other fertilizers (except plant ash) that the peasants applied were organic fertilizers that did not damage the soil texture and kept the soil fertile for a long time (see Appendix).

Taking the Jianghan Plain as a whole, if the large amount of topsoil that was removed for dike work was offset by the deposits of enriching silt, and if most fields were enriched by the application of organic fertilizers that did not damage the soil texture, then it was only waterlogging that degraded the quality of paddy fields. However, based on proper agricultural technology, the fertility of waterlogged paddy fields can be recovered by reducing the underground water level, covering the land with pond sludge (*Hanchuanxian jian zhi* 1959, 35), and applying suitable fertilizers.[32] This is completely different from the over-reclamation of upstream mountains, which destroyed virgin forest, caused soil erosion, and left denuded mountains: such land was hard, if not impossible, to restore. In other words, from the angle of soil fertility, the Jianghan agricultural system based on extensive dike systems was sustainable.

As I have argued, the dike systems of the Jianghan Plain in the Qing and the Republic suffered from many managerial problems that led to the degradation of the local environment, which, in turn, impeded the growth of the local economy. But many of the factors that contributed to poor management were controllable and could have been rectified. Remedies might have included such things as upper-level government agencies collecting a unified dike fee, abolishing surcharges, and rooting out corruption. The frequent water calamities and the environmental degradation caused by water-control projects were controllable and reducible.

The most important form of water control in the Jianghan Plain were the dike systems, which were different from the irrigation and drainage systems emphasized by both Perkins and Elvin. Irrigation and drainage systems, which were very important in other areas, directly influence the yield of crops. But the dike systems in the Jianghan Plain – even though they were involved with irrigation and drainage – mainly functioned to maintain relatively stable farming, not to increase the yield. In the long run, the yield of rice, the primary crop in the Jianghan Plain, did not sharply decline even under a degraded environment, although it did fluctuate widely from year to year (see Appendix). This again demonstrates that production from paddy fields in the Jianghan Plain was sustainable. Since the paddy fields were the principle form of farmland in the Jianghan Plain, the simple black-and-white dichotomy of sustainable versus unsustainable growth cannot explain the history of Jianghan agriculture.

The dike systems and the related frequent water calamities did degrade the local environment and caused many problems that had a negative impact on the local economy. But it is hard to simply attribute this to "unsustainability."

One look at the farmland reveals that the application of various organic fertilizers did not damage the soil texture or degrade soil fertility: production was sustainable. In fact, in an interview published a decade after his "three-thousand-years" article, even Elvin admitted that pre-modern Chinese agriculture of course was sustainable (Bao 2004a).

Ironically, it has been since the 1970s and, particularly, since the 1980s (when the state withdrew its control of agricultural production from the village level), that the soil in China became widely contaminated by the use of polluted water and the extensive application of agrochemicals such as fertilizers and pesticides (Edmonds 1994, 145-49).[33] This highlights the sustainability of agriculture in traditional China, when farmers relied on organic fertilizers (as well as proper cropping systems) to maintain soil fertility.[34]

Conclusion

The dike systems were an important prerequisite for the growth of Jianghan agriculture and were the basic safeguard of the local economy. But extensive dike construction had some deleterious side effects, such as covering farmland, removing topsoil, reducing the quality of paddy fields, and causing conflicting demands between controlling high water and farming. As more and more dikes were built, both the workload and the dike fees increased. This led to an increase in the cost of dike management and, consequently, to an increase in the monetary burden of the dike fees, which were largely borne by the local peasants. All of this took its toll on the local economy.

Although the local people spent a huge amount of time, capital, and materials on dikes, the return on their investment was also huge in terms of the protection the dikes afforded them. If they had not invested in the dikes, they would have had far smaller (and fewer) harvests – to the extent that their very survival as a society would have been in question. In the PRC, in theory, the monetary investment of the provincial and central governments in the Jianghan dikes accounted for less than 1 percent of the yearly gross income from local agriculture. Before 1949, it was the regional differences and individual inequities in the dike fees, the lack of centralized investment, and dike affair-related surcharges and corruption that increased the monetary burden of dike management in some places in the Jianghan Plain. This burden and the frequent dike ruptures impeded the growth of the local economy.

The dike systems and related water calamities also caused the degradation of the local environment. Taking the territory as a whole, this degradation contributed to the decline of the local economy. However, based on the careful use of farmland and the maintenance of soil fertility, Jianghan agriculture was still sustainable. When dikes broke, the result was sometimes catastrophic loss to the local economy; but often losses could be recouped, and the economy could recover. The most important means of production in farming – soil – remained undamaged, with the exception of waterlogged paddy fields. The quality of waterlogged paddy fields, however, could be recovered by reducing the underground water level and applying suitable fertilizers. This differs from the over-reclamation of upstream mountains, which caused the loss of virgin forests and soil erosion, and left barren hills – destruction that was virtually irreversible (or, at best, would take decades or centuries to undo). Whereas the damaged economy of the Jianghan Plain would recover once the problems of environmental management (dike management, water-way improvement, etc.) were overcome.[35]

4 Agriculture, Commercialization, and Environmental Adaptability

Because of the ever-present threat of water calamities in the Jianghan Plain, the changing environment played a decisive role in the rural economy over the course of the Qing and the Republic. The Jianghan peasants were extremely responsive to their changing circumstances, and the construction of dikes was one of their responses. Dike building was usually a collective effort, but here I focus on the economic behaviour of individual peasants. Their individual responses to the environment, particularly to changes caused by water calamities, make it clear that they did their best to adapt, even when water-logging became as serious a problem as flooding. However, long-term environmental degradation restricted the effectiveness of their actions.

In pre-1949 China, staple food grains made up the bulk of agricultural production, and agriculture was the primary engine of the rural economy, providing foods as well as materials needed for most important handicrafts. This was no less true of the Jianghan Plain than of elsewhere in China. Scholars have devoted much attention to agricultural production, focusing on food grains and, particularly, the cultivation of rice in this area. They have provided detailed studies of many aspects of rice production, examining varieties, yields, cropping systems, farming techniques, and the relation between rice production and *yuan* land in the Jianghan Plain in the Ming-Qing era. They argue that, as early as the late Ming (the mid-sixteenth century), the Jianghan Plain had become a new centre of rice production. Together with the Lake Dongting Plain, it became one of the country's major granaries, giving rise to the saying: "If Hunan-Hubei has a good harvest, the entire empire will be fed" *(Huguang shu, tianxia zu)*. Researchers who discuss the production and export of food grain in Hunan-Hubei focus on this saying, which remained popular into the early years of the PRC. According to them, the soil was fertile in the Jianghan-Dongting Plain, the eastern Hubei plain, the central Hunan basin, and the hillsides of Hunan. Rice was the predominant crop in these areas, and its relatively high yield created a large surplus that had the potential to be sold commercially. In addition, the location of the Hunan-Hubei region, particularly Hankou (a major entrepôt in Central China in the Qing), helped it to become a transit centre for rice shipped along the Yangzi River. And its own surplus rice found a ready market in the Yangzi delta, where demand was increasing (Zhang Jianmin 1987b; Tan Tianxing 1987; Zhang Guoxiong 1993; Mei, Zhang, and Yan 1995, 136-82; Wu 1995, 23-42; Gong 1996).

Most of these researchers have paid more attention to agricultural production in the Hunan-Hubei region than in the Jianghan Plain. Many of them mention rice only in reference to food grain and seldom discuss dryland grain crops such as wheat and barley. Or they conflate rice with food grain in general and cultivated land with paddy fields. Since dry land accounts for more than a third of the cultivated land in the Jianghan Plain in the period under study, paddy fields were not the only type of cultivated land, nor was rice synonymous with food grain. Most important, few scholars have considered the role of environmental instability in the production of food grain in the Jianghan Plain.

Agricultural production, of course, depends heavily on the natural environment. In the Jianghan Plain, a frequently inundated area, the types and varieties of food grain crops and the cropping systems were all closely related to the local conditions, which clearly reflects the crucial role of environmental adaptability in shaping Jianghan peasant decision making.

In the Jianghan Plain, beginning in the middle of the Qing dynasty, immigration was no longer an important source of population growth and rice was no longer an important export. However, natural population growth continued unabated, and, in response, so, too, did the reclamation of more and more *yuan*. Consequently, flooding became more frequent and waterlogging more serious, which led directly to a decline in the local economy. How was the economic behaviour of peasants affected by this changing environment? How and why did they make their economic decisions?

In this chapter I seek answers to these questions. I probe the economic behaviour of the peasants in the Jianghan Plain as they responded to population pressure, environmental instability, and market expansion. Focusing on crop choices and the domestic textile industry, I consider how peasants responded to the changes in the environment and the market in the Qing and the Republic, and I explore the importance of an interactive relationship between human beings and nature in the rural economy. I show that, although issues of survival were more important in peasant economic decision making than market considerations, their survival strategies and their participation in the market were intertwined.

Overview of Food Grain Crops in the Jianghan Plain

Varieties of Food Grain Crops

The most available sources on the types and varieties of crop in the Qing are records from the local products *(wuchan)* section of traditional gazetteers. As local histories, gazetteers documented everything that compilers regarded as important or special to the local area (e.g., fragrant rice *[xiangdao]*, a rare variety but one recorded in many gazetteers [Zhang 1991]). The more records there were of a particular crop, the more important it was.

In almost every Qing gazetteer in the Jianghan area, rice was the first crop listed in the local products section, and it had the largest number of varieties. One gazetteer listed up to thirty-three varieties, while other crops only had one or at most a few varieties (*Jingzhou fu zhi* 1880, 6: 1a). There were even different genotypes of rice, such as glutinous rice, indica rice, and japonica rice (which had different types and amounts of starch), and early-season rice, middle-season rice, and late-season rice (which were harvested at different times of the year). No other crop had this degree of differentiation. There can be no doubt that rice was the most important food grain crop in almost every county of the Jianghan Plain.

The cultivation of rice in the Jianghan Plain has a long history. Archaeological findings show that rice had already become a popular crop in the Jianghan area in the Neolithic Age (Ding 1959; Wu, Liu, and Zhao 2010). By the Ming-Qing era, the number of the varieties of rice had increased substantially, and the single cropping system was typical (Zhang 1991). As we will see, this remained unchanged in the Republic.

Although rice was the leading food grain crop in the Jianghan Plain, there were some regional differences in choice of crops. Rice was all-important in paddy field areas, but *mai* (a general term for wheat, barley, buckwheat, etc.) or other dryland food grain crops were important in dryland areas, which accounted for about 40 percent of the total cultivated land in the Jianghan Plain in the Qing (Zhang 1992b). Actually, the rich diversity of food grain crops in the Jianghan Plain was demonstrated not by paddy field crops but by dryland crops. The latter included wheat, barley, buckwheat, Chinese sorghum *(gaoliang),* maize, sesame, millets, and many kinds of beans (Chinese peasants traditionally treated beans as food grain crops).

The records in gazetteers confirm that *mai* was the second largest and second most widely distributed food grain crop in the Jianghan Plain in the Qing. One late Qing gazetteer records five varieties of wheat, five varieties of barley, and two kinds of buckwheat (*Jingzhou fu zhi* 1880, 6: 1a). Though *mai* was widely distributed, the acreage devoted to it and other dryland food grain crops such as millet, Chinese sorghum, sesame, and beans was unclear. These crops were generally categorized as "miscellaneous grains" *(zaliang)*, functioned as indispensable supplements to the local people's daily diet, and were used for such things as the making of cakes and wine and the extraction of edible oil. As a gazetteer of Zhijiang declares: "Millet, beans, Chinese sorghum, and sesame are miscellaneous grains for the local people. They are used in cooking, in making wine and are extracted as [edible] oil. They are daily necessities. Most of them are grown in mountain [hilly] land and shoaly land" (*Zhijiang xian zhi* 1866, 7: 1a). Millet *(su [Setaria italica])* was particularly important; in fact, it was just as important as rice in some areas (e.g., *Jingzhou fu zhi* 1757, 18: 2a). Beans, a large group, functioned as a food grain, vegetable, or source of edible oil. However, New World crops – namely, maize and the sweet potato – were not at all important in the Jianghan Plain.[1]

Proportion of Various Food Grain Crops
Because of a dearth of data, it is hard to get an accurate picture of the acreage and output of individual grain crops in the Qing; the relative importance of each crop described above is only a rough estimate. However, statistics are available for the Republican era. According to these figures, rice and *mai* were, respectively, the number one and number two food grain crops in terms of output. Maize moved into the sixth position, but the sweet potato was still of negligible importance (Table 9).

This table demonstrates that, during the Republic, rice was both the most important food grain crop and the most important crop overall in the Jianghan Plain. Other major food grain crops included wheat, barley, soybeans, and sorghum. Although the percentage of the output of each non-rice crop is not large, the total output of all non-rice food grains accounts for about one-third of the total food grain output in the Jianghan Plain. In other words, the output of rice only accounted for about two-thirds of the food grain output in the Jianghan Plain in the Republic.

Environmental Adaptability of Different Crops
That rice is grown in paddy fields and dryland crops on dry land seems self-evident. However, the situation was not so simple in the Jianghan Plain. Since gazetteers indicate that rice was the single most important local crop, let us first discuss the environmental adaptability of the various varieties of rice.

Paddy rice, with its need for large amounts of water, can grow only in places that have easy access to irrigation and drainage. According to a gazetteer of

Table 9

Estimate of the output of major food grain crops in the Jianghan Plain, 1936

Food grain crops	Estimated output	Percentage of each crop
Rice	31,440.0	66.05
Wheat	6,340.0	13.32
Barley	3,508.0	7.37
Soybeans	1,985.5	4.17
Sorghum	1,440.0	3.03
Maize	999.5	2.10
Broad beans	801.0	1.68
Peas	510.0	1.07
Sesame	459.0	0.96
Sweet potatoes	120.0	0.25
Total	47,603.0	100.00

Notes: Unit: 1,000 *shi dan.*

Since the data presented in this table are the result of a provincial survey, they only cover some general crops that were raised throughout the whole province. They do not, for example, include certain local crops that had special importance in the Jianghan area, such as buckwheat and lake millet (see Chapter 7). Although these crops did not challenge the dominant position of rice in the Jianghan Plain, they were nonetheless important in this frequently inundated area.

Source: Hubei sheng zhi tudi liyong yu liangshi wenti (1977 [1938], inset between 24208-09) (n.b., these page numbers are numbers in a series of reprints of handwritten works, hence their huge volume. The original page numbers of each book are missing). The Jianghan Plain in the above table includes the counties of Wuchang, Hankou, Hanyang, Xiaogan, Yunmeng, Hanchuan, Yingcheng, Tianmen, Mianyang, Zhongxiang, Jingshan, Jingmen, Qianjiang, Jianli, Shishou, Gong'an, Songzhi, Zhijiang, Jiangling, and Dangyang. The total estimated output has been calculated by the present author.

Hanchuan, "in this county, no matter if it is mountain [hilly] land or lakefront land, rice should grow if the land can be drained and irrigated" (*Hanchuan tuji zhengshi* 1895, 4: 36b).[2] On fields with basic drainage and irrigation systems, different varieties were cultivated in different locations, depending on when they matured. The Jianghan peasants knew that "high land and sloping fields were suitable for [the cultivation of] early-season rice, and lake land was suitable for [the cultivation of] late-season rice" (*Jingzhou fu zhi* 1880, 6: 1a).[3]

Rice can be grown not only in paddy fields but also on dry land (i.e., *handao* or *ludao,* dryland rice). But since water was generally readily available and there were many paddy fields in the Jianghan Plain, the cultivation of dryland rice was extremely limited. It has only been found in a few places, such as Hanchuan: "*Ludao* ... is sown late but ripens early. Its grain is large but short, the yield is very low, few people grow it in our county" (*Hanchuan tuji zhengshi* 1895, 4: 36b).[4] From this example, it appears that its low yield was the primary reason that peasants chose not to cultivate dryland rice; later, however, we find that this was not always the case.

In addition to the general ability of rice to adapt to its environment, there are two specific groups of rice, direct-seeding rice and deepwater rice, that display obvious and extreme environmental adaptability. Direct seeding rice includes awned varieties (i.e., varieties that have long awns on one end of their grains) such as *mangzao* (awned early), *mangcao* (awned weed), *mangdao* (awned rice), and *zhagu* (zha rice), which were prevalent in the Han River valley, along with *sagu* ("casting rice"), which was seen in both Jingzhou Prefecture and Hanyang Prefecture.

According to a gazetteer of Hanyang, "*mangcao* is cast over the field; there is no need for transplanting [its seedlings]. It ripens the earliest and is usually cultivated in low places" (*Hanyang fu zhi* 1747, 28: 2a). Obviously, the local peasants chose it mainly because it ripens early and could be harvested before the coming of summer high water. The same strategy was used by the peasants in late Qing Hunan (Perdue 1987, 117). But, due to its awn and the method of seeding, its yield was not high.[5] Thus, peasant cropping choice was constrained by environmental conditions – more specifically, by seasonal high water.

Zhagu (zha rice) also has a relatively short growing period and can resist water. Unlike awned varieties, which were sown before the coming of the summer high water, *zha* rice was sown after the summer high water had subsided. The local peasants chose it if it was too late to grow other types of food grain crops after the high water. In the words of one gazetteer:

> There is another variety called *zhagu*. There is no need to soak its seeds and transplant [its seedlings] when cultivating it. Just plough the paddy field and cast the seeds. It will ripen in fifty to sixty days. The people who live in the lake area usually grow it if there is not enough time to grow other types of rice after the high water has receded. (*Xiaogan xian zhi* 1883, 5: 30b)

A span of fifty to sixty days is less than the actual period leading up to maturity, but it emphasizes the brevity of the growing period. Since the growing period is short, the yield cannot be high. Thus, the yield was not necessarily the primary consideration in peasant decision making: they also considered whether the crop would ripen early and whether it was water-resistant (and would thus increase the possibility of a harvest). In such an unstable environment, these are more rational motivations than high yield.

The last variety in this group is *sagu*.

> According to the gazetteers of Jingzhou Prefecture, in addition to early and late season rice, there are three kinds of *sagu*, named *Yunnan zao* (Yunnan early), *maobanzi* (hair valve), and *dongnianzi* (frozen glutinous rice), which all ripen twice a year. Casting means sowing by broadcast with no need for transplanting. There is no difference from the cultivation of *zhagu*, but it may have other differences since it says it ripens twice a year. (*Hubei tong zhi* 1921, 779)

No mention is made of any special environmental adaptability. But from the record of the Lake Dongting area, we know that *sagu* was grown in newly silted fields (Peng 1977 [1938], 39356-57), a type of field that is not suitable for normal paddy rice. Since newly silted fields were common in the Jianghan Plain (particularly in the Han River valley) well into the Republic, varieties of *sagu*, which ripened early, were still widely cultivated (*Honghu xian zhi* 1992, 105).

The second group of rice consists of deepwater rice, which can tolerate deep water when being transplanted and during its growing period. Its varieties include *qingnian* (green nian) and *qing zhanzi* (green champa).

> *Qingnian:* [the peasants of the] lake area have started to grow it, transplanting its seedlings after the middle of the fourth lunar month. [Its seedlings] are two or more *chi* in length. It will grow as long as its head can be kept about one *cun* [1 *cun* = 3.2 cm.] above the water surface when transplanting. The harvest is slightly more than that of the early-season rice, and [when cooked] it is fragrant and soft. (*Hanyang fu zhi* 1747, 28: 3b)

As for *qing zhanzi*, it "can resist water; the locals call it *qiu shui zhang* (grows with the rise of water). It can still be transplanted even when the water is more than one *chi* in depth" (*Hanchuan tuji zhengshi* 1895, 4: 36a). Both *qingnian* and *qing zhanzi* are very tolerant of deep water and have similar names. It is possible that they may be one variety with two different names. According to the newly compiled gazetteer of Xiaogan, *qingnian* was still a major variety of middle-season rice cultivated in Xiaogan in the Republic (*Xiaogan shi zhi* 1992, 128). In Honghu, *qingnian* was still cultivated as a deepwater rice in the Republic due to its ability to tolerate high water. It can grow with the rise of water to up to more than two metres in height. This makes it adaptable to low-lake paddy fields (*Honghu xian zhi* 1992, 105).[6] Again, we see how the local peasants dealt with seasonal high waters, how they adapted to their unstable environment.

This kind of environmental adaptation can also be found in dryland food grain crops. Since dry land accounted for about 40 percent of the total cultivated land of the Jianghan Plain, dryland crops were of great importance and were widely distributed. In almost all of the *wuchan* sections of the gazetteers, *mai* is the second food grain crop mentioned. However, during the Qing, the cultivation of *mai* was still spreading, and this was related to the flood-prone local environment. Mai Zhu, a governor general of Hubei-Hunan, once reported:

> Before the fourth year of the reign of Yongzheng [1723-35], few people in Hubei grew *mai*. After the flood in the fifth year [of the reign of Yongzheng], I came to Hubei to ask the local officials to advise the people to do their best to grow *mai*. In the following year, the high water only came after the *mai* harvest. The locals benefited from it a lot; therefore there are more people who grow *mai* since then ... There is much lakefront land in Hubei ... Recently the people of Hubei have all come to know that *mai* will ripen before the coming of the summer high water. Even if there is a huge amount of high water, the wheat and barley have already been harvested. [The locals] have enough to eat and there is no need to worry about hunger. [They] therefore grow *mai* everywhere on lakefront land, where they had never grown *mai* before ... The former waste lakefront land is now fertile land. [The locals] also benefit from this. (*Yongzheng zhupi yuzhi* 1965, 2: 94b-95a [Mai Zhu, 1734, the 29th day of the eighth lunar month])

Here, Mai Zhu exaggerates his achievement as the results from introducing one crop cannot be seen in such a short time. In fact, seven years later, another official reported that, in the Han River valley, the land under *mai* was not very extensive: "Everywhere, barley has been harvested and wheat is still in the process of being harvested [in a rush] ... Since [the locals] do not grow [wheat/barley] very much, the loss is limited" (Shuli dianlibu 1991, 246). Mai Zhu's report, however, at least tells us that *mai* had spread to lakefront land (the same process occurred in the Lake Dongting Plain, where, under the influence of local officials, the number of counties that grew wheat increased from ten in 1752 to thirty-three in 1837 [Perdue 1987, 125]), and the primary reason for this was that *mai* could be harvested before the coming of the summer high water. It is clear that the cultivation of *mai* was another way that the peasants adapted to seasonal high water.

Whether the *mai* in Mai Zhu's memorial refers to wheat or barley or both, barley was particularly important in some dryland areas. Although barley can ripen even earlier than wheat, its quality as a food is inferior. Some Zhijiang peasants preferred barley to wheat because barley matured relatively quickly, and they took barley as a staple food (*Zhijiang xian zhi* 1990, 121). The peasants of Hanchuan also considered this advantage when they chose barley over wheat: "As for barley ... the yield is relatively low, [but] the peasants [grow it] simply because it ripens early and can relieve famine. Most of the peasants grow [the variety that can] ripen in the fourth lunar month" (*Hanchuan tuji zhengshi* 1895, 4: 40b). That the peasants chose barley despite its inferior quality as food and its low yield again illustrates that the ripening time, not the yield, was the first priority in their decision making. In this way the local people avoided the damage that might have been caused by seasonal high water. And, most important, they had something to eat during the temporary food shortage in the late spring and early summer, when the new crop is still growing and the old one has all been consumed. It is for this reason that, during the Republic, Qianjiang, a county with a great deal of flood-prone dry land, had between 250,000 to 300,000 *mu* under barley, enough to supply half of the grain consumed annually by the local people (*Qianjiang xian zhi* 1990, 232). In Hanchuan in the Republic, barley was also a staple food for the people who lived in cotton-growing areas. They chose early-season barley because any crop harvested late could be hit by water calamities (*Hanchuan xian zhi* 1992, 126).

Another locally important dryland crop, and one that provincial officials frequently mentioned in their memorials, was Chinese sorghum, which was usually grown in low-lying places or on river beaches because of its ability to survive days of submersion. For example, after an inundation in Qianjiang and Tianmen counties in 1806, "the places that raise sorghum still had a harvest" (Shuili dianlibu 1991, 563). In the Republic, the local people usually grew sorghum on beachland along the Han River and the Dongjing River (*Qianjiang xian zhi* 1990, 233). It was reported that both Mianyang and Tianmen had more than 200,000 *mu* of land under sorghum in 1917 (Hu 1920, 1: 35, 68). Even in low-lying lands that had been waterlogged for a long time, a harvest of spring sorghum was still possible after the land had been dried for a winter (*Zhijiang xian zhi* 1990, 118).

Although the various and scattered sources substantially disagree about the yields of these dryland crops, it is clear that they were much lower than those of rice (Table 10). Nonetheless, the local peasants grew them in order to have a relatively reliable supply of food, particularly during famine years.

Clearly, the peasants of the Jianghan Plain usually chose varieties that were suitable to their inundation-prone environment. These varieties included early-season rice and *mai* that could be harvested before the coming of the seasonal high water, directly seeding rice with a short growing period, and

Table 10

Yields of non-rice food grain crops in the Jianghan Plain in the Republic

Grains	Yields	Sources
Wheat	0.8-2 *shi* [95.2-238.1 *jin*]	*Hubei xianzheng gaikuang* 1934, 68, 760, 1055
	120 *jin*	*Hanchuan xian jian zhi* 1959, 32
	7 *dou* [83.3 *jin*]	*Xiaogan shi zhi* 1992, 128
	100 *jin*	*Wuhan shi zhi nongye* 1989, 273
Barley	120 *jin*	*Hanchuan xian jian zhi* 1959, 32
	76-100 *jin*	*Qianjiang xian zhi* 1990, 232
	5 *dou* [59.5 *jin*]	*Xiaogan shi zhi* 1992, 128
Soybeans	1 *shi* [159.4 *jin*]	*Hubei xianzheng gaikuang* 1934, 760
	160 *jin*	*Hanchuan xian jian zhi* 1959, 32
Sorghum	80 *jin*	*Qianjiang xian zhi* 1990, 233
	0.8-1 *shi* [124.2-155.3 *jin*]	*Hubei xianzheng gaikuang* 1934, 760, 858
Millet *[su]*	2 *shi* [310.5 *jin*]	*Hubei xianzheng gaikuang* 1934, 760

Note: The conversion rates of different crops in this table are: 1 Qing *shi* = 1.035 *shi shi*, 1 *shi shi* = 115 *shi jin* (wheat and barley), 154 *shi jin* (soybeans), and 150 *shi jin* (sorghum and millet). See Xu Daofu (1983, 344).

deepwater rice and Chinese sorghum, which are water-resistant. In almost all cases, environmental adaptability, rather than yield, was the local people's major consideration.

These records show that, in the Jianghan Plain in the Qing and the Republic, particularly in areas along rivers and adjacent to lakes, peasants chose their crops very carefully, mindful of the water-rich surroundings. Although it is impossible to know exactly how much land was devoted to the various crops discussed above, frequent water calamities and the repeated inundation of hundreds of *yuan* and millions of *mu* of farmland (see below) obviously forced the local peasants to consider the need for relatively unpalatable but reliable crops when deciding what to plant. Whether they regularly grew water-resistant crops or varieties to deal with seasonal high water, or replanted various miscellaneous grains and famine-relief crops after water receded or in famine years (see Chapter 7), their priority was reliability, not market value or high yield. The principle was safety first.

Environmental Adaptability of the Cropping Systems
Environmental adaptability emerged even more clearly in the cropping systems in the Jianghan Plain. During the Qing and the Republic, in both paddy

fields and dry land, the single cropping system predominated, supplemented by auxiliary double cropping systems and occasionally by multi-year cropping systems. This is different from both the North China Plain, where a multi-year-multi-crops system prevailed (mostly three-crops-in-two-years rotation [Liang 1989, 492-93; Li 2005, 27-29]), and the Yangzi delta, where a double cropping system predominated. The formation and popularity of the single cropping system in the Jianghan Plain was very closely related to the local environment.

Paddy Field Cropping Systems

The single cropping system in the paddy fields of the Jianghan Plain included three types: (1) one season of early rice, (2) one season of late rice, or (usually) (3) one season of middle-season rice. In areas of the Han River valley prone to flooding, the peasants chose to plant early-season rice in order to have a harvest before the coming of the summer high water. Varieties of early season rice included *wushi zao* (fifty-day early) and *qishi zao* (seventy-day early) (*Jingzhou fu zhi* 1880, 6: 1a). Their growing period, of course, should not be understood as exactly fifty or seventy days; the names simply suggest that these varieties ripened quickly.

Wushi zao and another similar variety, *liushi zao* (sixty-day early), were still cultivated in the Republic (Zeng 1984, 2: 133). The peasants of Honghu called them *hong sagu* (red casting rice). The seeds of these varieties were known to sprout vigorously. They produced hardy seedlings, and they ripened quickly during the late period of milking. They could ripen before July and August (i.e., before the coming of the major summer high waters of the Yangzi and the Dongjing Rivers). They became one of the most popular varieties of early-season rice grown in lake areas (*Honghu xian zhi* 1992, 105).

The varieties of middle-season rice also depended on the local environment. The peasants of Qianjiang in the Republic grew *qingnian* in lake areas where water was deep, and they rushed to plant *dongnian* (winter nian) after the retreat of floods in years of water calamities: both involved a single cropping of rice (*Qianjiang xian zhi* 1990, 228). In Honghu, before 1949, *qingnian* was the most popular variety of late-ripening middle-season rice. In low-lying lake fields, however, both *qingnian* and *hong sagu* could be harvested if the water was not unusually high; if it was, peasants would lose the harvest (*Honghu xian zhi* 1992, 105).

In addition to the single cropping of rice, there was limited double cropping of rice (i.e., harvests occurring twice per year on the same plot), which included continuous cropping of rice and rice ratooning.[7] There are some records from the Qing dynasty on the continuous cropping of rice, and it was generally found in the Han River valley. Some frequently cited examples are, in fact, not necessarily referring to the double cropping of rice. For example, in Jiangxia, "there are an early rice and a late rice. The early rice is transplanted after the harvest of *mai,* and it is harvested in the middle of the sixth lunar month. Late rice is transplanted after the early rice has been harvested, and is harvested in mid-autumn" (*Jiangxia xian zhi* 1869, 5: 36b). We cannot be sure this refers to the double cropping of rice because the source does not make it clear whether the early rice and the late rice (or even the wheat) were grown on the same plot. However, the gazetteer of Hanyang Prefecture provides a clear description of the double cropping of rice: "The late rice should be grown in fields after the early rice has been harvested; [the late rice] is transplanted after the beginning of the autumn. The peak of the grain [of late rice] has an awn similar to barley. Its husk is slightly dark, and its husked grain is particularly fragrant" (*Hanyang fu zhi* 1747, 28: 3b). The distribution of the ratooning rice is the same. For example, in Hanchuan, "there is a kind of early rice that will regenerate leaves from its roots after [the first] harvest and will ripen. It is called *dao sun* (ratooning rice) ... Though its yield is only a third of that of the first harvest, the labour is easy" (*Hanchuan tuji zhengshi* 1895, 4: 36a).

Although the meteorological conditions (temperature, heat, and sunlight) in the Jianghan Plain were adequate for the double cropping of rice, the water conditions limited the acreage under double cropping. First, the double cropping of rice needs relatively sophisticated and effective drainage and irrigation; however, in the Qing and the Republic many paddy fields in the Jianghan Plain did not have ready access to drainage and irrigation (*Mianyang xian zhi* 1989, 90), mainly because of the frequent floods. Second, the yield from the double cropping of rice is low. Thus, although the double cropping system of rice was undertaken in more than one-third of the counties in the Jianghan Plain, its acreage was limited.[8] By the same token, the acreage devoted to the cropping system of three-harvests-in-one-year was even more limited: it was seen mostly on high-quality *yuan* land such as that in southern Xiaogan and Hanyang in the Republican era (*Xiaogan shi zhi* 1992, 128; *Hubei xian-zheng gaikuang* 1934, 68). Under this system there was one harvest of wheat and two harvests of rice within one year on the same plot.

One season of wheat and two seasons of rice meant that, in some places, wheat was also cultivated in paddy fields. This then raises the issue of the rotation of dryland crops and paddy field crops. In the Yangzi delta in late imperial times, the rotation of dryland crops (wheat) and paddy field crops (rice) was common, and the transformation of paddy fields into dry land was not unusual. Many local peasants moved from the cultivation of rice to the cultivation of non-grain cash crops, mainly cotton and mulberry trees. In contrast, in the Jianghan Plain in the Qing and the Republic the rotation of non-grain cash crops and food grain crops was rare. Most of the multi-cropping systems involved the rotation of food grain crops. When peasants of the Yangzi delta transformed their rice fields into cotton land, the farming system was completely changed from a paddy field farming system into a dryland farming system. Moreover, when peasants made this switch, it was usually for more than one year; indeed, often paddy fields were permanently transformed into dry land. This change required a good irrigation system. In the Jianghan Plain, however, the farming system was more influenced by local natural conditions. The Jianghan peasants could usually only harvest dryland crops on paddy fields if there was relatively little spring rain; they could then grow rice again the next summer. Few of them completely changed their paddy fields into dry land.

The primary reason for this is the low elevation and high underground water table in many areas of the Jianghan Plain. The single pattern of the rota-tion of paddy field crops and dryland crops in the Jianghan Plain in the Qing and the Republic was the rotation of rice and wheat: one season of rice was alternated with one season of wheat (*Zhijiang xian zhi* 1866, 7: 1a), or two seasons of rice were followed by one season of wheat. In general, because of the hostile environment, the acreage under the rotation of rice and wheat would not have been very large. As a Hankou gazetteer reports: "All of the flat land is low-lying and wet; little [of it] is suitable for the cultivation of *mai*. [Therefore, the peasants] only transplant rice seedlings" (*Hankou xiaozhi* 1915, fengsu zhi: 1). Actually, in the whole of Hubei Province, before 1949 wheat was only occasionally grown in paddy fields (*Hubei sheng zhi nongye* I 1994, 187). This is, at least in part, because of the high level of underground water.[9] Moreover, since the local peasants were not accustomed to planting wheat in paddy fields, the acreage of paddy fields devoted to wheat would not have greatly increased.[10]

Thus, in those places where crops were rotated in paddy fields, the crops were rice and a dryland crop, such as wheat. Most of the dryland crops in this system were winter crops. As stated above, the majority of the rice grown in the Jianghan Plain was middle-season rice. In the Republic, after the middle-season rice was harvested, many paddy fields under middle-season rice were left fallow to soak up water throughout the winter and so to restore soil fertility. This kind of paddy field was usually low-lying (*Jiangling xian zhi* 1990, 269).

Paddy fields on relatively high terrain were either allowed to dry in the winter or the peasants grew green manure crops or winter grain crops such as wheat, beans, rape, and so on. In many places, the harvest of these winter grain crops depended on the amount and the timing of the spring rain. If the spring rain came early and was sufficient, the local peasants would plough in these winter grain crops as green manure (or soak them as base manure) and then plant a crop of middle-season rice. In this case, these winter grain crops improved soil fertility. Even more effective as green manure was the broad bean, which draws nitrogen from the air through its root nodules and so enriches soil fertility. If the spring rain came late or rainfall was insufficient, the peasants would let these crops ripen; after harvesting them, they transplanted the seedlings of middle-season rice into the fields. This kind of cropping system was called *shuang bao xian* (double insurance) and was common in the Republic in many places (e.g., *Tianmen xian zhi* 1989, 199; *Jingmen shi zhi* 1994, 247). In Zhijiang in the Republic, the local peasants even adjusted the normal cropping system of paddy fields in the summer, depending on the water supply: if there had been enough rainfall, they would transplant rice; if there had not been enough rainfall, they would grow dryland crops (*Zhijiang xian zhi* 1990, 117, 119). These examples illustrate how the cropping system in the Jianghan Plain was shaped by local conditions. It was driven by environmental uncertainty and was completely different from the cropping system (from paddy fields to dryland [cotton]) seen in the Yangzi delta in Ming-Qing times.

Dryland Cropping Systems

Although dryland crops were less important in the Jianghan Plain than they were in the North China Plain, they were as important as, if not more important, in the Jianghan Plain than they were in the Yangzi delta. The dryland cropping systems in the Jianghan Plain included both a single cropping system and a double or multi-year cropping system; however, the majority of land was under a single cropping system that focused on food grain crops. Not all dry land was necessarily higher than paddy fields; like paddy fields, low-lying dry land was also prone to seasonal high water. This was particularly true of land located outside the river dikes (i.e., on river beaches), which would be flooded every year. The local peasants had to grow crops that could be harvested before the annual high water arrived. In double or multi-year cropping systems, the winter crops were usually *mai*, but the summer crops varied. The land under this kind of cropping system was usually "miscellaneous grain" land; its profile of crops depended not only on the growing characteristics of the crops in question but also on the terrain or the environmental stability of the land. Before the 1940s, cotton was mainly single cropped: after the cotton harvest, the land was left fallow or it was planted with a green manure. Double cropping (of cotton with wheat) was very limited (*Hubei sheng zhi nongye I* 1994, 187, 223).

To sum up, in the Jianghan Plain in the Qing and the Republic, the major cropping system was the single cropping system, supplemented by some double cropping on the part of a relatively small number of cultivators in both paddy fields and dry land. These cropping systems emerged out of the need to adapt to the unstable environment. This flood-prone environment constrained peasants from transforming paddy fields into dry land, a common phenomenon in the Yangzi delta in the Ming-Qing era.

Limits of Crop Choice and Peasant Response

The Jianghan peasants, particularly those who lived along rivers and close to lakes,[11] had generations of experience in dealing with water. A Qing provincial official of Hubei observes that, in this area: "The land near rivers and close to lakes is inundated whenever water comes. [The locals then] replant something on it after the water recedes ... The locals are accustomed to this." Another notes: "In counties such as Qianjiang that are located along the lower reaches of the Han River, the land is inundated whenever water comes; the locals know how to handle it" (Shuili dianlibu 1991, 492, 563). By "water" they obviously mean seasonal high water, and they suggest that the locals have a sophisticated approach to their water-rich environment.

That sophistication was most apparent, and most needed, in areas close to lakes and thus prone to inundation. In 1802, the governor of Hubei found that the people of Tianmen, Mianyang, and Hanchuan counties knew that "lakefront *yuan* would be submerged whenever the water came ... Therefore they usually only planted late rice and miscellaneous grains after they harvested the *mai* [wheat or barley]" (Shuili dianlibu 1991, 534). The same was done with the land outside the major dikes (river beaches), which was usually devoted to dryland grain crops.[12]

The floods caused by dike ruptures and the waterlogging caused by seasonal high water, floods, and heavy rain or natural seepage from rivers also affected agricultural production. Peasants responded in ways appropriate to their specific situation, particularly by choosing suitable crops. But the crop choice was not the sole response. The discussion that follows analyzes their behaviour in a larger context and discusses additional ways they adapted to the local environment, such as changing how they made a living and even building so-called *fengtian* (floating fields).

Limits of Crop Choice and Waterlogging

In responding to their precarious circumstances, the local peasants wisely chose suitable crops and replanted crops after high water had receded. However, the harvest of replanted crops was never as good as that of a regular planting.[13] The later the time of replanting, the smaller the harvest. In a 1773 memorial, one observer records:

> I checked one after another, in Hanchuan, Tianmen, Jiangling, and Jianli ... The late autumn grains are replanted after the water recedes in these areas. [The peasants] may get 70 to 80 percent of the regular harvest ... The lands of Mianyang, however, are the lowest-lying, and the water in inundated fields recedes slowly, delaying the replanting time. As a result, late rice and miscellaneous grains cannot completely ripen ... [The peasants there thus] get only 60 percent [of a regular harvest]. (Shuili dianlibu 1991, 451)

A second inundation after replanting would reduce yields even more. In a 1794 memorial, an official writes:

> In the counties of Anlu Prefecture along the Han River ... This year, the peasants of each county are happy because the summer grain is ripening. Unfortunately, the Han River rose twice between the sixth and seventh lunar months, causing many *yuan* in Qianjiang and other places to be inundated. [The locals] just gradually drained these *yuan* and immediately replanted miscellaneous grain crops. On the first of the eighth lunar month, the Han River unexpectedly rose again, causing many *yuan* to be inundated again. (Shuili dianlibu 1991, 513)

In 1794, some *yuan* were flooded three times (Shuili dianlibu 1991, 514). Conditions could thus undermine peasant strategies of crop choice since the key to a successful replanting is a short period of submersion. As the governor general of Hunan-Hubei observed in 1816: "Low-lying places in the lower valley [of the Han River] will be submerged whenever the Yangzi and the Han Rivers fully rise. Only if [the high water] recedes and [the land] drains very quickly can [the locals] replant the autumn crop" (ibid., 616). But it was not always easy to replant in time. For example, in 1788, replanting after a flood was delayed by the slow recession of the water. According to the official who went to survey the situation after the flood: "Most of the land along the post road was still submerged. Even where the water had drained, it will be hard to have an autumn harvest. After the middle of the eighth lunar month, the water will return to the main river course, and the long-term waterlogging will be over. At that time, because the fields are damp, [people] can grow wheat and legumes and expect a spring harvest" (ibid., 480).

After the heavy flood of 1788, the local people had increasing difficulty draining waterlogged land. In 1807, the governor general of Hunan-Hubei found that about 4 million *mu* of land – a huge area – had failed to drain promptly; some fields in the Hubei basin had been waterlogged for twenty years (ibid., 569-70). As the riverbed of the Han River rose, the drainage of rainwater amassed nearby became even more problematic. Although water-logging was not new to the Jianghan Plain, it had obviously become more common and more serious. Frequent inundation and waterlogging combined to produce long-term environmental degradation.

As the severity of waterlogging grew through the nineteenth century, re-planting became less successful. In 1816, for example, 593 *yuan* in the counties of Hanchuan, Mianyang, Qianjiang, Tianmen, Jiangling, Gong'an, and Jianli were inundated once or twice, with the loss of the entire harvest. Because the process of draining the land either proceeded too slowly or began too late, the replanted crops did not have time to ripen (ibid., 618).[14] In some *yuan*, the waterlogging was so extensive that the water that had entered in the summer and autumn did not drain out until the following winter or spring (*Qing jingshi wenbian* 1992 [1889], 117: 8b).

To make matters worse, even without inundation, peasants who inhabited the middle region of the Jianghan Plain still suffered from waterlogging. An 1817 memorial provides a detailed description:

> Hubei is usually called a *zeguo* [marshy kingdom], while Jiangling, Qianjiang, Jianli, and Mianyang in particular are low-lying, and are located between two great water systems, the Yangzi River and the Han River. For only a few months in the winter and spring is the land located inside the dikes higher than the water level outside the dikes [of the river]. For the rest of the year, the water level outside is higher than the land inside. The security [of these *yuan*] depends entirely on the dike systems. Whenever the river rises in the summer and autumn, if a dike breaks, many *yuan* will be submerged; the water will not drain. Even if the dike systems are solid and prevent river water from inun-dating the *yuan*, the rainwater that accumulates inside the *yuan* still cannot be drained. (Shuili dianlibu 1991, 623)

In other words, for more than half the year, the land in the centre of the Jianghan Plain was below the water level of the Yangzi and Han Rivers. Given the natural seepage of river water into the *yuan*, which this memorial does not mention, the waterlogging may have been even more severe.

Twenty-one years later, in 1838, another memorial reported that some land protected by *yuan* dikes was as much as ten metres or so lower than the outside water level. Any break would therefore cause a serious, large-scale inundation, and a single flood would cause waterlogging problems for years thereafter (ibid., 810). The local people found they could no longer recover from flooding as easily as they had done in the past. It was during this period – in the 1830s – that the residents of Tianmen, Hanchuan, Mianyang, and Jianli started to flee the area in large numbers. In some places, nearly the entire population left (ibid., 819).

It is clear that, in the Jianghan Plain, changes in the environment were paramount when it came to determining peasant behaviour. And these changes elicited a variety of responses.

Changing One's Way of Making a Living

If the environment changed radically, the local people sometimes adapted by changing how they made a living. One of the most popular strategies was to turn from farming to fishing. Living in an area studded with lakes, many Jianghan residents fished, usually as a sideline. As the number of *yuan* increased, more and more people became cultivators who relied on farming for their livelihood. But once their *yuan* were heavily inundated and became hard to drain, some would temporarily return to fishing.[15]

In response to heavy or recurrent floods, the local people sometimes simply returned their land to the lakes. This is what they did, for example, with the Diaocha *yuan*. Reclaimed from Lake Diaocha, it was the largest official *yuan* in Hanchuan in the early Qing. It was encircled by about seventy-five hundred *zhang* of dikes and contained within it thirteen small *yuan*. In the reign of Qianlong (1736-95), three new *yuan* were built on the eastern, western, and northern sides of Diaocha *yuan*, respectively. Every year, the *yuan* on the southern side were drained into the lakes located within the Diaocha *yuan*, making the large *yuan* itself very difficult to drain. Three heavy floods – in 1761, 1764, and 1765 – badly damaged the Diaocha *yuan*. The dikes around it were so thin (three to six *chi* high and two to five *chi* wide on top) that the local people found it difficult to ensure their integrity. They grew tired of being called in for emergency repairs every year and, at some point, began to consider themselves fishers. They asked the government to classify them as such. Moreover, the money sent to aid the local people exceeded the tax collected from this *yuan*. In the end, the Board of Works verified that, in 1767, the local people had returned the Diaocha *yuan* to Lake Diaocha (*Xu xingshui jinjian* 1937, 3585; *Hanchuan xian zhi* 1873, 9: 17b-18b). Other large *yuan* returned to lakes during the Qing included the Shiba li *yuan* in

Hanchuan and the Xiaojianghu *yuan* in Jingmen (Zhang Jianmin 2001, 362). One former market town in Songzi in the 1870s and the Zhengzhu *yuan* (and six or more other *yuan*) in Honghu were also turned back to lakes between 1869 and 1872 (*Songzi xian zhi* 1982 [1937], 85; *Honghu xian zhi* 1992, 59). Lake Chen, located on the border of Mianyang and Tianmen, was formed in the Ming dynasty after water flooded some *yuan* land and was partly reclaimed as *yuan* land at the end of the Qing and the early Republic (LS 19-2-2676). Xiaojiahu *yuan,* located in Mianyang and with an acreage of about ten thousand *mu,* was turned into a lake in 1931 (*Mianyang xian zhi* 1989, 123).

There were, however, other alternatives to dealing with life in frequently and severely flooded areas. The residents of the lower reaches of the Han River created an ingenious system called *fengtian,* or "floating fields." According to one record:

> Hanchuan is surrounded by water on all four sides. The people who live on the lake take the water as their home. They usually knit together *jiaocao* [a kind of aquatic grass] to make a raft *(pai)* and cover it with cogongrass *(maoci).* The whole household lives on the raft, which is called a *jiao* raft *(jiaopai).* It rises and falls with the water level. The people farm and raise livestock on it. (*Hanchuan xian zhi* 1873, 6: 15a)

Although this source gives no dimensions, such a *jiao* raft would have had to be quite large to sustain crops and livestock. In 1170, the poet Lu You (1983, 2: 24ab), who had seen similar floating fields in southeast Hubei, describes one as "about 10 *zhang* in width and 50 *zhang* in length [i.e., roughly 30 by 150 metres], with 30 to 40 families living on it." Whereas Lu You recorded the floating fields as a curiosity, by the time of the Qing dynasty the *jiao* rafts were shown in illustrations as densely dotting the water in Mianyang (*Hubei An Xiang Yun dao shuili ji'an* n.d., II: 10b-11a). Such depictions suggest that *jiao* rafts were common in this region and can be understood as a way of dealing with frequent floods.

In sum, the local people adapted to their unstable environment by relying on crops that were water resistant (or that would mature before or after the seasonal high water) and by replanting various types of crops after high water had receded. All these sources of nourishment had low yields or were considered relatively undesirable as food; they were thus of little commercial value. We should not idealize the effectiveness of these strategies, particularly under the twin conditions of severe floods and waterlogging. If the environmental pressure was too great, the local people had to find other solutions, such as creating floating fields or abandoning farming in favour of fishing.

Thus, in the Qing and the Republic, the environment was a critical determinant of the economic behaviour of many peasants in the Jianghan Plain.

Peasant Economic Behaviour: Environment versus Market

As we have seen, the peasants of the Jianghan Plain were sophisticated in their responses to the environment. To this point, we have only considered their subsistence efforts: the source materials indicate that almost all of the replanted crops were food grains, while unusual crops such as aquatic plants were farmed or collected because they were edible (see Chapter 7). Even the decision to become fishers was made in order to survive in an environment unfavourable to cultivation (see Chapter 6). Here, I turn to an examination of peasant involvement in non-grain cash products.

In late imperial China, grain and cotton cloth were the two most important rural products that entered the long-distance trade in commodities. According to Xu Xinwu and Wu Chengmin, the domestic market of grain and cotton cloth greatly expanded in Ming-Qing times, particularly in the Qing. During the mid-Qing, the average annual total of rice that circulated in long-distance markets was 36 million *shi,* of which 6 million *shi* was tributary and military rice and 30 million *shi* was commercial – three times more than the amount traded in the late Ming. The Yangzi delta was the most important grain importer. The second most important commodity at that time was cotton cloth. Forty-five million bolts, or 15 percent of commercial cotton cloth, entered the long-distance market (Xu and Wu 2000, 167-73).

As an area that produced both rice and cotton cloth (as well as raw cotton), one might expect that the Jianghan Plain would have responded positively to this expanding market. But, as Wu shows, most of the cotton cloth traded long distance came from the Yangzi delta; the quantity contributed by the Jianghan Plain is not clear, but it was only a very small share (Xu and Wu 2000, 173). Nor did the Jianghan Plain export much rice after the early Qing,[16] and before the twentieth century even the cotton it produced was primarily for local consumption, mainly for the personal use of peasant families (Xu 1991). As we see below, whether peasant households became involved in the market depended on a host of factors.

As has been seen, beginning in the early Ming, many outsiders moved into the Jianghan Plain. Most were refugees from wars or other calamities or came from densely populated areas. Primarily, these people hoped to survive by reclaiming wasteland. All, of course, hoped for a better life. The plain's proneness to flooding forced them to adjust and to respond to the changes of an unfamiliar environment. What remains to be explored is how, if at all, the peasants of the region participated in Ming-Qing trends associated with rural commercialization – and to what ends. As it turns out, some peasants were involved in the market and produced non-grain cash crops, but environmental constraints severely limited such activities.

Production of Cotton and Making of Cotton Cloth

In the Jianghan Plain, as generally in rural China in the Qing and the Republic, cotton was the main non-grain cash crop and cotton cloth was one of the leading rural commercial products. Several popular types of cotton cloth were produced in the Jianghan Plain, each of which had a special market outlet on the frontier.[17] However, as previously mentioned, the amount of cloth entering the long-distance market before the mid-nineteenth century was very small. Before the early twentieth century, cotton in the Jianghan Plain usually went to make cloth that was consumed locally; little of it was sold and shipped out (Xu 1991).

The cotton plant cannot withstand water; it can grow well only on dry land with specific soil qualities. Because cotton can be easily damaged by flood-water, it is best grown on relatively high ground but not on land that is of low fertility or on hard-to-irrigate hills. In Hanchuan by the end of the Qing, cotton was cultivated in many *yuan* but on only 20 to 30 percent of the hilly land (*Hanchuan tuji zhengshi* 1895, 5: 2b).

The weaving of cotton cloth was one of the major non-farming productive activities of peasant households, and it was usually undertaken by women and children. In Shishou, "in the eighth lunar month … after the harvest of the early-season rice, women and children get together to pick cotton to prepare for spinning and weaving … In the tenth lunar month … women spin and weave in order to provide thick porridge and protection against the cold in the winter." Apparently, the rural households in Shishou (which also grew cotton) sold part of their cotton cloth, but the income from its sale was not high for it only helped to "provide thick porridge." And even diligent and hardworking households could do no better than "keep from getting cold" (*Shishou xian zhi* 1866, 3: 55a, 61a).

Similarly, the making of cotton cloth in Hanyang was the task of women and children as well as elders. Hanyang produced something called *koubu* (*kou* cotton cloth): "In the southern part of the county in the spring, in addition to farming, every family relies on this [weaving]. Women, children and the elders work on this, and the looms are clicking. Each person can make one *pi* [bolt] of cloth per day: one *pi* is 15 to 16 *chi* in length" (*Hanyang xian zhi* 1748, 10: 1b). Somewhat unusually, in Hanchuan, even men wove: "Right after the work on the fields is over, men, women, and the old and young all work together [weaving cotton cloth]. Some of them do it day and night; the clicking of looms can be heard from the neighbouring houses" (*Hanchuan xian zhi* 1873, 6: 19b).

Although the handicraft weaving of cotton cloth was widespread in the Jianghan Plain countryside, it was as a supplement to farming not as a main source of livelihood. According to a mid-nineteenth century gazetteer: "Cotton is cultivated in this county [Zhijiang] ... [and] the residents also partially engage in cotton cloth making; families without [real] property even fully rely on it" (*Zhijiang xian zhi* 1866, 7: 7b-8a). In other words, the locals who farmed wove cloth in their spare time (engaging "partially" in this handicraft), but families "without property" (and therefore without farms) relied on weaving. Those with land did not have to produce for the market; those without land did.

Even this kind of rural production was circumscribed, or conditioned, by the local environment. In Jianli in the late Qing, for example, a gazetteer reports: "*Jibei dabu* [Jibei great cotton cloth] woven [by the locals] is sold to Sichuan and Guizhou to the west, and to Guangdong to the south; the benefit is great. If there were no floods, [cotton] would be a good product on fertile land" (*Jianli xian zhi* 1872, 8: 1a). Profitable sales of cotton cloth (woven, the description implies, from the cotton grown by the locals) required both fertile land and the absence of floods.

According to Xu Kaixi, although weaving home-grown cotton was second only to the cultivation of rice as the most important rural productive activity in Ming-Qing Hubei, the cotton cloth that most rural households wove was for their own use. The surplus was traded locally, and only a small quantity entered the long-distance market. Moreover, although Hubei exported a limited amount of raw cotton, there was no place in the province that specialized in cotton cultivation until the mid-Qing (Xu 1991). That is to say, market incentives did not induce the people of Hubei, including the residents of the Jianghan Plain, to give up grain farming. Even in the Yangzi delta in the Republic, most villagers who cultivated non-grain cash crops did not devote all of their land to them, usually reserving a plot of land for grain to ensure that their basic needs would be met. Only after they had planted enough grain for subsistence did they consider growing cash crops on the rest of their land. Rural commercialization was thus accompanied by steps to ensure survival (Cao 1996, 123). Only in the early twentieth century, as markets at home and abroad expanded, the quality of cotton improved, and foreign capital became involved, did Hubei come to rival Jiangsu as a major cotton-producing province (Xu 1991).

Although Xu investigates the role played by outside factors in the sharp increase in cotton production in Hubei, he does not take into account environmental change. The latter, however, may have been just as important as the former. Some of the rise in cotton cultivation in the 1920s was accounted for by Jingzhou, a prefecture that encompassed seven counties (Jiangling, Shishou, Gong'an, Jianli, Songzi, Zhijiang, and Yidu), where the acreage under cotton more than doubled from 1.44 million *mu* in 1919 to 3.5 million *mu* in 1928 (Xu 1990, 71). Not coincidentally, throughout this period, the Jingjiang Great Dike held. In fact, from 1871 to 1931, there was no major break in this dike, largely because Ouchi *kou* and Songzi *kou* had been formed. These two *kou* discharged the excess floodwater of the Yangzi River into Lake Dongting, thereby substantially easing pressure on the dike (Cheng 1990; *Hubei shuili zhi* 2000, 373). That a part of the Jianghan Plain, particularly Jiangling (the seat of Jingzhou Prefecture), avoided frequent inundation was a very important precondition for the expansion of cotton cultivation there. Yet water calamities in the Jianghan area as a whole became no less frequent; indeed, the Han River dike was gradually weakening, and waterlogging had become more serious. Waterlogging usually had little effect on cotton, however, because it was normally grown on relatively high, dry land. For this reason, the counties in the Han River valley that were blessed with such land – Tianmen, Mianyang, Qianjiang, Xiaogan, Hanyang, and Hanchuan – also produced and exported raw cotton.[18]

Cotton was important in the local economy – particularly in Hanchuan, where, "if both the Yangzi River and the Han River were stable, in addition to grains, the cultivation of cotton was common. There were many rich merchants who came here in groups with cash to trade for cotton. [Some of the locals] depended on this [trade] for [paying] their rent and tax, [and] for their daily life" (*Hanchuan xian zhi* 1873, 6: 19b). "Our county," another Hanchuan gazetteer explains, "has more water than hills, and more products come from lake areas. Although all kinds of food grain crops – rice, millet, beans, etc. – are produced in the county, it is not self-sufficient in grains even in a bumper year" (*Hanchuan tuji zhengshi* 1895, 4: 35a). The local people had to find some other means of making a livelihood, such as producing cotton or weaving cotton cloth. However, this county had much less high, dry land than low-lying fields: "Seven or eight out of ten of our local products come from low-lying areas or lake areas; only two or three out of ten come from higher areas" (*Hanchuan xian zhi* 1873, 6: 18a). This meant that land suitable for cotton was also limited.

At the same time, water calamities were very frequent in Hanchuan. Of the thirty-five that occurred from 1875 to 1949, nineteen were caused by dike breaks (*Hanchuan xian jian zhi* 1959, 17-19). Under these conditions, peasants who cultivated cotton ran a very high risk. As a gazetteer explains: "Once [the county] is hit by floods, the income [from the cultivation of cotton] becomes too little to make ends meet" (*Hanchuan xian zhi* 1873, 6: 19b). In the Republic, frequent floods and droughts made the production of cotton in Hubei extremely unstable (Xu 1991). Large floods, such as those in 1931 and 1935 in central Hubei, caused great damage to cotton in the fields. In 1931, many cotton fields were flooded, and output sharply declined. Hankou's cotton exports (drawn mainly from Hubei) fell to 360,000 *dan*; in comparison, annual exports from 1923 to 1929 exceeded 1 million *dan*. In 1935, the Jingjiang Great Dike broke in many places, and eight or nine out of ten of the surrounding cotton fields were destroyed (Zeng 1984, 1: 44, 47).

Of course, household textile production was less affected by changes in the environment. Even if a flood damaged the cotton in the fields or if cotton was not cultivated at all, a rural household, just like an urban household, could still buy raw cotton on the market. This is exactly what happened in the counties of the Han River. In the early twentieth century, the market for domestic cloth generally declined throughout most of China under competitive pressure from foreign yarn and cloth, while Hubei continued to export a huge amount. According to a survey before the War of Resistance against Japan (1937-45), the highest annual output of domestic cotton cloth in Hubei amounted to 30 million or more bolts, of which 7 to 8 million were exported from Wuhan each year (*Hubei jindai nongcun fuye ziliao* 1987, 147). Even if only half of these bolts were produced in the Jianghan Plain, that would amount to 3.5 to 4 million bolts, or more than 4 million bolts if exports from Shashi were included.[19] This was far in excess of the Jianghan Plain's exports in the mid-Qing. Although the market for Jianghan cotton cloth was concentrated in northwestern and southwestern China (where cotton cloth produced in the Han River counties was particularly in demand), it reached the provinces of Guangdong, Jiangxi, Anhui, and Henan as well. Most of the cotton cloth exported to these places originated in the counties of the Han River valley (Zeng 1984, 1: 78). Although the environment there was much more unstable than in the Yangzi River valley, it had less effect on spinning and weaving than on cotton cultivation. The story of raising cotton and of producing cotton cloth thus makes clear the impact of various factors, particularly the environment, on local people's involvement in the market.

The historical record reveals how the local people made their economic decisions in the face of particular environmental and market conditions. Their experience suggests that inhabitants of an area with an unstable environment, such as the Jianghan Plain, first sought to adapt to the environment, with market considerations being secondary. Those in an area with a relatively stable environment, such as the Yangzi delta, had a greater opportunity to become involved in the market. But even here vigorous rural commercialization was the result of the locals' effort to ensure subsistence rather than to pursue market-generated profits (Huang 1990).

It is safe to say that the major goal of the peasants of the Jianghan Plain was survival (ensured by growing grain), not profit.[20] Whether or not local residents became involved in the market was highly conditional on their flood-prone environment. Frequent floods and waterlogging guaranteed that peasant economic behaviour was primarily a response to changes in the local environment. That the environment severely constrained the market behaviour of the Jianghan peasants is clearly demonstrated by the story of cotton production and the economic behaviour associated with it.

Intertwining of Market Participation and Survival Strategies

From the above analysis, it does not follow that, during the Qing dynasty and the Republic, the Jianghan Plain wholly lacked a market dynamic. On the contrary, it was in the vanguard of rural commercialization in Hubei and was an important exporter of agricultural products. But this type of commercialization was always subject to environmental constraints. If the market had been the peasants' primary consideration, then they would have substantially expanded the cultivation of cotton in the Qing. But this did not happen. Moreover, the significant growth of the acreage devoted to cotton in the Republic is directly attributable to the relative stability of the Jingjiang Great Dike.

Commercialization in rural China could be market-driven, survival-driven, or disaster-driven. The North China Plain, for example, had a highly developed factor market characterized by the buying and selling of labour and land to achieve a balance between the two (Zhou 2000, 30-32). Fuelling this market was the frequency of natural disasters, particularly droughts, in the area (Xia 2001, 314-29).

We find a similar pattern of disaster-driven agricultural production in the Jianghan Plain in the Qing and the Republic. For example, on land that was repeatedly inundated, the local people cultivated water-resistant crops, such as deepwater rice, instead of what they considered to be "normal" crops. If the land was seriously flooded, the local people turned to fishing. Their choices were thus determined by extreme changes in the local environment: the peasants had to adapt production to the environment.

As we have seen, both the water-resistant and the replanted crops selected were edible: the local people rarely replanted non-grain cash crops. This choice demonstrates that their aim was to produce food for their own consumption rather than for exchange on the market. The main non-grain cash crop – cotton – was usually grown at relatively high elevations, but the peasants still had to take into account the risk of a high-water season severe enough to destroy the crop. Peasants knew that there would be high water every year. What they could not predict was its magnitude and, consequently, the damage it might cause.

Clearly, the primary concern of the peasants who lived in the Jianghan Plain was adapting to the environment. They could not pursue maximum profit without bearing in mind the conditions determined by the environment, particularly if they lived at lower elevations. I am not arguing for environmental determinism, which would see the Jianghan peasants as lacking agency (as their use of dikes demonstrates, adaptation includes changing the environment); rather, my point is that peasants could not overcome environmental problems through the market.

The economic strategies of Jianghan peasants can be characterized as minimizing risk but maximizing utility, not profit. For peasants living in an environment so unstable that their survival was in jeopardy, profit had to be a secondary consideration. Even though they could for the most part manage the instability, they could deal only with the normal high water. If water calamities grew out of control, the local peasants lost their harvest, their property, or even their lives. We should not overstate the effectiveness of their response.

Nor should we see strategies as purely market- or environment-driven. In practice, the two can work together. In Hanchuan, a resource-poor region under very great population pressure, the local people also participated in the market – with the primary goal of obtaining cash so that they could buy food. Moreover, peasants who farmed in different locations might also have different responses to the market and the environment. For instance, peasants on high land had the opportunity to cultivate cotton and may have made choices with an eye on the market; peasants at lower elevations had to first pay close attention to changes in the environment and adjust their crop selection accordingly. Thus, the behaviour of Jianghan peasants should be understood primarily as an expression of the dictates of survival as they behaved in such a way as to optimize their use of resources.

They could also combine their consciousness of risk with involvement in the market: for rural households that cultivated more cotton than they could use and those that wove more cotton cloth than they needed, the market played an important role. Such households fell into two types: the first focused only on growing cotton or weaving cotton cloth and would do whatever was necessary to maximize returns; the second engaged only sporadically in cultivating cotton or weaving cloth, activities that did not provide a sole income. For the members of the second type of household, this production was merely a sideline, and maximizing their return came a distant second to securing their food supply, particularly if they lived close to rivers or lakes.

In the case of the North China Plain and the Yangzi delta, as Philip Huang (1985, 1990) argues, population pressure resulted in involutionary commercialization; the market could not overcome population pressure. In the Jianghan Plain, the changing environment greatly shaped the economic behaviour of local residents. There, population pressure was expressed not through the market but through the environment as that pressure, and the subsequent activities of the local people, resulted in long-term environmental deterioration.

Conclusion

From both the environmental features of the varieties of rice and the characteristics of the cropping systems in the Jianghan Plain since the Qing, it can be seen that the demands of environmental adaptability largely shaped the decision making of local peasants. First, they chose from among many varieties of rice (e.g., early-season rice, direct-seeding rice, and deepwater rice), all of which were adapted to particular water conditions. All of them, as well as barley and many other food grain crops such as buckwheat, were also chosen because of their environmental adaptability rather than their yield. Second, peasants devised a series of cropping systems that could accommodate their unstable environment, such as the dominant single cropping system of middle-season rice and the supplementary "double-insurance" cropping system involving the rotation of rice and another dryland crop. But both the rotation of rice and wheat, and the change from paddy fields (and the cultivation of rice) to dry land (and the cultivation of cotton/mulberry), which were common in the Yangzi delta, were rare in the Jianghan Plain, an area that was characterized by frequent floods and a high water table. Third, precisely because of these environmental restrictions, both paddy fields and dry land were mostly worked according to the single cropping system, supplemented by the double cropping system.

In the Jianghan Plain in the Qing and the Republic, environmental change played a more important role in shaping the economic behaviour of peasants than did market incentives. The local people chose crops mainly in response to environmental changes in order to ensure a subsistence food supply. Schultz (1964) believes that the market was the overriding factor in economic growth; however, in a preindustrial society, the agricultural system is an organic whole comprising many other key elements, including climate, top-ography, and population. We cannot focus on just one factor when analyzing economic growth.

Also in the Jianghan Plain in the Qing and the Republic, some local peas-ants were indeed involved in the market, but their involvement was deter-mined not so much by the rate of return or market incentives as by macro changes in the environment. Their greatest concern was the maximization of utility; that is, making choices that would enable them to best adapt to the environment and to minimize risk. Thus, for the most part, the Jianghan people chose crops mainly in response to environmental changes, their pur-pose being to ensure a subsistence food supply. Had they chosen to turn to the market, an unstable environment would have resulted, at best, in an uncertain output and income.

Although the paucity of data makes it impossible to differentiate Jianghan peasants according to their economic status and to analyze their different calculations in responding to market opportunities and in attempting to ensure survival (Scott 1976; Huang 1985), we can analyze how *where* peasants lived significantly influenced their economic behaviour. Peasants who lived at lower elevations or farmed land by lakes gave greater weight to the environ-ment; peasants on high or dry land had more opportunities to grow (non-grain) cash crops and gave greater weight to the market; peasants who farmed both low-lying and high land based their crop choices on the relative amount of each. But first all of them had to guarantee their food supply. After the mid-Qing, more and more people moved to even lower-lying places in order to enclose more *yuan*. Some turned to fishing as a means of easing the prob-lems caused by population pressure and environmental degradation, though doing so lowered their standard of living (see Chapter 6). Under these cir-cumstances, they first considered how best to use the available resources in order to minimize damage or loss. They pursued the maximization of utility, not the maximization of profit, within the local ecosystem.

Long-term environmental degradation has significantly affected eco-nomic growth in the Jianghan Plain since late imperial times. The behaviour of individual peasants reflected the constant threat of high water and floods, combined with concern over the increasing damage caused by waterlog-ging. They adapted ingeniously to the flood-prone environment but found themselves confronted with the growing problem of waterlogging. Under these circumstances, it is not surprising that market incentives were not the primary force behind changes in the Jianghan economy.

This is not to say that market incentives were irrelevant. Around the begin-ning of the twentieth century, as demand increased in both the domestic and international markets, the Jianghan peasants began to grow commercial cotton and to weave cotton cloth on a large scale. But this involvement in the market occurred within a context of higher population pressure (in the Han River valley) and a relatively stable environment (in the Yangzi River valley). No single factor – population pressure, environmental change, market incentive, peasant response – was dominant within the whole society and environment; rather, various factors interacted with each other as they formed and transformed the economy and society of the Jianghan Plain.

5 Tenancy and Environment

Landownership and rent varied throughout rural China. In the Yangzi delta relatively high agricultural productivity combined with a relatively stable ecosystem attracted the investments of absentee landlords, which led to a further concentration of land ownership. By contrast, in the North China Plain, the unstable ecosystem and low productivity of dryland crops combined with high population density resulted in repeated famines and wars. Investors there had little interest in land. These differences in land distribution and tenancy relationships in the Yangzi delta and the North China Plain were mainly the result of two contrasting ecosystems (Huang 1990, 40-43). The same differences can also be found by comparing smaller neighbouring regions within one province (such as southern Jiangsu with northern Jiangsu, northern Anhui with southern Anhui, and northwest Shandong with southern Shandong). In other words, the general pattern of tenancy in China (high in the south and low in the north) concealed great differences due to varied ecosystems among smaller areas within one large area, one province, or even one county (Xia 2000, 212-13; Xia 2001, 296-99).

In order to understand tenancy relationships in China we need to pay attention to the role of spatial differences and environmental conditions. In the Jianghan Plain in the Qing and the Republic, land distribution, rent deposit requirements, the form of rent, rental rates, and even the relations of landlords and tenants were all shaped by the environment.

Such an approach fundamentally differs from the CCP's representation of the relations of agricultural production in pre-1949 rural China, whereby land was supposedly inequitably distributed between the exploiting classes (landlords and rich peasants) and the exploited classes (poor peasants and hired hands). The landlords and rich peasants accounted for only 8 percent of the rural population (in terms of households) but owned 70 to 80 percent of the farmland, while the remaining rural population owned only 20 to 30 percent of the farmland (Mao 1975, 4: 164). In the eyes of the CCP, in the power relations between landlords (or employers) and tenants (or employees), the former were always the dominant party. Ownership and control of land thus became one of the core issues to be resolved through the CCP's revolutionary movement. Moreover, the CCP's representation, which focused on class relations, had strong political and emotional implications. It emphasized rural exploitation in the form of rent, the necessity of overthrowing this exploitative system, and the seriousness of the land problem and the pressing need for solutions. It did not highlight non-political factors such as the environment; rather, it presented a generalized picture of rural China and neglected local differences. As it happens, in the Jianghan Plain in the Republic, not many peasants had no land at all, and less than 10 percent of landlords were absentee landlords. This is a subject to which we will return below.

In many respects, Western scholarship on tenancy in traditional China presents a mirror image of the CCP's ideologically driven approach, but instead of emphasizing class exploitation it focuses on the role of the market. Dwight Perkins (1969, 87-101), for instance, concludes that, though there was frequent buying and selling of land in the past six centuries, the form of land distribution and the pattern of tenancy (high in the south and low in the north) underwent little change. The major adjusting factor was the market: peasants lost (i.e., sold) their land in disastrous years and redeemed it (i.e., purchased it back) in prosperous years. But, according to John R. Shepherd (1988), Perkins's "debt-sale paradigm" fails to recognize the role the shift from owner operation to managerial and rental landlordism, labour immigration, and reclamation played in the formation of spatial and temporal variations of tenancy in late imperial and Republican China. Based on a careful analysis, Xia Mingfang (2001, 319) also argues that, although disasters caused a relative surplus in the market supply of land, they also caused a relatively shrunken market demand for land (see also Shepherd 1988, 408). It is clear that regional differences and environmental differences are crucial to understanding tenancy relationships in rural China.

The subject of tenancy relationships in the Jianghan Plain has been almost universally ignored. Tan Tianxing (1992) is one of the few scholars who addresses tenancy relationships and their connection with local customs in Hubei-Hunan during the early Qing. According to Tan, at that time, the rent rate might have been lower than the 50 percent that is generally accepted by scholars; tenancy was just for one year, with permanent tenure being rare; and, though most tenants paid fixed rent in kind, payment in cash was becoming more common. Hunan-Hubei led the country in requiring rent deposits from tenants. At the same time, relations between landlords and tenants loosened during the Qing, and we even see the emergence of the phenomenon known as "renting and cultivating by force" (*qiang dian, ba zhong*, meaning the tenant forced the landlord to rent land to him so that he could grow crops). Tan analyzes the relationship between these changes and the development of agricultural production.

However, Tan takes most of his examples from mountainous areas, ignoring the significant differences between plains and mountains in tenancy relationships and the level of agricultural production. Moreover, he discusses only the general situation regarding tenancy relationships in the early Qing, failing to pay attention to changes throughout that dynasty. Finally, and most important, he does not consider the role of the environment in shaping and changing tenancy relationships.

Land Distribution

Before discussing tenancy relationships, it is necessary to consider land distribution as it was this that formed the basis of those relationships. Except for some scattered data from the Yangzi delta, China lacks a systematic record of land distribution before the 1920s and 1930s. For the Jianghan Plain, we have several surveys from the Republican era, which form the basis for my analysis of land distribution. These, unfortunately, are not village-based surveys but county-based surveys. They include one 1933 survey that was compiled and published by the Department of Civil Affairs, Government of Hubei (*Hubei xianzheng gaikuang* 1934, 1-20); one 1938 survey organized by the Committee of Rural Surveys of Hubei, for which thirty thousand people were mobilized to work on the survey for five months (*Wuchang xian* 1938, 1); and some other surveys carried out by individuals. The results of these county-based surveys should be more accurate than those of province-based surveys. In general, due to Hubei's great regional diversity, I eschew province-wide data.[1]

With regard to the Jianghan Plain, we lack detailed anthropological field surveys, such as those that Mantetsu carried out in the Yangzi delta and the North China Plain. Because of this we cannot focus on the household level. The statistics in many of the county-based Republican surveys used here are very rough and sometimes even contradictory. For this reason, my analysis usually does not focus on specific numbers but, rather, on the general picture that emerges from these surveys.

For the sake of comparison, I cite the "feudal production relations" section from new gazetteers, which briefly describes tenancy relationships and/or landownership at the turn of the 1950s. These data are by far the most comprehensive with regard to the relations of agricultural production, particularly landownership, around 1950 since, during the Land Reform campaign, the CCP recorded all land for redistribution.

As mentioned earlier, the CCP maintains that, during the Republic, land-lords and rich peasants accounted for about 8 percent of the rural households but owned 70 to 80 percent of China's farmland; the rest of the rural popula-tion owned only 20 to 30 percent of cultivated land. Zhang Youyi (1988), however, challenges this, arguing that landless tenants accounted for only about 30 to 40 percent of rural households. Landlords and rich peasants, Zhang maintains, owned about 60 percent of the cultivated land, and the rest of the rural population, mainly poor peasants and middle peasants, owned 40 percent. Zhang also denies the existence of a long-term tendency towards the concentration of landownership. I do not discuss the long-term tendency of the distribution of landownership in the Jianghan Plain due to the limita-tions of the source materials but, rather, restrict myself to examining land distribution during the Republic. The results of this show that the percentage of cultivated land owned by landlords and rich peasants was even less than the 60 percent figure offered by Zhang Youyi, who based his research on nationwide data.

First, let us look at the structure of rural households in the Jianghan Plain in the 1930s. According to surveys in many counties of the Jianghan Plain, more than half of the rural households were owner-peasants. Taking the Jianghan Plain as a whole, about 60.3 percent of rural households were cat-egorized as owner-peasants, and an additional 12.8 percent were "half owner-peasants" (peasants who farmed some land but who also needed to rent land from others or hired out part of their labour) (Table 11).

As the "Note" in the original source concerning the data in A ("Number and percentage of households") in Table 11 mentions, these data are only estimates. However, they roughly reflect the real situation of land distribution. The data in B ("Percentage of households") come from other sources but were also based on estimates (with the exception of five counties). Despite these limitations, the data are rigorous enough to show that the percentage of owner-peasants was quite high.[2] From the surveys we also see that the dis-tinctions between owner-peasant, half owner-peasant, and tenant-peasant were not very clear. In Dangyang, for example, there was a kind of owner-peasant-landlord, "most of whom come from tenant-peasants. Thus although they rent out part of their lands, they have a spirit of industriousness and do work that is no less than that of tenants" (Zhang 1957, 443).

In the 1930s, a national survey conducted by the National Land Commission divided Chinese rural households into no fewer than ten categories. According to this survey, which investigated 113,549 households in eleven counties of Hubei, these categories were: landlord (0.97 percent of the households), landlord-owner-peasant (2.39 percent), landlord-owner-peasant-tenant

Table 11

Category and percentage of households in the Jianghan Plain in the 1930s

		A: Number and percentage of households						B: Percentage of households		
County	Total	Owner-peasant		Half owner-peasant		Tenants		Owner peasant	Half owner-peasant	Tenants
		Number	%	Number	%	Number	%			
Wuchang	37,960	18,980	50	11,388	30	7,592	20	68.78	19.07	12.15
Hanyang	28,710	20,097	70	4,306	15	4,307*	15	65.6	26.3	8.1
Xiaogan	102,700	82,160	80			20,540	20	80		
Yunmeng	34,920	24,444	70			10,476	30	65.77	26.34	7.89
Hanchuan	19,760	15,808	80			3,952	20	80		20
Yingcheng	23,520	11,760	50			11,760	50	52.97	35.12	11.91
Jingmen	76,300	53,410	70			22,890	30			
Zhongxiang	54,500	10,900	20	27,250	50	16,350	30	20	50	30
Jingshan	81,120	48,672	60			32,448	40	60		40
Tianmen	93,810	65,667	70	23,453	25	4,690	5	60		30
Mianyang	123,240	86,268	70			36,972	30	70		30
Qianjiang	71,080	46,913	66			24,167	34	66.7		33.3
Jianli	64,400	32,200	50	16,100	25	16,100	25	82	15.7	2.3
Shishou	33,020	23,114	70			9,906	30			
Gong'an	33,800	6,760	20	6,760	20	20,280	60	20	40	40
Jiangling**	109,350	56,862	52	31,712	29	20,776	19			

Songzi	40,320	16,128	40	16,128	40	8,064	20	40	40	20
Zhijiang	17,640	8,820***	50	3,528	20	5,292	30	50	20	30
Dangyang	52,800	34,320	65			18,480	35	66.7		33.3
Total	1,100,750	663,283	60.3	140,625	12.8	295,042	26.8			20

Notes:

* The original number was 7,307. According to its percentage, it should be 4,307.

** The percentage of each category of rural households of Jiangling is taken from another survey (*Hubei sheng zhi tudi liyong yu liangshi wenti* 1977 [1938], 24,134). There were different percentages for three years: I selected the percentage for 1934.

*** The original number was 3,528. According to its percentage, it should be 8,820.

Sources:

A. *Hubei sheng zhi tudi liyong yu liangshi wenti* (1977 [1938], 24131-33). ("Note" in the original source: The number of households in the column of households was calculated on the basis of the percentage of different households and the number of the total households. Tenants in some counties were included in the category of half owner-peasants.)

B. *Wuchang xian* 1938, 16; *Hanyang xian* 1938, 14; *Yunmeng xian* 1938, 9; *Yingcheng xian* 1938, 14; *Jianli xian* 1938, 11. Others are from *Hubei xianzheng gaikuang* (1934): Xiaogan, 647; Hanchuan, 785; Zhongxiang, 860; Jingshan, 834; Tianmen, 761; Mianyang, 810; Qianjiang, 884; Gong'an, 1,007; Songzi, 1,056; Zhijiang, 1,032; Dangyang, 1,350.

(0.17 percent), landlord-tenant (0.03 percent), owner-peasant (48.26 percent), owner-peasant-tenant (28 percent), tenant (14.98 percent), tenant-agricultural labourer (0.01 percent), agricultural labourer (0.56 percent), and others (4.63 percent) (Tudi weiyuanhui 1937, 34). It is clear that in Hubei owner-peasants were the majority and that people who really had no land at all (tenants and agricultural labourers) were rare.[3] Since the ownership of farmland was scattered, a contemporary researcher even argues that the economic problems in rural Hubei were caused not by an unequal distribution of land, as was commonly thought, but by the fragmentation of farmland (i.e., plots were scattered) (Cheng 1977 [1938], 45,508).[4] Thus, households that were clearly identified as "landlord" during the Land Reform (i.e., those that only rented out land and lived on rent) may have been rare.[5] Much more common were households that rented out some land but that also farmed their own land or were tenants of other people. A lack of clear-cut class distinctions and dispersion of landownership rights have also been found to have been very common in central Shaanxi and in the provinces of Hebei and Shandong.[6]

In gathering land distribution data, the Guomindang (GMD, the Nationalist Party) government used the categories of owner-peasant, half owner-peasant, and tenant-peasant. As this emphasizes the distribution of rental patterns, not class status, it is understandable that it leaves the status of rural people rather murky.[7] Thus, these data do not tell us exactly how much land was owned by landlords, rich peasants, middle peasants, and poor peasants, respectively, in the 1930s. The CCP's Land Reform records, on the other hand, contain not only the most comprehensive data by far regarding landownership in the Republic but also classify peasants by class status.[8] What these records tell us is that status was very complicated.[9] Moreover, landlords and rich peasants together actually owned less cultivated land than did the rest of the rural population.

According to the CCP's Land Reform records for thirteen counties in the Jianghan Plain, before the Land Reform, landlords and rich peasants accounted for 8.04 percent of the rural households and 9.17 percent of the rural population, but they only owned 40.76 percent of the cultivated land. On the other hand, the rest of the rural population accounted for 91.96 percent of the rural households and 90.83 percent of the rural population, and they owned 59.24 percent of the cultivated land (Table 12). These percentages are close to the percentages of Hubei Province as a whole before the Land Reform: landlords and rich peasants accounted for 11 percent of the rural population but owned 46.4 percent of the cultivated land, while all other classes accounted for 89 percent of the rural population and owned 53.6 percent of the cultivated land (*Hubei shengqing* 1987, 89).[10]

Table 12

Land distribution in thirteen counties of the Jianghan Plain on the eve of the Land Reform

Class status	Households		Population			Cultivated land (*mu*)			
	Number	%	Amount	%		Amount	%	Per household	Per capita
Landlords	45,266	3.84	201,526	4.27		3,701,536.83	28.49	81.77	18.37
Rich peasants	49,476	4.20	231,156	4.90		1,594,363.28	12.27	32.23	6.90
Middle peasants	371,540	31.52	1,573,044	33.35		4,787,733.26	36.85	12.89	3.04
Poor peasants and hired labourers	660,606	56.03	2,524,957	53.53		2,394,118.90	18.43	3.62	0.95
Small land lessors*	11,358	0.96	36,062	0.77		184,457.00	1.42	16.24	5.12
Other	40,691	3.45	150,517	3.19		329,784.09	2.54	8.11	2.19
Total	1,178,937		4,717,262			12,991,993.36		11.02	2.75

Notes: Unit: household, person, *mu*

* According to the Land Reform regulations, "the status of revolutionary army men, dependents of martyrs, workers, staff members, professional workers, vendors and other people who engage in other occupations or lack labour and therefore need to rent out their small piece of land should be determined by their occupations, or they should be categorized as small land lessors, not landlords." As for the maximum amount of land owned per person in a family, it should not exceed 200 percent of the average amount of land owned per person in that locality (Du 1996, 293-94).

Sources: Data are from the newly compiled gazetteers of these counties: *Gong'an xian zhi* (1990, 129); *Wuchang xian zhi* (1989, 191); *Honghu xian zhi* (1992, 101); *Jingmen shi zhi* (1994, 211); *Xiaogan shi zhi* (1992, 126); *Mianyang xian zhi* (1989, 84) (n.b., the source only includes eighteen townships, not the whole county); *Dangyang xian zhi* (1992, 145); *Qianjiang xian zhi* (1990, 222); *Shishou xian zhi* (1990, 157); *Jianli xian zhi* (1959, 70); *Tianmen xian zhi* (1989, 174); *Songzi xian zhi* (1986, 278); and *Zhijiang xian zhi* (1990, 107). I added the figures of these thirteen counties to calculate the percentage of cultivated land per household and per capita.

The percentage of land owned by landlords and rich peasants was relatively high in the four counties of Gong'an, Jingmen, Songzi, and Shishou (72, 63.83, 59.40, and 59.39 percent, respectively). All of them except Jingmen are located on the southern side of the Yangzi River and are relatively more stable than counties in the lower reaches of the Han River, an area subject to relatively frequent inundation. The same was true in Jingmen, a Han River county, which was located in the middle reaches of the river and was not prone to frequent floods. But these high percentages contributed to the overall high percentage of land owned by landlords and rich peasants in the Jianghan Plain as a whole. Looking at all those counties for which there are data, we find that the percentage of cultivated land owned by landlords and rich peasants varied greatly, from as low as 11.93 percent in Hanchuan to as high as 72 percent in Gong'an, but in most places it was lower than 40 percent (Table 13).

Of those counties where the percentage of land owned by landlords and rich peasants was relatively low, four of them – Hanchuan, Tianmen, Mianyang, and Qianjiang – were located in the Han River valley. All four of these counties were well known as particularly prone to heavy flooding. Jianli was located in the Yangzi River valley, but it was also prone to heavy inundation because of its low elevation and great number of *yuan*. In fact, in 1950 it was found that, compared to mountain areas in Hubei, there was not much land concentration in the area along the Han River in its middle and lower reaches (SZ 34-2-247). All of this suggests that the concentration of landownership in a particular area was directly related to the stability of its environment.[11]

In the Jianghan Plain the ratio of landlord and rich peasant households to all rural households varied from about 5 to 12 percent (see Table 13). Ninety percent or more of the rural population consisted of people who were *not* landlords or rich peasants. This is similar to the standard interpretation of classes in rural China in the Republic. But there is one very big difference: compared to the Yangzi delta, the percentage of absentee landlords in Hubei was very low. About 83 percent of the landlords in Hubei lived in villages, and an even greater percentage of landlords in the Jianghan Plain did so. As for the occupation of resident landlords, many of them managed farms and were rural gentry (*Hubei sheng zhi tudi liyong yu liangshi wenti* 1977 [1938], 24267).[12]

Absentee landlords usually lived and did business in nearby towns or cities. In Wuchang County, for example, most large landlords ran businesses in the city of Wuhan and either had tenants cultivate their lands (*Hubei xianzheng gaikuang* 1934, 42) or had agents (*zhuangtou, er di zhu*) who located

Table 13

Percentage of the households, population, and cultivated land of landlords, rich peasants, and the rest of the rural population in the Jianghan Plain on the eve of the Land Reform

County	Landlords and rich peasants			Rest of the rural population		
	% of households	% of population	% of land	% of households	% of population	% of land
Hanchuan		3.73	11.93		96.27	88.07
Jianli	7.90	9.20	19.00	92.10	91.80	81.00
Tianmen	6.42	7.63	20.90	93.58	92.37	79.10
Qianjiang	5.09	7.42	24.00	94.91	92.58	76.00
Wuchang	6.87	6.07	24.81	93.13	93.93	75.19
Shashi *	8.28		24.98	91.72		75.02
Mianyang	9.00	10.50	27.50	91.00	89.50	72.50
Jingshan **			21.00			70.00
Zhijiang	6.50	7.90	35.70	93.50	92.10	64.30
Wuhan *	7.15		36.28	92.85		63.72
Hanyang		8.90	36.90		91.10	63.10
Dangyang	10.50	11.55	37.50	89.50	88.45	62.50
Zhongxiang	7.88		43.39	92.12		56.61
Xiaogan	11.78	12.70	44.26	88.22	87.30	55.74
Honghu	9.29	10.00	54.90	90.71	90.00	45.10
Shishou	6.03	6.30	59.39	93.96	93.70	40.61
Songzi	7.50	9.00	59.40	92.50	91.00	40.60
Jingmen	8.08	7.44	63.83	91.92	92.56	36.17
Gong'an	8.83	11.40	72.00	91.17	88.60	28.00

Notes:
* For both Wuhan and Shashi, data exist only for the rural suburbs.
** In Jingshan, we have data from only one township, and 9 percent of its land was either owned by outside landlords or was public property.

Sources: Hanchuan xian zhi (1992, 106); *Jingshan xian zhi* (1990, 94); *Nongye zhi* [Shashi] (1993, 26); *Hanyang xian zhi* (1989, 165); *Wuhan shi zhi nongye* (1989, 52); *Zhongxiang xian zhi* (1990, 282) (n.b., does not include townships that did not undergo land reform). The sources of other counties are the same as those cited in Table 12.

potential tenants. This was because many rural residents were newcomers (*Wuhan shi zhi nongye* 1989, 51).[13] In Hanchuan in the Republic, some merchants purchased peasant land at low prices in famine years and then rented it out at high prices; some of these merchants did not even know where their newly purchased land was located (*Hanchuan xian jian zhi* 1959, 31). But these people were few, and the land they owned was limited; even if all the landlords of Hanchuan were absentee landlords, only about 12 percent of Hanchuan's land was owned by landlords and rich peasants (*Hanchuan xian zhi* 1992, 106). One can be sure that the owners of this 12 percent of the land included, but were not exclusively, absentee landlords. Also, in Hanyang, some landlords who were fully involved in running businesses outside their villages and had no time to farm asked their relatives to farm for them (*Hangyang xian* 1938, 14).[14]

With all these data, it is possible to discern, at least in approximate form, the features of land distribution in the Jianghan Plain before 1949. Landlords and rich peasants together accounted for 9.17 percent of the rural population and owned 40.76 percent of the cultivated land, while the rest of the rural population owned 59.24 percent of it. In general, the more frequent a place was subject to flooding, the lower its concentration of landownership. By the same token, the class status of the rural population was not very clear, though it is certain that the majority were owner-peasants. Most landlords were middle and small landlords who lived in the villages and engaged in farming; only a few were absentee landlords who ran businesses in the city.

Rent Deposits

A rent deposit was a sum of money (usually the equivalent of one year's rent) the tenant paid to the landlord at the start of the tenancy. If the tenant failed to pay the rent, the landlord could take the deposit as rent. Once the tenancy ended, if the tenant was not in arrears in paying rent, the landlord was to return the deposit.

In the early Qing, the practice of tenants paying rent deposits was apparently more prevalent in Hunan-Hubei than in many other places in the country (Tan 1992). Rent deposits were also found in the counties of the Jianghan Plain at that time. In Jingmen, for example, a tenant named Wang Taichang, whose brother said: "[Wang] … rented some land from Xiao Lishan, and paid him a tael of *shang zhuang li yin* [literally, "gift-money for going to the fields"]. [Wang] didn't owe him any [back] rent for any year. [But] last winter Xiao Lishan suddenly rented his farmland to Chen." Here *shang zhuang li yin* was a rent deposit. In Mianyang, this was called *shang zhuang qian* (literally, "money for going to the fields"). Tenant Xiao Guangshou declared: "I rented 4.7 *mu* of paddy field from Zhang Shimei for a couple of years. I had to pay [Zhang] *shang zhuang qian* at the beginning." In Jiangling it was called *xie tian li* ("gift for signing a land contract") as tenant Lü Wanxiu said that he had helped his brother Lü Lieshan with 1.6 *dan* of *gaoliang* as *xie tian li* to sublet 6.6 *mu* of land from Wang Sudan (Zhongguo diyi lishi danganguan and Zhongguo shehui kexueyuan lishi yanjiusuo [hereafter Zhongguo diyi]

1982, 404, 412, 707). In this last example, *xie tian li* looks like a kind of compensation for the transfer of a land contract; however, later on Wang asked that the *xie tian li* be returned, which means that it was a kind of rent deposit.

Although it is hard to deduce the extent of the practice of rent deposits in the Jianghan Plain in the early Qing based on these three examples, it is certain that this practice did exist there at this time. There are two possible reasons for this. First, the local environment had not yet become severely degraded; indeed, the Jianghan area was still able to attract immigrants to reclaim lakeside wasteland. It would have been difficult for all those newcomers to reclaim land and put it under the plough immediately, thus at least some of them would have had to rent land from local landlords. But the local landlords did not quite trust them, and, consequently, they demanded rent deposits (*Minshi xiguan diaocha baogao lu* [hereafter *Minshi xiguan*] 2000, 662). Second, it is possible that competition among local residents or between them and the new immigrants forced tenants to accept landlords' demands for rent deposits. Under these circumstances, it was the landlords who set the terms of land leases. All of the three examples mentioned above involved disputes caused by landlords unilaterally ending a land rental contract and transferring it to another tenant, with the original tenant then demanding the rent deposit be refunded. These cases also suggest that, unlike in the Yangzi delta, the payment of rent deposits did not lead to permanent tenure.[15]

With the concomitant increase of population and *yuan* enclosure and the worsening environmental conditions in the middle and late Qing, rent deposit requirements continued to be widespread in Hubei Province (*zhongguo tudi renkou zudian zhidu zhi tongji fenxi* 1978, 88-89), including in the Jianghan Plain, into the early twentieth century.[16] But, after that, they disappeared in some counties, such as Jiangling and Hanchuan (see Table 14).

These records reveal some regular patterns in the distribution of rent deposit requirements. First, some of the counties in which rent deposits were required had a relatively low percentage of owner-peasants. If more than two-thirds of a county's rural population were owner-peasants, then the practice of rent deposits was absent, with Wuchang being an exception. In this county, only peasants who rented fertile land were required to pay a rent deposit. It is likely that the demand to rent this kind of land was high, thus giving landlords some extra bargaining power.

Second, counties in which rent deposits were required were usually located in the Yangzi River valley, while counties with no rent deposit requirements were usually located in the Han River valley, with the exception of Jingmen and Jingshan. As discussed in Chapter 1, floods were more frequent in the

Table 14

The distribution of rent deposits in the Jianghan Plain in the 1930s

	Counties along the Han River			Counties along the Yangzi River	
County	Rental deposit	% of owner-peasant	County	Rental deposit	% of owner-peasant
Hanyang	No*	65.6	Wuchang	On fertile land	68.78
Xiaogan	No	80	Jiangling	No	
Yunmeng	No, occasionally	65.77	Jianli	No***	82
Hanchuan	No, occasionally**	80	Shishou	Yes	
Yingcheng		52.97	Gong'an	Yes	20
Tianmen		60	Zhijiang	Occasionally	50
Mianyang		70	Songzi	Occasionally	40
Jingshan	Yes	60	Dangyang		66.7
Zhongxiang	Yes	20			
Qianjiang	No, occasionally*	66.7			

Notes: This table presents data that indicate only the general situation in each county. In other words, if the table shows that "Yes," the practice of rent deposits was found in a particular county, that does not mean that every landlord in that county required a rental deposit. Similarly, "No" does not mean that no landlord in that county required a rental deposit.

*   Another source claims that Hanyang and Qianjiang had rental deposit requirements. It offers no explanation regarding Hanyang, only mentioning that the amount of the rental deposit equalled the amount of one year's rent. For Qianjiang, the rental deposit was a sum of money deposited by newcomers from outside the community who sought to rent land. It seems the landlords did not quite trust these outsiders, hence the rental deposit served as a kind of security for rent payment and for protection against any damage to land or other property (*Minshi xiguan* 2000, 652, 662).

** According to one source, only where land was scarce and tenants were relatively numerous or landlords were "cunning" would rent deposits be required (*Hanchuan xian zhi* 1992, 107).

*** A newly compiled gazetteer contradicts this and says that this county also had rental deposit requirements. The landlords, the gazetteer claims, demanded deposits in order to secure rent and to force peasants to fertilize the land -- in short, to "exploit" tenants (*Jianli xian zhi* 1959, 71).

Sources: For rental deposit, see *Wuchang xian* (1938, 16); *Hanyang xian* (1938, 14); *Yingcheng xian* (1938, 14); and *Hubei xian zheng gai kuang* (1934). Percentage of owner-peasants the same as found in data B, Table 11.

Han River valley than in the Yangzi River valley, and, in the late Qing, the damage caused by floods was also more severe in the former than in the latter. In other words, counties in the Han River valley were less environmentally stable than those in the Yangzi River valley. The percentage of rented-out land was higher in environmentally stable areas than in environmentally unstable areas. This is clear when one compares not only the Yangzi River valley to the Han River valley but also, for example, the Yangzi delta to the North China Plain.

In counties with a relatively high percentage of owner-peasants, the competition or demand for land to rent would have been comparatively weak. The demand for land would also have been comparatively weak in areas subject to frequent floods. In such areas, the requirement of a rent deposit would have made it even more difficult to find tenants. In fact, rent deposits were usually not required in the Han River valley counties. Jingshan and Jingmen were exceptions to this because only a portion of their land close to the Han River was prone to frequent floods. Much of their land was at a high elevation (i.e., hills and mountains) and was not seriously affected by the annual high water of the Han River. And, not surprisingly, we find that rent deposits were required in these two counties.

Jiangling was an exception to the pattern in the Yangzi River valley. It should have had a relatively stable environment since, in the late nineteenth century, the formation of Ouchi *kou* and Songzi *kou,* which discharged high water from the Yangzi River into Lake Dongting, reduced the pressure of high water on the Jingjiang Great Dike. But Jiangling was also affected by the Han River, which was less stable than the Yangzi River, and the environmental situation of the Yangzi River valley worsened in the 1930s. We thus see that both of these two features are closely related to the differences in their environmental conditions.[17]

From the early Qing to the Republic, there was a tendency for the rent deposit practice to become less prevalent in the Jianghan Plain, partly due to decreasing environmental stability. By the Republic, rent deposits were usually only found in counties that were relatively infrequently inundated.

Tenancy Relationships and Rental Rates

Sharecropping was the major form of rent in early Qing Hubei. A frequently cited example involves a case from Xiaogan, a county on the northern Jianghan Plain: "[Li] Jinru rents two *dou* of land from [monk] Chenyuan. [They always] divide the harvest in half, and [Li] never fails to pay [his] rent" (Zhongguo diyi 1982, 53). This passage describes a common form of rent found throughout Chinese history; that is, landlords and tenants each taking a half share. Another example mentions a certain Wu Renyu, a tenant in Jiangling in the mid-eighteenth century, who paid rent in cash (Zhongguo renmin daxue Qing shi yanjiu suo, dang'an xi Zhongguo zhengzhi zhidu shi jiaoyanshi [hereafter Zhongguo renmin] 1979, 70). However, we know nothing about the form of rent payment in other counties of the Jianghan Plain at that time. It is uncertain how the form of tenancy relationships varied from one county to another. Regional differences do not become clear until the early twentieth century, after many surveys had been conducted (Table 15).

As can be seen from Table 15, tenancy relationships in the Jianghan Plain in the early Republic had the following characteristics. First, both rent in kind and in cash were widely distributed over the Jianghan Plain.[18] Within any single county, only in relatively commercialized areas and on dry land did tenants pay rent in cash; in all other areas, and for paddy fields, rent was paid in kind. Second, sharecropping was still common in some counties (as seen from the original records), with the ratio (the percentage of harvest taken by landlords and tenants, respectively) ranging from 3:7 to 6:4 or 7:3. Third, in many cases, the amount of fixed rent in kind depended on land quality (the higher the grade of land, the more the landlords took [*Wuhan shi zhi nongye* 1989, 51]); if the land was poor, rent could be lower than half the harvest.

Various sources support the last point. In Wuchang, for example, according to a Republican survey, fixed rent was one-third of the harvest of the early-season rice (*Wuchang xian* 1938, 16). In Songzi, it was one-quarter of the harvest in the late Qing but increased by one-third to 40 percent in the 1930s due to increasing (natural and human-made) disasters and surcharges (*Songzi xian zhi* 1986, 278, 689). In Jingmen before 1949 it was 30 to 40 percent of a single harvest (*Jingmen shi zhi* 1994, 211). In all cases, the rent was less than half of the harvest. This is because not all places required that rent be paid on every harvest within one year. It is clear from Table 15 that, in some places, tenants only paid rent for the major crops and that they retained the entire harvest of the secondary crops. This is similar to the custom in the Yangzi delta, according to which tenants usually did not pay rent for the spring harvest.[19] On the other hand, it is unclear whether rent was paid on each harvest in those places that were under double cropping. Even when rent was paid from one harvest, the amount was usually not as high as 50 percent of the harvest. The rent on paddy fields in some counties is a case in point: on average it was from 43 percent to 48 percent of the harvest (*Hubei sheng zhi tudi liyong yu liangshi wenti* 1977 [1938], 24271).

The data in Table 15 clearly show that fixed rent in kind from the regular harvest did not reach 50 percent,[20] the figure that most orthodox Marxist scholars take as the "standard" for China. The reason for this discrepancy is that these scholars focus on class analysis to the exclusion of environmental analysis. Class analysis notwithstanding, from the above examples, it can be seen that the local environment in the Jianghan Plain greatly influenced the structure of various forms of tenancy relationships.

Under a sharecropping system, both landlords and tenants must bear some risks.[21] In the Jianghan Plain, sharecropping remained a common – and from

Table 15

The major form of tenancy relationships in the Jianghan Plain in the 1930s

| County | Rent in kind | | Rent in cash (per *mu*) |
	Sharecropping	Fixed rent (per *mu*)	
Wuchang	6:4, 5:5, or 4:6	⅓ of early season rice	1-3 yuan in advanced commercial area
Hanyang	8:2, 7:3, 6:4, 5:5	1.3 *shi* (unhusked rice)	2.6-4 yuan (rent paid in advance), paddy field
Xiaogan	6:4 or 5:5*	1.25 *shi* (unhusked rice), rent paid in advance	2.5-4 yuan (rent paid in advance), dry land
Yunmeng		1-1.5 *shi* (unhusked rice)	2.88-6.25 yuan
Hanchuan		1-1.6 *shi* (unhusked rice)	1.1-3 yuan (before 1934)
Yingcheng	7:3, 6:4, or 5:5**	1-1.5 *shi* (unhusked rice)	5 yuan (dry land)
Tianmen		0.7-1 *shi* (unhusked rice), wheat 0.5 *shi*	Exists
Mianyang	3:7		1.5-3 yuan
Jingshan		4-7 *dou* (unhusked rice)	
Zhongxiang	Not more than 1 *shi*	Exists	
Qianjiang		3-5 *dou* (unhusked rice or wheat)	1-2 yuan
Jiangling		0.4-1.5 *shi* (unhusked rice)	
Jingmen	4:6		
Jianli	3:7 or 4:6, 5:5	1-2 *shi* (unhusked rice)	Exists
Shishou	5:5 or 4:6	1.2-1.4 *shi* (unhusked rice)	
Zhijiang	4:6 or 5:5	1-1.2 *shi* (unhusked rice)	24 *chuan* (dry land)

Notes: In general, the amount of rent in this table is that paid for one *mu*. In the pair of shares, such as 4:6, the first is the share landlords take, the second is the share tenants take. For fixed rent, the amount usually varied depending on land quality.

* Tenants contribute labour and implements; landlords contribute land, a share of the seeds, and fertilizer. In this county, there was another form of labour-rent exchange. A tenant worked free for a landlord for about two months in busy seasons; in return, the tenant could rent 2.4-2.8 *mu* of land from that landlord without payment. Also in this county, tenants only paid rent for the major crops, and they took the whole harvest of secondary crops (*Xiaogan xian jian zhi* 1959, 27).

** A Republican survey mentions that there was only one kind of sharecropping (i.e., 5:5) and that it was only applied to rice; the tenants kept all other miscellaneous grains and straw (*Hubei xianzheng gaikuang* 1934, 729).

Sources: Wuchang (fixed rent, rent in cash) (*Wuchang xian* 1938, 16); Hanyang (sharecropping) (*Hanyang xian zhi chugao* 1960, 32); Hanchuan (*Hanchuan xian jian zhi* 1959, 31); Yingcheng (*Yingcheng xian zhi* 1992, 131); Jianli (*Jianli xian* 1938, 11; *Jianli xian zhi* 1959, 71); Shishou (*Shishou fang zhi* 1958, 106). All other information comes from *Hubei xianzheng gaikuang* (1934): Wuchang, 42; Hanyang, 69; Xiaogan, 647; Yunmeng, 698; Tianmen, 761; Hanchuan, 785; Mianyang, 810; Jingshan, 834; Qianjiang, 884; Jiangling, 907; Jingmen, 926; Zhijiang, 1032.

the tenants' perspective, a popular – pattern of rent in an environment characterized by frequent water calamities, particularly floods. The more frequent the floods in a county, the bigger the tenants' share of the harvest, as in Jianli and Mianyang. Mianyang was located in the very centre of the Jianghan Plain and could be inundated by either the Yangzi River or the Han River. Some tenants in this county took more than 70 percent of the harvest of the major crop and all of some secondary products, such as straw (*Hubei xianzheng gaikuang* 1934, 810). Although Jianli was located in the Yangzi River valley, it was also frequently inundated because of its relatively low elevation and the fact that it had many *yuan*. In Jianli, sharecropping involved a 3:7 split of the major crop between the landlord and the tenant, with the tenant keeping the entire harvest of the secondary crops (*Jianli xian* 1938: 11).

There was another very conspicuous and revealing custom in Jianli: the rental rate depended on the elevation of the plot (*Hubei xianzheng gaikuang* 1934, 955).[22] This differs completely from the general custom, which holds that the amount of rent depends on the fertility of the plot. What accounts for this difference is the fact that, in Jianli, people took into consideration the potential threat of floods. Obviously, in this flood-prone county, the size and predictability of a harvest depended more on the elevation of the land than on its fertility. So, too, did the amount of rent. Jianli was not the only county with this custom. In Dangyang, for example, the amount of rent also depended on a plot's vulnerability to flooding or drought in addition to its fertility (*Dangyang xian zhi* 1992, 145).

The effect of frequent floods on the pattern of rent in the Jianghan Plain can be seen from the relatively low rate of fixed rent in kind. In many cases, this form of rent was not completely immune to change. In Hanyang, for example, some landlords were said to have taken a fixed rent *(ganke)* from land on which harvests were uncertain; the tenants had to pay the fixed rent no matter the size of the harvest (*Hanyang xian zhi chugao* 1960, 32). This definitely put the tenants in a disadvantageous position, while it allowed the landlords to reduce their risk of losing rent. But this example is mentioned in a newly compiled gazetteer. According to an early Republican survey, in lean or poor years, if the total harvest was less than the agreed rent, the landlord and the tenant would split the harvest 60:40 (*Minshi xiguan* 2000, 658).[23]

Even if we grant that there may have been some landlords who insisted on fixed rent no matter what happened, in practice, things were not so simple. First of all, we do not really know the exact amount of rent the tenants had to pay in the Hanyang case mentioned above. Considering the unstable environment of this county, the amount might not have been too great. In many cases, fixed rent in kind was less than half the harvest. This should be considered evidence that, at least to some extent, landlords yielded to tenants.

Second, in some counties, such as Tianmen and Jianli, it was possible for tenants to get the amount of fixed rent reduced when a poor harvest was the result of calamities.[24] The landlords, of course, would go to the field to examine the harvest in person once a calamity-related poor harvest had been claimed (*Jianli xian* 1938, 11; *Hubei xianzheng gaikuang* 1934, 955). This means that, in fact, the amount of fixed rent in kind was not exactly "fixed." In Zhijiang, rent was subject to change in yet another way. If there was a calamity that resulted in a poor harvest, which the landlord verified by a personal inspection, fixed rent in kind could be changed to sharecropping (*Hubei xianzheng gaikuang* 1934, 1032). The common practice of commuting rent in this way was in accordance with the rural economic structure of the Jianghan Plain. Since the majority of landlords in the Jianghan Plain were village residents and many of them also farmed, it was easy for them to go to fields to check the harvest. But that would have been difficult for absentee landlords. All of these examples show that the frequent floods in the Jianghan Plain had forced landlords and tenants to find a rental system acceptable to both parties. If rents were rigidly fixed, tenants would be in truly desperate circumstances in case of a poor harvest, and poor harvests were common due to frequent floods. Under such conditions, tenants would lose their interest in renting the land. By the same token, if rents were rigidly fixed, landlords would feel insufficiently compensated if there was a good harvest – and, due to the deposits of rich sludge, the harvests after floods were usually better than regular harvests. Thus, even in Songzi, a county with both lake areas and mountainous areas, sharecropping was adopted in frequently inundated lake areas (*Songzi xian zhi* 1986, 278).

Finally, in counties such as Xiaogan and Hanyang, where fixed rent remained "fixed" even when the area was hit by floods (as implied by the CCP's new gazetteers), tenants still found ways to reduce the rent. One method was to pay rent at a discounted rate. For example, in Hanyang, for an agreed rent of thirteen *dou,* tenants paid only 8 or 9 *dou;* the same was the case in Xiaogan, where an agreed rent of 1.25 *shi* (1 *shi* = 10 *dou*) of rice was usually paid only to the tune of 8 or 9 *dou.* It seems that, in general, landlords could do nothing regarding this kind of virtual rent resistance besides complain that "tenants are usually 'crafty'" *(dianhu duo piwan)* (*Hubei xianzheng gaikuang* 1934, 69, 647).[25] In Gong'an in the 1850s, the tenants who rented school lands (which usually bore fixed rent) frequently refused to pay rent, using the excuse of severe water calamities (*Gong'an xian zhi* 1874, 4: 4b).

The record of rent disputes in Hunan-Hubei in the early Qing show that a rental contract was needed for the establishment of almost all forms of tenancy. Furthermore, the duration of tenancy varied: usually it was over one year, very rarely was it permanent. Early in the twentieth century, tenancy in the Jianghan Plain varied (mostly by one or three years, with limited permanent tenure (Cheng 1977 [1938], 45,515), and land contracts were required in almost all counties (although oral contracts were also acceptable in some places).[26] No matter what kind of contract was involved, an intermediary was needed as a witness and guarantor. The contracts did not always guarantee tenants' rental rights. In some places, landlords could not easily terminate a contract; in other places, they could break a contract at any time. Even within one county, contracts varied. In Xiaogan, for example, it was rare for large landlords to break a contract, while the owners of small plots could change tenants at will (*Hubei xianzheng gaikuang* 1934, 647). In Wuchang, however, it was the owners of fertile land who changed their tenants at will, plus they required a rent deposit equivalent to one year's rent. Even so, peasants were willing to rent (*Wuchang xian* 1938, 16).

Since contracts were backed by custom, a landlord who broke a contract before the harvest had to pay the tenant at least for the seed and fertilizer (this was the case in Hanyang). In Qianjiang, it was unusual for a landlord to break a contract before the harvest. If he did so, he or the successor tenant had to pay the former tenant the whole harvest plus the cost of fertilizer (*Minshi xiguan* 2000, 652, 662).

Permanent tenure was found only in some counties. In Jiangling it was termed *ruandian* (soft contract rent), as opposed to *yingdian* (hard contract rent) (i.e., contracts that permitted landlords to change tenants at any time). Landlords entered into soft contracts because the tenants inherited the right to farm the land that was the subject of those contracts (*Hubei xianzheng gaikuang* 1934, 907). In Wuchang, it was said that most of the tenants who secured permanent tenure rights did so because they had contributed labour to the reclamation of the subject land or had paid a *pi tou* (rent deposit) in earlier years (*Wuchang xian* 1938, 16).[27] According to early Republican surveys, permanent tenure was also found in Hanyang and Jingzhou. In Hanyang, some land was distinguished according to whether it was *li* (inside) or *mian* (facing out). *Li* refers to the right of rent collection, which belonged to the landlord; *mian* refers to the right of farming, which belonged to the tenant. The landlord could not cancel a tenancy at will, but tenants could freely transfer the right to rent (*Minshi xiguan* 2000, 336).

The pattern of rental contracts and types of tenure relationships in the Jianghan Plain seems to be intimately related to frequent floods. Because of frequent dike ruptures, farmland was constantly in danger of being trans-formed or even erased. Fertile land might vanish after a flood, or low-lying lakeside fields might dry up and later be reclaimed as fertile land. This made landownership uncertain. By the same token, even the property of a household was hard to secure for long. In the fourth administrative district of Hanyang, for example, "nearly no house was older than ten years" – this because of Hanyang's low elevation and its frequent water calamities (*Hanyang xian* 1938, 6). In fact, in the Jianghan Plain few rich families managed to stay rich for many generations.[28] This was very different from the Yangzi delta, where there were many established families that had been wealthy and prominent for centuries.[29] It was the unstable environment that made permanent tenure hard to sustain in the Jianghan Plain. Although the percentage of permanent tenure in Hubei was higher than in the North China Plain, it was far lower than in the Yangzi delta.[30]

Thus it is safe to say that the unstable environment in the Jianghan Plain had a great effect on tenancy relationships. First, the higher the frequency of floods, the greater the share of the crop the tenants would get. Second, the amount of rent depended on the elevation of land as well as on its fertility. Finally, fixed rent could be reduced in amount or changed to sharecropping (with the approval of the landlord) or paid at a discounted rate (without the approval of the landlord) if the harvest was poor due mainly to water calam-ities.[31] The rental system was a means of dealing with uncertainty and risk.

Labour Service and the Landlord-Tenant Relationship

Labour service continued to exist in the Jianghan Plain into the early twentieth century. According to various gazetteers compiled after 1949, it was found in Shishou, Jianli, Xiaogan, and some other counties. Reportedly, it involved such things as tenants working for their landlords without compensation in busy seasons, offering wine and meat to landlords when they came to check the harvest or signed the land contract, and giving seasonal, fresh agricultural products to landlords (*Shishou fang zhi* 1958, 106; *Jianli xian zhi* 1959, 71; *Xiaogan xian jian zhi* 1959, 27).

Republican surveys, however, show that tenants provided no such extra services in some of these counties. Many Republican surveyors found that the custom had gradually diminished since the late Qing in other counties, such as Zhijiang, Songzi (*Hubei xianzheng gaikuang* 1934, 1032, 1056), and Wuchang (*Wuchang xian* 1938, 17). We know that both the newly compiled gazetteers and Republican surveys represent political positions as the CCP's guiding ideology led the compilers of the new gazetteers to emphasize rural exploitation from the angle of class relations, while the Republican surveys tended to take a more positive view of rural life. In many respects, the Republican surveys and the post-1949 gazetteers were looking at the same phenomena but from different perspectives. In Jianli, for example, according to a Republican survey, tenants provided no labour service (*Hubei xianzheng gaikuang* 1934, 955); but, according to a newly compiled gazetteer, they either had to offer labour service to landlords or suffer "extra exploitation," which included offering free labour service and gifts to landlords during festival times (*Jianli xian zhi* 1959, 71). It is true that such labour services and gift-giving amounted to "exploitation," but exchanges of labour and gifts were popular in rural communities and also occurred among fellow villagers. A Republican gazetteer makes it clear that, in Songzi, it was the custom for tenants to give gifts to their landlords during festivals. But many landlords did not demand that their tenants do so; it was only some "evil gentry" who would be displeased if they did not receive gifts (*Songzi xian zhi* 1982 [1937], 241). Some Qing officials in Hunan tolerated this kind of exchange because "these non-contractual gifts and services served to maintain rural stability" (Perdue 1987, 153). Thus, in the view of many Republican surveyors, the relations between tenants and landlords were good, as in Jianli, where it was claimed that, "among landlords and tenants, there were profound [good] relations" (*Hubei xianzheng gaikuang* 1934, 955).

Some landlords and tenants were relatives. For this reason, in Hanyang it was found that "relations between the landlords and the tenants were very harmonious" (*Hanyang xian* 1938, 14). Their relations may not have been exactly "harmonious," but at least they were relatively personal and not hostile. As has been stated, a rent deposit was needed to rent fertile land in Wuchang, but "there were some landlords and tenants who were on good terms, and so there was no need to pay a rent deposit" (*Hubei xianzheng gaikuang* 1934, 42). Since some landlords of Dangyang had once been tenants themselves, they reportedly did not put on airs or look down on tenants and hired hands (Zhang 1957, 443). In Zhongxin Township in Jingmen, the general relationship between landlords and tenants was characterized by "lenient consanguinity." Tenants particularly appreciated landlords who rented land to them when they were in desperate circumstances; during the Land Reform, these people found it hard to believe that their hard-working landlords had amassed wealth by exploiting peasants (Wu 2007, 47). In Hanchuan, the records even mention the phenomenon of the landlord and the tenant both owning the same piece of land. This was termed *zutian* (rental land). The rental of such land needed to be recorded in a contract in order to differentiate it from *qintian* (personal land), which was land owned solely by the landlord and over which he had the absolute right to change tenants (*Hubei xianzheng gaikuang* 1934, 785). Clearly, relations between landlords and tenants in the Jianghan Plain could sometimes be highly personal.

These kinds of personal relations could also be found among landlords (or employers) and hired labourers (or employees). Many Republican surveys report that employees were well treated by their employers (e.g., in Jianli). This was particularly so for so-called *dang jia chang gong,* chief yearly labourers who took care of their employer's household (Songzi) (*Hubei xianzheng gaikuang* 1934, 955, 1056). If a hired labourer got sick, the employer was expected to provide support, including medical care. Exactly how much care was provided varied depending on the length of the hiring period, the work attitude of the employee (whether or not he/she was hard-working), and the personal relations between the employer and the employee (*Minshi xiguan* 2000, 669). And the employers usually provided yearly labourers with some basic apparel, such as one or two suits of clothes, one towel, one straw hat, and/or one pair of socks and shoes (*Hubei xianzheng gaikuang* 1934, 699, 729, 785). This is, of course, far different from the image of the poor servant who was treated as a slave by the master's household – though this was sometimes the case (*Nongye zhi* 1993, 26).

Overall, the picture of the Jianghan Plain was unlike that seen in both the Yangzi delta and the North China Plain. In the Yangzi delta, tenants usually made their rent payments to agents of absentee landlords, and they might not have any direct, personal contact with landlords. In the North China Plain in the Republic, owing to population pressure and rural commercialization, personal relations were increasingly replaced by purely economic relations (Huang 1985, 202-16). A mountain of literature would also have us believe that relations between landlords and tenants in the North China Plain were inevitably conflicted (e.g., Crook and Crook 1959; Hinton 1997 [1966]).

Although we do not know how many landlords and tenants had the kind of good relations mentioned by Republican surveyors, the fact that the examples are widely distributed (Hanyang, Wuchang, Jianli, and Dangyang) is sufficient to suggest that respectful, and sometimes cordial, relations were common in the Jianghan Plain during the Republic. Under such circumstances, it seems certain that landlord-tenant relations were not as hostile as indicated by the "renting-and-cultivating-by-force" phenomenon in the early Qing mentioned by Tan (1992). Nor were they as coercive as Chinese Marxist scholars maintain. After calamities rent could be reduced, or paid at a discounted rate, or transformed into sharecropping. In other words, landlords and tenants could – and did – compromise with one another. In the relations between landlords and tenants, the former did not completely overpower the latter. In such counties as Hanchuan, Hanyang, and Xiaogan, where sharecropping was common, some tenants and landlords even shared the land or other production materials. In Hanyang, for instance, some landlords contributed farmland, seeds, and fertilizer, and tenants contributed labour and implements (*Hanyang xian* 1938, 14). In Xiaogan, some landlords offered land, and tenants contributed labour and implements, and both shared in the cost of seeds and fertilizer (*Xiaoganxian jian zhi* 1959, 27). Clearly, in some places the relations between landlords and tenants were the outcome of negotiation and cooperation, not of a clash between two classes that were poles apart. Both landlords and tenants lived in the same community (and many of them were kin), and they had to follow the same customs and moral standards (Wu 2007, 47-48).[32] It would be difficult for a bellicose tenant to rent land from a landlord; it would also be difficult for an offensive employer to hire new hands. Usually, those who were ungenerous to tenants or employees were this way because of personality flaws: they were not necessarily the natural enemies of the poor peasants that the communist revolutionary ideology portrayed.[33]

In the Jianghan Plain, both the rarity of permanent tenure and the negotiating power of tenants were related to the local environmental situation, particularly to frequent floods. Though the relationship between labour service and the unstable environment remains unclear, over time the incidence of labour service decreased. Finally, many landlords and tenants maintained a reasonable relationship or at least a patron-client relationship (Eisenstadt and Roniger 1984, 139-40).

Conclusion

Based on an analysis of many county-level surveys, we find that, in the Jianghan Plain before the Land Reform, landlords and rich peasants accounted for about 9 percent of the total rural population but owned about 41 percent of the total cultivated land, while the rest of the rural population owned the remaining 59 percent. Class status was variable, and classes were not sharply and clearly divided. Landlords might also rent land from others, and hired labourers might also own a piece of land. But the majority of the rural population consisted of owner-peasants. Most landlords were middle and small landlords who lived in the villages and engaged in farming. All of this differs from the CCP's classic representation of rural society before 1949, which focuses on class relations and exploitation on the part of landlords and rich peasants, and ignores non-political factors such as the environment. On the other hand, Western scholarship tends to look at China from a market perspective and, consequently, considers economic factors as the key determinants of the pattern and change of land distribution and tenancy relationships.

Both the CCP's Marxist analysis and the Western scholars' market analysis virtually ignore the role of the local environment in the formation and evolution of the pattern of land distribution and tenancy relationship. The story of the Jianghan Plain shows that, as in the Yangzi delta and the North China Plain, environmental conditions shaped the relations of agricultural production, particularly those of land distribution and tenancy. First, the environment bore a close relationship to the extent of land concentration: the more frequently a county suffered from floods, the lower the concentration of landownership, and vice versa. Second, permanent tenure and the practice of requiring rent deposits were not directly related. In the Jianghan Plain, rent deposits were relatively common, but permanent tenure was not. The major reasons for this include the frequent flooding, which made it difficult for the local people to maintain landownership rights or, indeed, property for long periods of time. Moreover, rent deposits were usually only required in counties blessed with a relatively stable environment.

Third, the unstable environment affected the forms of rent payments and the amount of rent or share of harvest taken by each party. Where share-cropping was practised, the higher the frequency of floods in a particular place, the bigger the tenants' share. The rental rate depended less on the fertility of the land than its elevation. In fact, in Jiangling and Jianli it was found that even the price of farmland relied on its elevation: the higher the elevation of the land the higher its price (*Hubei xianzheng gaikuang* 1934, 907, 954). Where fixed rent was practised, landlords were expected to reduce the rent to some extent or to change to sharecropping once a calamity-related poor harvest had been claimed. If this did not happen, the tenants would pay the rent at a discounted rate. In other words, both landlords and tenants sought to bargain with each other in different ways in order to reach an acceptable balance of power, and there was an accommodation of interests between the powerful and the weak. The relations between landlords and tenants were thus neither impersonal economic relations (common in the Yangzi delta) nor hostile (common on the North China Plain); rather, at least sometimes, they were personal and close.

In sum, the unstable environment had a direct and crucial effect on the formation, evolution, and pattern of the relations of agricultural production, particularly land distribution and tenancy, in the Jianghan Plain in the Qing and the Republic. The relations of agricultural production were not simply "feudal" land relations in the form of class exploitation, as Chinese Marxist scholars contend, nor landlord-tenant relations that were mainly shaped by economic factors, as Western scholars who offer a market-based analysis would lead us to believe.

6 Fisheries and the Peasant Economy

The middle and lower Yangzi River valley plain is well known in China as "a land of fish and rice" *(yu mi zhi xiang)*. In fact, as early as the Han dynasty (206 BCE-220 CE), the middle and lower reaches of the Yangzi River were described as places where the local people "have rice as their main dish and their soup contains fish" *(fan dao geng yu)* (Sima 1990, 2119). The Jianghan Plain was even richer in aquatic products, owing to its abundance of surface water. In later centuries, right up to the late Qing, historians and compilers of local gazetteers continued to use this expression. In the Republic, Hubei ranked first among the freshwater fishing areas of China (Zeng 1984, 2: 255).

Researchers examining the structure of the rural economy in the province of Hubei argue that the domestic cotton textile industry was the most important non-farming productive activity of rural households in late imperial times and the Republican era. They describe the rural economy as a combination of farming and weaving (Xu 1991, 101; Mei 1993). But neither focuses on the Jianghan Plain nor pays any special attention to the fishing economy. This lack of attention has puzzled some readers who, aware of the phrase "a land of fish and rice," wondered where all the fish of the Jianghan Plain had gone.[1] Recently, researchers have become aware of this lacuna and consequently have started to address the issue of the fishing economy of the middle Yangzi River valley in the Ming-Qing era.

Zhang Jianmin is one of the first scholars to have recognized the importance of fisheries for the economy of Hubei. In *A Comprehensive History of Hubei: Ming and Qing Dynasties,* he treats fisheries as one of the principal sectors of Hubei's diversified economy, whose importance is on par with the production of cash crops such as cotton and ramie. He shows that, in the Ming-Qing era, there were two kinds of fishers living along Hubei's rivers and lakes: full-time fishers and part-time fishers. The latter – who supplemented crop production with fishing, especially in years of water calamities – were more numerous. The aquatic products (fresh fish, salted fish, dried fish, etc.) of Hubei were not only consumed locally but also sold in other places and were even shipped to the imperial court as tribute (mostly salted fish). Indeed, the aquatic products were so rich that the Ming government established in Hubei the country's largest number of river-tax-stations for collecting fishing taxes (Zhang 1999, 335-65).

Yin Lingling goes further than Zhang, pointing out that, in the Ming-Qing era, the local socio-economic structure of the Hubei-Hunan Plain transformed from a fishing economy into an agrarian economy. According to Yin, in the early Ming, fisheries still played a very important role in the local economy, and "population, lakes, fisheries, and agriculture together formed a relatively stable ecological economic system." But, with the increase of population and the consequent increase of *yuan*, the agrarian economy became more and more dominant in the local economy and, by the mid-Qing, fisheries had become relatively insignificant (Yin 2001b, 400-20; Yin 2004, 7-9, 17-19).

Although both Zhang Jianmin and Yin Lingling recognize the significance of fishing in Hubei and on the Hubei-Hunan Plain, neither of them focuses solely on the Jianghan Plain.[2] In addition, Yin's analysis of the transformation of the local economy may exaggerate the importance of the fishery in the early Ming and underestimate its importance in and after the mid-Qing. Moreover, both scholars devote little or no detailed discussion to such issues as how fisheries were involved in the local people's economic life, the different relations of production between fishing and farming, how fishers lived, and how all of these factors related to the local environment and the changes it underwent.

This chapter addresses these questions. Guided by available source materials, it focuses on the late Qing and the Republic and relies mainly on the newly compiled local gazetteers.[3] Using these, it traces the relationship of fisheries and the environment into the early and mid-Qing. It also offers a more environmental than an economic analysis, consequently leaving aside such topics as the returns of fishing.

Although the water-rich environment offered opportunities for Jianghan people to engage in fishing, in late imperial and Republican times many of them were actually forced to do so since they suffered from frequent water calamities and heavy dike fees and lacked sufficient arable land. In general, there was more reclaimable land in the Lake Dongting Plain than in the Jianghan Plain at that time. But some reports indicate that, at the end of the nineteenth century (1897), after the reclamation of most reclaimable land, many local peasants also gave up farming and turned to fishing (Perdue 1987, 87). As peasants moved from farming to fishing, they reduced the population pressure on the land. However, in the process they suffered a lowering of their standard of living. In this they had little choice: the alternative for most of them would have been starvation.

Acreage under Water and Full-Time and Part-Time Fishers

Hubei is so studded with lakes that it was once called "the province of a thousand lakes." In the early 1950s, Hubei had 1,332 lakes with an area of more than one hundred *mu;* by the mid-1980s, the number of such lakes had been reduced to 843 (*Hubei sheng zhi shuili* 1995, 1). In addition, Hubei has 1,195 rivers (that are longer than five kilometres), most of which are tributaries of the Yangzi and the Han Rivers. In the 1990s, Hubei had 0.19 kilometres of river for every square kilometre of its territory (*Hubei sheng zhi dili* 1997, 493). Many of these lakes and rivers are located in the Jianghan Plain. In the four-lake area, a region of 11,548 square kilometres in the very centre of the Jianghan Plain, there are about three thousand square kilometres of water surface (*Hubei sheng zhi shuili* 1995, 343). In other words, 26 percent of the region is under water. In the county of Honghu, there were forty-one rivers in 1951, not including the Yangzi, the Dongjing, and some deserted river courses, making 0.24 kilometre of river per square kilometre of territory. Adding in Honghu's 2.2 million *mu* of lakes, the area under water in this county accounted for no less than 55 percent of its entire territory (*Honghu xian zhi* 1992, 59-62). Considering the large number of reclaimed lakes and vanished rivers in the Jianghan Plain, the area under water in the Qing and the Republic would have been larger than what was the case in the mid-twentieth century.

The area under water today includes five major categories – lakes, rivers, irrigation and drainage canals, reservoirs, and weirs and ponds (sometimes also including fishponds). Since there were few large irrigation and drainage canals in the Jianghan Plain before 1949, and small reservoirs or weirs/ponds were only used for irrigation, in the Qing and the Republic fishing was limited mostly to lakes and rivers. It is true that a large number of reservoirs were built in the late twentieth century and have been used to raise fish, but they did not exist in the Republic. Therefore, this chapter mainly discusses lakes and rivers, the major sites of fishing in the Republic and before.

Although we lack accurate figures on the area under water in the Jianghan Plain before the twentieth century, we can get a rough picture of the extent of water by looking at data from some counties in the Jianghan Plain in the twentieth century (see Table 16).

The data in Table 16 show only the proportion of water surface or lake surface for the entire territory of a county, including agricultural land (i.e.,

Table 16

The proportion of water surface to the total area of some counties in the Jianghan Plain

County	Time (year)	Water surface	Lake surface	Water or lake surface as a % of total territory
Honghu	1951		2,174,400 *mu*	55.0
Shishou	1958	673,385 *mu*		31.8
Hanchuan	1959		1,120,771 *mu*	24.8
Gong'an	Late Qing, Republic			23.2
Yingcheng	Republic	342,000 *mu*		22.2
Jianli	1950s	603.5 km²		20.7
Qianjiang	1937		298.6 km²	~ 20.0
Yunmeng	20th century or more	100,000 *mu*		14.0
Songzi	1982	349,800 *mu*		10.7
Tianmen	1917		190 km²	7.3
Hanyang	Republic		342,000 *mu*	
Jiangling	1947		1,079,800 *mu*	
Xiaogan	1950s	510,000 *mu*		

Sources: *Honghu xian zhi* (1992, 59, 62); *Hanyang xian zhi* (1989, 163); *Shishou fang zhi* (1958, 20); *Hanchuan xian jian zhi* (1959, 11); *Gong'an xian zhi* (1990, 172); *Yingcheng xian zhi* (1992, 198); *Jianli xian zhi* (1959, 16); *Qianjiang xian zhi* (1990, 321); *Yunmeng xian zhi* (1994, 205); *Songzi xian zhi* (1986, 285); *Tianmen xian zhi* (1989, 110); *Jiangling xian zhi* (1990, 83); *Xiaogan shi zhi* (1992, 177).

cultivated land, water surface, forests, grasslands, and gardens [*Jingzhou diqu zhi* 1996, 111]) and non-agricultural land. If we were to compare the water surface with the acreage under cultivation, the proportion of water surface would be even higher. According to a land survey conducted in 1981-83, what was then Jingzhou District had a water surface of 8,365,808 *mu*,[4] which accounted for about 19.4 percent of the whole territory of the district but amounted to 39.4 percent of its cultivated land (Wang 1989, 10-12).[5] In other words, for almost every three *mu* of cultivated land there were two *mu* of water surface. Although this was the general situation of Jingzhou District in the 1980s, the proportion of water surface to total area varied from county to county. Also, the survey did not include counties outside Jingzhou District, such as Dangyang, Zhijiang, Xiaogan, Hanchuan, Yunmeng, Yingcheng, Hanyang, and Jiangxia (Wuchang). Some of these counties (e.g., Hanchuan) had an unusually large water surface.

In an area with such a high density of rivers and lakes, it was perhaps inevitable that fisheries became an inseparable part of local life. The most important type of fishery in the Jianghan Plain, right down to 1949, was natural fishing. Some people fished mainly in rivers, others in lakes, a difference known as "inward-lakes" fishers and "outward-rivers" fishers (*Gong'an xian zhi* 1990, 178). According to the importance of fishing to their income, fishing people can also be divided into what were called whole fishing households and half-fishing households – that is, households that fished full-time and those that fished part-time. The former usually spent all year round on rivers and lakes fishing, and lived on their fishing boats. Part-time fishing people usually fished in nearby rivers and lakes in the off-season. It was the existence of a large number of part-time fishing people in the Jianghan Plain that highlighted the water-rich character of local life. The proportion of fishing households to all rural households or the entire population of a county varied from 3.46 to 70 percent, depending on location (see Table 17).

Table 17 only lists counties in the Jianghan Plain for which data on fishing households are available; counties not on the list did not necessarily lack fishers. But there are sufficient data to confirm that the fishing population in the Jianghan Plain in the Republic was significant. Taken together, the data in Table 17 provide a conservative estimate that about 10 percent of rural households in the Jianghan Plain were also fishing households (full-time or part-time) (see details below). For example, more than one-third of the rural population in Hanchuan in the Republic consisted of full-time fishers. However, in terms of households, fishing households (both full-time and part-time) made up about 70 percent of the total households of this county (*Hanchuan xian zhi* 1992, 176). Lake Diaocha, one of the most famous fishing areas in Hubei, is located mainly in this county.

The Jianghan Plain as a whole, with its high density of rivers and lakes, had about one-fifth or so of its whole territory covered by water. The ratio was higher than 50 percent in some counties. All this made it possible for many households to take up either full-time or part-time fishing: perhaps 10 percent or so of all households engaged in fishing, full or part time.[6]

Fisheries in the Rural Economy of the Jianghan Plain

With 20 percent or so of its territory covered with water, and with around 10 percent of its rural households engaged in fishing, the Jianghan Plain had a distinctive rural economy. It is generally thought that Chinese rural society in late imperial times, at least before the Opium War (1839-42), was a traditional society characterized by, as a very popular expression put it, "men ploughing and women weaving" *(nan'geng nüzhi).* The "ploughing" here

Table 17

The proportion of fishing households to all rural households or population in some counties in the Jianghan Plain in the Republican era

County	Time	Fishing households Total	Fishing households Full-time	As a % of all rural households of the county	As a % of the rural population of the county
Wuchang	1930s	4,146		6.4	
Hanyang	1930s	5,530		9	
Hanchuan	1948		158,330*	70	39.33
Yunmeng	1930s	1,734		3.46	
Yingcheng	1930s	2,731			
Honghu	1949	6,000	1,357		
Jingmen	1949		1,630		
Zhongxiang	Republic		300		
Qianjiang	1949	11,390*			8.14***
Jianli	1937	10,524		12	
Shishou	Republic		12,000*		5.4 (20 **)
Gong'an	1949		483		

Notes:
*   Refers to population, not households.
**   Refers to the part-time fishing population.
*** Refers to the percentage of the whole labour force of a county.

Sources: Wuchang xian (1938, 36); *Hanyang xian* (1938, 56); *Yunmeng xian* (1938, 26); *Yingcheng xian* (1938, 38); *Hanchuan xian zhi* (1992, 176); *Honghu xian shuichan zhi* (1986, 55); *Jingmen shi zhi* (1994, 296); *Zhongxiang xian zhi* (1990, 365); *Qianjiang xian zhi* (1990, 330); *Jianli xian* (1938, 36); *Shishou xian zhi* (1990, 200, 205); *Gong'an xian zhi* (1990, 178).

generally refers to farming, or, more specifically, crop production; and "weaving" refers to the household cotton textile industry, the major household non-farming productive activity of rural China. This combination of farming and household handicrafts was also common in most places, including both the Yangzi delta and the North China Plain (excluding households that worked full time at spinning and weaving, which were not very common in the countryside).

Researchers have tended to believe that the household cotton textile industry was the leading non-farming productive activity in rural Hubei in the Ming-Qing era (Xu 1991, 101). But this understanding of the rural economy of Hubei Province fails to take fisheries into account and overlooks the relationship of regional differences (such as those associated with mountains, plains, and lake areas) and the distribution of the domestic cotton textile industry. If we take these differences into account and focus on the Jianghan Plain, a quite different picture emerges. In the Republic, for example, in some places in the Jianghan Plain, the number of rural households that engaged in fishing as their major non-farming productive activity was greater than the number of rural households that produced cotton textiles (Table 18a). Hence, in these places, fishing was far more important than the domestic cotton textile industry.

The five counties listed in Table 18b – Wuchang, Hanyang, Yunmeng, Yingcheng, and Jianli – were extensively surveyed by the GMD government of Hubei. The domestic cotton textile industry was the major non-farming productive activity of rural households in Wuchang, Yunmeng, and Yingcheng.[7] Read together, the data from these five counties indicate that the domestic cotton textile industry ranked as the number one household non-farming productive activity. However, a close look at the location of these counties and the history of cotton textile production there reveals a picture that differs from the generally accepted portrait of "men ploughing and women weaving."

The number of households that engaged in fishing as their major non-farm productive activity (including full-time fishing households) in both Jianli and Hanyang counties exceeded the number of households engaged in other non-farming productive activities (see Table 18b). In Hanyang, the number of fishing households was ten times the number of households that spun and wove cotton cloth as their major non-farming productive activity, and in Jianli it was two and one half times the number. Significantly, both Hanyang and Jianli were generally thought to be very important producers of domestic cotton textiles, including the famous cotton textiles known as *jibei dabu*, which were produced in Jianli (*Jianli xian zhi* 1872, 8: 1a), and *koubu*, which were produced in Hanyang (*Hanyang xian zhi* 1748, 10: 1b).

Even the data for Wuchang presented in Table 18b indirectly show the importance of fishing in the local economy. Since Wuchang was the capital of Hubei, one might expect to find a large number of peasants in the surrounding rural areas engaged in peddling and providing various kinds of services. But these people were less numerous than those who engaged in fishing as their major non-farming productive activity.

Moreover, the number of rural households that engaged in non-farming productive activities listed in Table 18b accounts for only a small part of all rural households in these counties, which may suggest that the survey was incomplete, particularly when one looks at the small number of rural households engaged in the domestic cotton textile industry in Hanyang and Jianli and the small number of rural households engaged in fishing in Yunmeng

Table 18a

The number of rural households engaged in non-farming productive activities in selected counties of the Jianghan Plain, 1930s

Number of rural households in different non-farming productive activities

County	Fishing		Domestic cotton textile		Peddling		Small handicraft industry		Other	
	Households	%	Households	%	Households	%	Households	%	Households	%
Wuchang	4,146	6.36	9,058	13.88	833	1.28	2,045	3.15	939	1.44
Hanyang	5,530	9.36	510	0.86	1,710	2.90			1,553*	2.63
Jianli	10,524	11.84	4,134	4.65	7,197	8.10			1,867**	2.1
Yunmeng	1,734	3.46	19,359	51.31	3,350	8.88				
Yingcheng	2,731	5.86	6,760	14.50	5,324	11.27	1,470	3.15	1,337***	2.87

Table 18b

Comparison of rural households' non-farming productive activities in fishing and domestic cotton textile industry in selected counties of the Jianghan Plain, 1930s

County	Total number of rural households in the county	Households with cotton spinning and weaving as major non-farming productive activity	Households with fishing as major non-farming productive activity
Wuchang	65,243	9,058	4,146
Hanyang	59,058	510	5,530
Yunmeng	33,776	19,359	1,734
Yingcheng	46,613	6,760	2,731
Jianli	88,918	4,134	10,524
Total	293,608	39,821	24,665
%		13.56	8.40

Notes:
* Including 674 households of woodcutters.
** Including 899 households of silkworm raisers.
*** Including 624 households of miners.
Sources: Wuchang xian (1938, 16, 56); *Hanyang xian* (1938, 32, 37); *Yunmeng xian* (1938, 26); *Yingcheng xian* (1938, 38); *Jianli xian* (1938, 36). The percentages in the table are the proportion of households in each kind of non-farming productive activity to all rural households. They have been calculated to two decimal points by the present author based on original data.

and Yingcheng.[8] Indeed, another survey (which does not provide household statistics) shows a very different picture of these four counties; however, taking the Jianghan Plain as a whole, fishing was clearly one of the most important non-farming productive activities of rural households in the 1930s (see Table 19).

The source for Table 19 lists fishing as first among non-farming productive activities in ten counties. Each of these counties was either the site of a great number of lakes, or situated along the Yangzi River or the Han River, or both; hence the importance of fisheries. There are no data for two counties, Shishou and Gong'an, in this source. However, because a large part of each county was located between the Yangzi River and Lake Dongting, and because both counties had many lakes, it seems likely that fishing would have been important there. The Yangzi River runs through the middle of Shishou. The least straight portion of the Yangzi is located in this county. Shishou also has many lakes. Here, the area under water was large, as was the number of part-time fishing households (see Table 16 and Table 17). As for Gong'an, according to a late Qing gazetteer: "There are many lakes in the county, and the people who own lakes call on fishing households to fish in the off-season in autumn/winter" (*Gong'an xian zhi* 1874, 4: 37b).

Table 19

Non-farming productive activities of rural households in the Jianghan Plain, 1930s

Counties along the Han River		Counties along the Yangzi River	
County	Non-farming productive activities	County	Non-farming productive activities
Hanyang	Doing business, cloth making	Wuchang	Doing business, fishing
Hanchuan	Fishing	Jianli	Textile industry, peddling, trade
Yunmeng	Fishing	Gong'an	N.A.
Xiaogan	Peddling	Shishou	N.A.
Yingcheng	Fishing, handicraft industry, mining, doing business	Zhijiang	Fishing, commercial boating, paper making, textile industry
Mianyang	Fishing, textile industry, raising chickens and pigs	Jiangling	Fishing, textile industry, wood cutting, leather making
Zhong-xiang	Fishing, wood cutting, textile production, silk-worm raising	Songzi	Fishing, peddling, handicraft industry
Tianmen	Fishing, weaving, peddling	Dangyang	Textile production
Jingshan	Peddling, trading		
Qianjiang	Fishing, textile production		
Jingmen	Leather making, raising [poultry for] eggs		

Note: The reason for the order of non-farming productive activities of each county in the list is not clear in the original source. (According to the source, the list was taken from *Hubei xianzheng gaikuang* [1934], but it is not exactly the same. Furthermore, there is no indication of what is meant by "business.") One can surmise that the first item on the list was the most important one or the largest group.

Source: Hubei sheng zhi tudi liyong yu liangshi wenti (1977 [1938], 24142-45).

Fishing was not the most important non-farming productive activity of rural households in Xiaogan, Jingshan, Jingmen, and Dangyang, but none of these counties was located at the very centre of the Jianghan Plain. They had relatively few lakes and the parts of their territory that were contiguous to the Yangzi River and the Han River were relatively small.[9]

Surprisingly, the survey reported in Table 19 lists fishing as the only non-farming productive activity of rural households in Yunmeng, as the most important non-farming productive activity of rural households in Yingcheng, and as the second most important non-farming productive activity of rural households in Wuchang, but it does not mention fishing among the rural households of Hanyang and Jianli at all. This is inconsistent with the data presented in Table 18a and Table 18b. Although information culled from these sorts of surveys can provide a general picture of how widespread fishing as a secondary occupation was on the Jianghan Plain, it cannot be precisely quantified. Still, even the data in Table 19 show that, in more than half the counties, fishing was the most important non-farming productive activity of rural households. It is apparent that fishing *was* important among non-farming productive activities of rural households in much of the Jianghan Plain in the Republic – a conclusion also evident in Table 18a and Table 18b.

As we can see, according to the available Republican surveys, the structure of the rural economy in much of the Jianghan Plain includes fishing along with farming and weaving. In fact, in describing the customs of the county of Honghu in the late Qing, the newly compiled county gazetteer had this to say:

> The common people [of Honghu] are industrious, thrifty, and hard working. [They] know farming and fishing very well. If they are forced to move out of the area because of flooding, [they] long for their homeland. They will return to their homeland immediately after the flood subsides and begin rebuilding. (*Honghu xian zhi* 1992, 531)

It is clear that, in the view of the compilers of this gazetteer, an important characteristic of the people of Honghu (which was part of Mianyang in the late Qing) was that its people "know farming and fishing very well." In other words, they combined farming and fishing, not farming and weaving.

This, then, was the situation in the Jianghan Plain in the late Qing and the Republic. How did this situation differ from those of earlier times? Many lakes and tributaries that had existed as late as the middle of the Qing dynasty began to vanish by the late Qing due to the extensive reclamation of lake-fronts and the blockage of river outlets. The acreage under water was decreasing in the late Qing and the Republic. According to one source, during the Ming-Qing period, the largest amount of water surface of lakes in the Jianghan area was 26,000 square kilometres; this decreased to 10,000 square kilometres or so by the end of the Qing and to 8,330 square kilometres by the end of the Republic (Guan 1983, 35). If it is true that, as Yin Lingling argues, the Hubei-Hunan Plain transformed from a fishing economy into an agrarian economy during the Ming-Qing era, then fishing must have contributed a bigger share to the local economy prior to the late Qing and the Republic. The combination of farming and fishing in the Jianghan Plain should have been much more pronounced before the late Qing.

This argument is supported by evidence contained in local gazetteers. In Qianjiang, for example, a Qing gazetteer points out that, in this county, "in the plain, with its huge marsh, the local peasants either hire out [as agricultural labourers] or go into fishing." And, in the late Qing and the Republic, because of frequent water calamities, farming and fishing each constituted half of most households' economy. Thus the saying: "The children make hooks, and the old women make [fishing] nets" (*Qianjiang xian zhi* 1990, 322). In Shishou, "[the people] engage in farming and fishing but not trading; there is no big difference [in this respect] between the present and the past" (*Shishou xian zhi* 1866, 3: 57b). The sources thus highlight the combination of farming and fishing, not the combination of farming and weaving, though each county, as far as we know, had households that spun and wove. Of course the records do not lead to the conclusion that fishing always accompanied farming, but they do make it clear that, before the late Qing, fishing was of great importance in the local economy.

To return to the conventional view that links farming and weaving, one would have to conclude that, as it does not take fishing into account, it exaggerates the number of households that engaged in the domestic cotton textile industry. This is not to say that the rural household textile industry in the Jianghan Plain was unimportant. Some rural households may have spun and wove and fished at the same time. In many cases, it was the women, the elderly, and the young who spun and wove, while it was the adult males who fished. This was particularly the case for part-time fishing people. This, for example, was the case in the village of Xiaojiawan, in Hanyang, in the late Qing, where men engaged in fishing and women engaged in weaving (of cotton, ramie, etc.) (*Hanyang xian zhi* 1989, 237). A late-Qing Hanyang gazetteer also mentions that, in this county, since the late Ming, "[the rural men] fish when they do not farm, but rarely engage in business or peddling ... [While] the rural women only engage in the textile industry" (*Hanyang xian zhi* 1868, 9: 2a). Apparently there was no conflict in the gender division of labour with regard to fishing and weaving: they could co-exist.

Moreover, inasmuch as all the statistics cited above are from county-level surveys or studies, they conceal regional differences within each county. Areas along rivers and close to lakes, on the one hand, and dryland areas, on the other, had very different environmental conditions. Thus, the residents of these two kinds of areas would have had different priorities when choosing a handicraft or other major non-farming endeavour in the slack season. The residents of watery areas usually took up fishing, while the residents of dryland areas preferred to take up cotton spinning and weaving (*Hanchuan xian zhi* 1873, 6: 14a-15a; *Qianjiang xian zhi* 1990, 592). Since most of the Jianghan Plain was close to either lakes or rivers, many households would engage in both fishing (conducted by male adults) and/or weaving (conducted by females) as well as farming. Thus, their economy was structured around a combination of farming, weaving, and fishing.

Water Surface Ownership

Like cultivated land, the majority of lakes and even some rivers in the Jianghan Plain were privately owned. The only exceptions were public water surfaces – those owned by the government and those without a registered owner – which covered only a small area of the plain. Privately owned water surfaces can be further divided into those owned by one household, multiple households, and entire lineages.[10]

In general, fishing in privately owned waters without permission was not allowed. The local people could only fish free in public waters or on water surfaces that lacked a registered owner. In mid-Qing Hanyang, for example, someone once forcibly occupied seventeen public lakes, but the governor of Hubei felt these lakes were the property of all those who lived around them. The lakes were eventually returned to the local residents (*Hanyang xian zhi* 1889, 1: 14b-15a). However, it seems that there were few bodies of water with no owner. A record of such a body of water was found in Jingshan in the Republic, where it was said that some "rivers and lakes had no owner," and so the local people could freely fish in these waters and sell their catch without hindrance. Reportedly, not many people in this county fished (*Jingshan xian zhi* 1990, 171, 184). Some county governments took over the ownership of some lakes in the Republic and, thereafter, the fishers paid lake taxes. In fact, the lakes were contracted to some individuals, which amounted to a covert form of private ownership (*Shishou xian zhi* 1990, 207).

Most bodies of water in the Republic were privately owned. Almost all new county gazetteers mention that the majority of local lakes were owned by "lake tyrants" *(hu ba)*, landlords, and lineages (e.g., *Mianyang xian zhi* 1989, 123, 592).[11] These so-called lake tyrants owned about 80 percent of the lake surfaces in Jianli (*Jianli xian zhi* 1959, 92) and almost all the lake surfaces in Hanyang (*Hanyang xian zhi* 1989, 163). The lakes in Jiangling were even called "family lakes" *(jiahu)* (*Jiangling xian zhi* 1990, 303), and fishers had to pay lake fees and boat fees to fish in them (this was a right guaranteed by the Fishery Law [LS 1-5-597]). In addition, in some places the water-grass land and reed land that surrounded lakes and bordered rivers were usually also privately owned (*Hanyang xian zhi* 1989, 163-64; *Hanchuan xian zhi* 1992, 106).

Some lake owners were also landlords: they owned cultivated land as well as water resources. Those who owned lakes but no farmland were rare since they would have had to live on the water in a boat. "Lake tyrants" would probably have owned more or larger boats than ordinary fishers, but the available sources do not document the existence of this kind of landless lake tyrant in the Jianghan Plain. Typically, these lake tyrant-landlords were the heads of lineages and owned both farmland and lake surfaces.

It appears that lineages were very active in lake areas. It was common for powerful households, in the name of their lineages, to become entangled in feuds. In Honghu, one function of lineages was to manage lineage-owned lakes (*Honghu xian zhi* 1992, 531). In Hanyang, powerful lineages occupied huge areas of water and profited from it (Guo 1988). In the counties of Xiaogan and Hanchuan, fishers of different lineages frequently fought for the control of fishing areas (*Xiaogan shi zhi* 1992, 129; *Hanchuan xian zhi* 1992, 197). In Jianli, opposing lineages became involved in lawsuits and violent struggles for the control of lakes (*Jianli xian zhi* 1959, 93). In some extreme cases, these so-called lake tyrants or fishing tyrants even maintained private militias.[12] Although fighting was also common among the peasants of the Jianghan Plain, particularly in the lower Han River valley, the goals were different. The fishers who clashed with one another were struggling for the control and ownership of lakes for the sake of establishing or strengthening their own power (or that of their lineage) in the community, while the peasants on the land were struggling for the control of waterways for the sake of their own *yuan*.

Although the role of "lake tyrant" in local administration is unclear, it is certain that they had as strong and direct an authority over village affairs as did the gentry-landlords in the North China Plain, and they were even more powerful than their Yangzi delta counterparts.[13] It appears that the lake tyrants and fishing tyrants in the Jianghan Plain had sufficient power to forcibly occupy a large amount of lake surface, particularly in the Republic.

A Jianli gazetteer vividly describes their power as virtually limitless in the Republic: "[Their] fists are the boundary, and [their] teeth are the stakes" (*Jianli xian zhi* 1959, 92). They even brazenly seized farmland around the edges of the lake when the water level rose. In Hanyang, during the same period, after the water level of the lake rose, the boundary of lake water became the boundary of farmland (now covered by lake water). After the lake water receded to its regular level, the farmland, once submerged, was then claimed by the lake owner (*Hanyang xian zhi chugao* 1960, 32). A similar land grab occurred in the Republic in Honghu, where the lake owners navigated their boats to seize farmland during the seasonal flooding: wherever they navigated their boats, the lake and the lands under the lake water became theirs. This was called *dang jiang quan di* (enclosing land by swinging the oars). Many large landlords who owned thousands of *mu* of land got rich this way (*Honghu xian zhi* 1992, 100). The prerequisite for this method was the ownership of the lake surface at its regular water level. This kind of forcible occupation was impossible on land.

Unlike land, which can be divided into plots of virtually any size or shape, bodies of water, particularly large ones such as lakes, are hard to divide into small plots, each potentially owned by a different individual. Thus it was common for several large lake tyrants or lineages to share ownership of a lake. Before 1949, Lake Xiaoyan on the border of Tianmen and Hanchuan, for example, was mainly shared by two large clans, the Xiaos (of Tianmen) and the Yans (of Hanchuan) (SZ 113-3-197). Lake Pai in Mianyang, with a surface area of 160,000 *mu*, was owned by five groups of households, or lineages, the members of each group having the same surname. Each of these groups had its own lake regulations (*Mianyang xian zhi* 1989, 123). Lake Diaocha in Hanchuan, which had a circumference of several hundred *li*, was owned by seven different lineages, or same-surname groups of households, each of which exclusively occupied a portion of the lake. The owners surnamed Huang occupied the southern part of the lake; the Pans and Xus occupied its eastern part; the Wangs and Mas occupied its northern part; and the Suns and Wangs occupied its western part. They divided the lake surface by turning part of it into a so-called preserved lake in which outsiders could fish only if they paid a fee (*Hanchuan xian zhi* 1992, 176).

Another very common method of sharing ownership involved taking turns being in charge of the water surface. The sections of the Yangzi River and the Ouchi River in the county of Shishou, for example, were "occupied" by the three lineages of He, Yan, and Chen.[14] Their agents collected fees from fishers in yearly turns (each boat that fished in these river sections had to pay three to five silver yuan per year). The lakes located in the *yuan* of Shishou were also occupied by powerful lineages, some of which took control by turn. On the first day of the seventh lunar month, which was known appropriately enough as "shifting lake day" (*zhuan hu ri*), control was handed over from one lineage to the next lineage in line. Lake Song in Shishou was even divided into eighty shares owned by four large lineages (*Shishou xian zhi* 1990, 207).

Like land, bodies of water could be traded and inherited. During the reign of the Yongzheng Emperor (1723-35), Wang Wenzuo's father, a resident of

Gong'an County, bought 130 *mu* of lake land and 100 *mu* or so of lake surface from Liu Tianpei's lineage in Jiangling County. In a trivial clash in 1744, Wang Wenzuo's son accidentally killed one young Liu. This death led to a lawsuit, which wound its way up to the Board of Punishments (Zhongguo diyi 1982, 720). This case reveals not only that the ownership of water surface was inheritable but also another, more important, piece of information: in the contract, the lake land and lake water were discussed separately, indicating that ownership of the two was clearly distinguished.

During the dry season, lake land and lake water were clearly separated and readily distinguishable, thus there should have been no dispute over ownership. But once the lake water level rose, the issue became complicated. While the level of the lakes of the Jianghan Plain rose and fell every year, the extent of the rise varied from year to year. If the ownership of the lake water and the nearby lake land was vested in two different parties, and the balance of power between them was uneven, the owner of the lake water (assuming he was the most powerful) could forcibly occupy the contiguous lake land. If the balance of power between the two owners was even, or if the weaker party did not easily give up, the rise of the lake water level could definitely spark a dispute.[15]

One such dispute occurred when the lake water reached its highest level and the owner of the lake water (by custom, "the lake" was defined by its water level in the dry season) tried to infringe on the ownership of lake land by picking lotus seeds and digging out lotus roots. By the same token, the owner of lake land tried to infringe on the ownership of lake water by catching fish and shrimps. Both parties hoped for petty gain at the expense of the other.[16]

In order to deal with this kind of dispute, the local customs of Hanyang clearly held that the ownership of lake land and lake water was separable. Even after the water rose, the owner of the lake land still held that ownership and had the right to harvest his lotus; the owner of the lake water still held that ownership and had the right to fish, no matter what the level of the water (i.e., fish were always the property of the lake owner, even when they were swimming in water that had risen and flooded lake land). And these kinds of rights were supposed to be clearly recorded in contracts. According to surveys made in the early Republic, this custom was found not only in Hanyang but also in almost all other counties of Hubei (*Minshi xiguan* 2000, 335).

This custom again shows the difference between the ownership of a body of water and the ownership of a piece of land. Sometimes cultivated land was subject to double ownership: one party owned the topsoil and another the subsoil (a common custom in the Yangzi delta but rarely seen in the Jianghan Plain). At first glance, this system seems very similar to the ownership of lake land and the ownership of lake water when the high-water level is reached, but in fact they are quite different. The owner of the topsoil owned the usufruct and was responsible for paying rent to the owner of the subsoil. The owner of the subsoil received the rent and paid the taxes. The two ownerships usually did not overlap, and to physically separate the topsoil and the subsoil of any plot of cultivated land was of course impossible. For their part, the owners of lake land and lake water had, simultaneously, both the right of usage and the right of ownership, and, of course, the lake land and lake water were clearly separable.

In the Republic, the surface water of the Jianghan Plain was generally privately owned, though who – large lake tyrants, small owners, or lineages – owned how much remains unclear. The owners were usually landlords and lineage heads. Relatively large lakes were often shared by several owners, who either separated the water surface among themselves or took control of it in yearly turns. The ownership of lake land and lake water, according to local custom, belonged to different parties. In all these respects, the ownership of surface water differed from the ownership of land.

Relations of Production on Water

Since water surfaces in the Jianghan Plain were privately owned, fishers had to pay owners fees for the use of water, just as tenants paid landlords rent for the use of land. However, unlike tenants, who could delay paying rent and reduce its amount in various ways, fishers seemingly lacked such power. According to the Qing gazetteers, two surveys of Honghu, in 1933 and 1947, respectively, and many post-1949 surveys, fishers in the Jianghan Plain in the late Qing and the Republic had to pay many fees and charges.

First, there was a "lake fee" or a "water fee,"[17] payment of which gained one permission to enter the lake. In Honghu, fishers first had to give some gifts to lake owners, and then had to pay 20 to 40 percent – usually 30 percent – of their catch as a "water fee" (*Honghu xian zhi* 1992, 163). The lake fee was 20 percent of the catch in Jianli (*Jianli xian zhi* 1959, 93). In Lake Diaocha in Hanchuan, fishers not surnamed Huang had to pay three to five silver yuan per boat per season in order to get permission to fish in the waters owned by the Huangs (*Hanchuan xian zhi* 1992, 176).

Second, there was the lake rent, payable at a rate that varied from area to area. In Hanyang, it was 4:6 or 3:7 (i.e., the lake owner got 60 or 70 percent of the catch) (*Hanyang xian zhi chugao* 1960, 32-33). It was usually 4:6 in Honghu, but it also could be as low as 7:3 or as high as 3:7. Most of the lakes in these examples were so-called preserved lakes, or forbidden lakes, in which fishers could enter only if they agreed to share their catch (*Honghu xian zhi* 1992, 163).[18]

Third, there were assorted fees and surcharges. In Honghu, these included a *guan shui fei* (closed water fee) and a *guo shui fei* (fee for passing through water), which usually amounted to 2 to 5 percent of the yearly catch (*Honghu xian zhi* 1992, 163). In Jianli, these fees included *yu er chu shui qian* (money for taking fish from the water), which amounted to 10 percent of the catch, and *yin gen qian* (interest on a loan), which amounted to 20 percent of the catch; and *guo shui piao* (ticket for passing across the water) (*Jianli xian zhi* 1959, 93). The fishing people of Xiaogan had to pay four *dan* of the catch per household (each boat was considered one "household") per year as the fee for fishing. If anyone entered the lake to fish without paying this fee, his boat and gear would be confiscated. And – after asking a member of the local gentry to intercede on his behalf – he had to offer a dinner and pay a fine as well as a fishing "tax" to the lake owner in order to get his boat and gear back (*Xiaogan shi zhi* 1992, 129). In addition to lake fees, the fishers of Qianjiang also had to pay numerous surcharges such as *piao er qian* (gourd money), *guo shui qian* (money for passing through the water), *gan zi fei* (fee for bamboo poles), and *kao po fei* (mooring fee) (*Qianjiang xian zhi* 1990, 329).

Fourth, in some areas fishers had to provide free labour. In Honghu, for instance, they had to render corveé labour to the lake owners (*Honghu xian zhi* 1992, 163). The fishers of Hanyang had to carry the sedan chairs and row the boats of lake owners. In addition, during the Spring Festival and other festivals they had to offer a meal to the lake owners or present them with gifts such as chickens, ducks, fish, and pork. Whenever a fishing family had a life-cycle event, such as a wedding or a funeral, it had to invite lake owners as the most honoured guests in order to ensure the right to fish the following year. Since lake owners were usually landlords and many part-time fishers may have been their tenants, in some places the latter were required to watch over lotus plants and row their boats for the landlords/lake owners (*Hanyang xian zhi chugao* 1960, 33-35; Zhongguo diyi 1982, 719).

Fifth, fish dealers and/or fishing shops charged a brokerage fee. The fishers of Honghu could sell their catch only to fishing shops run by the lake owners. These shops, weighing the fish with a large steelyard, took 8 percent of the catch as a brokerage fee (*Honghu xian zhi* 1992, 163). This fee was considerably higher in other places: 20 percent in Zhijiang (*Zhijiang xian zhi* 1990, 155), 25 percent in Jianli (*Jianli xian zhi* 1959, 93), and 30 percent in Xiaogan (*Xiaogan shi zhi* 1992, 129). It was said that the lake tyrants of Jianli used extremely large doctored steelyards to weigh fishers' catch (*Jianli xian zhi*

1994, 184). In Hanchuan, the large fishing tyrants surnamed Huang assigned the best fishing areas, ports, and large gear to fishers with the same surname. Fishers with other surnames had to pay lake fees in advance and agree to sell their catch to the assigned fishing shops if they wanted to fish in these areas (*Hanchuan xian zhi* 1992, 176).[19] But some Republican sources also indicate that, if their catch was small, fishers usually sold their fish directly on the market, and some fishers sold all of their catch this way (Zeng 1984, 2: 264, 273).

In addition to all these various fees and surcharges, which were paid to lake owners, fishers had to pay fishing taxes and fishing tribute to the government. In the Ming dynasty, Hubei once had the largest number of river-tax stations in the country. Many of those stations still existed in the Qing. In Mianyang, for example, there were eleven such stations that specialized in collecting river/lake taxes (*Mianyang xian zhi* 1989, 123). The lake tax and fishing tax collected from thirty-four lakes in Wuchang in the period between 1862 and 1874 was 3,528 taels (*Wuchang xian zhi* 1989, 263). In the Han River valley in the Qing, the counties of Tianmen, Zhongxiang, Qianjiang, Yingcheng, and Xiaogan, along with the county of Jiangling in the Yangzi River valley, had to pay a special surcharge called *ma tie yin* ("coarse iron money"), which was to fund cosmetics for the imperial palace maids and the amount of which varied from county to county.[20] This surcharge was usually small, but sometimes it could be exorbitant. For example, in Xiaogan, the assigned amount was one hundred taels for the whole county, but the real charge was much higher than this. And, ridiculously, this surcharge continued into the Republic, after the imperial system – and its palace maids – were no more (*Xiaogan shi zhi* 1992, 125, 129).

In the Republic, some county governments ordered that fishing boats be registered for taxation. For example, the tax was two to three silver yuan per boat per year in Hanchuan, and an additional two silver yuan per person for fishing boats that came from other counties (*Hanchuan xian zhi* 1992, 176). In Zhijiang, the county government issued annual licences to fishing households, one licence per boat; the fishing taxes and the licensing fee were collected at the same time (*Zhijiang xian zhi* 1990, 155). So the fishing people of Hanyang said: "Once the fresh fish are taken from the water they feed three parties: the government, the fishing shops, and the lake tyrants" (*xianyu chushui yang sanjia: guanfu, yuhang he huba*) (*Hanyang xian zhi* 1989, 185). If this is true, it was the fishers who were directly responsible for the fishing tax – something that would have differentiated this system from that of land ownership, according to which land owners were directly responsible for the land tax.

Although fishing people had to pay part of their catch to lake owners, just as tenants paid part of their harvests to landlords, not every single fisher had to pay all the fees and charges just discussed. It is unclear who – full-time fishers and/or part-time fishers – had to pay which kinds of fees and charges. Nonetheless, it is clear that, whether one was a full-time or a part-time fisher, one had to pay one or more of these charges. One source indicates that, before 1949, the fishing people of Mianyang had to pay nine kinds of "fishing taxes," though it is unclear what these were (*Hubei sheng zhi nongye* II 1999, 194). Because water surfaces were privately owned, it is most likely that no distinction was made between full-time fishers and part-time fishers when it came to paying fees and surcharges to use private waters. In any case, some fishers, particularly full-time fishers, may have had to hand over most of their catch. Thus, there was clear class stratification among the residents of lake areas, just as there was in ordinary rural society. After the Land Reform in the early 1950s, the CCP launched the so-called "democratic reform of the water" *(shuishang minzhu gaige)* to determine the class status of fishing people. In Jianli, for example, the "pure" *(chun,* full) fishers and "half" *(ban)* fishers were divided according to class status: poor fishers, middle fishers, rich fishers, and lake owners (Table 20a).

The proportion of lake owners and rich fishers to the fishing households as a whole in Jianli was similar to the proportion of landlords and rich peasants to all rural households. The distribution of each class was similar too: the richest, or highest status, comprised the fewest households, and the poorest comprised the most. The only slight difference between fishers and peasants is that the percentage of poor fishers among all the fishing households was higher than the percentage of poor peasants among all the rural households (see Chapter 5).

But there are no figures on hired fishers that can be compared to those that were gathered for hired labourers. As we know, hired labourers were those who had little or no means of production (particularly arable land) and had to hire themselves out in order to survive. If we take only the ownership of the means of production into account, then the majority of the fishing people would have fallen into the category of hired fishers as they did not own the basic means of production (i.e., a body of water). But they did own their own boats and (presumably) fishing gear, so in that regard they were more like tenants who had their own implements but who rented land than they were like hired labourers (who had nothing). Probably for these reasons, fishers (especially full-time fishers) were not exactly equivalent to peasants, and this may explain why there was no category or class known as "hired fishers."

Table 20a

The class status of the fishing people of Jianli		
Total number of fishing households....................................		4,516
Among them.....................................	Pure	408
	Half	4,108
Status (household)...............................	Poor fishers	2,552
	Middle fishers	1,792
	Rich fishers	154
	Lake owners	18
Among them: large fishing merchants (households)		25

Table 20b

The labour force structure of fishing households in Jianli County		
Total number of fishing households....................................		4,516
Population.......................................	Sub-total	23,809
	Male	13,041
	Female	10,768
Labour force.....................................	Subtotal	12,075
	Whole labourer	6,377
	Half labourer	5,698
Fishing boats...		4,714

Source: Jianli xian zhi (1959, 95). The criteria for defining class status remain unclear.

As for part-time fishers, they were peasants, and thus were typically divided into rich, middle, and poor. Whatever category they belonged to, however, they all owned a fishing boat, whether big or small, in good condition or bad. In fact, in Honghu in the early 1950s, fishing boats were listed as one of the "six major agricultural implements" (*Honghu xian zhi* 1992, 98). Large and expensive fishing gear, on the other hand, was mostly owned by lake owners. Just as some landlords farmed, some fishing tyrants or lake owners may have fished. But the available data do not indicate that in the Jianghan Plain there were lake owners or large fishing merchants who provided fishing boats and hired fishers, as was done in the coastal fishing areas.[21]

Life of the Fishing People

One of the basic characteristics of the relations of production on water – that is, the lack of the essential means of production – implies that fishing people had a harder life than did peasants, though the latter certainly did not live well. The following discussion examines some basic aspects of the life of fishing people (particularly those who engaged in fishing full-time) in an unstable environment.

First, let us examine the housing of fishing people. Most full-time fishing people lived on their boats (*Hubei sheng zhi nongye I* 1994, 17), even though the condition of their boats may have been very poor (*Hanchuan xian zhi* 1992, 662). Even if they had houses on the land, they were typically dilapidated, as in Jianli, where "the wind sweeps the floor, the moon serves as a lamp, and a half piece of reed mat covers the entrance" (*feng saodi, yue dian deng, banpian luwei yan jiamen*) (*Jianli xian zhi* 1959, 92). This description, taken from the 1959 gazetteer of Jianli, may have been an exaggeration prompted by the CCP's tendency to use an extreme example to typify the whole. Still, it may well have been at least partly true. Because fishing people usually lived on the margins of rivers and lakes, their houses were easily damaged by frequent floods. In Hanchuan, for example, the majority of the houses in lake areas were thatched shacks or straw sheds. Some dwellings were even made of wormwood, reed mats, and sorghum straw (*Hanchuan xian zhi* 1992, 662). Some fishing people did not even have shacks of this quality but, rather, lived in primitive hovels (*Honghu xian zhi* 1992, 536). On the other hand, fishing people (particularly those who fished full-time) could not afford brick- and tile-roofed houses; brick houses in fact did not withstand water as well as do thatched cottages.

Full-time fishing people lived on their fishing boats year in and year out and drifted over the water, following the shoals of fish (*Mianyang xian zhi* 1989, 121). Part-time fishers may also have lived on their boats for long periods. Exactly how long depended on how important fishing was to their household income. In Yunmeng in 1938, a Republican survey shows that, annually, part-time fishers spent about one hundred days on farming and two hundred days on fishing (*Yunmeng xian zhi* 1994, 206). Obviously, almost all the income of full-time fishers and part of that of part-time fishers depended on their catch. Again, unlike many peasant households, which were on the whole self-sufficient, in most cases fishing people, particularly those who fished full-time, could not directly consume all of their catch. They had to sell at least some of it – either as fresh fish consumed locally or as dried fish sent to neighbouring areas or provinces (Zeng 1984, 2: 258)[22] – to buy part or most of their daily necessities. It is not clear what species they caught; however, according to Republican reports, the popular species in Hubei include carp, mackerel, bream, and Chinese perch (Zeng 1984, 2: 255).

Basically, fishing people relied on manual gear. A 1964 survey indicates that, in Honghu, there were fifty-five kinds of traditional fishing gear, including a variety of nets, hooks, and spears. Most fishing was carried out by two people in one boat, although some needed no boat and others needed multiple boats (*Honghu xian zhi* 1992, 151-52). Understandably, the catch of each fishing boat varied widely according to whether it was operated full-time or part-time, the size of the boat, the quality of different fishing spots, the seasons, and so on. According to a Republican survey of Zhijiang, each fishing boat needed two people to operate it. The so-called *zeng* fishing boats *(zeng chuan)* could carry ten to twenty tons and could haul in a yearly catch of five to six thousand *jin*. The smaller net-boat *(wang chuan)* could catch about two to three thousand *jin* per year (*Zhijiang xian zhi* 1990, 155). In this case, we do not know how much of the catch had to be paid out as fees and in the form of other charges.

In Honghu, however, a 1932 investigation of ten full-time fishing households in Zhangjiafang village found that each fishing boat could catch twenty-four thousand *jin* of mixed fish per year. About 70 percent of the catch – namely, 16,800 *jin* – was paid to the lake owners as their assigned share (i.e., as lake rent), and another 2,520 *jin* was paid as a "lake patrolling fee," leaving only 4,680 *jin*. But if we take into account other costs, such as the depreciation of the fishing boat and gear and other surcharges, then almost nothing is left. In the end, a fishing family with three members was so poor that the adults were shabbily dressed and the child went naked in summer, and both adults and child went barefoot all year round (*Honghu xian zhi* 1992, 163-64). Thus, in many areas, the local people referred to fishing people as "fishing beggars" *(yu huazi)* (*Jingzhou diqu zhi* 1996, 183; *Wuchang xian zhi* 1989, 263).[23]

Moreover, fishers, no matter whether they were full-time or part-time, constantly faced the threat of snail fever (schistosomiasis). Since they worked on water for a long time every year, and the lakes of the Jianghan Plain were heavily infested with snail fever, they ran a relatively great risk of being infected. Once infected, few of them could afford even a minimal amount of medicine; consequently, innumerable fishers died (*Shishou xian zhi* 1990, 205). Many villages were completely wiped out by this terrible disease in the late Qing and the Republic (*Mianyang xian zhi* 1989, 580). Not surprisingly, the people who lived along the lower reaches of the Han River said that they lived with "three clubs hanging over their heads: evil tyrants, water calamities, and the big belly disease [snail fever]" *(huqu renmin toushang santiao gun: e'ba, shuizai, daduzi bing)* (*Hubei sheng zhi shuili* 1995, 350). Of these three "clubs," only one – "evil tyrants" – may be seen as ideologically loaded. Water calamities and snail fever, no matter from which ideological perspective one views them, were truly disastrous. The "three clubs" metaphor enables us to imagine just how poor were the lives of fishing people in an unstable environment.

Generally speaking, the fishers of the Jianghan Plain did seem to lead a poorer life than the peasants. This has been cited as one of the major reasons so many fishing people in the Honghu area joined the communist revolutionary movement in the 1920s and 1930s (*Honghu xian shuichan zhi* 1986, 188-89). In fact, even the government of Hubei acknowledged the contribution of the fishing people, particularly those who worked full-time, to the victory of the Communist Revolution in 1949 (SZ 68-2-234).

If before 1949 the fishing people of the Jianghan Plain generally lived at or below the standard of poor peasants (*Hubei sheng zhi nongye I* 1994, 43-44),[24] why is it that they did not shun fishing altogether? The answer lies in the fact that the large acreage under water provided opportunities for income aside from farming. Furthermore, some households turned to fishing out of desperation. For instance, some households simply could not cope with the frequent water calamities and heavy dike fees. Mostly, however, the answer lies in the increasing population pressure in the Jianghan Plain.

Frequent water calamities forced the local peasants to turn from farming to fishing, and they did this in two different ways. First, they turned their farmland into lakes. In the mid-Qing, the residents around Lake Diaocha, for example, were forced to turn their *yuan* into a lake because it was so frequently submerged. Thus, they effectively transformed themselves into fishing people. Second, after serious floods, some peasants temporarily took up fishing. After the 1931 flood in Songzi, a county on the periphery of the Jianghan Plain, full-time fishers increased from three hundred households to thousands (*Songzi xian zhi* 1982 [1937], 232). Even in 1954, after the record-breaking floods of that year, the number of fishing households increased by more than thirty thousand in Hanchuan and by more than eleven thousand in Qianjiang (*Hanchuan xian zhi* 1992, 176; *Qianjiang xian zhi* 1990, 330).

The heavy dike fees also drove some local peasants into fishing. In the counties located on the south side of the Yangzi River, for example, in the mid-nineteenth century many residents fled their homes and turned to living on the water because they could not afford to pay the dike fee (Song 1954, 59). However, population pressure was the most common reason for peasants to turn to fishing. Since some of them lacked enough land to feed themselves, they had to engage in fishing in the off-season in order to make ends meet. In Hanyang in the Ming dynasty, for example, each year many residents switched between farming and fishing, depending on the season: "[They] farm in spring and summer and fish in autumn and winter ... When the spring water rises, the peasants move to the land to cultivate and reclaim it, and after the water subsides in autumn-winter they move to the lake to fish in order to support themselves." In the early Qing, however, they had no land to return to when spring water came, and some of them had to collect aquatic plants in order to survive (*Hanyang fu zhi* 1747, 16: 4a). The same situation obtained in Qianjiang: "[This county] definitely has no spare land due to the high density of its population and the scarcity of arable land. [The residents of] areas that have been waterlogged a long time failed at farming and [had to] make a living by fishing" (*Qianjiang xian zhi* 1879, 8: 1b). In the Republic in Mianyang, many full-time fishing people lacked arable land and made a living by fishing; some part-time fishers either consumed their catch or sold it (*Mianyang xian zhi* 1989, 121). Some peasants of Hanchuan in the late Qing only owned a little infertile farmland, thus, after the autumn harvest, whole families went out to the rivers and lakes to fish and returned to farm the following spring (*Hanchuan xian zhi* 1873, 6: 15a). During times of war in the Republic, the income some peasants received from their small plots of land could only support them for four months (*Hanchuan xian zhi* 1992, 659). Consequently, after the autumn harvest, entire families went to neighbouring counties to "pick lotus, fish, collect clams, and hunt for tortoises for subsistence, and still returned home to farm in the spring ploughing"(*Hanchuan xian jian zhi* 1959, 32). In both cases, the peasants considered this behaviour to be usual. In fact, in lake areas of Hubei in the Republic, many people became fishers for the simple reason that they lost their land (SZ 68-2-234). Records of the Land Reform show that many fishers had no land at all, while others rented very limited land (SZ 37-1-280; SZ 37-1-332).

Conclusion

Fisheries played an important role in the rural economy in the Jianghan Plain in the late Qing and the Republic. That is the basis of the phrase "a land of fish and rice": such a combination was directly related to local environmental conditions.

The rivers and lakes of the Jianghan Plain accounted for one-fifth or so of its entire territory. For roughly every three *mu* of cultivated land there were two *mu* of surface water. In this water-rich environment, about 10 percent of the rural households took up fishing as their major non-farming productive activity.

The high density of rivers and lakes and the large number of full-time and part-time fishing households in the Jianghan Plain determined the importance of fisheries in the local economy. For the rural households that lived along rivers and close to lakes, fishing was more important than the domestic cotton textile industry. Only in dryland areas were cotton spinning and weaving the major non-farming productive activities of rural households. Since in the Jianghan Plain the areas along the rivers and close to lakes were more extensive than dryland areas, a combination of farming, weaving, and fishing became a distinguishing characteristic of the structure of the rural economy. This is different from the combination of farming and weaving typical of the rural economy of traditional China as a whole.

Bodies of lake water in the Jianghan Plain were generally privately owned, and the owners were usually landlords and/or lineages. The ownership of lake land and the ownership of lake water were separated according to local custom, which differed from the dual ownership of farmland (which allowed for separate ownership of topsoil and subsoil as the two are physically inseparable).

With water being privately owned, the majority of the fishing people lacked the essential means of production (i.e., a body of water). Full-time fishing people had an even lower standard of living than poor peasants and hired labourers, who may have owned one or several plots of arable land. Whether households engaged in fishing full-time or part-time, they tended to be locked in poverty (as a result of various fees and charges for access to water) and were condemned to ill health by dint of working on water plagued with diseases such as snail fever. Jianghan's frequent water calamities, occasionally large dike fees, and population pressure combined to transform some peasants into fishing people.

7 A Water-Rich Society: Socio-Economic Life in a Marshy Kingdom

In the "marshy kingdom" that was the Jianghan Plain, the abundance of rivers and lakes, the networked waterways, the never-ending dike building and *yuan* enclosure, the frequent water calamities, and, subsequently, the changing environment all shaped the rural economy and society. The many lakes and rivers in the plain created the means to augment daily subsistence and even to make life possible in times of famine. But the changeable environment caused unstable harvests and, in general, was not conducive to economic growth. Although this is not the whole picture, it reminds us once again that, when discussing agrarian history, we must consider the ways in which the environment changed. If we do not do so, we will not be able to understand rural society and its vicissitudes.

In their fight to control the water and reclaim land, the people of the Jianghan Plain constantly adapted and changed their environment, and the changed environment, in turn, reshaped their behaviour, which can be seen not only in dike building and crop choice but also in their daily life (e.g., their choices in diet, housing styles, the distribution of villages, the gendered division of labour, means of local transportation) and in the socio-economic and political features of local society (e.g., a litigious and belligerent tradition and the popularity of *yuan*-centred rural communities).

Impact of Water Calamities on the Local Society and Economy

Loss of Lives and Property and the Spread of Diseases
In this water-rich plain, the local people frequently suffered from water calamites that destroyed *yuan;* flooded villages, towns, and even cities; swamped hundreds of thousands of *mu* of farmland; and claimed lives. In some cases, hundreds of rivulets and lakes topped and turned the Jianghan Plain into an inland sea. The inundation of 1788, for example, broke the Wancheng dike in twenty-two places. The resultant floodwater poured into Jingzhou City through two of its gates and destroyed almost all the houses inside, ten thousand or so soldiers and civilians died (*Jingjiang dadi zhi* 1989, 62). In 1870,

all of Baili islet in Zhijiang was flooded and the northern part of Jingzhou was inundated. The flood of 1931 was so huge that the Jianghan Plain was turned into an inland sea and linked up with Lake Dongting. Ninety percent of its dikes were broken or topped, thousands of houses were destroyed, about 5 million *mu* of farmland was inundated, 3 million people became refugees, and the entire city of Wuhan (particularly Hankou) was engulfed in water. In 1935, another huge flood attacked the Jianghan Plain: almost all the *yuan* in the middle Han River valley were inundated, killing ninety-six thousand people (*Jiangling difang zhi* 1984, 15; *Hubei sheng zhi shuili* 1995, 215-19).

In the aftermath of a severe flood would come epidemics of malaria, cholera, and particularly schistosomiasis (snail fever). In the early nineteenth century, many residents living along the south bank of the Jing River fled, driven out by frequent floods and the ensuing poverty and epidemic diseases (Wang 1832, 1: 16a). Often people lost their lives due to the hunger and diseases that immediately followed an inundation. In 1931, in Mianyang alone, 180,000 people died because of the inundation of that year (through drowning, starvation, and illness) (*Honghu xian zhi* 1963, 32). In the first half of the twentieth century, records reveal that, in Jingzhou, snail fever alone caused the disappearance of 1,794 small villages, the destruction of 23,000 or so families, and the death of at least 104,276 people (*Jingzhou diqu zhi* 1996, 2).

In the Jianghan Plain, the water sat in low-lying locations for a protracted time in the summer and autumn and did not dry up until winter or spring. This kind of wet-dry switch provided favourable conditions for the breeding of oncomelania, a kind of freshwater snail, which is the intermediate host of schistosome (*Hubei sheng zhi shuili* 1995, 342). The earliest victim of snail fever in the Jianghan area was found in a Western Han (206 BCE-24CE) tomb (Wu Zhongbi 1982). According to recent research, over the past two centuries, the spread of snail fever in the Yangzi River valley, particularly the mid-Yangzi where the Jianghan Plain is located, has been directly and closely related to floodwaters (Jiang and Gong 1998). Many state-owned farms in the post-1949 Jianghan Plain were established on wasteland that had been destroyed by floods or abandoned due to snail fever (*Wusan nongchang zhi* 1987, 384).

Growth or Decline of Farmland and Fluctuations in Agricultural Productivity

Because the Yangzi River follows a meandering course through the Jianghan Plain, rushing currents frequently scoured out one side of the river bank and caused its collapse. The collapsed earth was soon deposited on the other side of the same section of the river. An early Qing (1653) survey found that, in

Shishou, 326,300 *mu* of land from three *yuan* in this county had collapsed into the Yangzi River (*Shishou xian zhi* 1866, 3: 6a). In 1764, it was reported that some land from twelve islets in Jiayu County had been swept into the Yangzi River. At the same time, across the river in Mianyang, about 7,120 *mu* of islet land had been gradually created; the registered land on this islet continued to grow and reached 10,330 *mu* in 1809 (Shuili dianlibu 1991, 607). In the middle of the nineteenth century, an Englishman who travelled along the Yangzi River in Hubei found that water constantly worked on the banks, causing the collapse of the alluvial soil, and that the annual high water increasingly brought fresh deposits, "thereby steadily raising the level of the land between the river and the embankments" (Blakiston 1862, 286n). Thus, in Shishou, although its administrative boundaries did not change in the late Qing and the Republic, the amount of registered land fluctuated as a result of the contingent collapse and/or creation of islet land, frequent water calamities, and swings of the course of the Yangzi River (*Shishou xian zhi* 1990, 159). According to Qing regulations, the islet land in Jiangling, Gong'an, Shishou, and Jianli of Jingzhou Prefecture had to be re-measured every five years because of the loss of old land and the silting of new land (*Jingzhou fu zhi* 1880, 14: 5ab).

The same pattern of loss of land and deposition of land occurred along the Han River. An early Qing gazetteer mentions that, because Qianjiang County "is located on the lower reaches of the Han River, its terrain is low and there are frequent collapses and silting. Thus people have no permanent property that lasts for more than a hundred years ... Whenever the water rises and the dike breaks, high places and low places are transformed, one into the other. The so-called domain of our county [in fact] cannot be verified [i.e., its boundaries cannot be identified]" (*Qianjiang xian zhi* 1879, 3: 29a). In Hanyang, residents were tired of re-measuring their land every five years because of frequent loss of land and silting of river banks (*Hanyang xian zhi* 1889, 1: 17b).

Although the Jianghan people constantly built dikes to protect themselves, they nonetheless suffered from frequent water calamities, particularly in the lower reaches of the Han River. The frequent inundations destroyed some farmland while the silt carried by floodwater was deposited on low-lying land and hence created new farmland and/or enriched previously infertile land. Under these conditions, some former fertile lands became lakes, and some former lakes became fertile land. Thus incessant water calamities caused frequent increases or decreases in the amount of available farmland and affected the productivity of the land in general. For example, a late Qing Mianyang gazetteer comments: "Formerly [some lands in this department] were upper grade land but now [they] are lakes and wasteland, while some former wasteland is now fertile land" (*Mianyang zhou zhi* 1894, 4: 39b).

In many cases, neither the size of any particular *yuan* nor its structure was stable. One *yuan* or a part of it could be completely destroyed by heavy flooding, while, at the same time, some newly reclaimable land would be formed by deposited sludge after a flood or the deposition of river beach land. As one county gazetteer records in early Qing Qianjiang: "30 *mu* of paddy fields in Honghua *yuan* ... and 33 *mu* of paddy fields in Bianjiang *yuan* ... now have collapsed into the river" (*Qianjiang xian zhi* 1694, 5: 29a).

This process also caused a change in the distribution of lands in a certain area. The acreage of paddy fields in Qianjiang in the early seventeenth century, for example, was nine times that of dry land (*Anlu fu zhi* 1669, 5: 29ab). In the Republic, however, the acreage of dry land in this county was 1.67 times that of paddy fields (*Qianjiang xian zhi* 1990, 221). This demonstrates a dramatic change of the landscape in Qianjiang County within three centuries.

Such changes and water calamities naturally resulted in uncertain harvests. The yield of grain crops in the Jianghan Plain was relatively high, but many gazetteers record that the yield and, subsequently, the yearly output were unstable. In Xiaogan in the early Qing, for example: "If the dike holds then the land is covered with green [i.e., vegetation or crops]; if the dike breaks then it turns into water," while "whenever there is a good year, the harvest is twice [the normal harvest]" (*Hubei tong zhi* 1921, 1141). In Jianli in the Qing: "Grain is usually stored outside in good years ... it is really a good place [to live]. Once [it] has been flooded, however, houses would drift away, or even some cadavers would float on the water" (*Jianli xian zhi* 1872, 8: 1a). Since the land was so fertile and the harvest so huge in good years, the local peasants found themselves with so much grain that they had nowhere to store it except outdoors. In the end, if there was no flooding, the harvest of this county was twice that of neighbouring counties: "If there is one good year within ten years, it would be a good place [to live]" (*Jianli xian zhi* 1872, 4: 1a, 11: 11a). A popular saying in the Han River valley is as follows: "In Shahu and Mianyang, nine out of ten years are lean years; if there is a good year, the dogs will refuse to eat [polished] glutinous rice gruel" (*Shahu Mianyang zhou, shinian jiu bushou; ruoshi yinian shou, gou dou buchi nuomizhou*). This does not mean that there were always nine years of water calamities each decade but simply that water calamities were very frequent and that yields and output were relatively high but unstable (depending on the presence or absence of water calamities) (see Appendix). For this reason, famine-relief crops and wild edible plants became very important.

Cultivation of Famine-Relief Crops and Role of Aquatic Products

Because of their water-rich surroundings and the increasing water calamities in the Qing and the Republic, the Jianghan peasants not only carefully chose crops and cropping systems that suited their precarious circumstances but also cultivated famine-relief crops and grew or collected aquatic products to relieve hunger. In Chapter 4 we see that they chose crops such as early-season rice and *mai,* which could be harvested before the coming of the seasonal high water; deepwater rice, which can grow in deep water; and Chinese sorghum, which can survive days of submersion. They also applied such cropping systems as the dominant single cropping pattern of middle-season rice and the supplementary "double-insurance" cropping pattern that could accommodate their unstable environment. Here I discuss their cultivation of famine-relief crops and the growth or collection of locally rich aquatic products.

Cultivation of Famine-Relief Crops

After floodwater had receded, the Jianghan peasants usually replanted various crops, such as buckwheat, beans, millet, and even vegetables (the specific varieties depended on the location and the season) as famine-relief crops. For example, in 1777, according to archival records:

> In lakeside *yuan* in Jingzhou ... because they are very low-lying, late rice is only planted in the early and middle of the sixth lunar month after the rainy season. Because the water level of the autumn high water gradually rises again in the Han River and floods over the dikes, some low-lying land inside *yuan* are again inundated. [The locals] quickly drain the water and replant miscellaneous grain crops. (Shuili dianlibu 1991, 462)

It is unclear what these "miscellaneous grain crops" were, but buckwheat was mentioned in many other records. Although as a food buckwheat is of poor quality and its yield is low,[1] it can be grown on almost any land and in almost any season; it therefore was often used to replant lake land after a late autumn flood. In 1747 in Mianyang, Qianjiang, and Tianmen, for example, once the floodwater had receded, the local people "quickly replanted buckwheat, beans and vegetables. [In this way they] could still look forward to a harvest, and avoid a famine" (Shuili dianlibu 1991, 282). A 1917 survey shows that at least five counties in the Jianghan area (Xiakou [Hankou], Jingshan, Qianjiang, Tianmen, and Songzi) had more than twenty thousand *mu* of farmland (196,548 *mu,* or 9.2 percent of its sown area in Jingshan) under buckwheat in that year (Hu 1920, 1: 27, 63, 65, 67, 104). Buckwheat was frequently grown in Qianjiang after floods due to its short growing period (about seventy-two days). In that county in the Republican era, because of floods, about forty to fifty thousand *mu* were devoted to buckwheat each year. The acreage devoted to buckwheat was gradually reduced after 1954, and by 1985 it was only grown in a few scattered fields (*Qianjiang xian zhi* 1990, 233). In Zhijiang, the local people also traditionally resowed buckwheat in lake fields after floods receded, but it was no longer grown in Zhijiang in the 1980s (*Zhijiang xian zhi* 1990, 122).

As for millet *(ji)*, since it "resists waterlogging, after the water has dissipated, peasants grow it on newly silted land without any preparation of the land. [This] saves labour. Since [millet] ripens early, [it is] a kind of famine relief crop" (*Hanchuan tuji zhengshi* 1895, 4: 38a). A kind of wild millet, locally called *huji* (lake millet), was also grown in many places to cope with water calamities (*Jingzhou fu zhi* 1880, 6: 1b). Similarly, vegetables were replanted not because they were nutritious but because they could prevent hunger. A 1795 memorial regarding the counties of Jingmen, Tianmen, Qianjiang, and Mianyang describes the locals as "also try[ing] to drain low-lying places and replanting miscellaneous grain and radishes, all of which can be used to fill the stomach" (Shuili dianlibu 1991, 519).

Raising dryland "miscellaneous grain" as hunger relief crops was common in the Jianghan Plain. In Hanchuan in 1920, for example, miscellaneous grain (excluding wheat and barley) accounted for 51.2 percent of the acreage under food grains. Since most of these grains ripen quickly, they were grown for hunger relief (*Hanchuan xian zhi* 1992, 126-27).

Growth and/or Collection of Aquatic Products as Substitute Foods

When faced with the likelihood of famine, the Jianghan peasants took advantage of the great number of rivers and lakes dotted all over the Jianghan Plain by growing or collecting various aquatic plants, such as lotus *(lian)*, water chestnuts *(lingjiao)*, and wild rice *(gumi* or *jiaomi)*.[2] Some of these plants, such as *jiaomi*, were grown (or collected) during famine years as a substitute for rice. A late Qing gazetteer of Hanchuan, a county frequently hit by floods, contains a detailed record of such products:

> *Jiaomi* is a water food grain and grows in lakes and marshes ... Its seeds can be cooked as [dry] food or cooked as porridge. The local people collect it [and use it] as grain in famine years ... *Lingjiaocai* (water chestnuts) ... people collect ... in famine years; they dry it and then mix it with rice as food ... *Shuihe*, like *lingjiaocai*, which is mostly found in lakes and marshes in our county, grows with [the rise of] water ... In famine years people collect its stems and mix it

with rice powder to cook gruel to relieve hunger or to serve [by itself] as a dish. *Fanteng* has leaves similar to but smaller than those of spinach; it is a trailing plant ... and mostly grows on the borders of farmland. In famine years, people dig out its roots, boil and eat them; or they chop up the roots [to make them resemble] grains of rice. These are dried and stir-fried as a food to appease hunger. (*Hanchuan tuji zhengshi* 1895, 5: 20a-21a)

All of these plants, except for *fanteng*, are aquatic products. Residents of the Han River valley were not alone in eating *jiaomi*; the practice was also seen in the Yangzi River valley counties. In Jiangling, for instance, "*jiaobai* appears in the autumn; it is locally called *jiaogua*. [It] ripens in the autumn and forms *diaohu* seeds, called *jiaomi*, which are fragrant when cooked. It usually grows in lakes and marshes in low-lying areas" (*Jiangling xian zhi* 1794, 22: 16b). Because most Jianghan counties had similar physiographical conditions, their inhabitants also grew or collected *gumi/jiaomi*.[3]

Residents of Hanchuan continued this tradition in the Republic. Every year during the spring famine or when they suffered from flood or drought, the poor peasants would rely on wild vegetables, wild lotus, and water chestnuts to relieve hunger. They usually mixed non-staple food grains and vegetables with staple grains; some of them ate chaff and vegetables for half a year and ate grains for the other half. According to a 1937 yearbook, the poor peasants of Hanchuan mostly relied on side production and fishing. After the War of Resistance against Japan (1937-45), the harvests of these poor peasants could only support their families for four months. Therefore, after the autumn harvest, they would bring their families to neighbouring counties to "dig lotus roots, catch fish, and collect freshwater mussels." The following spring, they returned home to resume farming (*Hanchuan xian zhi* 1992, 659, 662).

This custom was widespread in other counties as well. Lake Lingjiao, in Jiangling, is rich in water chestnuts. In 1930, famine victims from the surrounding area (the source indicates that this encompassed one hundred square kilometres) came to the lake to collect water chestnuts to appease their hunger (*Lingjiaohu nongchang zhi* 1991, 86). In Yingcheng before 1949 residents also ate water chestnuts in famine years (*Yingcheng xian zhi* 1992, 203). In Qianjiang during the Republic, people suffered from frequent water calamities and had difficulty making a living. It was said that if it were not for aquatic products, they would have died long ago (*Qianjiang shuili zhi* 1997, 343). In Shishou in the late Qing and the Republic, lotus was grown in every lake and pond. Some of them were planted, but most grew wild. Rural residents ate lotus roots as a vegetable in good years but consumed them as a staple "grain" in famine years. They also ate wild water chestnuts (which were poorer in quality than lotus roots) as a non-staple food in good years but as a staple in famine years (*Shishou xian zhi* 1990, 203-4).

In Mianyang, one of the most frequently flooded administrative units in the area, before 1949 the peasants supplemented their staples (rice, millet, wheat, beans, sorghum, and buckwheat) with vegetables in normal years. In years with poor harvests or famine years, poor peasants mostly relied on fishing (fish, shrimp, and freshwater mussels) and gathering (water chestnuts, lotus roots, and wild vegetables). Some simply fled and turned to begging in order to survive (*Mianyang xian zhi* 1989, 591-92).

As foods these famine-relief crops are certainly inferior in quality to paddy rice and other regular crops, as the local people clearly understood. For example, buckwheat was widely grown in the Jianghan Plain and served as a hunger-relief crop. A late Qing Hanchuan gazetteer, however, records that a variety of buckwheat tastes bitter and that one should steam out its yellow juice before eating it. It was certainly a low-grade food but it could at least sustain life (*Hanchuan tuji zhengshi* 1895, 4: 41b). Another Hanchuan gazetteer even recognizes the utility of some normally undesirable crops, *baizi* (barnyard grass) and *shenzi*, when water calamities struck: "Among [the various types of] late rice, there is a variety called *baizi*, which is sown in the early autumn and ripens in the ninth lunar month. [Another is] similar to baizi, called shenzi, which is sown in the first or second lunar month, and ripens in the fifth lunar month. [This is] a kind of coarse food. People occasionally grow it after waterlogging, because it ripens early and requires little labour" (*Hanchuan xian zhi* 1873, 6: 18b).

Barnyard grass is a weed found in rice fields. It thrives even under bad conditions. In my own experience, *baizi* is coarse, tastes bad, and is hard to digest. Peasants knew these were low-quality crops and would make a miserable meal, but they apparently had no alternative. In Jiangling in 1960, some cadres who suffered from a food shortage collected baizi to supplement their rations (*Jiangling xian zhi* 1990, 28). In Yingcheng in the late Qing, *baizi, ji,* and *gumi* were widely planted in lake areas (*Yingcheng zhi* 1882, 1: 45a).

As for *jiaomi*, the governor general of Huguang reported in 1658 that, in the lower reaches of the Han River, because the water rises suddenly and washes away farmlands and houses, the local poor people had to eat *jiaomi.* He tried some himself and found that it was "utterly impossible to swallow" (Chen Zhenhan et al. 1989, 2: 646).

Regardless of their quality, it was due to these famine-relief crops and local aquatic products that the Jianghan peasants were better able to endure famine than were poor peasants in the North China Plain, where two successive years of drought could result in life-long poverty (Huang 1985, 299). In the 1930s,

Table 21

Yearly per capita consumption of food grain in selected counties in the 1930s

County	Total	Husked rice	Wheat	Barley	Beans	Millet	Sweet potato	Maize	Sorghum	Flour
Wuchang	413.00	310.00	42.00	27.00	9.00	2.00	20.00			3.00
Hanyang	392.00	257.00	45.00	43.00	18.00			18.00	11.00	
Yunmeng	312.80	217.00	35.90	33.60	11.60	12.60				2.10
Yingcheng	322.40	264.80	22.50	24.60	2.00	8.10				0.40
Jianli	347.00	240.00	21.00	22.00	29.00	29.00	1.00		5.00	
Total	1787.20	1288.80	166.40	150.20	69.60	51.70	21.00	18.00	16.00	5.50
Average	357.44	257.76	33.28	30.04	13.92	10.34	4.20	3.60	3.20	1.10
%		72.11	9.31	8.40	3.89	2.89	1.18	1.01	0.90	0.31

Note: Unit: shi jin. 1 shi jin = 500 grams or 1.1 pound.

Sources: Wuchang xian (1938, 44); Hanyang xian (1938, 29); Yunmeng xian (1938, 20); Yingcheng xian (1938, 29); Jianli xian (1938, 28).

the local peasants of the Lake Dongting Plain said that they could recover from one year's flood only after three good years (Peng 1977 [1938], 39353).

Water-Rich Surroundings and Daily Life of the Local People

Food and Diet

By cultivating a wide and diverse variety of crops and taking advantage of the abundance of wild plants and aquatic products, the Jianghan people, despite the frequent water calamities, attained near self-sufficiency in food production during the Qing and the Republic. At the level of individual peasant households, self-sufficiency in grains would have been even greater since peasants were adept at adjusting their diet to meet changing circumstances.

As stated earlier, rice accounted for two-thirds of the output of grain in the Jianghan Plain, with miscellaneous grains accounting for the remaining one-third (see Table 9). This proportion was reflected in the consumption patterns of the local people. According to a survey in the 1930s, in the Jianghan Plain husked rice accounted for more than 70 percent of the local people's daily consumption of grains, with miscellaneous grains accounting for the rest (Table 21).

Although Table 21 mentions nine kinds of "food grain crops" (actually, flour is not a crop, and "beans" is only a general classification), it is clear that husked rice, the primary food of the residents of the Jianghan Plain in the 1930s, accounted for 72.11 percent (i.e., 257.76 *jin*) of their yearly consumption, and miscellaneous grains accounted for the balance (i.e., 99.68 *jin*).

This, of course, is only a very rough estimate (under normal conditions), and the total is probably slightly high: since Wuchang was the capital of Hubei and Hanyang was close to it, and farmland in Jianli was predominantly devoted to rice paddies, the consumption level of food grain in Wuchang and Hanyang and the consumption level of husked rice in Jianli might have been higher than in other counties. Also, diet varied regionally, even within one county. Furthermore, it differed in different years, seasons, and families. In general, in these counties of the Jianghan Plain (as their gazetteers show), peasants of areas where paddy fields predominated relied more on rice, while peasants in areas dominated by dry land relied more on miscellaneous grains; the rich ate more rice, while the poor ate more miscellaneous grains; peasants ate more rice in a good year but more miscellaneous grains and vegetables in a lean year; and peasants ate three meals with rice per day during the busy season but two meals (one of rice and one of porridge) per day in the off-season (e.g., *Xiaogan shi zhi* 1992, 844; *Tianmen xian zhi* 1989, 844). Given this dietary structure, self-sufficiency in grains should have been even higher, though this by no means suggests that peasants had a comfortable standard of living – in fact, it was lower than that of their Yangzi delta counterparts. Still, despite suffering frequent water calamites in the Qing and the Republic, the people of the Jianghan Plain were quite capable of sustaining themselves insofar as grains were considered, and they were sophisticated with regard to adjusting their diet to a range of situations.

Housing and Distribution of Villages

The water-rich setting of the Jianghan Plain determined the local style of housing. The residents of lake areas usually built their houses on relatively high land. A Qing provincial official of Hubei reports: "My colleagues and I surveyed the counties of Anlu prefecture along the Han River, and found that the water rises every summer and autumn; that is normal. The local people know how to avoid [the water] and usually build their houses on high places, thus [they] seldom suffer from water calamities" (Shuili dianlibu 1991, 513).

Local gazetteers record many instances of this kind of environmental adaptation. For instance, in Tianmen in the Qing and in Mianyang in the Republic villages were usually located in elevated places (*Tianmen xian zhi* 1765, 1: 36a; *Mianyang chenchangqu xiangtu zhi* 1987, 269). These high places were called so-and-so *tai* (i.e., Majia tai, Zhoujia tai, etc.) or *taizi* in local dialect (*Jianghu nongchang zhi* 1988, 6; Lu and Han 2011). In some places, an entire (natural) village was situated on a *tai* or *taizi* (which are the same) (*Renmin dayuan nongchang zhi* 1988, 17). If there were no satisfactory high places, the local people sometimes built high platforms on which to build their houses. In Hanchuan, for example: "The people's households usually are built on *duntai. Dun[tai]* is [a high platform] the local people built of earth" (*Hanchuan xian zhi* 1873, 10: 8a). In Mianyang, before 1949, people mostly built high platforms on which to build their houses to protect against water calamities (*Mianyang xian zhi* 1990, 598).

Tai/Taizi were common in the Jianghan Plain, particularly in the Han River valley. Although a few occurred naturally, most were human-made. Thus the names of many villages in the Han River valley bear the word *tai* (*Jianghu nongchang zhi* 1988, 6; Lu and Han 2011). In Yangma Village, a typical *tai* or *taizi* (for one household) was usually around 1.5 metres high (although *taizi* located outside dikes were about two or more metres high as they faced a greater threat of flooding), with an area of one hundred or more square metres. Since it was difficult for a family to build a *taizi* on its own, help from relatives, neighbours, and friends was crucial. Before 1949, some families were too poor to build a *taizi,* so they just built their houses on dikes (Chen 2007).

During the Qing dynasty and the Republic, most of the houses of Jianghan people were wood-framed, with thatched roofs of cogongrass and walls of a mixture of reeds, bamboo, earth, and grass (e.g., *Hanchuan xian zhi* 1992, 662; *Tianmen xian zhi* 1989, 846). Such materials were particularly suited for a setting subject to frequent floods. As a Hanchuan gazetteer explains: "If soaked by floodwater for a long time, even the *duntai* will usually collapse. Thus many of the residents build their houses with bamboo and cogongrass and simple walls, and when the high water comes in summer and autumn, [they] take apart their houses and go to live in other places, or flee on boats" (*Hanchuan xian zhi* 1873, 10: 8a). Frequent inundation forced residents of many villages of Zhijiang and lake areas of Dangyang to build shacks of reeds or Chinese sorghum straw (*Zhijiang xian zhi* 1990, 783; *Dangyang xian zhi* 1992, 770). In Mianyang, some residents just dismantled the walls of their houses and secured the frame with wire to ensure they would not float away on the floodwater. This enabled them to easily "rebuild" their houses after the floodwater receded (*Mianyang xian zhi* 1989, 598).

This kind of housing also shaped the distribution of villages in the Jianghan area. Understandably, most of these *taizi* or villages were small and usually isolated from one another. For example, from 1938 to 1948, snail fever led to the destruction of "520 *tai* (villages) and 13,264 households" in Qianjiang, which means that there were, on average, only twenty-six households per *tai* (village). In 1935, ruptures occurred in two locations in this county: one had three *tai* with twelve households; the other had four *tai* with twenty-one households. These *tai* were even smaller: on average each *tai* had only 4.7 households (*Qianjiang shuili zhi* 1997, 94, 232). In the core area of the Jianghan Plain, until the Republican era, most villages were of this type – small and "scattered villages" situated on relatively high but isolated *taizi* or along the dikes (Lu and Han 2011). This is very different from the North China Plain, where villages were usually much larger. Even in the Yangzi delta, villages (usually located along rivers) seem to have been larger than those in the Jianghan Plain (Fei 1962[1939], 17-19).

Settlement, Gender, and the Division of Labour

Although the construction of dikes was one of the most important public projects in the Jianghan area, it is clear that, before the Republican period, women were usually not involved in dike work. In fact, in late imperial China, women had few opportunities to work outside the homestead. For instance, they could not serve as officials: all government personnel, including *yamen* runners, were men. Thus, when the compilers of traditional gazetteers provided figures on changes in population, sometimes they were referring to men only; changes in the number of women were ignored (women literally did not count) (Zhang 1992a). But in fact, in the Jianghan Plain, women played an important role in the economy. In many places they wove and in some places they fished. And gradually, during the Republic, they began to work in the fields. The factors that determined the division of labour include geographical variation, level of economic development, and socio-political change.

One reason women were mostly limited to domestic industries (especially textiles) was that they usually had bound feet, making it difficult for them to work in the fields. In Yingcheng in the late Qing, only in rare cases did women work in the fields; here, as in most other places, it was men who made up the bulk of the labour force (*Yingcheng xian zhi* 1992, 137). It was even harder for women to work in the fields if they lived in places where paddy fields predominated. Thus, in Tianmen at the end of the Qing and the early Republic, in dryland areas, both men and women worked in the fields, though heavy tasks like tilling and shouldering loads were conducted by the former. In paddy field areas, however, only men worked in the fields, while the women took care of family chores and weaving (*Tianmen xian zhi* 1989, 843). However, in Dangyang, a hilly county on the western edge of the Jianghan Plain, women not only worked in the fields but were also the major labour force. In the Republic, more than half of this county's labour force consisted of women (*Dangyang xian zhi* 1992, 152), an exceptionally high percentage and one that cannot be found anywhere else in the Jianghan Plain before 1949.

In fishing households, whether women were involved in fishing or not depended on whether the household fished part-time or full-time. In full-time fishing households, where families lived on their boats, women were naturally involved in fishing; women from part-time fishing households, however, may have stayed home to weave instead of going out to fish. This, at least, was the case in the village of Xiaojiawan in Hanyang, where men fished and women wove (*Hanyang xian zhi* 1989, 237).

Some villagers from the counties near the city of Wuhan found work outside their villages, thus leaving the women to till the land. In the 1930s, when the economy of Wuhan declined for a time, many male migrant workers returned to the villages. But they had become accustomed to urban life and were reluctant to return to working in the fields. Eventually, it was the women who took up the slack and began tilling the land, while the men, it was said, remained indolent (*Hanyang xian* 1938, 5).

Political and social change in China in the twentieth century also brought changes to women's economic role. The custom of foot-binding began to be abandoned early in the Republic. In Yingcheng, for example, some women no longer bound their feet in the Republic and went to the fields to provide supplementary labour (*Yingcheng xian zhi* 1992, 137). The same thing occurred in Songzi: by 1949, half of this county's labour force consisted of women (*Songzi xian zhi* 1986, 281). In Zhijiang, because many men were seized as coolie labourers or cannon fodder during the Republic, women with unbound feet shouldered the farm work (*Zhijiang xian zhi* 1990, 110).

There were few outside job opportunities for poor women in rural society, except as day labourers or servants. But female day labourers usually earned less than men. In Mianyang in the Republic, female labourers were paid 0.15 yuan a day, while male labourers received 0.25 yuan (*Hubei xianzheng gaikuang* 1934, 810). Female servants earned less than male servants. In Jingshan in the Republic, the wages of a female servant maid were less than half of what a year-long male labourer was paid (*Jingshan xian zhi* 1990, 95). In Tianmen in the Republic, female servants, as well as child labourers, earned nothing but a meal (*Tianmen xian zhi* 1989, 174).

Fisheries, Fuel, and Transportation

As we have seen, fishing was important in the Jianghan Plain. Some residents gave up lives as farmers to live on the water as full-time fishers. Others changed their occupation to suit the season, farming in the busy agricultural season and fishing in the off-season. This lifestyle eased the population pressure on the land and shaped the structure of the local economy, which combined farming, weaving, and fishing. While serious inundation made farming extremely difficult if not impossible, it benefited fishing, ensuring a plentiful catch (LS 19-2-2440). In addition to fish, the large amount of water also provided an abundance of other aquatic products that provided relief during water calamities.

The islets, river beaches, and lakefront areas that had not been reclaimed provided fuel for the local people. Before 1949, this was important in rural Jianghan, where mineral fuel such as coal was uncommon. The basic fuel in rural Jianghan was plant matter, particularly straw (*Hanyang xian zhi* 1989, 482; *Suohe zhen zhi* 1991, 277-78). In Jiangling, for instance, until the end of the Qing, "aside from coal that was imported from other places, the rest [of the fuel] such as willow and reeds all come from the islets of the county" (*Jiangling xian xiangtu zhi* 1959 [1909], 2). Most fuel in Jianli in the Republic also consisted of reeds and wild grass (*Jianli xian* 1938, 2), mostly growing on islets and river beaches. In Xiaogan and Hanchuan during the Republic, different powerful groups or lineages fought each other for control over the use of lakefront grasslands for fuel (as well as for building materials and green manure) (*Xiaogan xian jian zhi* 1959, 56; *Hanchuan xian zhi* 1992, 197). This function of islets, river beaches, and lakefront land was particularly import-ant for the local residents of lake areas and paddy field areas, where rice straw alone could not fulfill the need for fuel. The rich vegetal fuel in the Jianghan Plain again demonstrates that the living situation in this area was superior to that in the North China Plain (such as in the Huang-Yun area, where the villagers had to search out the last bits of wild grass for cooking and heating [Pomeranz 1993, 123-37]).

Finally, the net-like waterways and dikes also influenced the local means of transportation and the location of market towns. In Mianyang and Jianli, for example, boats were the most important means of transportation before 1949. There were so many waterways, and water transportation was so con-venient, that land transportation became less important. Some peasants thus completely depended on boats to get around and used *yuan* dikes for animal-drawn transportation in the absence of regular land routes (*Jianli xian* 1938, 2, 14; *Mianyang xian zhi* 1989, 598). In Shishou, before 1949 boats were also important for long-distance travel (*Shishou xian zhi* 1992, 633).

Almost everywhere in traditional China, passengers depended on ferry-boats to cross small rivers and lakes. But ferries were particularly common and important in the Jianghan area. According to gazetteers, there were fifty-four ferries in Tianmen in the mid-Qing, thirty-three in Shishou, nine-teen in Hanchuan, and fifteen in Songzi in the late Qing (*Tianmen xian zhi* 1765, 2: 26b-30a; *Shishou xian zhi* 1866, 1: 27a-28b; *Hanchuan xian zhi* 1873, 8: 33b-35a; *Songzi xian zhi* 1869, 2: 13a-14a). In Jingzhou there were no fewer than 474 ferries (245 were officially recorded in gazetteers) in the late Qing and about six hundred in the Republic (*Jingzhou hangyun shi* 1996, 120). The establishment and management of ferries was one of the major administra-tive duties of local government in the Qing (Wu 2008). In Jingshan in the Republic, ferries varied from small boats that could only carry ten-plus pas-sengers to larger ones that could carry more than a hundred (*Jingshan xian zhi* 1990, 262).

Ferries were either state-owned, privately owned, or owned by charities. At the end of the Republican era, there were eleven charitable ferries along one river in Songzi alone. One charitable ferry set up by a widow in this county in 1862 had benefited the locals for eight decades (*Songzi jiaotong zhi* 1984, 39, 154). Charitable ferries were free or charged only a small fee. Some private ferries were also free. Thus, in Shishou in the Republic: "[A person with] no money can also cross over the river." The number of major ferries in Shishou had increased to thirty-nine during this time (*Hubei jindai nongcun fuye ziliao xuanji* 1987, 265). In this custom we see the subsistence principle of a moral economy, not the profit-seeking principle touted by the market.

A late Qing stele records that, for about a thousand years (from the Song dynasty to 1900), a charitable ferry in Shishou, owned by a local lineage, was either free or charged only a small fee under special circumstances (e.g., around the Spring Festival) (*Jingzhou gonglu shi* 1993, 68-69). As charities typically provide goods and services such as food, medicine and medical care, and schools, all of which are essential to the maintenance of life and the continuation of normal society, the fact that there were charitable ferries would suggest that ferries were essential to the maintenance of society in the Jianghan Plain.

As for the ferries that charged a fee, there was no uniform standard regarding how much should be charged; rather, fees varied by location, depending on the difficulty or ease of the crossing. In Jingzhou before 1949, there were two ways for passengers to pay ferry fees: one was by paying cash (or materials with equal value, such as a chicken's egg), and the other was by paying a *huashui* (ferry fee). The latter applied to people who lived nearby. When they took the ferry, they did not have to pay a fee; instead, after the fall harvest, the ferry operator went from village to village collecting *huashui* from each household. It did not matter how many times one took the ferry, and it was completely up to the head of the household to decide how much to pay and whether to pay in cash or in kind (i.e., grain). Reportedly, disputes were rare (*Jingzhou diqu shuiyun zhi* 1989, 232-33).

Because of the importance of water transportation, most of the famous market towns in the Jianghan Plain in the Qing and the Republic were located along rivers: Tiaoguan (Tiaoxian kou) and Ouchi in Shishou, Zhuhe in Jianli, Haoxue in Jiangling, Yuekou in Tianmen, and Xindi and Xiantao in Mianyang, as well as Shashi (see Map 1). Not only market towns but also county seat towns were mostly located along rivers. In the reign of Kangxi, for example, of the seventy counties and departments of Hubei, sixty had their seat towns located along rivers (*Hubei hangyun shi* 1995, 186).

Locating towns next to rivers, however, had its drawbacks. Dikes could break, and the absence or presence of water calamities caused ups and downs in the business conducted in market towns. For instance, the frequent floods during the Qing dynasty caused periodic depressions in Shashi (Chen Guanlong 1989). Some smaller market towns were even deserted because of floods (*Gong'an xian zhi* 1874, 2: 18ab). Ouchi in Shishou, however, became a flourishing market town in the late nineteenth century and the early twentieth century because of the formation of the Ouchi River (after the formation of Ouchi outlet, see Chapter 1) in the 1850s, but it declined after the Japanese invasion in 1943 (plus silting up) (*Ouchi zhen zhi* 1985, 53-54; *Shishou jiaotong zhi* 1990, 28-29). The destruction brought by the Japanese invaders and the change of waterways combined to wipe out nineteen market towns in Qianjiang from 1938 to 1947 (*Qianjiang xian zhi* 1990, 91).

Socio-Economic and Political Features of a Dike-*Yuan* Society

Litigation

Subject to frequent water calamities, the local residents in the Jianghan Plain became entangled in countless lawsuits – lawsuits among *yuan* residents for control over farmland and lawsuits among different *yuan* for control over waterways.

First, because of frequent inundation, changes of river courses and waterways, and the collapse and silting up of riverbanks, the legal ownership of much of the land in the Jianghan Plain was unclear. Since the silting up of river harbours and lake islets created reclaimable land, it also created lawsuits among people who wanted to reclaim it (*Hanchuan tuji zhengshi* 1895, 4: 19b; Zhang 2005, 192-94). Other similar disputes in the Qing include lawsuits over the control of land ownership between immigrants and the natives, among the immigrants, and between powerful families and commoners (Peng 1990, 184). Some argue that it was immigrants from the province of Jiangxi who brought the custom of litigiousness to the Hunan-Hubei area after the Ming dynasty (Fang 2004).

Second, the use of waterways for different purposes could also cause lawsuits. For example, in the Qing dynasty the Sima family of Gong'an once dug a small, ten-*li*-long canal for fishing; however, during the high-water seasons, the water flooded the surrounding farmland, with the result that every year people tried to block the mouth of the canal before the arrival of the high water. But the canal became deeper and wider and hence harder to block. The local people hoped to build a stone sluice gate and sued the Sima family in the local court. The case dragged on for years without resolution since, by paying a bribe, the Simas were able to boycott the proceedings. The case was finally referred to the provincial court only because, in 1799, the Sima family killed one of the people who rushed to block the canal to protect the farmland when floodwater came (Shuili dianliabu 1991, 523).

Third, more commonly, residents of some *yuan* fought for control over the management of a certain dike and waterways. For instance, Baili islet in Zhijiang was turned into a wasteland for thirty years in the early Qing because of a lawsuit (*Zhijiang xian zhi* 1990, 165-66). In another example, two groups of *yuan* in Jiangling were involved in a lawsuit over drainage and irrigation that dragged on for fifty-one years, from the reign of Qianlong to the reign of Daoguang. The problem remained unresolved until the Republic (*Jiangling xian shuili zhi* 1984, 165). To mention yet another example, in the 1930s, the various *yuan* in Xiaogan struggled among themselves over the building of *yuan* dikes and a dam and engaged in lawsuits that continued for a decade (*Xiaogan shi zhi* 1992, 211).

Some dishonest gentry even extorted fellow villagers by filing lawsuits: they used dike affairs and water control as an excuse to benefit themselves by forcing villagers to pay surcharges for dike maintenance. If people thought they were being overcharged for dike work (or were otherwise being treated unfairly) and refused to submit to extortion, and if local officials did not see things their way, these gentry would go to the local, provincial, or even central government to sue (*Xiangdi cheng'an* 1969, 2: 206b-207a). In one case, some poor people went all the way to the capital to accuse the local *yamen* clerks of overcharging for land tax (*Hanchuan xian zhi* 1873, 10: 9ab).

Fourth, there were some large, famous lawsuits involving many *yuan*. Some of these continued for decades. In the late Qing, for example, court battles were fought between Penggong *yuan* and Qishier *yuan*, which lay along the boundary of Tianmen, Mianyang, and Hanchuan (*Hubei sheng zhi shuili* 1995, 8). The most famous lawsuit involving the *Zekou* (*Ze* outlet) in the Han River lasted for about seven decades. The issue was simple: the people of Jiangling, Qianjiang, Jianli, and Mianyang, who lived on the south side of the Han River, wanted to close the Zekou; the people of Tianmen, Hanchuan, and Hanyang, who lived on the north side of the Han River, wanted it to remain open. From 1844 to 1913, thirteen lawsuits were filed. As the dispute dragged on, some of those who led the blockage of Zekou lost their positions or were exiled or even beheaded (*Da zekou cheng'an* 2004). The people of Hubei who lived along the Han River were notorious for being litigious.

The involvement of high-ranking officials who were natives raised the stakes in these cases. The final formation of four southward outlets on the Jing River at the end of the nineteenth century created newly deposited soil, which attracted people who wanted to reclaim it. People in Nanxian and Huarong, in Hunan Province, enclosed a certain Tianhu *yuan* in 1926. But people of Gong'an, Shishou, and Jianli, all in Hubei Province, worried that this would cause their land to be flooded. They asked the governments of both Hunan and Hubei to destroy this new *yuan*. Many important figures who had been born in either Hunan or Hubei joined the conflict in support of their respective province. This, of course, made the case even more complicated, and the lawsuit eventually wound its way up to the central government. Both sides battled for twenty years, and the case remained unresolved at the end of the Republican era (LS 1-5-1389; LS 6-2-964; Wu Xianming 1982; He 1983). The same was the case in Shishou and Jiangling, where residents had struggled over the blockage/opening of the mouth of the Xiaozhiyuan rivulet for about two hundred years, from the mid-Qing to the early PRC (LS 31-4-1726; SZ 34-2-117).

Bellicosity

Lawsuits not only took time but also often failed to solve real problems. More often local people were directly involved in finding a solution by fighting with each other. In a word, they were not only litigious but also bellicose. The residents of Qianjiang, for example, were praised as simple by a late Ming gazetteer. In fact, the gazetteer makes them sound positively timid: they did not dare to object to the local officials about anything (see *Qianjiang xian zhi* 1694, 8: 1b-2a); however, during the Qing dynasty, they frequently fought with their neighbours in Mianyang and Jianli (Peng and Zhang 1993, 222, 225). In Mianyang itself, seven upstream *yuan* and seventeen downstream *yuan* fought for forty years in the mid-Qing over control of drainage, a struggle that claimed many lives (Shuili dianlibu 1991, 583). In the late Qing, residents of *yuan* in the Lake Pai area frequently fought for the control of a sluice gate: they battled with fishing tridents, knives, spears, and blunderbusses. Not surprisingly, lives were lost (*Mianyang chenchangqu xiangtu zhi* 1987, 297-98).

In the Republic, some people who lived on one side of the Han River deliberately opened *(daojue)* the dike on the opposite side of the river to safeguard themselves against an impending flood (LS 31-4-221). This kind of deliberate opening of dikes also occurred along the Yangzi River in the Qing and the Republic. According to a Songzi gazetteer, some people intentionally opened up other people's dikes in order to safeguard their own *yuan* without thinking of the consequences for those whose land would be inundated (*Songzi xian zhi* 1982 [1937], 87). And, according to an 1876 gazetteer of the Wancheng dike in Jingzhou, someone once deliberately opened up a *yuan* dike in order to silt up his low-lying land within the *yuan,* which may have been good for him but flooded the land of those whom the dike had protected (Ni 1885 [1876], juanmo: 8b-9a). In still another instance, in 1890, due to a dispute, some people in Jianli even stealthily opened the dike of the Dongjing River in Luojiawan, causing its rupture (*Jianli difang zhi* 1991, 52). The same thing also occurred in the Huang-Yun area of North China, where, in 1917, the residents who lived on the west bank of the Grand Canal "deliberately broke the dikes on the east bank," inundating about 2 million *mu* of land (Pomeranz 1993, 173).

In 1935, the dike on the south side of the Yangzi River burst at Luojiatan. A local individual who owned thousands of *mu* of land in a *yuan* at that spot decided to take a chance and try to enrich his farmland with the sludge he thought would be deposited by floodwater. With this in mind, he forbade people to strengthen the *yuan* dike.[4] The dike broke, and the *yuan* was flooded. After the floodwater receded, thousands of *mu* of fertile land were covered not by sludge but by white sand. The land remained useless until the late 1950s (*Hubei shuili zhi* 2000, 191). In this case, nobody benefited from the rupture.

With the intensification of environmental deterioration, conflicts over the control of waterways became more violent. To illustrate, let us consider a few cases, all of which involve the Chailin River. In 1839, a rupture of the Chailin River dike at Zibeiyuan led to a feud between residents of hundreds of *yuan* who lived along the river. For decades after that the residents on the south side of the river and the residents on the north side of the river clashed over the blockage of this rupture (*Dongjinghe difang zhi* 1994, 70). Feuds occasionally broke out among the residents of Jianli, who lived on the upper reaches of the Chailin River and insisted on leaving the rupture unrepaired, and the residents of Mianyang, who lived on the lower reaches and insisted that the rupture be blocked. It was said that each side hated the other so much that even relatives (who lived in different counties) considered each other as enemies. Occasionally feuds turned into full-blown battles. In 1881, clashes between fully armed residents of Jianli and Mianyang reportedly caused thousands of deaths (Peng and Zhang 1993, 225). In 1882, the magistrate of Jiangling led his people in reopening the blocked Zibeiyuan by force, with the result that farmland on the south side of the Chailin River was flooded. This eventually led to a huge feud among residents of about sixteen hundred *yuan* in five counties who lived on either side of the river. The conflict was not quelled until the central government issued a special fund of 140,000 taels for dredging the river and building sluice gates (*Dongjinghe difang zhi* 1994, 70).

Within Jianli, throughout the Qing and Republic, hundreds of *yuan* dikes were built independently without a comprehensive plan, with residents of each *yuan* building dikes to protect their own *yuan* from floods. This led to frequent disputes and feuds over the control of irrigation and drainage (*Jianli difang zhi* 1991, 80). For instance, several *yuan* along the Lao Linchang River in this county struggled for hundreds of years, from the end of the Ming dynasty to the early twentieth century, over the issue of dredging the river. Beginning in 1926, they began to battle for control over a single section of the dike. The residents of *yuan* located on the upper reaches wanted to break the dike to drain their *yuan* of water; the residents of *yuan* on the lower reaches wanted to preserve the dike to protect their *yuan* from floods. The fighting continued for years. Weapons were used, many people were killed, and a huge amount of money was spent on lawsuits. The upper *yuan* people and the lower *yuan* people were said to have hated each other as enemies (*Jianli xian zhi* 1959, 119-20).

Even in Songzi, a county on the periphery of the Jianghan Plain and far from the Han River (but along the Yangzi River), "residents in the southwest where mountains were close were simple and honest ... [but] residents in the southeast where water was close were bellicose" (*Songzi xian zhi* 1696, 4: 1b). In the early nineteenth century, more and more conflicts arose as ruptures became more frequent and subsequently dike fees mushroomed (*Songzi xian zhi* 1982 [1937], 75).

These examples show that lawsuits and fighting over water control between enraged residents in the Jianghan area were a result of long-term environmental deterioration caused by extensive dike building and over-enclosure of *yuan*. With more and more people involved in lawsuits, and lawsuits becoming more and more frequent, the residents along the Han River in the Qing were increasingly litigious. In fact, filing lawsuits related to water control became one of the most notorious customs of Hubei Province.

Organizational Units of the Rural Community

As has been pointed out, the Jianghan peasants originally built dikes to adapt to their water-rich setting. As time passed, however, the dike systems gradually became an inseparable part of local community, particularly the *yuan,* which became the basis of socio-economic organization. In many cases, people were organized by *yuan* for the purposes of dealing with dike management, maintaining social order, collecting taxes, worshipping water deities, and governing rural communities.

Since *yuan* dikes were originally built to protect people's land from flooding, it was natural for all residents of any given *yuan* to work together to maintain the *yuan* dike. Since inundation affected everyone within range of water, everyone, including the rich (particularly the gentry), in the community should work together to deal with the floodwater. As has been noted, in addition to serving as leaders, supervisors, and funders of dike work, the gentry (especially scholars or degree holders), at least in theory, had to pay regular dike fees. According to local officials as well as local customs, dike fees were set aside to protect the community, and every member of that community was expected to pay his or her share (Ni 1885 [1876], 6, jingfei I: 9b-10a; *Gong'an xian zhi* 1874, 3: 76a-81a). So the gentry were not exempt from dike fees, though they were indeed exempt from some regular taxes and labour service. Even the banner soldiers (i.e., members of the national army) stationed at Jingzhou were required to pay dike fees, though they were usually reluctant to do so (Ni 1885 [1876], 6, jingfei I: 8ab, 14ab). This meant that almost everyone (i.e., every adult male) in the community was involved in the construction and maintenance of the dike systems, particularly *yuan* dikes.

The cohesiveness of the *yuan* community directly determined whether it would be protected from floods. If the residents of a *yuan* could unite to safeguard their *yuan* dike, as did the people of Baiju *yuan* and Hulu *yuan* in Jiangling County in the early Qing, there would be fewer water calamities (*Jiangling xian zhi* 1794, 8: 11a). Reflecting the patterns of cooperation and conflict discussed in Chapter 2, in Qianjiang, some neighbouring *yuan* that benefited from the same dike joined forces in maintaining it. In Tianmen and Mianyang, on the other hand, some *yuan* failed to cooperate with each other in maintaining their dike, leaving each individual household responsible for its own share and thus putting the entire *yuan* in jeopardy (*Hubei An Xiang Yun dao shuili ji'an* n.d., II: 2b-3a).

For this reason, Lu Xiqi (2004) divides the Jianghan Plain – from the angle of water control – into four geographical zones consisting of roughly concentric circles: (1) the "living zone" (the high places within *yuan*, where people preferred to locate their farmsteads); (2) the "productive zone" (where, typically, crops were raised); (3) the "cooperative zone" (where multiple *yuan* were linked together); and (4) the "survival zone" (the area encircled by major dikes). The cooperation of neighbouring *yuan* in Qianjiang even resulted in a regional quasi-military administration during the Taiping Rebellion, whereby the local people were organized to defend themselves against the Taiping army. The cooperating *yuan* (a "cooperative zone") formed a military unit, a *tuan* (bureau). The military units under the *tuan* were *qi* (teams), and there was one in each *yuan*. In Xiangyin County in the Lake Dongting Plain, the militia bureaus *(tuanlianju)* established in the late nineteenth century were also mostly organized around *yuan* (Perdue 1982, 763).

Attentive readers may have already realized that in the above discussion, the Jianghan people frequently sued and battled on the basis of *yuan*. One of the largest group conflicts occurred in the late Qing, when, for about five decades, residents along the Chailin River, from five different counties, feuded over its closing and/or dredging. Sources only indicate that these people were from sixteen hundred *yuan*; no villages are named (*Zai xu xingshui jinjian* 1970 [1942], 473; *Dongjinghe difang zhi* 1994, 70). In fact, *yuan* served as one of the major bases for organization when the Jianghan people fought against each other in violent conflicts over water control in the Qing and the Republic (Zhang 2013).

As long ago as the early Qing, *yuan* functioned as the basic unit of regular land tax collection in Qianjiang County. Until the middle of the nineteenth century, this was the case in Hanchuan, Mianyang, and Jianli (*Qianjiang xian zhi* 1879, 3: 11a-29a; Lu 2011, 385-98). It is well known that the unit of area varied wildly in different regions in rural China; it was even different in neighbouring *yuan* in the Jianghan Plain. In 1938, when, for the purpose of water control, the government of Hanyang County decided to combine two neighbouring *yuan* into one, the residents of one *yuan* strongly opposed this and argued that these two *yuan*, though adjacent to each other, were actually very different – society was organized differently, and even the unit of area (the unit in one *yuan* was 1.5 times the unit in the other) was different (LS 31-4-1403).

Because the Jianghan Plain is vulnerable to water calamities, the local residents built many temples in which to worship water deities in the hope of engaging their protection (Yang and Chen 2008, 314-50). In Sanhe *yuan*, Songzi, in the 1940s, worshipping water deities was a routine practice during annual repair and flood control (Lü 2011); and the temples in which this occurred became the social and religious centres of *yuan* residents (Lu Xiqi 2011, 434). Regarding the worship of water deities, Gao Yan (2012, 79-93) further argues that this reinforced the *yuan* as a cultural unit in the Jianghan Plain, at least in the late Qing. According to her, the direct relation between a certain *yuan* and a certain water deity or several deities was still not apparent in the Ming dynasty and the early Qing; however, in the late Qing, gazetteers were usually clear about which temple was located in which *yuan*. Gao claims that residents of different *yuan* worshipped different water deities, and this custom served to form a sense of community among *yuan* residents, particularly those who lived in larger *yuan* consisting of multiple villages.

From a water-control perspective, what is the relationship between rural governance and the management of *yuan*, especially in multiple-village *yuan*? The relationship between water-control organizations and the rural administrative system in general is significant. Japanese scholars have made a rich contribution to the topic, particularly regarding the so-called water-control community. Morita, for example, insists that a rural administrative system is a precondition for the organization of water control. However, Elvin (1975, 91) questions this. In the Qing dynasty, in some places in the Jianghan Plain, it seems that these organizations were independent from the rural administrative system, but in other places they overlapped with it. For example, in Jiangling, sometimes the *lizhang* (the headmen of a *li* – a village unit) were also in charge of calling up labourers for dike work (*Qing jingshi wenbian*

1992 [1889], 117: 17b), and some *baozheng* (headmen of a *bao* – a rural administrative unit) were also in charge of collecting dike fees (Ni 1885 [1876], 6 jingfei I: 10b). Whether they were parallel to or overlapped with the rural administrative systems, it is certain that these organizations were deeply rooted in rural society, particularly in the management of *yuan*.

In the Republic, it became clear that these organizations overlapped. In 1938, the government of Hubei issued a new regulation, which held that people's *yuan* were required to set up a bureau of dike repair and flood control, which was to include a director, a deputy director, some dike managers *(didong)*, and dike maintainers *(dibao)*. According to this regulation, the dike manager was to be selected from among the current *lianbao zhuren* (directors of security) and *baozhang* (heads of bao), and dike maintainers were to be selected from among the current *baojia zhang* (heads of the baojia [a rural administration system based on households]) (LS 36-2-15). In some *yuan* of Hanchuan and Hanyang, several people held the positions of *baozhang* and *dibao* simultaneously (LS 36-1-69). Thus it is no wonder that, in one *yuan* of Songzi, the people who served in the dike management organizations were those who also served in the rural administrative system (Lü 2011). The directors of such bureaus were supposedly "publicly elected" by the local people, but in at least one case a former township head was directly appointed by the county magistrate of Hanyang as the director of the Bureau of Dike Repair and Flood Control of one *yuan* in that county (LS 31-4-1407). These directors were usually very powerful figures in their communities: they could force peasants to pay dike fees by taking away their oxen and quilts, and sometimes they even arrested and tortured these people (LS 31-4-60a; LS 31-4-1408).

In the Han River valley, it was found that, as early as the early Qing, the *yuan* frequently replaced the *baojia*, or village, as the basic rural political unit (Lu 2004; Lu 2011). This was also true in places such as Gong'an, where the *yuan* was and still is an administrative unit (*Gong'an xian zhi* 1990, 68-69).

It is apparent that, in Jianghan society, the *yuan* functioned as the basic unit of the rural community. Thus, in Qing memorials and Republican archives, we frequently find the local residents referred to as *yuan min* (*yuan* people) rather than as *cun min* (villagers). In fact, more commonly, the local people identified themselves according to the *yuan* in which they lived (Lu Xiqi 2011, 438), not according to which village. Even today, many places in the Jianghan Plain are still named according to *yuan* (e.g., Luocheng *yuan*, Zhangcheng *yuan*, Sanhe *yuan*, and Gufu *yuan* in Shishou) (*Hubei sheng shishou xian diming zhi* 1983, 492-93). In Qianjiang, although many *yuan* disappeared after the 1950s due to the construction of water-control projects, their names remained (*Qianjiang shuili* zhi 1997, 131).

Since *yuan* and the dike systems played such an important role and were so deeply involved in local society, it is not an exaggeration to describe Jianghan society as "a dike-*yuan* society" *(diyuan shehui)* (Zhang and Zuo 2001, 386).[5] In this society, *yuan* functioned as the basic unit of dike management, social order, tax collection, rural administration, and even religion. The peasants in the Jianghan Plain in the Qing and the Republic lived in *yuan* communities, which is not the picture painted by William Skinner (1964-65), who argues that Chinese peasants lived in rural market communities.

Conclusion

In many respects, society and the economy across the Jianghan Plain – thanks to its water-rich surroundings – were remarkably uniform. Water calamities were not only frequent but widespread, causing not only the loss of lives and property and the spread of disease but also a fluctuation in the amount of available farmland and uncertainty about harvests. Harvests were good when there were no floods but poor when there were. Yields, and productivity in general, were relatively high but unstable. In poor or famine years, the locals benefited from their various famine-relief crops and rich local aquatic products.

The daily life of the local people also bears the imprint of their water-rich surroundings. In different years, areas, and within different families, residents adjusted their food consumption and dietary habits accordingly; they built their houses and set up villages on relatively high places and used building materials that would not easily float away; they took advantage of the water for fishing and transportation; though women in general engaged in weaving, some women who lived in dryland areas worked in the fields; and so forth.

To protect themselves and their property from floods and to reclaim ever more land, the local people built more and more dikes. The struggle over water control led to Jianghan society being marked by litigiousness and bellicosity. The increasing number and intensity of conflicts over land ownership and water control demonstrated that this society suffered not only environmental deterioration but also social deterioration. Because the majority of the people of the Jianghan Plain were protected by dikes and lived in *yuan,* the dike systems constantly shaped and reshaped almost all aspects of local society. In many places, the *yuan* became the basic unit of rural organization and governance.

Conclusion

During the Qing dynasty and the Republic, tremendous changes in lake-river relations and water-land relations caused by extensive dike building and frequent water calamities constantly reshaped the environment of the Jianghan Plain, forcing peasants to adapt their productive practices and daily lives. Their ingenious and sophisticated responses to their altered circumstances, in turn, precipitated further environmental changes. These recurrent changes led to and intertwined with changes in socio-economic structures, thereby shaping the formation and transformation of the society and economy of the Jianghan Plain over time. All this demonstrates that environmental factors, more than class relations or market dynamics, defined the agrarian economy of the Jianghan Plain in the Qing and the Republic.

Environmental Change and Peasant Response

From an environmental perspective, the essential significance of the Jianghan experience is the sophisticated response of the Jianghan people to their precarious environment, or the flexibility of the Jianghan peasants to changing circumstances. One of the most obvious environmental changes involved the degradation of the local water system because of human action, which resulted in more frequent and severe water calamities, with which the local residents were increasingly incapable of contending. The rising number of water calamities in the Jianghan Plain in the Qing and the Republic can apparently be attributed to the deforestation, under population pressure, of neighbouring upstream mountains (which increased land erosion and silted up downstream riverbeds) and the over-reclamation of *yuan* within the plain (which shrank the flood diversion area). The more essential reason, however, was environmental mismanagement in general and corrupt, incompetent, and conflicting styles of dike management in particular.

Because the Jianghan Plain is a flat area studded with lakes and criss-crossed by rivers and waterways, stable water-control systems, particularly the dike systems, were a prerequisite for stable farming. As a matter of public welfare, water-control projects required the involvement of the provincial and central governments, particularly when projects crossed local jurisdictional boundaries. But state control over the dikes of the Jianghan Plain in the Qing and the Republic was inadequate and ineffective with regard to addressing the mounting problems.

Although the government placed greater emphasis on and became more deeply involved in dike management in the late Qing – for example, it increased the types and amount of government funds allocated for dike work – here, as elsewhere, it intentionally excluded most of the river dikes in the Jianghan Plain from its purview, instead leaving them to the local governments and the local residents to manage and maintain. In the Republic, the management of some major dikes in the Jianghan Plain was assigned to provincial authorities, but separating the responsibility for the annual repair of the dikes from high water control merely exacerbated the instability of hydraulic conditions and caused even more frequent floods. In the long run, at the local level, conflict over dike management was more common than was cooperation as the parties involved struggled to secure their conflicting interests. Widespread corruption further compromised the quality of dike management from the early Qing to the Republic.

The politics of dike management also reflected the relationships between peasants, rural communities, and the state. In order to ensure the integrity of the dike systems, members of a rural community had to share the responsibility for high water control in the summer and autumn and for annual repairs in the winter and spring. But individual peasants usually placed their own interests first, inevitably creating friction with their neighbours and tension in their communities. As the situation got worse, everybody looked only to their immediate interests, and the state did little to resolve their conflicts. In theory, the state was responsible for managing the environment and for regulating individual and community behaviour. To discharge this responsibility effectively, however, more was required than simply monitoring the condition of some major dikes and providing sporadic flood relief.

For individual villagers, regional differences, unequal dike fees, lack of centralized investment, and dike-related surcharges all added to the monetary burden of dike management. The solution to all these problems rested solely in powerful and effective management by higher levels of government. Nevertheless, the state exercised limited influence over local communities in pre-1949 rural China.

As the dikes became increasingly poorly managed, they deteriorated: the result was not only higher expenses for management as well as maintenance and repair but also more water calamities, which degraded the local environment. The declining ability of the dike systems to control the high waters led to changes in the local environment that were too severe for individual responses to cope with effectively. Before the early nineteenth century, agricultural production in the Jianghan Plain could quickly recover from high water. Because the high water receded quickly, affected communities could often resow or replant crops immediately after it retreated, and the crops could benefit from the rich sludge that had been deposited. By the mid-nineteenth century, however, the disorder of internal *yuan* waterways and the rise of riverbeds outside the *yuan* prevented high water from receding as quickly, and waterlogging thus became a more serious problem. Under these conditions, even a minor flood could cause a lean year. Yet, this degradation did not necessarily force the Jianghan economy into a pattern of unsustainable growth. Once problems of environmental management – mismanagement of dikes, the disorder of waterways, and the decline of soil quality in waterlogged fields – were overcome, the damaged economy of the Jianghan Plain would recover and eventually resume its growth.

For their part, the local peasants in the Jianghan Plain addressed their water-rich and precarious environment actively and with great sophistication. Their responses included extensive dike building, the cultivation of water-resistant crops, and the pursuit of fishing. Constructing extensive dikes was their primary way of adapting to the local environment. The people who lived along the Yangzi and the Han Rivers initially built river dikes to protect their farmland from seasonal high water; they also built *yuan* dikes to enclose lakeside and riverside wasteland. These dikes safeguarded farmland but also blocked the original waterways and, thereby, encouraged more frequent floods – to which the locals responded by building more and stronger dikes. Eventually, most of their farmland came under the protection of the dike systems. These activities, however, inevitably caused conflicts between individual interests and the collective good. Individuals may have benefited from their behaviour in the short term; however, in an area rich in hydraulic problems, such behaviour, particularly the widespread over-enclosure of *yuan*, resulted in long-term environmental deterioration.

In addition to constructing dikes, peasants cultivated water-resistant crops. They chose early-ripening crops such as early-season rice and *mai*; crops that can survive short periods of submersion, like Chinese sorghum; and even crops that can grow in deep water, like deepwater rice. Moreover, they developed a cropping system suited to their environment: a dominant single cropping system of middle-season rice in paddy fields and a supplementary "double-insurance" cropping system in both paddy fields and on dry land. They were motivated by the quest for environmental adaptability more than by the quest for high yield. In famine years, peasants sustained themselves by cultivating famine-relief crops and collecting aquatic products.

They also used whatever organic fertilizers were available to maintain the soil fertility. For this reason, in the Qing and the Republic, the Jianghan Plain saw no overall decline in soil quality (except for waterlogged fields) and no obvious fluctuation in the yield (per unit of area) of rice. Once a field was inundated, however, the yield and, subsequently, the yearly output of rice, as well as many other crops, would be greatly reduced. Thus, in flood years, both the yield and output might drop; however, if there was no flooding, the yield and output would recover. In other words, the environmental degradation of the Jianghan Plain significantly damaged agricultural production in flood years but not in normal years. In the long run, the result was relatively high but unstable yields and output, a key indicator of economic fluctuation.

Moreover, during the slack season in this water-rich plain, when the peasants were not farming, those who lived along the rivers and close to lakes tended to engage in fishing. Thus, large numbers of part-time fishing households were added to the full-time fishing households in the region. In contrast, peasants who lived in dryland areas were more likely to engage in the household cotton textile industry as their non-farming productive activity. However, since the Jianghan Plain was particularly dense with lakes and rivers, a great many people lived either along rivers or close to lakes, and, consequently, in many places more peasants engaged in fishing than in the household textile industry. As a result, the rural economy in the Jianghan Plain had a tripartite structure – farming, fishing, and weaving – rather than simply a combination of farming and weaving.

The Jianghan peasants' choices of food grain crops were determined mainly by environmental considerations, but they also cultivated and sold non-grain cash crops, particularly cotton. Although their crop selection can be viewed as a response to market opportunities, peasants also had to adapt to and were restricted by their environment – and the need for such adaptation was a greater concern for peasants on low-lying land. But everyone – whether the land they farmed was high, low-lying, or a mixture of the two – had to first guarantee their food supply. The Jianghan peasants certainly considered the market when making decisions about their agricultural production, but only after taking the environment into account. Failure to adapt to an unstable environment would result in uncertain output and income – or hunger or even death.

These priorities were also seen among people who made a living by weaving cotton cloth. The residents of Hanchuan, for instance, commonly wove cotton cloth not in pursuit of profit but as a way to maintain subsistence in the face of population pressure, a shortage of land, and environmental instability. Hanchuan was subject to frequent flooding, which made it unsuitable for cotton cultivation, but the floodwater had relatively little effect on domestic textile production. Thus, although the maximization of resource use in the Jianghan Plain might have been consistent with the predictions of classical economics, the local people were seeking to maximize not profit but utility.

Furthermore, although the local people built the dike systems to adapt to their flood-prone environment, there were clear free-rider problems in the use of the dike systems. Downstream residents often refused to pay dike fees or to contribute their labour to the upstream dike that protected them, as did residents who lived far away from dikes. And the rich, who had relatively more land protected by the dike systems, paid a disproportionately small dike fee. The solution to such problems lies in effective management.

The Republican data show that, in this environmentally unstable plain, the concentration of land ownership was inversely proportional to the frequency of water calamities: the more a place was prone to floods or waterlogging, the lower the land concentration. The rate charged for renting land depended not only on a field's fertility but also on its elevation. The more unstable the environment, the lower the landlord's share of the harvest, and the more ready landlords were to reduce rent or change fixed rents to sharecropping when calamity struck. Landlords and tenants negotiated as they sought a mutually acceptable balance of power. Thus, even tenancy relationships were shaped by the environment. The relations of agricultural production were not simply feudal forms of class exploitation, as Chinese Marxist scholars argue; nor were landlord-tenant relations mainly shaped by economic factors, as proponents of the market interpretation have maintained.

But we must not exaggerate the influence of the environment here. Indeed, a comprehensive consideration of environmental conditions, market variables, class exploitation, and population pressure is required to make clear their relative importance in determining the pattern of land distribution and tenancy relationships. In the Jianghan Plain in the Qing and the Republic, I believe that an unstable environment under population pressure constitutes the most important factor.

In highlighting one factor, we cannot ignore others. At the turn of the twentieth century, for instance, the relative stability of the Jingjiang Great Dike partly contributed to the expansion of cotton cultivation in the Jianghan Plain. It was the combination of market opportunities, population pressure, and relative environmental stability that caused the sharp increase in cotton cultivation in counties of the Yangzi River valley in the early twentieth century, while the combination of market opportunities, population pressure, and environmental instability aided the increase of cotton cloth making in the counties of the Han River valley at the turn of the twentieth century. Once recurrent floods again damaged the environment, however, even when market demand and population pressure remained constant, cotton cultivation declined.

A similar combination of factors can be seen in the local peasants' involvement in fishing. In an area with a high density of lakes and rivers, it was natural for many residents to fish. Since the early Ming, with the never-ending *yuan* enclosure of lakeside land in response to the pressure of an increasing population, fewer people relied on fishing. But beginning in the late eighteenth century, and particularly in the late nineteenth century and the early twentieth century, more peasants turned to fishing for their survival. Frequent water calamities, exorbitant dike fees, and population pressure on the land forced them to change to a lifestyle that entailed lower living standards.

Ceaseless *yuan* enclosure and dike building not only played a large part in the increase in water calamities but also generated conflicts over the control of waterways. In the long run, dikes gradually became entwined in, and constantly reshaped, almost every aspect of the locals' lives. The result was a unique dike-*yuan* society, in which the *yuan* functioned as important units of rural administration and dike management in some places, and *yuan* residents – particularly those who lived along the lower Han River – were generally litigious and bellicose. Population pressure and frequent water calamities were accompanied by worsening human relations. So it was not only the environment but also the relations among local residents in the Jianghan area that deteriorated in late imperial times, particularly towards the end of the Qing dynasty. Before the extensive construction of dikes, the local people generally lived in harmony with each other. But, as the number of dikes and subsequent floods grew, disagreements over who controlled the waterways became more frequent, and the ensuing feuds more bloody. Former friends and neighbours turned into enemies. As a result, people who lived close to water were generally more belligerent than those who lived close to mountains; people who lived in frequently flooded areas, such as the lower Han River valley, were particularly litigious and combative with regard to matters pertaining to control over waterways. This breakdown of the local community became a key measure of the social consequences of the environmental deterioration of the Jianghan area in the Qing and the Republic.

All this reminds us that numerous factors were interwoven in the formation and transformation of the rural economy and society of the Jianghan Plain. The Jianghan experience shows that, under population pressure, the behaviour of the local peasants included not only competing more strenuously for resources but also adapting to, destroying, reconstructing, and readapting to the local environment by building more dikes, reclaiming more lakefront land, and/or engaging in non-farming production such as fishing and weaving.

Although the change of the rural economy of the Jianghan Plain in the Qing and the Republic was also shaped by peasant rebellions (particularly the Taiping Rebellion), their effects were short-term.[1] In the long run, individual peasants probably cared more about water control than revolution, and environmental factors outweighed both the market and class struggle in determining their economic behaviour.

I do not mean to argue that the environment was an independent factor or a purely physical variable in the rural economy; rather, environmental factors interacted with many related socio-economic factors. The rural society and economy of the whole Jianghan Plain were formed and transformed by the interaction of population pressure, market forces, environmental change, state policies, community action, and individual peasant behaviour. Society and economy in the Jianghan Plain cannot be understood without taking into consideration these interactive human-nature relationships.

Government, Gentry, and Peasants in a Changing Society and Environment

The constantly changing environment and the full involvement of all the people of the Jianghan Plain created a complicated and interactive triangle of relations among the government, the local gentry, and the peasantry. Certainly none of them wanted the local environment to deteriorate, but that was what happened. This outcome was related not only to the conflicts among different interest groups but also to the behaviour of each individual within the same interest group (any particular individual may have belonged to different groups under different circumstances).

Both the Ming and the Qing sought to restore their war-torn economy in their respective early periods. Both pursued a policy of encouraging the reclamation of abandoned farmland and virgin land. This policy helped attract a great number of immigrants to the Jianghan Plain to reclaim its vast and fertile lakefront wastelands, which involved a great increase in the number of *yuan*. The government, the local gentry, and the peasants all benefited. The government found a place for war refugees and so helped stabilize society, and it also enjoyed growing tax revenues thanks to the newly reclaimed land. The local gentry (particularly those who had invested in reclamation) could get more rent, and the immigrants found refuge and, if they were fortunate, perhaps even a modicum of wealth. But the over-reclamation of land that followed the growth in the population and the subsequent water calamities caused many conflicts among different groups with diverse interests.

The most common and troublesome conflict was between the residents of the upper valley and the residents of the lower valley, as well as between those who lived on either side of the same section of a river. In both cases, the issue was whether to block or open an outlet or a river branch. In such conflicts, administrative units from the villages to the provinces could be involved. The second most frequent conflict was among the local gentry and the peasants. The third was between the peasants and the government. Each group did its best to further its interests.

The local gentry had a very specific role in most conflicts. They often led the local peasants in attacking their opponents (and sometimes even the state). In general, as time passed, conflicts became frequent and more violent. In the late Qing, it was not unusual for the residents of hundreds of *yuan* to be caught up in conflicts among different interest groups. When high-ranking officials who were natives of the Jianghan Plain got involved in support of their fellow villagers, things became more complicated and politicized. Some of these conflicts were even reported to the throne. But, on the whole, the Qing government, due to its inherent institutional weakness, failed to resolve these disputes.

First, the Qing government intentionally left the maintenance of the majority of the dike systems in the Jianghan Plain to the local people; it accepted responsibility only for a very limited section of the major dikes. It is unfair to say that the Qing government did not pay enough attention to Jianghan's dike system. On the contrary, it paid more and more attention to it by raising the ranks of responsible officials, by upping the classification of some major dikes, and by increasing the kinds of government funding. But the effectiveness of dike maintenance did not increase accordingly, and this was because of the inherent institutional weakness of the Qing state, whose officials often failed to follow regulations (e.g., not all responsible high-ranking officials went to the important dike sections in person during the flood season, as required) and which was riddled with corruption.

Second, since government funding was insufficient, the local people had to bear the burden of the majority of the dike fees (i.e., the earth fee and many other kinds of dike-related charges). That also offered an opportunity for *yamen* clerks or runners and some local gentry to embezzle dike fees. The local gentry stood side by side with their fellow villagers when they fought against other *yuan* or villages; but they might stand opposite their fellow villagers when they collected dike fees. Even fellow villagers may have had different responses to dike affairs: those who lived on relatively high terrain had little or no interest in the safety of the dikes, and the same was true of those who lived far away from them. The uneven monetary burden among the Jianghan people differs from what we would expect if Wang Yeh-chin is correct in claiming that the land tax in the Qing was kept low. The Jianghan experience shows that the low land tax was compensated by various fees – especially dike fees and related charges – which some poor households found exorbitant.

Third, the Qing government only found temporary solutions to Jianghan's problems. These included the realignment of the water systems and/or the banning of the enclosure of illegal *yuan*. The government understood the disadvantages of the over-reclamation of lakefront wasteland, and the local people wanted to avoid frequent floods. But the ban on the reclamation of illegal *yuan* was ineffective: the increasing population had to survive (by reclaiming lakefront wasteland), and some illegal *yuan* were owned by locally powerful individuals. In addition, reclaimed land was added to the tax rolls, giving local government a disincentive to enforce the ban. Later, the Qing government accepted the illegal enclosure of *yuan* as a fait accompli and only forbade the reclamation of newly silted land. However, due to unsolvable contradictions, such as that between long-term interests and immediate interests, between national interests and local interests, and between the government and the local gentry, this did not work either. In the end, more and more illegal *yuan* were built in the late Qing.

Even so, the increasing incidence of water calamities in the Jianghan Plain and the increasing importance of its economy worked together to draw more and more of the central government's attention to the integrity of its dike systems. The responsible officials at the prefectural and county levels could not usually afford to treat the dike systems lightly; indeed, even some governors of Hubei paid close attention to the dikes. In fact, local officials paid more attention to the dikes than to the introduction of new agricultural techniques and new varieties of crops. And once there was a disastrous flood, the central government would usually provide relief. For example, it provided relief to the people of the Jianghan Plain for about one-third of the Qing period, though some of this relief was not meaningful (Song 1989; Zhang 1993). The local peasants paid attention to the integrity of their *yuan* dike too, but sometimes they did not (or were unable to) deal with the dikes beyond the *yuan* dikes, particularly when they were involved in conflicts with other *yuan,* counties, prefectures, or even provinces.

In the triangular relationship between the government, the local gentry, and the peasants, conflict was more common than cooperation. In fact, how people identified with these three groups was not always clear since the same people, under various and varied circumstances, could belong to different interest groups. This, of course, rendered the conflicts particularly complicated. And all these conflicts were centred on the issue of dikes, the key issue in Jianghan society.

The Jianghan Plain, the Yangzi River Valley, and Rural China

The Jianghan Plain is not an isolated area. Socio-economic change has been unavoidably related to its immediate surroundings, particularly the Dongting Lake plain on the south bank of the Jing River and the northwestern Hubei mountains along the middle Han River valley. The Yangzi River, which runs through it, brought it into an even larger geographical unit – the Yangzi River valley. There is a built-in hydrological relationship between the upper reaches and lower reaches that has had a direct impact on the economy, society, and environment of the Jianghan Plain. The exchange of people and materials between the Jianghan Plain and the outside further linked it to other areas of the country.

From the Ming dynasty to the Republic, the Jianghan Plain underwent successive changes in its local environment, in its society, and in its economy. These include changes in such things as immigration, the export of grain, the cultivation of cotton and the production of cotton cloth, and the incidence of water calamities. All of these, in one way or another, were related to nationwide changes.

First, immigration to the Jianghan Plain was part of the western movement of population in late imperial China. In the Ming-Qing era, immigrants moved from eastern Hubei to the Jianghan Plain, and then spread step by step to southwestern and northwestern Hubei. This was part of the western movement of people from the lower Yangzi River valley to the middle and upper Yangzi River valley in late imperial times, a different movement from the southward migration from the Yellow River valley to the Yangzi River valley in early imperial times and the migration of Chinese people to many places in China and beyond in the nineteenth and twentieth centuries (Zhang Guoxiong 1995, 246-51). During this process, the Jianghan Plain was not a big source of emigrants but, rather, an abosrber of immigrants.

Second, the prosperity of rice production in the Jianghan Plain was part of the transformation of the production of the major food grain crops throughout Chinese history. Since the majority of migrants in Chinese history were peasants, the movement of population was also accompanied by a movement of major food grain crops. When the centre of China's population shifted from the dry lands of the Yellow River valley to the paddy fields of the Yangzi River valley, the major food grain crops of China also shifted from dryland crops such as wheat and millet to rice. During the Ming-Qing era, concomitant with the migration from the lower Yangzi River valley to the middle and upper Yangzi River valley, the centre of rice production shifted from the Yangzi Delta to Huguang (Hubei and Hunan) and the Sichuan basin, two new rice exporters in late imperial China. The export of rice from the middle and upper reaches of the Yangzi River, which included the Jianghan Plain, was also part of the nationwide circulation of grains, which also included the shipping of tribute grains from the Yangzi delta to Beijing via the Grand Canal in late imperial times and, in the late Qing, the shipping by sea of beans and wheat from Manchuria to the southeast coast. In the Yangzi River valley, there was another subsequent change: the extension of cotton production from the lower Yangzi to the middle Yangzi River valley. Hubei became the second largest cotton-producing province in the early Republic, while the Jianghan Plain was a major cotton production area in Hubei.

Third, the deteriorating environment of the Jianghan Plain was part of the westward shift of water calamities in the Yangzi River valley. The polder system (similar to that of the *yuan*) in the Yangzi delta reached its heyday as early as the Song dynasty, and the delta also suffered from worsened environmental conditions in Ming-Qing times. But the frequency of water calamities in the Yangzi delta was slightly lower than in the middle Yangzi River valley, in part due to the extensive construction of the seawall in the early Qing, which protected the delta from high tides. In contrast, by the mid-Qing the hydraulic situation of the middle Yangzi River valley, particularly the Jianghan Plain and the Lake Dongting Plain, became increasingly worse, mainly because of the over-reclamation of neighbouring mountains and extensive dike building and *yuan* enclosure on the plains. In the late Qing, central government officials paid more attention to the middle Yangzi River valley than they did to the rest of the Yangzi River valley. In short, the centre of gravity for water calamities shifted from the lower Yangzi River valley to the middle Yangzi River valley.[2]

So we see that the changes in the Jianghan Plain that were connected to nationwide changes included (1) immigration to the Jianghan Plain, which was part of the nationwide western migration; (2) the growth and prosperity of rice production in the Jianghan Plain, which was part of the transfer of the centre of rice production from the lower Yangzi to the middle and upper Yangzi; and (3) the frequent water calamities in the Jianghan Plain, which can be seen as a shift of such disasters from the Yangzi delta to the middle Yangzi River valley.[3]

These changes underline not only the fact that environmental and economic change in the Jianghan Plain was part and parcel of the pattern of nationwide environmental and economic change but also that the Jianghan Plain was in many respects similar to, and in many other respects different from, other areas of rural China, particularly the North China Plain and the Yangzi delta.

The Jianghan Pattern

Placing the Jianghan Plain within a larger context by comparing it with other areas of rural China helps not only to clarify its distinctive features but also to answer some larger questions. The Jianghan experience draws our attention to several significant developments in Chinese history. Changes in the Chinese landscape over the past three thousand years have been mainly caused by the expansion of farming areas as grasslands, mountainous lands, and lakefront wasteland were brought under cultivation. The history of Chinese agriculture (as well as of world agriculture generally) is a history of environmental change. Scholarly consensus is growing that Chinese civilization had multiple origins, but in its earliest period it flourished in the middle Yellow River valley and then gradually spread to the Yangzi River valley, Northeast China, and elsewhere. This expansion was followed by a reshaping of China's physical environment from north to south, from east to west, and from the heartland to the periphery. The transformation of the Jianghan Plain that began early in the Ming dynasty, and which was caused primarily by the construction of water-control projects such as dike building and *yuan* enclosures, is a small slice of this long history of Chinese environmental change.

In terms of the state-economy/agriculture relationship, Peter Perdue (1987, 250), in his research on Hunan, points out that "the imperial state was neither despotic nor laissez-faire, and its control over the agricultural economy was neither all-encompassing nor negligible." In other words, he challenges both the theory of oriental despotism and the theory of the limited state. The Jianghan experience supports his view. A comprehensive re-evaluation of oriental despotism would require another study; here I only highlight what is wrong with it. For example, contrary to the claim of oriental despotism that the Chinese government controlled all major water-control projects, the

central government actually wanted to avoid involvement in the management of most dikes in the Jianghan area. This policy contributed to the frequent water calamities in the area. Similarly, in Huang-Yun, according to
Pomeranz (1993), it was the government's "abandonment" that caused the
ecological decay (one major problem was a shortage of resources) and economic decline of the area. Both of these examples demonstrate the notable
but different role played by the state in the formation of environmental
problems and social and economic change in these areas. Even though it
suffered from the government's neglect and from environmental deterioration, the traditional agriculture of the Jianghan Plain was sustainable.
Throughout history, this is also true of Chinese agriculture in general. As
Robert Marks (2012, 334) argues in his survey of Chinese environmental
history, although China suffered long-term environmental degradation, "the
Chinese farming system itself was remarkably sustainable."

The Jianghan experience can help us understand the history of China in
other ways as well. Change in China's environment was directly related to
rural society and its economy. The Yellow River valley, China's political and
economic centre before the end of the Tang dynasty, for instance, did not
suffer much inundation following the Later Han because farmland was transformed to pasture by the nomadic people who had moved south and gained
control of the area. The introduction of grasslands largely reduced soil erosion
and the silting up of the Yellow River and, ultimately, lessened the frequency
of inundations. After the nomadic people left at the end of the Tang dynasty
and ethnic Han Chinese peasants began to farm the land again, both soil
erosion and flooding increased (Tan 1962). Even those who have viewed
Chinese history through the lens of class struggle cannot ignore the fact that
the political disorder that often plagued China as well as China's dynastic
cycles was related to environmental change. As Deng Yunte (1984 [1937],
144) pointed out long ago, almost all peasant uprisings in Chinese history
were caused by famines. Most of these famines were the result of environmental disasters (droughts, floods, etc.).

Throughout this book, I frequently compare the Jianghan Plain with the
North China Plain and the Yangzi delta, arguably the two most important
and thoroughly studied areas of rural China. Each has distinctive characteristics with respect to environmental stability, farming systems, water-control
systems, rural commercialization, and many other aspects. All of these were
shaped by their different environments.

Viewed from an environmental perspective, the Jianghan experience reveals
a pattern of rural development that differs from that of both the North China
Plain and the Yangzi delta. In the North China Plain, floods, droughts, and

plagues of locusts were very frequent; almost every year saw at least one or two disasters. Such disasters might last a very long time and affect a large area, severely damaging the local economy. A single rupture in the dikes of the Yellow River, for example, could submerge a major portion of the North China Plain.

To ensure a relatively steady income and supply of grain in such an unstable environment, the peasants of North China usually followed mixed-cropping systems. The most popular was a three-crops-in-two-years rotation of wheat, millet, sorghum, corn (by the late Qing), and cotton; but the yield of these crops was usually low because of the poor quality of the farmland owing to water shortages, salinization, a lack of fertilizers, and frequent natural disasters. The yield of food grain crops on average, for example, was about ten *dou,* or 150 *jin* per *mu,* in the Republic (Huang 1985, 141; Table 8.I). The living standard of the peasants was very low, and many of them struggled to survive. Recovery from disasters was a long and arduous process. Disasters and famines repeatedly drove the people to migrate; some severe disasters even fomented peasant rebellions. In the end, the entire socio-economy and environment of the North China Plain was characterized by extreme instability.[4]

In contrast, the environment of the Yangzi delta was relatively stable. During the period between 901 and 1900, regular waterlogging and drought occurred about once every two and a half years and once every four years, respectively (Huang 1990, 33; Table 2.I). The area rarely suffered from serious infestations of locusts. Nor did it witness disasters that nearly destroyed its economy or radically changed its environment, and the local people could recover from its relatively minor blows fairly quickly.

Taking advantage of their environment, the Yangzi delta peasants generally adopted a double cropping system, mostly of rice and wheat. Under this system, paddy fields and dry land became interchangeable as peasants replaced rice with cotton or mulberry trees. The yield in the Yangzi delta was likewise high. Rice (unhusked) on average yielded about 555 *jin* per *mu* in the Qing (Min 1984, 42). As inhabitants of one of the country's richest areas, the peasants of this region enjoyed the highest living standard in rural China. They might have had an interest in reducing their rent, but not in social revolution (Liu 2003). The Yangzi delta, in short, had a stable society and environment in pre-1949 rural China.

The Jianghan Plain was criss-crossed with protective dikes. When they broke, as they did with increasing frequency in the Qing and the Republic, the suffering and destruction could be severe. On average, every three years saw two water calamities (almost every year in the lower Han River valley), but droughts were less frequent, and locusts were only occasionally a problem. Sometimes the damage from inundation was very extensive. And it could take a long time for the locals to recover from water calamities, particularly waterlogging, which became an acute problem in the late Qing. However, in years of scarcity, the rich aquatic products from rivers and lakes provided famine-relief food. The Jianghan people could recover from disasters more quickly than peasants on the North China Plain but not as quickly as those in the Yangzi delta.

Though the alluvial soil of the Jianghan Plain was relatively fertile, the single cropping system predominated. The yield was higher than in the North China Plain but lower than in the Yangzi delta. Rice (unhusked), for example, yielded about 335 *jin* per *mu* in the Qing and the Republic (Appendix). The Jianghan peasants lived under more unstable and difficult conditions than did their Yangzi delta counterparts, but they were by and large better off than the peasants on the North China Plain. Although they did not resort to rebellion as frequently as did the North China peasants, they could be remarkably bellicose when it came to competing for control over waterways. Clearly, the society and environment of the Jianghan Plain was unstable.

Thus we see a distinctive regional pattern – the Jianghan pattern. Simply put, it was defined by high but unstable land productivity within an unstable environment. It thus differed markedly from the patterns both on the North China Plain (with its low and unstable land productivity within an unstable environment) and in the Yangzi delta (with its high and stable land productivity within a stable environment).[5] To be sure, there are more than three regional patterns of rural economy in pre-1949 China. However, by examining the similarities and differences between these three areas from an environmental perspective, we can see the Jianghan Plain within a broader environmental context. Exploring this context, I hope, will contribute to a more accurate understanding of the peasant economy in the Jianghan Plain and to a better understanding of the great diversity of rural China.

Appendix: The Yield of Rice in the Jianghan Plain in the Qing and the Republic

Studies of the yield of food grain crops of Hubei-Hunan in the Qing commonly equate rice with food grain crops and equate the yield/output of rice with the yield/output of all food grains. Few studies make any distinction between husked rice and unhusked rice; typically, the terms are used interchangeably and the calculation of the yield/output is based on only a few examples or even mere estimates (Tianxing 1987, 1988; Wu 1988; Zhang Guoxiong 1993, 1994b). As discussed in Chapter 4, there were many kinds of food grain crops; rice accounted for only about two-thirds of the output of food grains in the Jianghan Plain. In other words, the output of rice definitely did not equal the output of all food grains.

As for the yield of rice of the Jianghan Plain in the Qing, in an earlier study I mention that it experienced a slight decline from the early Qing to the late Qing but fluctuated around two *shi* per *mu* (Zhang 1991). I uncovered this yield in research based on the rent of school land. The result requires some caveats. First, my earlier study encompasses a somewhat different and larger area than is considered in this research. Second, it is hard to determine an exact yield based on piecemeal data of rents since the quality of the land and even the units for its measurement (the size of the *mu* or the amount of the *shi*) varied from county to county. Third, some gazetteers merely copied school land rent records from old gazetteers; thus the record may be centuries old. This makes our estimate of the yield of rice problematic. Here, I omit those samples that were not in the Jianghan Plain but add some new relevant samples and put them in possible periods. The results are listed in Table 22.

Table 22 shows, first, that the amount of rent varied from county to county. It could be as low as 0.6 *shi* per *mu* in Dangyang in the 1850s but as high as 1.52 *shi* per *mu* in Hanyang from the late Ming to the early Qing. This difference was unrelated to the general level of land productivity of those counties; rather, it was related to the quality of different school land.

Second, the rate of the rent of school land did not change substantially during the Qing, implying that the productivity of the land in question did not change much either. For instance, the rental rate in Jianli (a frequently

Table 22

Examples of rent charged (unhusked rice) for school land in the Jianghan Plain in the Qing

County	Late Ming -1735	1736-95	1796-1820	1821-50	1851-61	1862-74	1875-1908
Hanchuan	1						
Hanyang	1.19-1.52						
Xiaogan			0.821				
Jingshan	0.606		0.891				
Zhongxiang							1
Jingmen	1.015						
Jianli	0.675					0.671	
Shishou		0.8				1.38	
Gong'an		1.16					
Zhijiang				0.789			
Songzi					1.15		
Dangyang					0.6	0.751	0.738

Note: Unit: *shi/mu*

a. For unhusked rice, 1 Qing *shi* = 1.035 *shi shi* = 111.78 *shi jin* (1 *shi shi* = 108 *shi jin* [Xu Daofu 1983, 344]), or 123 pounds.

b. Almost all the data consisted of the amount of rent of school land. The original records were area followed by the amount of rent. I have made the necessary calculation (into Qing *shi/mu*).

c. The quality of school land is an issue open to question. According to Perkins (1969, 312), school land might not have been the best land, but it was better than poor land. The situation in the Jianghan Plain is more complex. In some cases, it is clear that school land was indeed poor land. Either it was of low soil fertility (*Hubei tong zhi* [1921, 1637]; *Gong'an xian zhi* [1874, 4: 2a-3a] or it was wasteland donated by individuals (*Jingmen zhili zhou zhi* 1868, 3[4]: 5a), although in some places the quality of school land varied (*Mianyang zhou zhi* 1894, 5: 11b). However, regardless of the quality of the school land, if we use rent data for the same kind of land, the result will be fewer miscalculations and better long-term comparisons.

Sources: Hanchuan: *Hanyang fu zhi* (1747, 22: 37a).

Hanyang: *Hubei tong zhi* (1921, 1602).

Xiaogan: *Hubei tong zhi* (1921, 1603).

Jingshan: *Hubei tong zhi* (1921, 1623-24). For the period between 1796 and 1820, there are four sources: 6.5 *shi* (19.5 *shi*) (acreage followed by rent, the same below), 11 *shi* (23 *shi*), 70.96 *shi* (212 *shi*), and 172.4 *shi* (512.63 *shi*). According to the same gazetteer, since 20 *shi* = 66 *mu*, then 1 *shi* = 3.3 *mu* (*Hubei tong zhi* 1921, 1623).

Zhongxiang: *Hubei tong zhi* (1921, 1622).

Jingmen: *Jingmen zhou zhi* (1754, 10: 24a). There are two sources: 80 *mu* (81.35 *shi*), and 10.5 *mu* (10.5 *shi*).

Jianli: *Jianli xian zhi* (1702, vol. 3-4); *Jianli xian zhi* (1872, 5: 45b-46a) (there are two sources: 62 *mu* [0.7 *shi* per *mu*], 25 *mu* [0.6 *shi* per *mu*]).

▶

◄ Table 22

Shishou: *Shishou xian zhi* (1866, 2: 9b); *Hubei tong zhi* (1921, 1637) (there are four sources for
the period between 1862 and 1874: 25.32 *mu* [38 *shi*], 13.2 *mu* [16 *shi*], 13.1 *mu* [18.4 *shi*],
and 9.1 *mu* [11.5 *shi*]).

Gong'an: *Hubei tong zhi* (1921, 1637) (there are three sources: 139 *mu* [166 *shi*], 11 *mu* [6 *shi*],
and 33.3 *mu* [40.7 *shi*]).

Zhijiang: *Hubei tong zhi* (1921, 1638) (there are two sources: 115 *mu* [92 *shi*], and 32 *mu*
[24 *shi*]).

Songzi: *Hubei tong zhi* (1921, 1638) (there are two sources: 6 *mu* [8 *shi*], and 46.19 *mu*
[52 *shi*]).

Dangyang: *Dangyang xian zhi* (1866, 5: 5ab) (11.1 *shi* [33.3 *shi*], 1 *shi* = 5 *mu*); *Dangyang xian
bu xu zhi* (1889, 1: 4a-8b).

inundated county) in the early Qing and the late Qing remained almost
the same. In the early Qing, there were 40 *mu* of school land with rent set at
27 *shi,* or 0.675 *shi* per *mu.* In the late Qing, there were 87 *mu* of school land,
with rent at 58.4 *shi,* or 0.671 *shi* per *mu* (*Jianli xian zhi* 1872, 5: 45b-46a),
the same as in the early Qing. This suggests that the yield of school land did
not change much, even in this flood-prone county.

There were some changes in Jingshan, Shishou, and Dangyang, where the
rental rate of school land increased from the mid-Qing to the late Qing
(except in Dangyang). But the low rental rate found in these three counties
was due to the poor land. The school land in Jingshan in the early Qing
bore a low rental rate (0.606 Qing *shi/mu*) because it was a piece of wasteland
without an owner; the school land in Shishou between 1736 and 1795 also
bore a low rental rate (0.8 Qing *shi/mu*), in this case because, thanks to water
calamities, the land was considered wasteland (*Hubei tong zhi* 1921, 1623,
1637). And the school land in Dangyang yielded a low rental rate (0.6 Qing
shi/mu) because the rent was reduced if there was a poor harvest (*Dangyang
xian zhi* 1886, 5: 5a). Therefore, for the moment, we cannot extrapolate too
much from the fact that rental rates for school land in these counties may
have increased. In any event, there were no cases either of the decline of
rental rates[1] or of rice yields.[2]

In the long run, the changing environment in the Jianghan Plain during
the Qing did not lead to significantly diminished rice yields. From Table 22
we can see that the rental rate of school land in the Jianghan Plain in the
Qing was around 1 *shi* per *mu* (as also evidenced by many records taken from
gazetteers). For the sake of comparison, if we take this as the general rental
rate during the Qing and transfer it to the yield, it works out to be about
335 *shi jin* per *mu,* an amount very close to the estimated average yield of
rice – that is, 323.3 *shi jin* per *mu* – in the Republic.[3] So it appears that, in

the Jianghan Plain in the Qing and the Republic, the unstable environment did not have a significant long-term negative impact on the yield of rice. Best or average yields for years without disaster saw no decline, and in some places floods (by depositing sludge) helped maintain average best/good yields for years that were spared a disaster.

This is understandable. It is true that the Jianghan Plain experienced frequent floods in the late Qing. However, the floods usually brought a rich deposit of sludge that replenished the soil's fertility. The inhabitants of land that did not experience frequent floods would maintain soil fertility (and consequently land productivity) through the use of suitable cropping systems and the application of fertilizers. As discussed in Chapter 4, the single cropping system was the major cropping system in the Jianghan Plain. In winter, after the harvest, paddy fields were either left fallow in order to restore soil fertility or covered with green manure. In addition to green manure, the fertilizers that Jianghan peasants applied in the late Qing and the Republic included human waste, animal manure, water grass, bean cakes (sesame bean cake, rapeseed bean cake, soybean cake, and cotton seed bean cake),[4] earth from old walls, plant ash, earth from stoves, crop straw, barnyard manure, farmyard manure, and pond sludge and river mud (e.g., *Gong'an xian zhi* 1990, 141; *Zhongxiang xian zhi* 1990, 314). With the exception of plant ash, all of these were organic fertilizers that could enrich the soil. As a result, the fertility of the soil did not decline under long-term environmental degradation.[5]

But in a single flood year, the yield of rice in inundated paddy fields would of course be reduced, and so would the output for that year. In other words, the effect of an unstable environment (mainly floods) on the yearly output of rice would be obvious since even a single dike rupture would reduce the output of affected paddy fields or completely destroy the crop. Water calamities were so frequent in this area that the output of rice (and other food grain as well) fluctuated from one year to the next. For example, in Jianli in the Qing, residents were satisfied if there was one good year of harvests every ten years (*Jianli xian zhi* 1872, 11: 11a). At the end of the Qing, the blockage of a broken dike would immediately result in a good harvest after years of poor harvests (Zeng 1987, 5:64).

The environment of the Jianghan Plain in the Qing and the Republic obviously deteriorated, but the yield of rice did not experience a parallel decline, suggesting that the deteriorating environment did not have a significant negative impact on the yield and output of rice in the years without water calamities. Its negative impact on yearly yield and output of rice (grains) in flooding years, however, was tremendous.

Glossary

Anlu	安陆（府）	danshou	单首
Baiju *yuan*	白莒垸	dao	稻
baixing	百姓	dao sun	稻荪
baiyi	白役	daojue	盗决
baizi	稗子	daoyuan	道员
ban	半	dianhu duo piwan	佃户多疲玩
bao	保	dianshi	典史
baojia	保甲	Diaocha *yuan*	汈汊垸
baojia zhang	保甲长	diaohu	雕胡
baolan	包揽	dibao	堤保
baogu shinian	保固十年	diding yin	地丁银
baozhang	保长	didong	堤董
baozheng	保正	difang ying	堤防营
celao	册老	dijia	堤甲
chang shui hu	敞水湖	dijiafa	堤甲法
Changjiang	长江	diju	堤局
Changjiang shuishi ying	长江水师营	dilao	堤老
Chengling ji	城陵矶	diqu	地区
chi	尺	ditou	堤头
chuan	串	diyuan	堤垸
chuanjuan/chuanli	船捐/船厘	diyuan shehui	堤垸社会
chun	纯	dizhang	堤长
cuifu	催夫	Dongjing he	东荆河
cun	寸	Dongjinghe difang	东荆河堤防委员
cun min	村民	weiyuanhui	会修防处
dabu	大布	xiufangchu	
daye	大业	dongnian	冬粘
dan	担	dongnianzi	冻黏子
dang jia chang gong	当家长工	dongshi	董事
dang jiang quan di	荡浆圈地	Dongting hu	洞庭湖
Dangyang	当阳（县）	dou	斗

duntai	墩台	Hanchuan	汉川（县）
er di zhu	二地主	*handao*	旱稻
fan dao geng yu	饭稻羹鱼	Hanshui	汉水
fang	方	Hanyang	汉阳（县）
fanteng	饭藤	Haoxue	郝穴
feng saodi, yue dian	风扫地，月点灯，	*hong sagu*	红撒谷
deng, banpian	半片芦苇掩家门	Honghu	洪湖（县）
luwei yan jiamen		*Honghu chiweidui*	洪湖赤卫队
fengtian	葑田	Huangpi	黄陂（县）
fu	府、夫	*huanxiang tuan*	还乡团
fumafei	夫马费	*huba*	湖霸
fumao	浮冒	*Huguang shu, tianxia zu*	湖广熟、天下足
fuqian	夫签	*huji*	湖稷
futou	夫头	*huke*	湖课
fuye	副业	Hulu yuan	葫芦垸
fuyi	夫役	*huqu renmin toushang*	湖区人民头上三
gan zi fei	竿子费	*santiao gun: e'ba,*	条棍：恶霸、水
ganke	干课	*shuizai, daduzi bing*	灾、大肚子病
gaoliang	高粱	*huashui*	划水
gong	弓、工	*huoli*	货厘
Gong'an	公安（县）	*ji*	稷
gongbu	工部	*jiahu*	家湖
guan du min xiu	官督民修	*jiancha*	监察
guan shui fei	关水费	Jiang	江
guan zheng guan xiu	官征官修	*Jianghan gongcheng ju*	江汉工程局
guan zheng min xiu	官征民修	Jianghan pingyuan	江汉平原
guandi	官堤	Jiangling	江陵（县）
guangong	官工	Jiangxia	江夏（县）
guanyuan	官垸	Jianli	监利（县）
guili	规礼	*jiaobai*	茭白
guimai fuqian jianmai	贵买夫签贱卖田	*jiaocao*	茭草
tian		*jiaogua*	茭瓜
guitian	归田	*jiaomi*	茭米
gumi	菰米	*jiaopai*	茭簰
gunshou	滚首	*Jibei dabu*	吉贝大布
guo shui qian	过水钱	*jin*	斤
guo shui fei	过水费	*jin bao yin*	金包银
guo shui piao	过水票	*jin shui hu*	禁水湖
Guomindang	国民党	Jingjiang	荆江
Han/Hanjiang	汉/汉江	*Jingjiang dadi*	荆江大堤

Jingjiang digong ju	荆江堤工局	*minyuan*	民垸
Jingmen	荆门（州）	*mu*	亩
Jingshan	京山（县）	*muyou*	幕友
jingshen	精神	*nan'geng nüzhi*	男耕女织
jingshu	经书	*ning shou tianzai,*	宁受天灾，
Jingzhou	荆州（府）	*bu shou renhai*	不受人害
Jingzhou shuili tongzhi	荆州水利同知	*nongmin gong*	农民工
Jingzhou shuishi ying	荆州水师营	Ouchi kou	藕池口
jiu qu hui chang	九曲回肠	*pai*	簰
Juhe	沮河	*pi*	匹
Juzhanghe	沮漳河	*pi tou*	批头
jundi	军堤	*piao er qian*	瓢儿钱
jushen	局绅	*qi*	旗
jushou	局首	*qi niu sa*	骑牛撒
kai tan	开坛	*qiang dian, ba zhong*	强佃霸种
kao po fei	靠坡费	Qianjiang	潜江（县）
kou	口	*qindi*	钦堤
koubu	扣布	*qing zhanzi*	青占子
lengjin tian	冷浸田	Qingjiang	清江
li	里	*qingnian*	青粘、青秥
lijia	里甲	*qintian*	亲田
lijin	厘金	*qishi zao*	七十早
lian	莲	*qiu shui zhang*	泅水长
lianbao zhuren	联保主任	*qiuxun*	秋汛
lingjiao	菱角	*renminbi*	人民币
liushi zao	六十早	*ruandian*	软佃
lizhang	里长	*sagu*	撒谷
ludao	稑稻	*sanhu*	散户
ma tie yin	麻铁银	*sanjian*	散监
mai	麦	*Shahu Mianyang zhou,*	沙湖沔阳州，
mangcao	芒草	*shinian jiu bushou;*	十年九不收，
mangdao	芒稻	*ruoshi yinian shou,*	若是一年收，
mangzao	芒早	*gou dou buchi*	狗都不吃糯米粥
maobanzi	毛瓣子	*nuomizhou*	
maoci	茅茨	*shandi*	山地
mian	面	*shang zhuang li yin*	上庄礼银
Mianyang	沔阳（州）	*shang zhuang qian*	上庄钱
min zheng min xiu	民征民修	Shashi	沙市
min'gong	民工	*shen*	绅
mindi	民堤	*sheng*	升

shenzi	糁子	*weitou*	圩头
shi	市、石	*weiyi*	圩役
shi dan	市担/石	*weiyue*	圩约
shi jin	市斤	*weizhang*	圩长
shi zhudi wei weitu	视筑堤为畏途	*wen*	文
Shishou	石首（县）	*wo gong*	硪工
shoushi	首事	*wuchan*	物产
shuang bao xian	双保险	Wuchang	武昌（府、县）
shuihai	水害	*wujin liuyin qitong*	五金六银七铜
shuihe	水荷	*batie*	八铁
shuike	水课	*wushi zao*	五十早
shuili	水利	*xian*	县
shuishang minzhu gaige	水上民主改革	*xiancheng*	县丞
siyuan	私垸	*xiangbao*	乡保
Songzi	松滋（县）	*xiangdao*	香稻
Songzi kou	松滋口	*xianyu chushui yang*	鲜鱼出水养三
su	粟	*sanjia: guanfu,*	家：官府、渔行
Su Hu shu, tianxia zu	苏湖熟、天下足	*yuhang he huba*	和湖霸
tai	台	*xiaobu*	小布
taizi	台子	Xiaogan	孝感（县）
tan yuan	滩垸	*Xiaogan bu*	孝感布
taohuaxun	桃花汛	*xiaohu*	小户
Tianmen	天门（县）	*xiaoyi*	效益
Tiaoguan/Tiaoxian kou	调关/调弦口	*xiaxun*	夏汛
Tongcheng *yuan*	通城垸	*xie tian li*	写田礼
tongzhi	同知	*xun*	汛
toujian	偷减	*xunjian*	巡检
tuan	团	*xunyuan*	汛员
tuanlianju	团练局	*xusuo*	需索
tudan	土单	*yanfu*	烟夫
tufei	土费	*yangshui*	洋税
tuju	土局	*yanli*	盐厘
tuniu	土牛	*yao di*	遥堤
tuquan	土券	*yi di wei ming*	以堤为命
tuzhang	土长	*yi gong dai zhen*	以工代赈
Wancheng di	万城堤	Yidu	宜都（县）
wang chuan	网船	*yin gen qian*	银根钱
wei	围、圩、卫	*yingdian*	硬佃
weijia	圩甲	*yinguan*	印官
weilao	圩老	*youfu*	游夫

yu er chushui qian	鱼儿出水钱	*zhagu*	□谷、□谷
yu huazi	渔花子	*zhang*	丈
yu mi zhi xiang	鱼米之乡	Zhanghe	漳河
yuan	垸、院	Zhicheng	枝城
yuan	元	*zhifu*	知府
yuan min	垸民	Zhijiang	枝江（县）
yuanfu	垸夫	Zhongxiang	钟祥（县）
yuanzhang	垸长	*zhou*	州
yuanzong	垸总、院总	*zhou yuan*	洲垸
yuba	渔霸	*zhoupan*	州判
yuetou	约头	*zhoutong*	州同
yuhang	渔行	*zhuan hu ri*	转湖日
Yunnan zao	云南早	*zhuangtou*	庄头
Yunmeng ze	云梦泽	*zhubu*	主簿
yutanzi	鱼坛子	Zhuhe	朱河
zaliang	杂粮	*zongjian*	总监
zeguo	泽国	*zongju*	总局
Zekou	泽口	*zongwei*	总圩
zeng chuan	缯船	*zutian*	租田

Notes

Introduction

1 For example, Chao (2004), Wang (2006), and Wang (2009). For a survey of Chinese works of environmental history, see Zhang (2003), Bao (2004b), and Chen (2011 [particularly studies on environmental history of the Yangzi River valley]). In the West, Mark Elvin is a pioneer and the leading figure in Chinese environmental history. On his brief generalizations about the field, see Bao (2004a).

2 The anthology was initially published in Chinese in 1995. An English version was published in 1998 (Elvin and Liu, 1998).

3 *Yuan* goes by several other names, including *wei*. In some places, *yuan* is understood as "dike," and thus "dike-*yuan*" *(diyuan)* frequently appears as a compound in the sources. *Yuan* may be translated "diked lands" (or "diked fields"), "embanked fields," "polders," or "enclosures." To minimize confusion, I leave the term untranslated throughout.

4 For comments on and critiques of these archival records and Mantetsu materials, see Huang (1982) and Huang (1985, 34-43). Li (2005) uses the exceptionally rich archive of Huailu County to draw a vivid picture of village governance in North China from the late nineteenth century to the early twentieth century.

5 The many substantial differences between the Yangzi delta and the North China Plain must be made clear because sometimes there is a tendency to assume that one pattern applies to China as a whole. Philip Huang (1990), among others, presents a detailed comparative analysis of the rural economy in these two areas over the past six centuries. In his recent research, Liu Chang (2007) compares the two areas in detail from the perspective of differential patterns of rural revolution.

6 For a selected bibliography of, and a brief introduction to, Japanese scholarship on water control in Chinese history, see Elvin et al. (1994, particularly 3-35).

7 In her recent dissertation, Gao Yan (2012) follows the model of Will (1985) and Perdue (1987) in discussing state-society relations in the Jianghan Plain, but she extends the time from the mid-Ming to 1949 and adds the environment as the third dimension in her analysis of a triangular state-society-environment relationship. According to her, the Qing government actually applied a laissez-faire policy in resource (water, land, *yuan*) management early in the dynasty, increasing its intervention since the mid-eighteenth century, when local ecological conditions worsened because of population pressure and excessive dike building. The effort of both the late Qing and the Republican governments, however, was ineffective due to their weakness, social chaos, and the conflicts between the locals and the state. As with Will and Perdue, peasant response is not her focus.

8 The memorials that reported legal cases might have a hidden bias – they were generally composed by a highly professional private secretary *(muyou)* in such a way as to keep the reporter's tendentiousness from being obvious (Gao 2000, 59-69). In such cases, one needs to carefully read reports and try to puzzle out the truth.

9 Many scholars – including Ho Ping-ti (1959) on Chinese demographic history, Dwight Perkins (1969) on China's agricultural development, and Philip Huang (1985, 1990) on rural China – have used contemporary data as a useful baseline to which more fragmentary historical data can be compared.

Chapter 1: Changes in the Environment of the Jianghan Plain

1 The extent of Jingzhou changed significantly over time. In the early Qing, Jingzhou was a prefecture containing eleven counties and two *zhou* (departments). In 1735, two departments and three counties were separated from it and placed in the newly established prefecture of Yichang. In 1792, another county was turned into Jingmen *zhou*. Seven counties remained (and they held most of the dike systems) in Jingzhou: Jiangling, Gong'an, Shishou, Jianli, Songzi, Zhijiang, and Yidu (*Jingzhou fu zhi* 1880, 1: 12a). Yidu is usually not discussed in this context, however, because it was later separated from Jingzhou (and is not a part of the Jianghan Plain). The capital of Jingzhou was Jiangling (see Map 1).

2 The district *(diqu)*, which was a level of government between the provincial government and county government in the PRC from the early 1950s to the mid-1990s, roughly equalled the prefecture in the Qing. The counties under the jurisdiction of Jingzhou District in 1993 were Jiangling, Songzi, Gong'an, Shishou, Jianli, Honghu, Xiantao (Mianyang), Qianjiang, Tianmen, Jingshan, and Zhongxiang (*Jingzhou diqu zhi* 1996, 51-52); all were located in the Jianghan Plain.

3 These data on the lands and their acreage are from Jingzhou District in the 1980s. Since this district included most of the Jianghan Plain discussed in this study, I use it as a rough approximation of that plain. No specific explanation is given when I use data on Jingzhou District in the 1980s to refer to the Jianghan Plain.

4 The argument over whether there was a *Yunmeng ze* (Yunmeng marsh) may have been caused by the conceptual confusion between *Yunmeng* and *Yunmeng ze*, or different understandings of *Yunmeng ze*. According to Tan Qixiang (1987, 105-25), *Yunmeng ze*, a royal hunting ground, was only one part of *Yunmeng*, and it was located in the eastward part of what is now Jiangling County. Shi Quan (1988, 29-35), on the other hand, argues that there were several *Yunmeng ze* at a certain time in history and that only one of them was famous. The location of this famous one, he believes, was changed from time to time. Historically, the kind of gigantic lake that included the whole Jianghan Plain (and even Lake Dongting) never existed.

5 In the late Qing there had been a protracted and intense debate over the diversion of the floodwater of the Jing River. In the late nineteenth century, those who insisted that the south of the Jing River be sacrificed (to protect the north of the Jing River) seemed to have the upper hand. So when there were two breaks in Ouchi and Songzi, the government did not block them, and these breaches gradually became two new outlets of the Yangzi River to Lake Dongting (Mei, Zhang, and Yan 1995, 125).

6 The earliest official record of the Dongjing River is in an 1833 memorial, but this river, under the same name, must have existed much earlier (Lu and Pan 2004, 123-29, esp. 127n3).

7 Due to physiographic differences along the river, it is possible for some rivers to have dikes on one bank but no dikes on another bank; the distance between dike and river also varied. Thus the length of dike on two sides of the same river section can be very different.

8 Historically, part of the lower reaches of the Dongjing River was, in fact, a natural flood diversion area for the Yangzi and the Han Rivers (*Hanyang xian zhi* 1989, 211).

9 Records show that the water level of the Han River was already higher than the surrounding lake land in Anlu Prefecture in the early Qing (*Mu ling shu* 1990 [1848], 9a: 40a); while, as early as 1439, the residents of Jingzhou had said that the Jing River water outside the west of Jingzhou City was more than ten *zhang* higher than Jingzhou City, a doubtful claim

(Zhang 1994a, 140n2), but it is very clear that, in 1788, the floodwater level of the Jing River was already higher than the Jingzhou City (Shuili dianlibu 1991, 481).

10   Usually one would, of course, say that the land and river between dikes on either side of a river are "inside the dikes," but the Jianghan people described them as "outside the dikes."

11   "Waterlogging" usually means that the underground water level is so high that the crops' root system is always submerged – a highly undesirable condition, even for rice. Though crops may not die, they cannot thrive.

12   This number may have been different in the Qing and the Republic, but it is likely that the difference was not great.

13   Water calamities and droughts were the two major disasters in Chinese history. But there is a big difference between the frequency of water calamities and droughts in the Jianghan Plain. Of the calamities of the Jianghan Plain in the Qing, for example, 87 percent were water calamities and 13 percent were droughts (Mei, Zhang, and Yan 1995, 190). Another source indicates that Hubei was plagued by thirty-five to forty-six floods but experienced only five to seven droughts from 1700 to 1949 (Qiao 1963, 22). For this reason, I focus my research on water calamities.

Chapter 2: Water Calamities and the Management of the Dike Systems

1   Dikes built and/or repaired by the government are government dikes; dikes built and/or repaired by local people are people's dikes.

2   According to a nineteenth-century gazetteer, the integrity of dikes was so important that no responsible person dared not act with great care (*Jianli xian zhi* 1872, 3: 5b). Lin Zexu (famous in China for his fight against the opium trade in Guangzhou), for instance, had witnessed the second-class assistant department magistrate of Mianyang standing in water as he took charge during a dike emergency. All responsible personnel carefully watched over dikes through the Jianghan area (Lin 1935, 140).

3   In the original Qing sources, *guangong* had two meanings, and the distinction between them is not clearly drawn. First, the term could refer to a dike whose annual repair the state supported (and thus the term could be translated as "government dike" or "government work"). Second, it might refer to any dike or dike project basically funded by the local people, though managed or supervised by officials and even though its repair was once funded by the government (and it could thus be translated as "official dike" or "official work"). For a detailed and vivid description of how the central government controlled and managed the Yellow River dikes and the Grand Canal, see, respectively, Randall Dodgen (2001) and Jane Kate Leonard (1996).

4   Although Liu Ts'ui-jung (1970) briefly mentions the role of the local people in dike management, she studies only a part of the Jianghan Plain in the late Qing. Zhang Jianmin also discusses the role of the local people, but he deals with both the Jianghan Plain and the Lake Dongting Plain. Moreover, he does not pay much attention to how the role of the people changed (Peng and Zhang 1993, 184-268). Neither Liu nor Zhang discusses dike management in the Republic.

5   The category "government personnel" includes anyone who served in the government system, such as formal officials (magistrates, prefects, etc.), informal officials and functionaries (*yamen* clerks, runners, etc.), and members of the military.

6   If a dike were to break within this ten-year period but the responsible official had moved to another position, both he and his successor would be fined. The ratio of the fine was 3:7 (the original county magistrate paid 30 percent, and the current county magistrate paid 70 percent [*Zai xu xingshui jinjian* 1970 (1942), 120]) or 6:4 (the original officials repaid 60 percent of the cost and the incumbent officials repaid 40 percent [Liu 1970, 5]).

7   For any newly built dike, whether an official dike or a people's dike, a period of ten "safe" years (i.e., years without serious problems) was required. If the cost for reconstruction or

annual repairs was over five thousand taels, the safety period was three years. If an official dike broke, the punishment was the same as the old case. For annual repairs of people's projects, the responsible local official would be stripped of his position. Both this official and the local gentry who undertook and led the project had to pay 40 percent of the cost, respectively, and the official who checked the project had to pay the remaining 20 percent (*Qing huidian shili* 1991 [1899], 929: 675-76).

8 The translations of such titles in this chapter are mostly from Liu (1970) and Will (1985).

9 They were the assistant magistrate of Jiangling (*Jiangling xiancheng*), the subcounty magistrate of Shashi (*Shashi xunjian*), and the subcounty magistrate of Haoxue (*Haoxue xunjian*) (*Jingzhou fu zhi* 1880, 18: 7b-8a).

10 Generally, the majority of the labour force consisted of local villagers; in very rare cases, some hired labourers were brought in from outside. For example, in the late Qing so-called *wo* workers *(wo gong)* (labourers who were good at ramming or tamping earth) from Hunan were hired to repair the Wancheng dike (*Jingzhou fu zhi* 1880, 17: 8a), and in the Republic labourers from Henan were hired to realign the course of the Han River (*Wuhan shi zhi nongye* 1989, 155). *Wo* workers were technical workers whose job met special requirements (*Hanyang xian shuili zhi* 1990, 163).

11 One source recorded that the so-called *youfu* were "evil persons" who used high water control as a pretext for trouble making (Hu 1999 [1838], 194). In Jiangling, *yanfu* were assigned to high water control of the Wancheng dike. Their tasks included preparing "earth oxen" (*tuniu*, earth piled for high water control) and planting trees along the dike. They were chosen by rotation from among those who lived close to the Wancheng dike to serve a one-year term (*Jiangling xian zhi* 1876, 8: 50a). This position was abolished in 1874 (*Jingjiang dadi zhi* 1989, 264). *Yanfu* also existed in Jianli, where they sent smoke signals in case of an emergency, hence their name (smoke labour) (*Jianli shuili zhi* 2005, 387).

12 The staff of these organizations include *zongju* (general bureau or heads of the bureau); *zongjian* (general supervisors or head supervisors); *sanjian* (secondary supervisors); *fuyi* (labourers) and others for annual repair; and *weilao, weijia,* and others for high water control (*Songzi xian zhi* 1869, 4: 12ab).

13 Since "government work," the term used by Qing sources, refers to dike construction or work that was funded by the government, while the money for the annual maintenance of the Wancheng dike was paid by the people of Jiangling (those who lived on the north side of the dike) on a prorated basis, the latter was not "government work." Nonetheless, the Wancheng dike was changed to an official dike after 1788 (because the government provided money for its reconstruction).

14 The annual dike repair was a very urgent task, and any problems – particularly breaks in the dike – had to be solved in the dry season of that year (usually the following winter and next spring). If the breaks were not blocked in the dry season, the result would be inundation the following year with the arrival of the summer high water. At the end of the Qing it had, in fact, become very difficult for the local people to pay their assigned dike fees on time, but the annual repair could not be delayed. In general, for official dikes, if the needed funds could not be collected from the local people on time, and the government (regardless of which level) had no funds for dike repair, the lower-level government unit would have to ask the upper-level government to divert any available funds to repair the dike. Later, the local people would have to repay this money. Because much of this money had to be returned, we can think of it as a loan. Some county governments even tried to borrow money from local merchants (Shu 1896, 6: 5b). In order to repair private dikes, the local people often took out a loan (*Xu xingshui jinjian* 1937, 3576). If they did not, no dike repairs would be carried out.

15 During and after the Taiping Rebellion, both the government and the local people were short of money. In Zhongxiang in 1858, a boat tax began to be levied as a regular tax. The

revenue from the boat tax was used to fund annual repairs to the Han River dike in this county (Peng and Zhang 1993, 218-19).

16 The *tuquan* was a special paper that recorded the name of the head of the household and the amount of the earth fee for which the household was responsible. The process of issuing *tuquan* was as follows: "[After the earth fee has been paid] ... [the government] immediately gives the payee a *quan*, [and] stamps the prefect's seal over the seal of county magistrate ... The name of the *lijia*, head of household, the amount of the earth fee, year, and the word 'completed' are recorded on the paper. The household sticks this paper on its door frame to show that it has paid last year's earth fee ... If there is no such paper on its door frame, then that household is resisting paying the earth fee, in which case the head is to be immediately arrested and fined double the earth fee as a warning to others" (Ni 1885 [1876], 6 jingfei 1, 6a).

17 But a mid-Qing gazetteer said that (the owner of) each *mu* of farmland in Tianmen had to pay 3 *wen* as a dike fee, which was held by county government for the repair of ruptured dikes (*Tianmen xian zhi* 1765, 3: 18b).

18 In 1759, for example, the gentry were encouraged to donate money to water conservancy projects. The rewards differed, depending on the amount of donation (*Qing huidian shili* 1991 [1899], 929: 673).

19 Zhang Jianmin divides them into five types: (1) money contributed by the local people, (2) government funds, (3) donations, (4) interest from special funds, and (5) the *lijin*. But, as he argues, these funds in fact came either from the government or from the local people generally (Peng and Zhang 1993, 208-19).

20 Wang Youdan concludes that there were five disadvantages to the co-repair of dikes. First, since the lower valley people had to travel a few hundred *li* away from home to build dikes, they had to bring their own tools and food (and sleep outside). Some of them died due to cold and hunger. Second, since *yamen* runners (or petty officials) were involved, extortion was unavoidable. Third, it was unfair to expect the lower valley people to rebuild or repair "other people's dikes" and abandon the maintenance of their own. Fourth, in cases in which silver instead of labour was used to meet one's share, the officials who handled the money would pocket some of it. Fifth, the exchange of official documents (in dealing with the dispute) would require time and result in inefficiency (*Qianjiang xian zhi* 1879, 10: 48ab).

21 An 1867 case records how the local people deliberately built private dikes. They usually built private *yuan* under the pretext of building a road. If someone investigated, they would say that what they had built was a road, not a dike. If no official discovered the truth, the local people would heighten their construction year by year until it became a private dike (Ni 1885 [1876], 8: 26a).

22 This kind of reluctance can also be seen in the maintenance of river dikes: even if they participated in dike works, those who lived far away from a river dike might not take their work seriously. Thus it would have been wise to have had those who lived close to dikes supervise and undertake dike works (particularly the annual repairs) because they would not risk their own lives by jerry-building and engaging in careless construction (*Jingshan xian zhi* 1882, 4: 3b).

23 In fact, it has been argued that corruption had become a built-in problem of the Qing government as early as the eighteenth century (Park 1997, 996-99). This is particularly true if we consider unregistered *yamen* runners – even though the government probably could not have functioned without these informal government personnel (Ch'u 1988 [1962]; Reed 2000).

24 The increasing burden of the dike fee in Jianli, for example, was partly a result of the enlargement of the earth bureau in this county. In the 1830s, Jianli first set up a county-level earth bureau to collect the earth fee. There were eight *shoushi* in this bureau, and each was paid four hundred *wen* a day for meals. Later, five subcounty branches of the earth bureau

were established in the countryside; each branch had three *shoushi,* and each *shoushi* received four hundred *wen* per day for meals. In total there were twenty-three *shoushi,* who were paid ninety-two hundred *wen* per day for meals. Lin Zexu thought that this was just a waste of money. He ordered the branches to be abolished and the meal fee to be reduced to three hundred *wen* per day per *shoushi* (Lin 1935, 101-6).

25 Dodgen (2001, 37-38) argues that critics exaggerated the corruption of the river bureaucracy (of the Grand Canal) in the early nineteenth century. This is possible. But local records show that the corruption associated with the dike fees in the Jianghan area in the nineteenth century was indeed a very serious problem.

26 Although in principle the method for maintaining *yuan* dikes was to share the responsibility evenly among the people who benefited from them, in practice it varied. There were three different ways of maintaining the dikes. First, several *yuan* that benefited from the same dike shared responsibility for its maintenance; second, one *yuan* assumed responsibility for a *yuan* dike and all *yuan* residents worked together; and third, one *yuan* took responsibility for a *yuan* dike, but each individual *yuan* household was responsible for one share (*Hubei An Xiang Yun dao shuili ji'an* n.d., II: 2b-3a). It is clear that the effectiveness of these methods tended to decrease as one moved from the first method to the third method.

27 For example, in *Qing huidian shili* (edited in the reign of Guangxu), the safety requirement only applied to the Qiaomaiwan dike in Jiangxia County, the Wancheng dike in Jingzhou, and the dikes along the Yangzi River in Hanyang (Peng and Zhang 1993, 206).

28 *Jin bao yin* means to build a dike with sand in the centre and covered with earth. Sand was not as solid as earth, but because years of repair had used up nearby earth, and because it was expensive to bring earth from afar as doing so would increase the already difficult-to-collect dike fee (*Xiangdi cheng'an* 1969, 1: 228b), readily available sand was used.

29 Table 6 shows that the Wancheng dike suffered only a few breaks after 1871. One of the major reasons for this was the formation of an outlet in Ouchi in the 1850s and another in Songzi in the 1870s that discharged floodwater into Lake Dongting and reduced the pressure on the Wancheng dike. The dike enjoyed about sixty years without a major break before a massive inundation in 1931 (*Jingjiang dadi zhi* 1989, 36-39; Cheng Pengju 1990; *Hubei shuili zhi* 2000, 373).

30 This high infrastructural power came into being in China after 1949. The Communist state, which has both a high degree of despotic power and a high degree of infrastructural power, has paid more attention than its predecessors to the maintenance of the dike systems in the Jianghan Plain. The CCP's ability to mobilize labour for dike projects and to make each person accountable for every metre of the dikes in high water control (*Jingjiang dadi zhi* 1989, 222-23) has ensured the integrity of the major dikes in the Jianghan Plain for more than half a century.

Chapter 3: The Dike Systems and the Jianghan Economy

1 In 1950, the PRC government announced that all land within one hundred metres on the outside of river dikes and fifty metres inside of river dikes was to be taken by the state for dike projects (*Jingjiang dadi zhi* 1989, 258). This suggests that, previously, most of these lands had not been owned by the state.

2 This calculation ignores the fact that the boundaries of Jingzhou were changed somewhat after 1949.

3 Hu Zuhe (1999 [1838], 202-5) recorded how to calculate the cost of moving earth for dike building via waterways, with boats used to move earth.

4 According to PRC regulations in Jianli, if it is deemed necessary to take earth from the inner side of a dike, it must be taken from beyond the safety zone. It was common to remove the soil from relatively high land and to transform dry land into paddy fields in order to avoid digging deep pits (*Jianli difang zhi* 1991, 203).

5 It is true that, with regard to size, the water-control projects in the Qing and the Republic could not compare to those in the first three decades of the PRC. But, on the other hand, this amount of earth was used only on regular repairs. The amount of earth used on the building of new dikes would be much more than this. Since many new dikes (major and minor) were built in the Qing and the Republic over the Jianghan area, the amount of farmland lost to dike projects in the Qing and the Republic would have been even larger.

6 The high water level of the Jing River has risen by 13.6 metres over the past five thousand years, mostly in the past several centuries (Zhou 1986). The Wancheng dike was progressively raised to accommodate the high water. According to one record, after the Wancheng dike was repaired in 1788, people set iron oxen (sculptures with talismanic power to ward off floods) on top of it. But four decades later, the iron oxen were more than one *zhang* below the top of the dike (Wang 1832, 1: 15a). According to another record, at the end of the nineteenth century, the arch of Fukang Gate of Shashi was already located in the middle of the Wancheng dike. In 1915 (thirty to forty years later), the gate was buried at the bottom of this dike, and only sixty- to seventy-year-old local residents knew where the gate was (*Jingjiang di zhi* 1937, 4: 16), which means that this dike had risen several metres within several decades.

7 Since the majority of *yuan* dikes were people's dikes, and hence not reported to the Board of Works, no record of their length is available. Hanchuan, however, was an exception. In the late Qing, it had thirty-five official *yuan* with 130,176 *zhang* of dikes and sixty-one people's *yuan* with 80,966.8 *zhang* of dikes, for a total of 211,142.8 *zhang*. This did not include the dikes of 155 small *yuan* since it was uncertain they still existed (*Hanchuan tuji zhengshi* 1895, 4: 4b-5a). In the same period, the Han River dike in this county was 41,130 *zhang* (Peng and Zhang 1993, 264). In other words, the recorded length of *yuan* dikes in this county in the late Qing was more than five times the length of its major dikes.

8 In the 1930s, however, it was found that the new, temporary bureaus that were set up to oversee dike works usually began repairs in spring and finished in late spring and early summer, when farming was busy (*Gailiang digong yijian shu* n.d., 2).

9 Levying the dike fee according to the land tax can also be understood as levying it according to farmland. This is because the land tax was levied on farmland. Theoretically, for farmland of the same grade, the larger the acreage, the greater the land tax, and the heavier the dike fee.

10 *Fang* is a measure of a volume of earth, and its size varies in different areas. According to a PRC gazetteer, 1 Qing *fang* is equal to 3.7 m^3 (*Jiangling difang zhi* 1984, 11); but, according to Hu Zuhe (1999 [1838], 207), 1 *fang* = 1 *zhang* × 1 *zhang* × 0.1 *zhang* or 3.28 m^3. The latter is the standard used in this chapter.

11 See Wang Baixin's discussions on dredging the Yangzi River (cited in Song 1954, 59). Though Wang may have exaggerated the situation (since he strongly opposed the building of dikes), it is certain that the heavy burden of the earth fee was a serious problem.

12 There is no explanation of the term *fuqian* in the original gazetteer. I surmise that it was a piece of paper or a wooden board on which was recorded the workload (how many *fang* of earth or how long a section of the dike) and the location of the portion of dike for which the individual household was responsible.

13 In some cases, peasants who participated in high water control also received a subsidy: for example, one hundred *wen* per day for meals and lighting, and an exemption from labour service. In some places, it was required that small or poor households (*xiaohu*) contribute their labour, while large or rich households (*daye*, with more than three hundred *mu* of cultivated land) contributed money, usually ten *wen* per *mu* in addition to providing meals to labourers during the high-water seasons. If labour was levied according to the amount of land owned, the rich families could not bear the cost; however, assigning labour

according to the household was considered much too unfair. Thus, rich households contributed an extra ten *wen* per *mu* of farmland (*Zai xu xingshui jinjian* 1970 [1942], 806, 814). In Jingshan, the people who participated in high water control were exempted from miscellaneous taxes and miscellaneous labour services (*Jingshan xian zhi* 1882, 4: 3ab).

14 In this case, "two harvests within one year" simply means that, in the province as a whole, there were harvests twice a year, not that there were harvests twice a year on the same plot (see Chapter 4).

15 *Mai* sometimes refers to wheat only, and sometimes to both wheat and barley, or even buckwheat. I use *mai* as a shorthand whenever the reference to a particular grain, or grains, is unclear.

16 Given the average yield of around two *shi* of unhusked rice in the Jianghan Plain during the Qing (see Appendix), this figure is probably not the yield of *mai* (which usually yields less than rice) but the output of both rice (two *shi*) and *mai* (one *shi*) per *mu*.

17 In the mid-nineteenth century, for instance, it was said that the food an average villager consumed in one month was worth 0.15 taels of silver (*Zai xu xingshui jinjian* 1970 [1942], 7: 193). In other words, an average villager needed only 1.8 taels of silver to cover the cost of one year's food. So if a dike project cost 100,000 taels of silver, the money could have been used to feed 55,555 people for one year.

18 During this period (1950-85) there was not much inflation at all in China, so we can ignore the change of relative prices.

19 This kind of comparison may be questionable since there are many other investments that contribute to the gross income of agriculture. I am not arguing that all the gross income of agriculture comes from the investment in dikes; rather, I am simply emphasizing the importance of the Jingjiang Great Dike. Agriculture as we know it would be impossible without the protection of this dike. Without the dike, no matter how many other investments the local peasants made, the gains would be small (because floods would destroy almost everything if it were not for the protection afforded by the dike).

20 The original source does not mention any investment in high water control on the part of the central government. However, judging from the total investment in the Jingjiang Great Dike, we can see that the investment in high water control had been very limited. For the moment, we can ignore it.

21 I use the term "theoretically" since these monies were not directly paid by the local peasants in the name of the dike fees. However, the local people frequently complained that the task of high water control and draining waterlogged fields was excessively burdensome. This may be because, first, there were some hidden costs (such as the expenditure of responsible cadres and some necessary materials) that are not reflected in the government's figures and, second, having to deal with high water control and dike repair and maintenance year in and year out drove people to the point of exhaustion.

22 The land tax in the Qing was levied according to the amount of land (measured in *mu*), while in the PRC, it was changed to a tax on the gross income from agriculture. However, in practice, the agricultural tax was collected on the basis of the regular output of local crops but was converted to the local staple food grain. In the Jianghan Plain, that would be rice (it was converted to cash after 1985) (*Jingzhou diqu zhi* 1996, 435-36). Thus, they are still roughly comparable.

23 According to official statistics, the amount of agricultural tax revenue has changed little since 1952, but the yield of crops has increased several fold. Thus, indeed, the tax rate has become lower and lower. But the real burden the Jianghan peasants have had to bear has increased since the early 1990s due mainly to many kinds of "legalized surcharges" (i.e., charges supported by the upper level government). Agricultural tax was officially abolished in Hubei in 2005. Unfortunately, a discussion of rural taxation since the 1990s is beyond the scope of the present research.

24 Thus, if the cost of such items (including labour) is taken into account, the investment would increase and the return on the investment in dikes would decrease.

25 In Republican Hubei, surcharges also usually exceeded (in some counties by seven- to eightfold) the regular land tax (Xiong [n.d.], 10).

26 The landlords were managers or supervisors of dike work. According to a saying in Hanyang: "[A person who owns] 30 *mu* of farmland [brings only] an umbrella, [a person who owns] 15 *mu* of farmland [brings only] a shovel, [a person who owns] 3-5 *mu* of farmland, arches his back to shoulder [the earth]" (*Hanyang xian zhi chugao* 1960, 34). A similar saying can be found in the Mianyang area in the Republic (*Honghu xian zhi* 1963, 121; *Mianyang chenchangqu xiangtu zhi* 1987, 299).

27 There is no reliable estimate of the damage caused by each inundation in the Jianghan Plain in the Qing and the Republic. Although it varied from inundation to inundation, sometimes the damage was serious.

28 In 1998, there was an extraordinarily high level of high water that destroyed some small *yuan* but did not break or over-flood any major dikes. Thus the Jianghan people did not suffer as much from the 1998 high water as they did from that in 1954.

29 Since the floods carried silt, they conceivably could have been used to fill in some low places. Indeed, someone suggested using the sediment of the Yangzi River water to fill low places in the Jianghan Plain north of the river (*Jingjiang dadi zhi* 1989, 12 [introduction of Lin Yishan]). Of course, this would have been a controlled, not a natural, silting.

30 In the Jingjiang Flood Diversion Area in 1954, after the floodwater receded, people found that the whole area was covered by a layer of sludge one-third of a metre or more thick (Li 2001, 102). In one *yuan* in Songzi, during the reign of Qianlong (1736-95) there was a tomb with a gravestone roughly one *zhang* (1 *zhang* = 10 *chi*) tall; by the late Qing, after many floods, there was only one *chi* or so of this gravestone still left above ground (*Songzi xian zhi* 1982 [1937], 81). Over the course of a hundred plus years the sludge had raised the land of that *yuan* by about three metres.

31 Xia Mingfang (2000, 59-62) provides more examples of this function of sludge. For instance, in Shanxi the harvest was closely related to the annual floodwater from surrounding rivers: the heavier the flood, the better the harvest the next year. And along Jiangsu's eastern coast the local peasants did not flee from the frequent floods because the deposited silt ensured good harvests.

32 When I was an agro-technician in the 1980s, I worked with the peasants to improve their waterlogged paddy fields (*lengjin tian* ["cold (water) soaked field"]) through the use of zinc fertilizer.

33 In Jingzhou, for example, the application of chemical fertilizers since the 1970s actually caused a reduction, not an increase, in soil fertility: 95 percent of farmlands lack nitrogen (N), 60.1 percent of farmlands seriously lack phosphorus (P), and 39.1 percent of farmlands lack potassium (K) (*Jingzhou diqu zhi* 1996, 361).

34 The symptoms of environmental unsustainability include climate change and greenhouse effect, ozone depletion, acid deposition, toxic pollution, species extinction, deforestation, land degradation, water depletion, fishery destruction, and non-renewable resource deple- tion, and so forth and so on (Ekins 2000, 7). Thus, the theory of sustainable development initially appeared as a reaction to the negative effects of industrial development on the environment. The pre-1949 Jianghan economy does not fall into this category.

35 I do not emphasize the role of technology in the maintenance of the dike systems. This does not mean that technology is unimportant, only that dike-related technology changed little over the past few centuries. Late Ming methods of dike construction and key points of high water control were still treated as the gold standard in the 1990s: the only difference involved an improvement in materials. In other words, dike technology was already very

advanced in the Ming (Zhang and Zuo 2001, 396). Human beings served as the sole power for dike work until the 1950s (*Jingjiang dadi zhi* 1989, 126). Probably for the same reason, past scholarship did not pay much attention to the role of technology in the control of frequent inundation in this area. In the Republic (after the 1930s), the management of major dikes in Hubei was taken over by the *Jianghan gongcheng ju*, a professional institution armed with powerful and advanced technology, but its effectiveness was very limited because it failed to mobilize the local people (*Hubei sheng zhi shuili* 1995, 22). At the end of the Qing and in the early Republic, Hunan also tried to use new technology to dredge Lake Dongting; however, due to a shortage of funds and weak management, this effort was in vain (Perdue 1987, 232, 246). These experiences again offer evidence that management is more important than technology in overcoming dike-related water calamities.

Chapter 4: Agriculture, Commercialization, and Environmental Adaptability

1 According to Ho Ping-ti (1959), New World crops played an important role in the increase of population in the Qing. But that is not the case in the Jianghan Plain. Although maize was recorded in the grain section of many local county gazetteers, in these counties, it was either scattered on land close to mountains and river beaches or, occasionally, grown on poor, hilly land (*Hanchuan tuji zhengshi* 1895, 4: 39b). This situation was very different from that in some high mountainous areas, where maize was grown as a staple food grain (*Hubei tong zhi* 1921, 779). In short, maize was not widely distributed in the Jianghan Plain in the Qing. The sweet potato was of even less importance as a food grain in the Jianghan Plain at that time, and only a few gazetteers mention it as occurring in places such as Zhijiang County. In fact, even in Zhijiang, only people who lived in mountainous areas ate it as a substitute for rice (and saved many lives) in lean years (*Zhijiang xian zhi* 1866, 7: 1b). In Shishou, there were only about two hundred *mu* of sweet potato at the beginning of the PRC (*Shishou xian zhi* 1990, 170). Both crops were introduced to Hubei and Hunan in the early Qing and mainly cultivated in mountainous areas (Gong 1993b). For these reasons, it is safe to say that neither maize nor sweet potato were at all important in the Jianghan Plain in the Qing.

2 A direct translation of *shandi* is "mountain land," but the mountains in this county were actually very low, and more like hills.

3 The "early-season rice" and "late-season rice" recorded in traditional gazetteers do not correspond to modern varieties similarly named; they were probably distinguished only by their time of transplanting (for more discussion, see Zhang [1991]).

4 *Handao* was also found in Xiaogan in the early PRC. The peasants there grew it as a way of coping with drought. Although it requires only half the water of paddy rice, the yield is low (*Xiaogan shi zhi* 1992, 164).

5 The awn (long ear on the end of grain) is a typical characteristic of wild (undomesticated) rice. That it was named "awn" probably means it clearly bore the characteristics of wild rice. The more times rice is transplanted (usually one or two times), the higher the yield. The yield of direct-seeding rice (which involves no transplanting) is the lowest.

6 According to You Xiuling (1995, 228-29), *qingnian* is a variety of deepwater rice that, biologically, closely resembles regular rice. He also mentions another variety of deepwater rice in this area, *qi niu sa*, literally, "broadcasting [rice] riding on the back of ox." In the 1950s, the people of Hanchuan asked the upper-level government to allot them the seeds of a variety of deepwater rice from Hunan, which was said to grow as much as four metres in height in water (SZ 113-3-197).

7 Records from gazetteers show the increasing distribution of the double cropping of rice in the whole Yangzi River valley in the Qing dynasty, but its acreage was limited (Min 1999, 2003).

8   According to a 1950 survey, in 1949 about 500,000 *mu* in Hubei was devoted to the double cropping of rice (*Hubei sheng zhi nongye I* 1994, 65). Even if all of this land were located in the Jianghan Plain (which was impossible), it would have accounted for only 5 percent of the paddy fields there, assuming that Jianghan's paddy fields amount to 10 million *mu* (that amount was around 9.73 million *mu* in the 1930s [*Hubei sheng zhi tudi liyong yu liangshi wenti* 1977 [1938], 24180-83). The success of the double cropping of rice on large acreage not only depends on the appropriate use of fertilizer and technology but also on picking the right variety to cultivate.

9   A high water table definitely affects the production of crops. It was observed that, if the water table of cotton land were 1 metre lower, the yield would range from 70 to 90 *jin;* if it were 1.3 to 2 metres lower, the yield would increase to 150 to 180 *jin.* If the underground water table of wheat land were less than 0.2 metre, the harvest of wheat would be almost totally lost (*Hubei nongye dili* 1980, 86).

10   Almost every new county gazetteer recorded that the major pattern of rice cropping in the Republic in the Jianghan Plain was single cropping (of middle-season rice). However, according to a survey of the 1950s, before 1949, the acreage of paddy fields under the rotation of middle-season rice and wheat in Hubei was very limited as people were not used to planting wheat in paddy fields (*Hubei sheng zhi nongye I* 1994, 187).

11   In emphasizing those who lived along rivers and close to lakes, I am not being very selective: the Jianghan Plain had one of the highest densities of lakes in the country. The greater Jianghan area (i.e., greater than the Jianghan Plain discussed in this book) had 1,066 lakes in the 1950s, with a surface area of 12.5 million *mu*, which accounted for one-sixth of the Jianghan Plain (*Hubei nongye dili* 1980, 80). The number in the Qing and the Republic was even higher.

12   In Shishou in the late Qing and the Republic, the local peasants harvested one season of dryland crop from the land outside the river dike before the coming of the summer high water and then, for the rest of the year, abandoned the land as wasteland (*Shishou xian zhi* 1990, 166).

13   Replanting can take two forms. In the first, some additional seeds (of the same crop) are sown after seedlings that have not sprouted as quickly as expected; in the second, the original sowing totally fails and, therefore, the crop (the same or another) must be completely resown.

14   Without knowing the exact number of *yuan* in the Jianghan Plain, we cannot calculate the percentage of *yuan* that lost their harvest. But if each *yuan* has an acreage of five thousand *mu* on average, which seems a reasonable estimate (Zhang Jiayan 2001), then 593 *yuan* would cover 2,965,000 *mu*, or roughly three times the registered land of Shishou in the Ming (949,064 *mu* [*Shishou xian zhi* 1866, 3: 4b]). Undoubtedly, the inundated acreage, or acreage of lost harvest, varied widely from year to year. (One must also keep in mind that the amount of registered land was usually less than that of the real acreage because the county or department government normally used large *mu* for reporting but small *mu* for taxation and then pocketed the difference. A large *mu* could be 1.5 to 8 times as large as the small *mu* [Liang 1980, 528].)

15   With regard to peasants' choice of market involvement and subsistence, Philip Huang (1985, 6-9) suggests an integrated analysis of different peasant groups. Due to limited data, I cannot offer such an analysis for the Jianghan Plain, but it is still possible to analyze the different behaviour of peasants who lived in different locations.

16   Since the late Ming, the middle Yangzi River valley exported more and more rice. In the end, the popular saying in Song-Yuan times, "If Suzhou and Huzhou have a good harvest, the entire empire will be fed" *(Su Hu shu, tianxia zu)* was replaced by the Ming-Qing saying: "If Hunan-Hubei has a good harvest, the entire empire will be fed" *(Huguang shu, tianxia zu).* Before the mid-Qing the Jianghan Plain was one of the most important providers

of commercial rice in Hunan-Hubei. Most of its export rice was shipped to the Yangzi delta for consumption and redistribution. It is estimated that, in 1734, about 10 million *shi* of (husked) rice were shipped from Hunan-Hubei to the Yangzi delta. Much of this rice was in fact produced in Hunan (Quan 1972, 573-74).

To be sure, some Jianghan rice continued to enter the long-distance market, and some was sold in the local market. Moreover, rice might be sold by landlords after having been received as rent or sold by peasants not for profit but to get cash in order to pay their taxes. In the 1930s, it was found that the unhusked rice produced in Hunan, Hubei, and Jiangxi and shipped to Hankou was mostly sold by poor peasants who needed to do so in order to survive (Zeng 1984 2: 137): it had nothing to do with "surplus grain," let alone with market-driven production.

17 The cotton cloth of Hanchuan, called *dabu* (great cotton cloth) and *xiaobu* (small cotton cloth), was either sold within Hubei Province or bought by merchants of the provinces of Shanxi, Shaanxi, Yunnan, and Guizhou (*Hanchuan xian zhi* 1873, 6: 19b). Xiaogan's cotton cloth bought by merchants from northwestern China was simply called *Xiaogan bu* (Xiaogan cotton cloth) (*Xiaogan xian zhi* 1883, 5: 39a).

18 According to a survey in the early 1930s, in many counties of the Jianghan Plain (Hanyang, Hanchuan, Yunmeng, Xiaogan, Qianjiang, Shishou, Tianmen, Mianyang, Songzhi, and Gong'an), cotton was the major product (*Hubei xianzheng gaikuang* 1934). Only a small part of this cotton was used by mills in Hubei; the majority was shipped to Shanghai to be used there or shipped abroad (*Hubei zhi mianhua* 1938).

19 For example, around 1900, about 140,000 to 150,000 *dan* of Jingzhou cloth was exported annually all over the country through Shashi and Jiangkou (Zeng 1984, 1: 78). From 1910 to 1937, Yunmeng alone exported 1.6 to 2.1 million bolts (1 bolt = 0.3 × 12 metres) of cotton cloth to Shanxi and Shaanxi annually. This trade only dried up after 1937 due to the Japanese invasion (*Yunmeng xian zhi* 1994, 284).

20 The new gazetteer of Zhongxiang, for example, simply indicates that, in the Republic, the local peasants usually grew everything they needed (*Zhongxiang xian zhi* 1990, 292). This suggests that the primary goal of the peasants was to be self-supporting, not to seek profit in the market.

Chapter 5: Tenancy and Environment

1 In this chapter I do not use John Lossing Buck's investigation, which was based on selected wealthier rural families from some large agricultural regions (Buck 1937, preface, ix). Such data are unavoidably problematic (Esherick 1981).

2 Most of the surveys used here mixed statistics with estimates. Not only were the surveys sometimes of questionable reliability, but they also differed greatly from one another. However, one aspect of the data is the same: the relatively high percentage of owner-peasants in Hubei's rural society. It was still higher in the Jianghan Plain.

3 This survey consisted partly of a letter investigation and partly of a personal investigation. Only three of these eleven counties – Jiangling, Zhijiang, and Wuchang – were located in the Jianghan Plain (Tudi weiyuanhui 1937, 2-7).

4 An early Qing official once bought 223.26 *mu* of land, consisting of 333 plots, in two locations in Jiangxia as school land (*Hubei tong zhi* 1921, 1597). In other words, each plot was only 0.67 *mu* (or 447 square metres) on average. In Jingshan, a school land property of 24.5 *mu* was divided into forty-one plots (*Hubei tong zhi* 1921, 1623), that is, each plot was only 0.6 *mu* (or 400 square metres) on average.

5 In citing the rural classification of the population, the newly compiled gazetteers rarely gave any figures about the number of landless people. It seems that virtually every rural household had some land. But the data of the Land Reform of one village in the Jianghan Plain show that about one-fifth of this village's households had no land. Most of these

landless households were categorized as "poor peasants" (Zhang 2009), and it is for this reason that the Land Reform records of the county in which this village was located had no landless households.

6 Qin Hui found that, in central Shaanxi in the Republic, almost every class hired labour and that both landlords and landless peasants were rare; the majority of rural people were middle peasants or owner-peasants (Qin and Jin 2010, 43-108). Xia Mingfang (2001, 311) found the same situation in the provinces of Hebei and Shandong.

7 "Class status" was a term used by the CCP during the Land Reform to identify the political classification of rural families, determined mainly by the extent of a family's property (land) and sources of income. Class status includes, from the richest to the poorest: landlord, rich peasant, middle peasant, poor peasant, and hired hand (or agricultural labourer). Once the class status of a family had been identified, every member of that family had the same class status, no matter the member's age or gender.

8 In fact, when it came to defining landlords, tenants, and so on, there were no major differences between the GMD and the CCP. According to the GMD's National Land Commission, landlords were those who owned land but rented it out; owner-peasants were those who owned land and cultivated it themselves; tenants were those who had no land but rented it from others; and agricultural labours were those who were without land and farmed for others (Tudi weiyuanhui 1937, 33). According to the Agrarian Reform Law of the People's Republic of China, landlords were those who lived off the rents of their lands; rich peasants were those who rented out some land but worked the rest themselves; middle peasants were those who worked their own land without the help of tenants or hired hands; poor peasants were tenants or owners of small plots who also rented land or hired out their labour; and agricultural labourers were those who generally had no land and worked for wages (Hinton 1997 [1966], 623-26).

9 According to the new gazetteer of Shashi, in a suburb of Shashi, before 1949, some rich peasants were owner-peasants who rented out part of their land; some owner-peasants also hired agricultural labourers. Middle peasants usually farmed only their own land, although some of them might rent a small piece of land. Poor peasants usually rented land from others and at the same time sold part of their labour. Only hired hands were landless and hired themselves out to landlords and rich peasants (*Nongye zhi* 1993, 26).

10 Actually, according to a 1952 national statistic of landownership before the Land Reform, landlords and rich peasants accounted for 6.87 percent of rural households and 9.41 percent of the rural population but owned 51.92 percent of the cultivated land (Du 1996, 4). The rest of the rural population owned almost half of all cultivated land. These percentages are even higher than those of Zhang Youyi. In other words, the CCP's own statistics clashed with its classic interpretation of rural classes. Very commonly, the newly compiled gazetteers highlighted some special examples to show how much land was owned by landlords. For example, in order to emphasize the seriousness of the problem of land concentration in the Republic, a new Hanyang gazetteer used this example: 90 percent of the farmland of Pengxin Township was owned by a single local landlord (*Hanyang xian zhi chugao* 1960, 31). But in fact, in 1948, only 35.5 percent of the entire farmland in this county was owned by landlords and rich peasants (*Hanyang xian zhi* 1989, 163).

11 In general, past scholarship has assumed that calamities increased the tendency towards land concentration. But Xia Mingfang (2001, 319) argues that, although calamities led to a relative surplus supply of land on the market, at the same time they also caused the demand for land to shrink. This helps explain the relationship between the frequent floods and the lack of land concentration in the Jianghan Plain. A similar argument can be made regarding the Lake Dongting Plain, where there is also a lack of land concentration. The reasons for this include frequent floods, heavy taxation, and an equal division of holdings among sons. Another survey further points out that, in the Lake Dongting Plain, there

were relatively more owner-peasants in old *yuan*, and there were more tenant-peasants in new *yuan* (Peng 1977 [1938], 39378-79, 39391-93).

12 Thus, the survey based on eleven counties in Hubei mentioned above indicates that 72.11 percent of the cultivated land was farmed by owners and only 27.89 percent was rented out (Cheng 1977 [1938], 45516).

13 It is unclear how a "large" landlord was defined in this context. One survey, however, defines Hubei's large landlords as those who owned more than 500 *mu* of land (Tudi weiyuanhui 1937, 32). The meaning of the term *er di zhu* (literally, "secondary landlords") differed from place to place. In Xiaogan, for instance, the *er di zhu* was someone who guaranteed that tenants would pay the rent: for this guarantee, tenants had to pay the *er di zhu* 10 to 20 percent of the harvest (*Xiaogan shi zhi* 1992, 126). In Shishou, however, *er di zhu* was those who rented land from landlords and then re-rented it to tenants; here tenants had to pay 30 percent of harvest to the *er di zhu* (*Shishou xian zhi* 1990, 157).

14 Since the mid-nineteenth century, some of them gradually severed their relations with the countryside and eventually became urban residents (Rowe 1990, 67-69).

15 Zhao Gang and Chen Zhongyi (1982, 407) insist that the rent deposit system was a source of permanent tenure: if a landlord did not return the rent deposit, then the tenant could rent the land forever; thus, the tenant acquired the right to permanent tenure. While that may be true in theory, in practice this was not always the case in the Jianghan Plain.

16 During the Republic, although in some counties, such as Xiaogan, tenants were not required to pay a rent deposit, they had to pay rent one season in advance (*Xiaogan shi zhi* 1992, 125). This can be understood as one way for landlords to guarantee their rent income in an environment of frequent floods.

17 One gazetteer claims that landlords demanded rent deposits as a security guarantee as well as to induce tenants to maintain the fertility of the land by fertilizing it (*Jianli xian zhi* 1959, 71). However, this is only a partial explanation. Otherwise it would be hard to explain why rent deposits were common in some regions but absent in others.

18 It is unclear from the data presented in this table how many landlords required which form of rent payment. Fan Shuzhi (1988, 658) contends that, in Hubei (in the Republic): "Share-cropping is more popular than fixed rent, and there are many labour services and surcharges, [all of which] reflect the backwardness of the tenancy relationships in Hubei." He argues that sharecropping was more common than fixed rent in Hubei, but he does not provide supporting statistics. If it is true that there was more sharecropping than fixed rent overall in Hubei, I would think that this was the result of environmental degradation.

19 Thus, if one includes the spring harvest in the total annual output, the rental rate (the amount of rent divided by the output of the land) in the Yangzi delta was 32 to 48 percent (mostly around 40 percent), not as high as the 50 to 80 percent that is usually cited (Zheng 1986, 46: Table 5).

20 This phenomenon has been found all over the country. Victor Lippit (1974, 61) argues that Chinese tenants usually paid 40 percent of the gross value of the agricultural output as rent, while Gao Wangling (2002) claims that this figure was probably only 40 percent or lower.

21 In the North China Plain, sharecropping was usually practised among relatives or close friends (Huang 1985, 204-7). It is unclear whether this was also the case in the Jianghan Plain.

22 Also in this county, the rent was reducible when calamity struck. But before agreeing to a reduction, the landlords would go to the fields in person to check the harvest (*Hubei xianzheng gaikuang* 1934, 955).

23 Many Republican surveys are not very reliable, but this one was guided by the principles of comprehensiveness and authenticity (Sui 2005, 52) and so should be comparatively sound.

24 This custom can be found in earlier times in the Jianghan Plain. For example, in the Qing dynasty, Cao Hongyuan of Xiaogan wanted his rent reduced after a drought (Zhongguo diyi 1988, 706-8).

25 A survey of Hanyang records that the landlords and the tenants agree to pay rent in rice [at the rate of] 1.3 *dan* after the autumn harvest, but "the tenants are usually crafty, and less than 10 percent of them pay their rent in full" (*Hubei xianzheng gaikuang* 1934, 69). This phenomenon was not only found in the Republic. As early as the 1800s, landlords of this county began to complain that there were more "crafty" tenants than docile ones (Zhongguo renmin 1979, 71).

26 According to the National Land Commission's survey of 17,354 households of eleven counties in Hubei, permanent tenure – which was particularly prevalent in mountainous western Hubei – was found on only 13.4 percent of rented land (Cheng 1977 [1938], 45514-15). Tenants on so-called *guitian* (redeemable land) pawned their land to a landlord then rented it back to cultivate, but the landlord would take the land if the tenant failed to redeem it on time (*Hanchuan xian zhi* 1992, 107).

27 There were two other kinds of permanent tenure in Hanyang and Zhongxiang. In Hanyang, the tenant paid a deposit on a piece of land and thus owned the topsoil right, or the seller of a plot of land retained the right to cultivate it. In both cases, tenants had the right to transfer land to other tenants. In Zhongxiang, if a landowner sold his land but recorded on the contract that he retained the right to cultivate it, then no one else had the right to cultivate it (*Minshi xiguan* 2000, 325, 336).

28 According to the newly compiled gazetteer of Jingshan County, in Guanqiao Township there was a large landlord surnamed Huang whose family had acquired a fortune during the reign of Jiajing (1522-66) and who owned land all over Jingshan and Zhongxiang. The land was transferred from one generation to another for about four centuries. This was a rare case. Since both Jingshan and Zhongxiang are located in the middle of the Han River valley, and more than half of their land lies in hills or mountains, it is possible that the Huang family's land was not subject to frequent flooding and so could be kept intact for centuries. Actually, the oldest son of the fourteenth generation of this family owned only 540 *mu* in 1940 – that hardly made him a very big landlord (*Jingshan xian zhi* 1990, 94).

29 For example, the Shen family in the Yangzi delta – who owned about one thousand *mu* – kept a record of land purchases and sales for 165 years (Hong 1988, 90-145).

30 The percentage of permanent tenure in the Jianghan Plain might have been even lower than that of Hubei as a whole due to Jianghan's frequent floods. As for tenancies, however, there were also differences between the North China Plain and the Jianghan Plain: the majority of tenancies were one year in the North China Plain but three to five years in the Jianghan Plain, due mainly to the latter's more stable environment. In the Yangzi delta, where the environment was relatively more stable, tenancy was much longer. According to a Republican survey, the percentage of cultivated land with permanent tenancy was 30.59 in Zhejiang, 40.86 in Jiangsu, 44.15 in Anhui, 4.47 in Shandong, 3.94 in Hebei, and 2.56 in Henan. In Hubei, the percentage was 13.4 (Tudi weiyuanhui 1937, 45).

31 In my research, water calamities are the main concern. The peasants of the Jianghan Plain sometimes endured drought, and rent could also be reduced after a drought, as was the case in Xiaogan in the mid-Qing (Zhongguo diyi 1988, 706).

32 For theoretical discussions on moral economy in rural society, see Scott (1976).

33 The CCP's revolutionary ideology of land relationships was based mostly on the rural experience of the North China Plain, where tenant-landlord relations were filled with violence. Played out against this historical backdrop, the Land Reform in the North China Plain was bloody and violent. But it was more peaceful in the Yangzi delta (Bernhardt 1992, 220-24) as well as in the Jianghan Plain.

Chapter 6: Fisheries and the Peasant Economy

1 I first encountered this question at Leiden University in 1996, when Dr. E.B. Vermeer of the Sinological Institute posed it to me during our discussion of my research on the agrarian history of the Jianghan Plain in the Ming-Qing era. At the time, I had no answer for him.

2 In other related articles they examined fishing taxation and the fishery in Hubei (Zhang 1998), the fishing economy of the Lake Dongting Plain, and the fishing economy of Hubei in the Ming (Yin 2000; Yin 2001a).

3 The ideological bias of these gazetteers is unmistakable, but they can still be of value if the data are carefully used. For example, their discussion of the relations of production with regard to water – that is, various taxes and fees – is most susceptible to political bias. Many new gazetteers record that fishers were exploited by lake owners via the payment of such fees and surcharges. If we overlook the word "exploitation," however, we can still accept the fact that fishers had to get permission to use lakes and that bodies of water were privately owned. In fact, the new gazetteers also frequently quote Republican surveys but express things in a different way.

4 The recorded water surface was 8,365,808 *mu*, but that included 855,016 *mu* of acreage under dikes (Wang 1989, 12). Thus, the net water surface was 7,510,792 *mu*.

5 The amount of cultivated land (21,231,137 *mu*) is from a field survey, which should be fairly accurate. According to official statistics, however, the cultivated land of Jingzhou District amounted to 14,196,200 *mu* in the 1980s (Wang 1989, 11) and 13,432,200 *mu* in 1993 (*Jingzhou diqu zhi* 1996, 111). Compared with these numbers, the water surface looks even larger (equal to 58.9 and 62.3 percent of cultivated land, respectively).

6 The figure of 10 percent is a rough estimate based on the very limited sources of Table 17 and Table 18b. The actual percentage should have been much higher, as can be seen from Table 19.

7 In the original Republican records, all non-farming production was lumped under the rubric of sideline production *(fuye)*. Today, in the PRC, fisheries are treated as a part of agriculture (i.e., farming, forestry, animal husbandry, household sideline production, and fisheries). For the sake of clarity, I prefer to use the term "non-farming production" or "non-farming productive activity" rather than the direct translation "sideline production."

8 As Table 16 shows, in the Republic, 22.2 percent of Yingcheng's territory was covered by water (*Yingcheng xian zhi* 1992, 198). It is hard to believe that only 5.86 percent of the rural households in this county engaged in fishing as their major non-farming productive activity.

9 Dangyang, however, would have had many people engaged in fishing since two minor rivers – the Juhe (Ju River) and the Zhanghe (Zhang River) – run through it.

10 The newly compiled gazetteers usually contend that lineage-owned lakes were probably really owned by the head of the lineage or by a powerful household in that lineage. Given that the compilers of the new gazetteers always emphasized exploitation by the ruling class (here the lake owners or, more precisely, the "lake tyrants"), the role of the head of the lineage in water surface ownership has probably been exaggerated, just as has the concentration of land ownership as described by the CCP (see Chapter 5). For this reason, it seems reasonable to believe that these lakes were owned by lineages as a whole rather than by only the head of lineage or a powerful household in that lineage.

11 "Lake tyrant" and "fishing tyrant" *(yuba)* are phrases used mostly in the new gazetteers. I use this CCP terminology to refer to the ownership of bodies of water, but this does not mean that I accept the ideology on which they are premised. A recent study finds that, in Hanchuan, some of these people were those who were responsible for making and carrying out regulations within their clans and that they may not have been wealthier than other clan members (Zhang 2005, 200n5).

12 In Shishou, for example, the large landlord Zhang Qiuming owned the Wangfeng yao (wasp waist) section of the Ouchi River. This section, where fish wintered, was called "the fish jar *[yutanzi]* of Shishou" and had an annual catch of 100,000 kilograms or more. Every year when the "jar" was opened (*kaitan,* i.e., when fishing starting), Zhang had gunners posted to drive off outsiders (*Shishou xian zhi* 1990, 207). In the film *The Red Guerrillas of Lake Hong,* or *The Red Guards of Lake Honghu* (Honghu chiweidui), the leading villain, Peng Batian (Peng Who Occupies the Sky), was a landlord, "lake tyrant," and "wicked gentry-man," and even commanded a personal militia, the *Huanxiangtuan* (Return-to-the-Villages Corps).

13 For example, in Jianli the heads of lake *bao* were powerful figures in the lake area (*Jianli xian zhi* 1959, 93). The *bao* was an administrative unit consisting of one hundred house-holds; thus, the lake *bao* would have consisted of one hundred fishing households. But the organization, number, and distribution of lake *bao* in the Jianghan Plain remain unclear.

14 It would be impossible for them to really "own" these rivers.

15 The lake land mentioned in this case would probably have been reclaimed land, while the lake land discussed in the following paragraphs more likely consisted of unreclaimed land (or even the lake bottom).

16 The lake lands involved in this dispute were still not good enough for the production of a regular crop (e.g., rice) – they grew only lotus – and they were not protected by a dike.

17 These terms were *huke* or *shuike,* which could be translated as "lake tax" and "water tax," respectively. According to a Republican source, *huke* was one of the unrecorded taxes levied by the county government (*Xiakou xian zhi* 1920, 3: 3a), and it was to be paid by the lake owner. Another source explains that *shuike* were taxes levied on surfaces of water (*Dangdai Zhongguo de shuichanye* 1991, 221). However, according to the PRC gazetteers, it seems both *huke* and *shuike* were paid to lake owners, not the state. It is for this reason that I translate these terms as "lake fee" and "water fee," respectively.

18 One source mentions that the fishers paid a water fee for the use of "open lakes" *(chang shui hu),* but the charge would be over 60 to 80 percent of their catch to lake owners for the use of "preserved lakes" *(jin shui hu)* (*Dangdai Zhongguo de shuichanye* 1991, 221).

19 These fishing shops were probably also run by "lake tyrants." The eight fishing shops of Hanchuan that were headed by a certain Huang Nan'gui controlled more than twenty doctored steelyards, and each steelyard controlled more than twenty fishing boats. They weighed the fish with a large (doctored) steelyard, paid a low price, and took a high broker-age commission. They also enclosed some parts of a large lake in the name of creating a "reservation," and then opened it to fishers for double the usual lake fee (*Hanchuan xian zhi* 1992, 176). In fact, according to a 1950 survey, the majority of fishing areas in Hubei were occupied by "evil lake tyrants" in the Republic, and they had astonishingly large doctored steelyards and changed the price at will. They controlled the catch and monopol-ized the fishing zones (Zeng 1984, 2: 264).

20 It was 2.72 taels in Tianmen (*Tianmen xian zhi* 1765, 3: 9a); 95.17 taels in Zhongxiang (*Zhongxiang xian zhi* 1795, 3: 21a); 59.2 taels in Yingcheng (*Yingcheng xian zhi* 1726, 5: 6b); 70 taels in Qianjiang (*Qianjiang xian zhi* 1879, 9: 33a); and 66.6 taels in Jiangling (*Jingzhou fu zhi* 1880, 14: 11b-12a). In each case, the levy was slightly higher in leap years. It is unclear from most sources just who – lake owners or fishers – was responsible for such taxes and tribute, except in Jiangling, where it is very clear that it was the latter's responsibility (*Jingzhou fu zhi* 1880, 14: 12a). It was most likely the same in other counties.

21 Two sources briefly indicate (with no detailed discussion) that some lake owners hired labourers to manage their fishing area (*Honghu xian shuichan zhi* 1986, 188) and that some poor fishers sold their boats to work for lake owners as hired labourers (*Hubei sheng zhi nongye 2* 1999, 192). In coastal areas, fishers who fished in the sea were divided into five

classes: fishing workers (who sold their labour), poor fishers (who owned some gear but also needed to rent gear or who sold their labour for survival), middle fishers (who themselves fished but also hired seasonal labour), fishing capitalists (who lived on the rental of fishing boats), and fishing tyrants (who lived on "exploitation"). Insofar as the relations of production were concerned, the fishing workers were similar to agricultural labourers (*Dangdai Zhongguo de shuichanye* 1991, 26).

22 However, according to the same source, in the late Qing and the Republic, the fishing trade *(yuhang)* was prevalent in rural towns and lake areas of Hubei but was a minor trade in Hankou. This may imply that fresh fish were usually consumed locally and that the volume of dried fish (around fifteen thousand *shi dan*) was not substantial (Zeng 1984, 2: 258, 264-65).

23 The term "fishing beggar" was also popular in many freshwater fishing zones in Republican China (*Dangdai Zhongguo de shuichanye* 1991, 221).

24 Considering that, because of environmental uncertainty, landlords and tenants could have good relations, the picture of unremitting conflict between the fish-tyrants and fishers painted by the new gazetteers is suspicious. At the moment we do not have enough materials to either confirm or disconfirm this suspicion. However, it would be easy to believe that the life of fishers, particularly full-time fishers, was, due to environmental constraints (e.g., spending an extended time on water, living in shabby thatched huts, and being prone to snail fever), harder than that of the peasants.

Chapter 7: A Water-Rich Society

1 According to a new gazetteer, in Shishou in 1949 the yield of buckwheat was fifty *jin* per *mu* versus 307 *jin* per *mu* for rice (*Shishou xian zhi* 1990, 168, 171).

2 To translate *gumi/jiaomi* as "wild rice" (as is usually done) is incorrect as they are completely different. *Gumi* is the grain of *gu* (*Zizania caducif lora* [L.]), while wild rice *[O. rufipogon W. Griffith]* is a variety of undomesticated rice that grows naturally in the wild.

3 *Gumi, jiaomi, diaohu,* and *jiaobai* refer to different parts of the same plant. *Gu* was first grown as a grain in China at least two thousand years ago; its seeds are called *gumi* (or *jiaomi, diaohu*). Later, people grew it only as a vegetable and consumed its stem, which was called *jiaobai* (*Zhongguo nongye baike quanshu: Nongye lishi juan* 1995, 75-76).

4 Based on the source materials, it seems this *yuan* dike also functioned as a river dike at this place.

5 In the Yangzi delta, the organization of water control also had a close relationship with local environmental/technological conditions and socio-economic structures (Elvin 1977).

Conclusion

1 For the Lake Dongting Plain, see Perdue (1987, 241-42).

2 In Huang-Yun, water calamities also shifted from the coastal area to the inland area after the government "abandoned" it (Pomeranz 1993).

3 Of course, all of these changes did not occur one after another; there was some overlap.

4 This is the common image of the North China Plain. Nonetheless, there was still much regional variation. Li Huaiyin (2005, 3-5), for example, points out that the ecosystem of eastern Hebei was actually much more stable than that of the rest of the North China Plain and that the local peasants enjoyed a better life and were less violent than other North China peasants.

5 The distinction between high and low, stable and unstable, is relative, not absolute. For example, the Yangzi delta also suffered floods and drought, but these disasters caused less damage than did the change of the course of the Yellow River and the sometimes decades-long droughts of the North China Plain. On the whole, dike ruptures and the linking of lakes and rivers were not common in the Yangzi delta. The disasters that struck the North

China Plain usually inflicted the heaviest human losses. The environment of the North China Plain, which also suffered frequent infestations of locusts, was very unstable. Mark Elvin suggests measuring environmental stability by determining the number of people who worked on water control and the number of years that were needed for a repair: the greater the cost and the shorter the time needed for repair, the less stable the environment. He considers droughts more serious than floods since, historically, droughts lasted longer, affected a larger area, and caused more severe damage (personal communication, University of California Los Angeles, 2001). If we judge the North China Plain, the Jianghan Plain, and the Yangzi delta by his standard, the North China Plain had the most unstable environment (with frequent droughts and floods and the need for the annual repair of the Yellow River dike), the Jianghan Plain was second (frequent dike ruptures, annual dike repairs, no severe drought), and the Yangzi Delta was third – that is, it had the most stable environment (no threat from large dike ruptures, no severe drought).

Appendix

1 Regarding rental rates, Dangyang may have been an exception. The rental rate of school land in the period between 1875 and 1908 was slightly lower than it was in the period between 1862 and 1874. One reason for this may be that there are too few examples from the latter period (*Dangyang xian bu xu zhi* 1889, 1: 4a-8b).

2 Here I assume the rate of rent of school land (as other lands by custom) in regular (non-flood) years remained the same over time. In other words, the rental rate experienced no change, although the real amount of rent collected may have changed, depending on the harvest (*Jingmen zhili zhou zhi* 1868, 3[4]: 5ab).

3 Shi Youmin (2001, 136) argues that, in Jiangxi, the rent of school land was half the yield. But other studies argue that the rental rate was lower. Here I take the rental rate of school land as 40 percent (a rental rate found in four villages in Hebei in the Republic [Shi 2003]). Thus, if the rent were one *shi* per *mu*, then the yield would be 2.5 *shi* per *mu*, or 335 *jin* per *mu* (1 Qing *shi*/Qing *mu* = 134 *jin* per *mu*). In Table 9, the estimated output of rice of the Jianghan Plain was 31.44 million *shi dan* or 3,144 million *shi jin*. According to the source of Table 9, the estimated acreage of rice in the Jianghan Plain was 9,725,000 *mu* (*Hubei sheng zhi tudi liyong yu liangshi wenti* 1977 [1938], 24180-82), thus the estimated average yield of rice was 323.3 *shi jin*. This is a general estimate based on the whole acreage and output; it should be more reliable than piecemeal data.

4 But not many people used bean cakes as they could not afford them (*Xiaogan xian jian zhi* 1959, 29).

5 According to Zhao Gang (1994), the improvement of agricultural technology could offset the negative impact of a deteriorating ecology on agricultural production. Thus, an increase of agricultural productivity does not mean that there was no ecological deterioration, but a decrease of agricultural productivity most likely means that there was. By comparing rental rates from rent books (the amount of rent taken from the same plots over a long period of time), Zhao found that agricultural productivity was decreasing in many places in the Qing, possibly caused by ecological deterioration.

References

Gazetteers

Traditional Gazetteers

Anlu fu zhi [Gazetteer of Anlu Prefecture]. 1669.
Dangyang xian bu xu zhi [Gazetteer of Dangyang County (addendum)]. 1889.
Dangyang xian zhi [Gazetteer of Dangyang County]. 1866.
Gong'an xian zhi [Gazetteer of Gong'an County]. 1874.
Hanchuan tuji zhengshi [Geography and products of Hanchuan County]. 1895.
Hanchuan xian zhi [Gazetteer of Hanchuan County]. 1873.
Hankou xiao zhi [Brief gazetteer of Hankou]. 1915.
Hanyang fu zhi [Gazetteer of Hanyang Prefecture]. 1747.
Hanyang xian zhi [Gazetteer of Hanyang County]. 1748.
Hanyang xian zhi [Gazetteer of Hanyang County]. 1868.
Hanyang xian zhi [Gazetteer of Hanyang County]. 1889.
Hubei tong zhi [General gazetteer of Hubei] [Lan Wenjin, ed]. 1921. Shanghai: Shangwu
    yinshuguan.
Jiangling xian xiangtu zhi [Local records of Jiangling County]. [Fu Bao, ed.] 1959 [1909].
    N.p.
Jiangling xian zhi [Gazetteer of Jiangling County]. 1794.
Jiangling xian zhi [Gazetteer of Jiangling County]. 1876.
Jiangxia xian zhi [Gazetteer of Jiangxia County]. 1869.
Jianli xian zhi [Gazetteer of Jianli County]. 1702.
Jianli xian zhi [Gazetteer of Jianli County]. 1872.
Jingmen zhili zhou zhi [Gazetteer of Jingmen Independent Department]. 1868.
Jingmen zhou zhi [Gazetteer of Jingmen Department]. 1754.
Jingshan xian zhi [Gazetteer of Jingshan County]. 1673.
Jingshan xian zhi [Gazetteer of Jingshan County]. 1882.
Jingzhou fu zhi [Gazetteer of Jingzhou Prefecture]. 1757.
Jingzhou fu zhi [Gazetteer of Jingzhou Prefecture]. 1880.
Mianyang zhou zhi [Gazetteer of Mianyang Department]. 1894.
Qianjiang xian zhi [Gazetteer of Qianjiang County]. 1694.
Qianjiang xian zhi [Gazetteer of Qianjiang County]. 1879.
Shishou xian zhi [Gazetteer of Shishou County]. 1866.
Songzi xian zhi [Gazetteer of Songzi County]. 1696.
Songzi xian zhi [Gazetteer of Songzi County]. 1869.
Songzi xian zhi [Gazetteer of Songzi County]. 1982 [1937]. N.p.
Tianmen xian zhi [Gazetteer of Tianmen County]. 1765.
Xiakou xian zhi [Gazetteer of Xiakou [Hankou] County]. 1920.
Xiaogan xian zhi [Gazetteer of Xiaogan County]. 1883.
Yingcheng xian zhi [Gazetteer of Yingcheng County]. 1726.

Yingcheng zhi [Gazetteer of Yingcheng]. 1882.
Zhijiang xian zhi [Gazetteer of Zhijiang County]. 1866.
Zhongxiang xian zhi [Gazetteer of Zhongxiang County]. 1795.
Zhongxiang xian zhi [Gazetteer of Zhongxiang County]. 1937.

New Gazetteers

Dangyang xian zhi [Gazetteer of Dangyang County]. 1992. Beijing: Zhongguo chengshi chubanshe.
Dongjinghe difang zhi [Gazetteer of the dikes of the Dongjing River]. 1994. Wuhan: Wuhan daxue chubanshe.
Gong'an xian zhi [Gazetteer of Gong'an County]. 1990. Beijing: Hanyu dacidian chubanshe.
Hanchuan xian jian zhi [A brief gazetteer of Hanchuan County]. 1959. Wuhan: Hubei renmin chubanshe.
Hanchuan xian zhi [Gazetteer of Hanchuan County]. 1992. Beijing: Zhongguo chengshi chubanshe.
Hanyang xian shuili zhi [Gazetteer of water conservancy in Hanyang County]. 1990. N.p.
Hanyang xian zhi [Gazetteer of Hanyang County]. 1989. Wuhan: Wuhan chubanshe.
Hanyang xian zhi chugao. [A draft gazetteer of Hanyang County]. 1960. Hanyang xian dang'an guan.
Honghu xian shuichan zhi [Gazetteer of the aquatic industry of Honghu County]. 1986. N.p.
Honghu xian zhi [Gazetteer of Honghu County]. 1992. Wuhan: Wuhan daxue chubanshe.
Honghu xian zhi 1949-1959[Gazetteer of Honghu County]. 1963. N.p.
Hubei sheng Shishou xian diming zhi [Survey of the names of places in Shishou, Hubei]. 1983. N.p.
Hubei sheng zhi dili [Gazetteer of Hubei Province: Geography. 2 vols.] 1997. Wuhan: Hubei renmin chubanshe.
Hubei sheng zhi nongye 1 [Gazetteer of Hubei Province: Agriculture. Vol. 1]. 1994. Wuhan: Hubei renmin chubanshe.
Hubei sheng zhi nongye 2 [Gazetteer of Hubei province: Agriculture. Vol. 2]. 1999. Wuhan: Hubei renmin chubanshe.
Hubei sheng zhi shuili [Gazetteer of Hubei Province: Water conservancy]. 1995. Wuhan: Hubei renmin chubanshe.
Hubei shuili zhi [Gazetteer of water conservancy in Hubei]. 2000. Beijing: Zhongguo shuili shuidian chubanshe.
Jianghu nongchang zhi [Gazetteer of Jianghu Farm]. 1988. N.p.
Jiangling difang zhi [Gazetteer of the dikes of Jiangling]. 1984. N.p.
Jiangling xian shuili zhi [Gazetteer of water conservancy in Jiangling County]. 1984. N.P.
Jiangling xian zhi [Gazetteer of Jiangling County]. 1990. Wuhan: Hubei renmin chubanshe.
Jianli difang zhi [Gazetteer of the dikes of Jianli]. 1991. Wuhan: Hubei renmin chubanshe.
Jianli shuili zhi [Gazetteer of water conservancy in Jianli]. 2005. Beijing: Zhongguo shuili shuidian chubanshe.
Jianli xian zhi [Gazetteer of Jianli County]. 1959. N.p.
Jianli xian zhi [Gazetteer of Jianli County]. 1994. Wuhan: Hubei renmin chubanshe.
Jingjiang dadi zhi [Gazetteer of the Jingjiang Great Dike]. 1989. Nanjing: Hehai daxue chubanshe.
Jingjiang fenhong gongcheng zhi [Gazetteer of the flood diversion project of the Yangzi River]. 2000. Beijing: Zhongguo shuili shuidian chubanshe.
Jingmen shi zhi [Gazetteer of Jingmen City]. 1994. Wuhan: Hubei kexue jishu chubanshe.
Jingshan xian zhi [Gazetteer of Jingshan County]. 1990. Wuhan: Hubei renmin chubanshe.

Jingzhou diqu shuiyun zhi [Gazetteer of water transportation of Jingzhou District]. 1989. Nanning: Guangxi renmin chubanshe.

Jingzhou diqu zhi [Gazetteer of Jingzhou District]. 1996. Beijing: Hongqi chubanshe.

Lingjiaohu nongchang zhi [Gazetteer of Lingjiaohu Farm]. 1991. Beijing: Zhongguo wenshi chubanshe.

Mianyang chenchangqu xiangtu zhi [Gazetteer of Chenchang Ward, Mianyang County]. 1987. N.p.

Mianyang xian zhi [Gazetteer of Mianyang County]. 1989. Wuhan: Huazhong shifan daxue chubanshe.

Nongye zhi [Shashi] [Gazetteer of agriculture, Shashi]. 1993. N.p.

Ouchi zhen zhi [Gazetteer of Ouchi Township]. 1985. N.p.

Qianjiang shuili zhi [Gazetteer of water conservancy in Qianjiang]. 1997. Beijing: Zhongguo shuili shuidian chubanshe.

Qianjiang xian zhi [Gazetteer of Qianjiang County]. 1990. Beijing: Zhongguo wenshi chubanshe.

Renmin Dayuan nongchang zhi [Gazetteer of People's Dayuan Farm]. 1988. N.p.

Shishou fang zhi [Gazetteer of Shishou County]. 1958. N.p.

Shishou jiaotong zhi [Gazetteer of transportation in Shishou]. 1990. Beijing: Hongqi chubanshe.

Shishou xian zhi [Gazetteer of Shishou County]. 1990. Beijing: Hongqi chubanshe.

Songzi jiaotong zhi [Gazetteer of transportation in Songzi]. 1984. N.p.

Songzi xian zhi [Gazetteer of Songzi County]. 1986. N.p.

Suohe zhen zhi [Gazetteer of Suohe Township]. 1991. N.p.

Tianmen shuili zhi [Gazetteer of water conservancy in Tianmen]. 1999. Beijing: Zhonghua shuju.

Tianmen xian zhi [Gazetteer of Tianmen County]. 1989. Wuhan: Hubei renmin chubanshe.

Wuchang xian zhi [Gazetteer of Wuchang County]. 1989. Wuhan: Wuhan daxue chubanshe.

Wuhan difang zhi [Gazetteer of the dikes in Wuhan]. 1986. N.p.

Wuhan shi zhi nongye [Gazetteer of Wuhan Municipality: Agriculture]. 1989. Wuhan: Wuhan daxue chubanshe.

Wusan nongchang zhi (1953-1985) [Gazetteer of Wusan Farm]. 1987. N.p.

Xiaogan diqu shuili zhi [Gazetteer of water conservancy in Xiaogan District]. 1996. Wuhan: Wuhan daxue chubanshe.

Xiaogan shi zhi [Gazetteer of Xiaogan City]. 1992. Beijing: Xinhua chubanshe.

Xiaogan xian jian zhi [A brief gazetteer of Xiaogan County]. 1959. Wuhan: Hubei renmin chubanshe.

Yingcheng xian zhi [Gazetteer of Yingcheng County]. 1992. Beijing: Zhongguo chengshi chubanshe.

Yunmeng xian zhi [Gazetteer of Yunmeng County]. 1994. Beijing: Sanlian shudian.

Zhijiang xian zhi [Gazetteer of Zhijiang County]. 1990. Beijing: Zhongguo chengshi jingji shehui chubanshe.

Zhongxiang shuili zhi [Gazetteer of water conservancy in Zhongxiang]. 1998. Beijing: Zhongguo shuili shuidian chubanshe.

Zhongxiang xian zhi [Gazetteer of Zhongxiang County]. 1990. Wuhan: Hubei renmin chubanshe.

Archival Sources

LS 1-3-566 *Zhu Bingkun tunmo dikuan qiangzhu buli* [Zhu Bingkun embezzled dike fees and was derelict in emergency building]. (Note: LS 1 is a category *[quanzong]* number, 3 is a subcategory *[mulu]* number, 566 is a file *[juan]* number, and *Zhu Bingkun tunmo dikuan qiangzhu buli* is a document title [I shortened or created some titles based on the contents of the document]. The same is true of the following archives: all come from the Hubei Provincial Archives.)

LS 1-4-452 *Guanyu qian Hubei shuiliju juzhang Chen Keming deng bei fu chengjie an yijue shu* [Resolution on the punishment of Chen Keming – the former director of the Bureau of Water Conservancy of Hubei – and others].

LS 1-5-597 *Yuye fa* [The fishery law]. 1929.

LS 1-5-607 *Ling yang te chi ge xian duiyu fangxun shiqing ying he zhong gong ji tong li hezuo yi zhong difang* [Each county should work together and fully cooperate in flood control to protect dikes]

LS 1-5-644 *Hubei sheng shuizai ji zhengji diaocha baogao* [Investigative report on the floods and relief in Hubei].

LS 1-5-781 *Kong yuandi gongcheng chuzhang Zhou Tianqu jie gong fei si an* [Accusing Zhou Tianqu, head of the *yuan* dike engineering bureau, of embezzling dike fees]

LS 1-5-838 *Shishou Zhanghui nan yuan kuikou an* [The case of the dike rupture in Zhanghui south *yuan* in Shishou]

LS 1-5-1389 *Zhongyangshe guanyu paohui Tianhu yuan an de xinwen* [Central News Agency's news about the destruction of Tianhu *yuan*].

LS 6-2-964 *Zuzhi fandui fuzhu Tianhu yuan lianhehui* [Organizing the union opposing the rebuilding of Tianhu *yuan*].

LS 19-2-2440 *Zhengli yuke banfa* [Methods to rectify fishery taxation].

LS 19-2-2676 *Tianmen-Mianyang Chenhu yutian zhangliang shi* [Matters concerning measuring the silted land of Lake Chen in Tianmen and Mianyang].

LS 19-8-55 (1) *Hubei shuili digong shiwu qingli weiyuanhui cheng bao qingli gong kui si kui an* [Report of the clearing committee of water conservancy and dike affairs in Hubei on governmental debt and private debt].

LS 31-4-58 *Hubei dikuan jielüe* [A brief history of dike fee collection in Hubei].

LS 31-4-60a *Shishou gongmin Chen Zuwu deng cheng kong Zhao Nan'gai an* [Chen Zuwu and others, citizens of Shishou, accuse Zhao Nan'gai (of corruption)].

LS 31-4-60b *Hanchuan xianzhang bian Wangjiayuan gandi xiuzhu an* [1946] [The magistrate of Hanchuan County defends his role in the building and maintenance of the Wangjiayuan dike].

LS 31-4-221 *Zhengli Hanshui xiayou hedi jihua caoan* [Draft plan for the realignment of dikes along the lower Han River valley].

LS 31-4-1403 *Hanyang Daxing yuan diwu jiufen* [Disputes over dike affairs in Daxing *yuan*, Hanyang County].

LS 31-4-1404 *Hanyang Yaodixiang yuan min jiufen* [Disputes among *yuan* residents of Yaodi Township, Hanyang County].

LS 31-4-1405 *Hanyang Changfeng yuan diwu jiufen* [Disputes over dike affairs in Changfeng *yuan*, Hanyang County].

LS 31-4-1407 *Hanyang Xihu yuan diwu jiufen* [Disputes over dike affairs in Xihu *yuan*, Hanyang County].

LS 31-4-1408 *Mianyang Yaoyuan xiufang zhuren yurou xiangmin* [A director of the bureau of dike repair and flood control in Yao *yuan*, Mianyang, bullies the local people].

LS 31-4-1531 *Hanchuan minyuan hezuo jiufen* [Disputes over cooperation in people's *yuan* in Hanchuan].

LS 31-4-1726 *Shishou Xiaozhiyuan jiufen* [Disputes over Xiaozhi riverlet in Shishou (multiple documents)].

LS 31-4-2007 *Chakan Mianyang xian da xiao xing shuili gongcheng gaikuang baogaoshu* [Report on the investigation of large and small water conservancy projects in Mianyang].

LS 36-1-69 *Hanchuan Hanyang Tongxing yuan diwu jiufen* [Disputes over dike affairs in Tongxing *yuan,* Hanchuan and Hanyang].

LS 36-2-15 *Hubei sheng ge xian min yuan xiufang chu zuzhi tongze* [General organization rule of the Bureau of Dike Repair and Flood Control of people's *yuan* in counties of Hubei].

SZ 34-2-117 *Hubei Shishou xian Jiaoziyuan xiaohe duse jingguo he chuli banfa* [The process for blocking the Jiaoziyuan riverlet in Shishou County, Hubei, and the method of handling the issue].

SZ 34-2-247 *Hubei sheng guanyu tudi wenti de baogao* [Reports on the land issue of Hubei].

SZ 37-1-280 *Hubei sheng Yingcheng xian zhu hu diaocha biao: Li Liangheng, Wu Xiubin* [Household investigation tables: (Households of) Li Liangheng and Wu Xiubin, Yingcheng County, Hubei Province].

SZ 37-1-332 *Hubei sheng Shishou xian zhu hu diaocha biao: (Sheng Anliang)* [Household investigation table: (Household of) Sheng Anliang, Shishou County, Hubei Province].

SZ 68-2-234 *Wei yumin fenpei tudi wenti tigong yijian* [Suggestions to distribute land to fishing people].

SZ 113-2-11 *Hubei sheng 1950 nian yi nian lai de difang gongzuo zongjie baogao* [Summary report of dike works of Hubei in the year 1950].

SZ 113-3-197 *Guanyu chuli Tianmen, Hanchuan liangxian linjie diqu de shuili he shuichan jiufen de baogao* [Report on the treatment of disputes over water control and fisheries in the border area of Tianmen and Hanchuan].

Other Sources

Ao Jiamei. 1990. "Jiushehui Hubei sheng caizheng gaiyi" [General recollection of Hubei's finance in the old society]. *Hubei wenshi ziliao* [Literary and historical materials of Hubei], 4: 1-12.

Bao Maohong. 2004a. "Zhongguo huanjing shi yanjiu: Yi Maoke jiaoshou fangtan" [Studies on the environmental history of China: An interview with Professor Mark Elvin]. *Zhongguo lishi dili luncong* [Collections of essays on Chinese historical geography] 1: 124-37.

–. 2004b. "Environmental History in China." *Environment and History* 10 [4]: 475-99.

Bernhardt, Kathryn. 1992. *Rents, Taxes, and Peasant Resistance: The Lower Yangzi Region, 1840-1950.* Stanford, CA: Stanford University Press.

Bishop, J.F. 1899. *The Yangtze Valley and Beyond.* London: John Murray, Albemarle Street.

Blakiston, Thomas Wright. 1862. *Five Months on the Yangtsze.* London: John Murray, Albemarle Street.

Buck, John Lossing. 1937. *Land Utilization in China.* Nanking: University of Nanking.

Cao Shuji and Li Yushang. 2006. *Shuyi, zhanzheng yu heping: Zhongguo de huanjing yu shehui bianqian, 1230-1960* [Plague, war and peace: Environment and social change in China, 1230-1960]. Ji'nan: Shandong huabao chubanshe.

Cao Xingsui. 1996. *Jiu Zhongguo Su'nan nongjia jingji yanjiu* [Traditional Chinese peasant economy in Southern Jiangsu]. Beijing: Zhongyang bianyi chubanshe.

Ch'u T'ung-tsu. 1988 [1962]. *Local Government in China under the Ch'ing.* Cambridge, MA: Council on East Asia Studies, Harvard University.

Changjiang liuyu guihua bangongshi, ed. 1979. *Changjiang shuili shilüe* [A brief history of water conservancy along the Yangzi River]. Beijing: Shuili dianli chubanshe.

Chao Xiaohong. 2004. *Shengtai huanjing yu Ming Qing shehui jingji* [Ecological environment and socio-economy of Ming-Qing times]. Hefei: Huangshan shushe.

Chen Guanlong. 1989. "Ming Qing shiqi Shashi shangpin shichang tansuo" [Exploration of the merchandise market of Shashi in the Ming-Qing era]. *Huazhong shifan daxue xue bao* [Journal of Huazhong Normal University] 1: 67-72.

Chen Jiyu, Wang Baocan, and Yu Zhiying. 1989. *Zhongguo haian fayu guocheng he yanbian guilü* [The developmental process and historical change of the Chinese seacoast]. Shanghai: Shanghai kexue jishu chubanshe.

Chen Tao. 2007. "Hongshui yu cunluo kongjian jiegou de yanbian: Jianghan pingyuan Yangma cun de taizi de shehuixue kaocha" [Floods and the evolution of the spatial structure of villages: A Sociological survey of Taizi in Yangma Village of the Jianghan Plain]. *Gujin nongye* [Ancient and modern agriculture] 2: 9-14.

Chen Xinli. 2011. "Changjiang liuyu huanjing shi yanjiu de huigu yu zhanwang" [Retrospect and prospect of studies on the environmental history of the Yangzi River valley]. In *Lishi shiqi Changjiang zhongyou diqu renlei huodong yu huanjing bianqian zhuanti yanjiu* [Monographic studies on human activities and environmental change in the history of the middle of the Yangzi River valley], ed. Zhang Jianmin and Lu Xiqi, 24-72. Wuhan: Wuhan daxue chubanshe.

Chen Zhenhan, Xiong Zhengwen, Li Chen, and Yin Hanzhang, eds. 1989. *Qingshilu jingjishi ziliao, 1644-1820, nongye bian, 2* [Data on economic history from the Qing records, agriculture. Vol. 2]. Beijing: Beijing daxue chubanshe.

Cheng Lichang. 1977 [1938]. *Hubei zhi nongye jinrong yu diquan yidong zhi guanxi* [The relationship between agricultural finance and changing landownership in Hubei]. Taipei: Chengwen chuban youxiangongsi.

Cheng Pengju. 1990. "Jingjiang dadi jueyi ji zhongyao xiuzhu de chubu fenxi" [A preliminary analysis of the breaks and overflooding of the Jingjiang Great Dike and its important construction]. In *Changjiang shuilishi lunwenji* [Collection of papers on the history of water conservancy along the Yangzi River], ed. Zhongguo shuili shi xuehui, 195-211. Nanjing: Hehai daxue chubanshe.

Chi Ch'ao-ting. 1963 [1936]. *Key Economic Areas in Chinese History: As Revealed in the Development of Public Works for Water-Control*. New York: Paragon Book Reprint Corp.

Crook, David, and Isabel Crook. 1959. *Revolution in a Chinese Village: Ten Mile Inn*. London: Routledge and Kegan Paul.

Da zekou cheng'an [Records on the large Zekou outlet]. 2004. Beijing: Xianzhuang shuju (reprint).

Dangdai Zhongguo de shuichanye [Aquatic industry in contemporary China]. 1991. Beijing: Dangdai Zhongguo chubanshe.

Deng Yunte. 1984 [1937]. *Zhongguo jiuhuang shi* [The history of disaster relief in China]. Shanghai: Shanghai shudian.

Ding Yin. 1959. "Jianghan pingyuan xin shiqi shidai hongshaotu zhong de daoguke kaocha" [Notes on the Neolithic rice husks unearthed in Hupei]. *Kaogu xuebao* [Acta Archaeologica Sinica] 4: 31-34.

Dodgen, Randall. 1991. "Hydraulic Evolution and Dynastic Decline: The Yellow River Conservancy, 1796-1855." *Late Imperial China* 12 [2]: 36-63.

—. 2001. *Controlling the Dragon: Confucian Engineers and the Yellow River in Late Imperial China*. Honolulu: University of Hawaii Press.

Du Runsheng, ed. 1996. *Zhongguo de tudi gaige* [Land reform in China]. Beijing: Dangdai Zhongguo chubanshe.

Edmonds, Richard Louis. 1994. *Patterns of China's Lost Harmony: A Survey of the Country's Environmental Degradation and Protection*. London: Routledge.

Eisenstadt, S.N., and L. Roniger. 1984. *Patrons, Clients and Friends: Interpersonal Relations and the Structure of Trust in Society*. Cambridge: Cambridge University Press.

Ekins, Paul. 2000. *Economic Growth and Environmental Sustainability: The Prospects for Green Growth*. London: Routledge.

Ellis, E.C., and S.M. Wang, 1997. "Sustainable Traditional Agriculture in the Tai Lake Region of China." *Agriculture, Ecosystems, and Environment* 61: 177-93.

Elvin, Mark. 1975. "On Water Control and Management during the Ming and Ch'ing Periods: A Review Article." *Ch'ing-shih wen-ti* (now *Late Imperial China*) 3 (3): 82-103.

–. 1977. "Market Towns and Waterways: The County of Shanghai from 1480-1910." In *The City in Late Imperial China*, ed. William G. Skinner, 441-73. Stanford, CA: Stanford University Press.

–. 1993. "Three Thousand Years of Unsustainable Growth: China's Environment from Archaic Times to the Present." *East Asian History* 6: 7-46.

–. 2004. *The Retreat of the Elephants: An Environmental History of China*. New Haven: Yale University Press.

Elvin, Mark, Hiroaki Nishioka, Keiko Tamura, and Joan Kwek, eds. 1994. *Japanese Studies on the History of Water Control in China: A Selected Bibliography*. Canberra: Institute of Advanced Studies, Australian National University.

Elvin, Mark, and Liu Ts'ui-jung, eds. 1998. *Sediments of Time: Environment and Society in Chinese History*. Cambridge: Cambridge University Press.

Esherick, Joseph W. 1981. "Number Games: A Note on Land Distribution in Prerevolutionary China." *Modern China* 7 (4): 387-411.

–. 1987. *The Origins of the Boxer Uprising*. Berkeley and Los Angeles: University of California Press.

Fan Shuzhi. 1988. *Zhongguo fengjian tudi guanxi fazhanshi* [A history of the development of Chinese feudal land relations]. Beijing: Renmin chubanshe.

Fang Zhiyuan. 2004. "Ming Qing xiang e gan diqu de 'song feng'" [The custom of litigiousness in Hunan, Hubei, and Jiangxi during the Ming-Qing era]. *Wenshi* [Literature and history] 3: 107-34.

Fei Hsiao-tung. 1962 [1939]. *Peasant Life in China: A Field Study of Country Life in the Yangtze Valley*. London: Routledge and Kegan Paul.

Feng Xianliang. 2002. *Ming Qing jiangnan diqu de huanjing biandong yu shehui kongzhi* [Environmental change and social control in the Yangzi delta in Ming-Qing Times]. Shanghai: Shanghai renmin chubanshe.

Finnane, Antonia. 1984. "Bureaucracy and Responsibility: A Reassessment of the River Administration under the Qing." *Papers on Far Eastern History* 30: 161-98.

Frank, Andre Gunder. 1998. *ReOrient: Global Economy in the Asian Age*. Berkeley and Los Angeles: University of California Press.

Fudan daxue lishi dili yanjiu zhongxin, ed. 2001. *Ziran zaihai yu Zhongguo shehui lishi jiegou* [Natural calamities and the structure of Chinese society and history]. Shanghai: Fudan daxue chubanshe.

Gailiang digong yijian shu [Suggestions on reforming dike works]. N.d. In *Qingli baogaoshu* [Report on checking up (on dike affairs)], ed. Eyuwan sansheng jiaofei zong silingbu and Hubei shuili digong shiwu qingli weiyuanhui, 1-5. N.p.

Gao, Yan. 2012. "Transformation of the Water Regime: State, Society and Ecology of the Jianghan Plain in Late Imperial and Modern China." PhD diss., Carnegie Mellon University. ProQuest, 3520084.

Gao Huanyue. 2000. *Qingdai xingming muyou yanjiu* [Studies on (magistrates') legal secretaries of the Qing dynasty]. Beijing: Zhongguo zhengfa daxue chubanshe.

Gao Wangling. 2002. "Dizu zhengshoulü de zai tantao" [A re-examination of rates of rent collection]. *Qingshi yanjiu* [The Qing history journal] 2: 17-23.

Gong Shengsheng. 1993a. "Qingdai lianghu diqu renkou yalixia de shengtai huanjing ehua jiqi duice" [The deterioration of the ecological environment and counter-measures under population pressure in the Qing in Hunan and Hubei]. *Zhongguo lishi dili luncong* 1: 69-94.

–. 1993b. "Qingdai lianghu diqu de yumi he ganshu" [Maize and sweet potato in Hubei-Hunan in the Qing dynasty]. *Zhongguo nongshi* [Agricultural history of China] 3: 47-57.

–. 1993c. "Qingdai lianghu renkou fazhan de shikong chayi yanjiu" [Studies of differences in time and space in the demographic development of Hunan-Hubei in the Qing]. *Zhongguo lishi dili luncong* 4: 109-45.

–. 1996. *Qingdai lianghu nongye dili* [Agricultural geography of Hunan and Hubei in the Qing dynasty]. Wuhan: Huazhong shifan daxue chubanshe.

Guan Qingtao. 1983. "Jianghan pingyuan jianghu lishi bianqian yu shuili shiye de fazhan" [Historical changes in rivers and lakes and the development of water conservancy in the Jianghan Plain]. *Hubei shuili zhi tongxun* [Bulletin of the gazetteers of water conservancy of Hubei] 5-6: 30-36.

Guo Xianzao. 1988. "Taibai hu zhi miaoshui ke" [The water tax of Lake Taibai]. *Hanyang xian wenshi ziliao* [Historical and cultural materials of Hanyang County] 3: 241-42.

Hanyang xian. 1938. *Hubei sheng nongcun diaocha baogao* 6 [Report of a rural survey of Hubei. Vol. 6]. 1938. Compiled and published by the Department of Statistics, Office of the Secretariat, Government of Hubei.

He Guozhong. 1983. "Tianhu yuan shuili jiufen shimo" [The history of the dispute over water control in the Tianhu *yuan*]. *Hubei shuili zhi tongxun* 1-2: 88-89.

–. 1984. "Hubei digong juan shimo" [The history of dike tax of Hubei]. *Hubei shuili zhi tongxun* 2: 53-59 [60].

Hinton, William. 1997 [1966]. *Fanshen: A Documentary of Revolution in a Chinese Village.* Berkeley: University of California Press.

Ho, Ping-ti. 1959. *Studies on the Population of China, 1368-1953.* Cambridge, MA: Harvard University Press.

Hong Huanchun. 1988. *Ming Qing Suzhou nongcun jingji ziliao* [Data on the rural economy of Suzhou in the Ming-Qing dynasties]. Nanjing: Jiangsu guji chubanshe.

Hsiao Kung-ch'uan. 1960. *Rural China: Imperial Control in the Nineteenth Century.* Seattle: University of Washington Press.

Hu Huanzong, ed. 1920. *Hubei quan sheng shiye zhi* [Gazetteer of industry of the whole of Hubei Province]. Zhongya yinshuguan.

Hu Zuhe, ed. 1999 [1838]. *Jingchu xiushu zhiyao* [Key to the management of the dike systems in Hubei]. Wuhan: Hubei renmin chubanshe.

Hua Zhong, ed. 1974. *Jianghan huqun* [Lake groups in the Jianghan area]. Wuhan: Hubei renmin chubanshe.

Huang, Philip C.C. 1982. "County Archives and the Study of Local Social History: Report on a Year's Research in China." *Modern China* 8 (1): 133-43.

–. 1985. *The Peasant Economy and Social Change in North China.* Stanford, CA: Stanford University Press.

–. 1990. *The Peasant Family and Rural Development in the Yangzi Delta, 1350-1988.* Stanford, CA: Stanford University Press.

Hubei An Xiang Yun dao shuili ji'an [A collection of papers on water conservancy in the circuits of Anlu, Xiangyang, and Yunyang]. N.d.

Hubei hangyun shi [History of shipping in Hubei]. 1995. Beijing: Renmin jiaotong chubanshe.

Hubei jindai nongcun fuye ziliao xuanji, 1840-1949 [A collection on rural household sidelines in modern Hubei]. 1987. N.p.

Hubei nongye dili [Agricultural geography of Hubei]. 1980. Wuhan: Hubei renmin chubanshe.

Hubei sheng ditu ce [Maps of Hubei Province]. 2000 [1998]. Ji'nan: Shandong sheng ditu chubanshe.

Hubei sheng Jingzhou bowuguan, ed. 1999. *Zaolingang yu Duijintai: Jingjiang dadi Jingzhou Mashan duan kaogu fajue baogao* [Zaolingang and Duijintai: Archaeological report on Mashan section of the Jingjiang Dyke project]. Beijing: Kexue chubanshe.

Hubei sheng zhi tudi liyong yu liangshi wenti [Land usage and issue of food grains in Hubei] [Author unknown]. 1977 [1938]. Taipei: Chengwen chuban youxian gongsi.

Hubei shengqing [General information on Hubei Province]. 1987. Wuhan: Hubei renmin chubanshe.

Hubei xianzheng gaikuang. 1934. [A survey of county administration of Hubei]. Compiled and published by the Department of Civil Affairs, Government of Hubei.

Hubei zhi mianhua [Cotton of Hubei]. 1938. N.p.

Isett, Christopher Mills. 2007. *State, Peasant, and Merchant in Qing Manchuria, 1644-1862.* Stanford, CA: Stanford University Press.

Jiang Ling and Gong Shengsheng. 1998. "Jindai Changjiang liuyu xuexichong bing de liuxing bianqian ji guilü" [The rule of the epidemics and changes of snail fever in the modern Yangzi River valley]. *Zhonghua yishi zazhi* [Chinese journal of medical history] 2: 90-93.

Jianli xian. 1938. *Hubei sheng nongcun diaocha baogao 8* [Report of a rural survey of Hubei. Vol. 8]. Compiled and published by the Department of Statistics, Office of Secretariat, Government of Hubei.

Jingjiang di zhi [Gazetteer of the Jingjiang Dike]. 1937. N.p.

Jingzhou gonglu shi [A history of highways in Jingzhou]. 1993. Beijing: Renmin jiaotong chubanshe.

Jingzhou hangyun shi [The history of shipping in Jingzhou]. 1996. Beijing: Renmin jiaotong chubanshe.

King, F.H. 1911. *Farmers of Forty Centuries or Permanent Agriculture in China, Korea and Japan.* Madison, WI: Democrat Printing.

Lan Yong. 1992. *Lishi shiqi xi'nan jingji kaifa yu shengtai bianqian* [Economic development and ecological change in the historical period in Southwest China]. Kunming: Yunnan jiaoyu chubanshe.

–. 2001. "Ming Qing Meizhou nongzuowu yinjin dui yaredai shandi jiegouxing pinkun xingcheng de yingxiang" [The effects of the introduction of New World crops on the formation of structural poverty in subtropical mountainous areas]. *Zhongguo nongshi* 4: 3-14.

Leonard, Jane Kate. 1996. *Controlling from Afar: The Daoguang Emperor's Management of the Grand Canal Crisis, 1824-1826.* Ann Arbor: Center for Chinese Studies, University of Michigan.

Leong, Sow-Theng. 1997. *Migration and Ethnicity in Chinese History: Hakkas, Pengmin, and Their Neighbors.* Stanford, CA: Stanford University Press.

Li, Huaiyin. 2005. *Village Governance in North China, 1875-1936.* Stanford, CA: Stanford University Press.

Li, Lillian M. 2007. *Fighting Famine in North China: State, Market, and Environmental Decline, 1690s-1990s.* Stanford, CA: Stanford University Press.

Li Shouhe. 2001. "Jingjiang fenhong gongcheng shouci qiyong ji" [The first usage of the Jingjiang flood diversion project]. *Hubei wenshi ziliao* 1: 90-102.

Li Wenzhi, ed. 1957. *Zhongguo jindai nongyeshi ziliao* 1, 1840-1911 [Source materials on the agricultural history of modern China], 1: 1840-1911]. Beijing: Sanlian shudian.

Liang Fangzhong. 1980. *Zhongguo lidai hukou, tiandi, tianfu tongji* [Statistics on households, land, and land tax in Chinese history]. Shanghai: Shanghai renmin chubanshe.

Liang Jiamian, ed. 1989. *Zhongguo nongye kexue jishu shigao* [A draft history of agricultural science and technology in China]. Beijing: Nongye chubanshe.

Lin Zexu. 1935 (Qing). *Lin wen zhong gong zhengshu* [Memorials of Lin Zexu]. Shanghai: Shangwu yinshuguan.

Lippit, Victor. 1974. *Land Reform and Economic Development in China: A Study of Institutional Change and Development Finance.* New York: International Arts and Science Press.

Liu, Chang. 2003. "Making Revolution in Jiangnan: Communists and the Yangzi Delta Countryside, 1927-1945." *Modern China* 29 (1): 3-37.

–. 2007. *Peasants and Revolution in Rural China: Rural Political Change in the North China Plain and the Yangzi Delta, 1850-1949.* London: Routledge.

Liu, Ts'ui-jung. 1970. "Dike Construction in Ch'ing-chou, a Study Based on the 'T'i-fang chih' Section of the Ching-chou Fu-chih." *Papers on China* 23: 1-27. Cambridge, MA: East Asian Research Center, Harvard University.

Liu Cui-rong, and Mark Elvin, eds. 1995. *Ji jian suo zhi: Zhongguo huanjingshi lunwenji* [Sediments of time: Environment and society in Chinese history]. Taipei: Institute of Economics, Academia Sinica.

Lu Hancai. 2005. *Tianmen ren zai Yinni* [People of Tianmen in Indonesia]. Wuhan: Wuhan chubanshe.

Lü Xingbang. 2011. "Jianghan pingyuan de diyuan shuili yu jiceng shehui, 1942-1949: Yi Hubei sheng Songzi xian Sanhe yuan wei zhongxin" [Water control of dike-*yuan* and grassroots society in the Jianghan Plain, 1942-1949: Centred on Sanhe *yuan*, Songzi County, Hubei]. *Gujin nongye* 1: 105-17.

Lu Xiqi. 2004. "Tai, yuan, dadi: Jianghan pingyuan shehui jingji quyu de xingcheng, fazhan yu zuhe" [Platforms, *yuan*, major dikes: The formation, development and combination of the socio-economic zones in the Jianghan Plain]. *Shixue yuekan* [Journal of historical sciences] 4: 16-17.

–. 2011. "Mingqing shiqi Jianghan pingyuan de weiyuan: Cong 'shuili gongcheng' dao 'shuili gongtongti'" [*Yuan* of the Jianghan Plain in the Ming-Qing era: From "water-control projects" to "water-control community." In Zhang Jianmin and Lu Xiqi, eds. *Lishi shiqi Changjiang zhongyou diqu renlei huodong yu huanjing bianqian zhuanti yanjiu* [Monographic studies on human activities and environmental change in the history of the middle of the Yangzi River valley], 348-439. Wuhan: Wuhan daxue chubanshe.

Lu Xiqi and Han Keke. 2011. "Sancun de xingcheng jiqi yanbian: Yi Jianghan pingyuan fudi de xiangcun juluo xingtai jiqi yanbian wei zhongxin" [The formation and evolution of scattered villages: Centred on the formation and evolution of rural villages in the inland Jianghan Plain]. *Zhongguo lishi dili luncong* 26 (4): 77-91, 104.

Lu Xiqi and Pan Sheng. 2004. *Hanshui zhongxiayou hedao bianqian yu difang* [The changes of the river course of the middle and lower reaches of the Han River and the dikes]. Wuhan: Wuhan daxue chubanshe.

Lu You. 1983 [Song]. *Ru shu ji* [Travels to Sichuan]. Taipei: Shangwu yinshuguan.

Luo Shiming and Han Chunru. 1990. "Ecological Agriculture in China." In *Sustainable Agricultural Systems*, ed. Clive A. Edwards, Rattan Lal, Patrick Madden, Robert H. Miller, and Gar House, 299-322. Ankeny, IA: Soil and Water Conservation Society.

Mann, Michael. 1984. "The Autonomous Power of the State: Its Origins, Mechanisms and Results." *Archives of European Sociology* 25: 185-213.

Mao Tse-tung. 1975. *Selected Works of Mao Tse-tung.* Vol. 4. Peking: Foreign Languages Press.

Marks, Robert B. 1998. *Tigers, Rice, Silk, and Silt: Environment and Economy in Late Imperial South China.* New York: Cambridge University Press.

–. 2002. *The Origins of the Modern World: A Global and Ecological Narrative.* Lanham, MD: Rowman and Littlefield.

–. 2012. *China: Its Environment and History.* Lanham, MD: Rowman and Littlefield.

Mazumdar, Sucheta. 1998. *Sugar and Society in China: Peasants, Technology, and the World Market.* Cambridge, MA: Harvard University Asia Center.

Mei Li. 1993. "Qingdai Hubei fangzhi ye de dili fenbu" [The geographical distribution of the textile industry of Hubei in the Qing]. *Hubei daxue xuebao* [Journal of Hubei University] 2: 105-9.

Mei Li, Zhang Guoxiong, and Yan Changgui. 1995. *Lianghu pingyuan kaifa tanyuan* [Exploring the origins of the development of the Hunan-Hubei Plain]. Nanchang: Jiangxi jiaoyu chubanshe.

Min Zongdian. 1984. "Song Ming Qing shiqi Taihu diqu shuidao mu chanliang de tantao" [A study of the per-*mu* yield of rice in the Lake Tai area during the Song, Ming, and Qing dynasties]. *Zhongguo nongshi* 3: 37-52.

—. 1999. "Cong fangzhi jizai kan Ming-Qing shiqi Woguo shuidao de fenbu" [Distribution of rice in our country in the Ming-Qing era as documented in local gazetteers]. *Gujin nongye* 1: 35-48.

—. 2003. "Ming-Qing shiqi Zhongguo nanfang daotian duoshu zhongzhi de fazhan" [The development of the multi-cropping of rice paddy in South China during the Ming-Qing era]. *Zhongguo nongshi* 3: 10-14.

Minshi xiguan diaocha baogao lu [Abstracts of reports on investigations of civil customs]. 2000. Beijing: Zhongguo zhengfa daxue chubanshe.

Morita Akira. 1960. "Shindai Kokō ni okeru chisui kangai no tenkai" [The development of control and irrigation in the Huguang Province under the Qing dynasty]. *Tōhōgaku* [Eastern studies] 20: 63-76.

—. 1974. *Shindai suiri shi kenkyū* [Studies in the history of water control during the Qing dynasty]. Tokyo: Aki shobo.

Mu ling shu [Handbook of the magistrate]. 1990 [1848]. Yangzhou: Jiangsu Guangling guji keyinshe.

Muscolino, Micah S. 2009. *Fishing Wars and Environmental Change in Late Imperial and Modern China*. Cambridge: Harvard University Asia Center.

Ni Wenwei, ed. 1885 [1876]. *Jingzhou wanchengdi zhi* [Gazetteer of the Wancheng dike in Jingzhou]. N.p.

Osborne, Anne. 1994. "The Local Politics of Land Reclamation in the Lower Yangzi Highlands." *Late Imperial China* 15 [1]: 1-46.

Park, Nancy. 1997. "Corruption in Eighteenth-Century China." *Journal of Asian Studies* 56 (4): 967-1005.

Peng Wenhe. 1977 [1938]. *Hunan hutian wenti* [Issues of lakeside land in Hunan]. Taipei: Chengwen chuban youxian gongsi.

Peng Yuxin. 1990. *Qingdai tudi kaiken shi* [The history of land reclamation in the Qing dynasty]. Beijing: Nongye chubanshe.

Peng Yuxin, and Zhang Jianmin. 1993. *Ming Qing Changjiang liuyu nongye shuili yanjiu* [Studies on agricultural water conservancy in the Yangzi River valley in Ming-Qing times]. Wuhan: Wuhan daxue chubanshe.

Perdue, Peter. 1982. "Water Control in the Dongting Lake Region during the Ming and Qing Periods." *Journal of Asian Studies* 41 (4): 747-65.

—. 1987. *Exhausting the Earth: State and Peasant in Hunan, 1500-1850*. Cambridge, MA: Council on East Asia Studies, Harvard University.

Perkins, Dwight. 1969. *Agricultural Development in China, 1368-1968*. Chicago: Aldine.

Perry, Elizabeth. 1980. *Rebels and Revolutionaries in North China, 1845-1945*. Stanford, CA: Stanford University Press.

Pietz, David A. 2002. *Engineering the State: The Huai River and Reconstruction in Nationalist China, 1927-1937*. New York: Routledge.

Pomeranz, Kenneth. 1993. *The Making of a Hinterland: State, Society, and Economy in Inland North China, 1853-1937*. Berkeley and Los Angeles: University of California Press.

—. 2000. *The Great Divergence: Europe, China, and the Making of the Modern World Economy*. Princeton, NJ: Princeton University Press.

Qiao Shengxi. 1963. "Hubei sheng lishi shang de shuihan wenti jiqi yu taiyang huodong duonian bianhua de guanxi" [The historical problem of inundation and drought in Hubei and its relationship to the variations in solar activities]. *Dili xuebao* [Acta geographica sinica] 1: 14-23.

Qin Hui and Jin Yan. 2010. *Tianyuan shi yu kuangxiang qu: Guanzhong moshi yu qian jindai shehui de zai renshi* [Idyll and rhapsody: the Central Shaanxi model and the re-recognition of modern Chinese society]. Beijing: Yuwen chubanshe.

Qing huidian shili [Statutes and cases of the Qing dynasty]. 1991 [1899]. Beijing: Zhonghua shuju.

Qing jingshi wenbian [Qing memorials on statecraft]. 1992 [1889]. Beijing: Zhonghua shuju.

Quan Hansheng. 1972. *Zhongguo jingjishi luncong* 2 [Studies on the economic history of China]. Hong Kong: Chinese University of Hong Kong, Xinya shuyuan.

Rawski, Evelyn S. 1975. "Agricultural Development in the Han River Highlands." *Ch'ing-shih wen-ti* (now *Late Imperial China*) 3 (4): 63-81.

Reed, Bradly. 2000. *Talons and Teeth: County Clerks and Runners in the Qing Dynasty.* Stanford, CA: Stanford University Press.

Richards, John F. 2003. *The Unending Frontier: An Environmental History of the Early Modern World.* Berkeley and Los Angeles: University of California Press.

Rowe, William. 1988. "Water Control and the Qing Political Process: The Fankou Dam Controversy, 1876-1883." *Modern China* 14 (4): 353-87.

–. 1990. "Success Stories: Lineage and Elite Status in Hanyang County, Hubei, c. 1368-1949." In *Chinese Local Elites and Patterns of Dominance*, ed. Joseph W. Esherick and Mary Backus Rankins, 51-81. Berkeley and Los Angeles: University of California Press.

Schoppa, Keith. 1989. *Xiang Lake: Nine Centuries of Chinese Life.* New Haven: Yale University Press.

Schultz, Theodore W. 1964. *Transforming Traditional Agriculture.* New Haven, CT: Yale University Press.

Scott, James. 1976. *The Moral Economy of the Peasant: Rebellion and Subsistence in Southeast Asia.* New Haven: Yale University Press.

Shepherd, John R. 1988. "Rethinking Tenancy: Explaining Spatial and Temporal Variation in Late Imperial and Republican China." *Comparative Studies in Society and History* 30 (3): 403-31.

Shi Quan. 1988. *Gudai Jingchu dili xintan* [New explorations into the ancient geography of Chu]. Wuhan: Wuhan daxue chubanshe.

Shi Youmin. 2001. "Qingdai Jiangxi xuetian de zudian xilun" [Analysis of the tenancy of school land in Jiangxi in the Qing]. *Nongye kaogu* [Agricultural archaeology] 1: 134-37.

Shi Zhihong. 2003. "Ershi shiji san si shi niandai Huabei pingyuan nongcun de zudian guanxi he guyong guanxi: Yi Hebei sheng Qingyuan xian si cun wei li" [Tenancy relationships and hiring relations on the North China Plain countryside in the 1930s and 1940s: The case of four villages in Qingyuan County, Hebei Province]. *Zhongguo jingji shi yanjiu* [Researches in Chinese Economic History] 1: 45-57.

Shu Hui, ed. 1896. *Jingzhou wancheng di xu zhi* [The sequel to the gazetteer of the Wancheng dike in Jingzhou]. N.p.

Shuili dianlibu shuiguansi kejisi, shuili shuidian kexue yanjiuyuan, eds. 1991. *Qingdai Changjiang liuyu xi'nan guoji heliu honglao dang'an shiliao* [Archival materials on flooding and water-logging of the Yangzi River and the international rivers in Southwestern China in the Qing dynasty]. Beijing: Zhonghua shuju.

Sima Qian. 1990 (Han). *Shiji (quanshu xinzhu)* [(New annotation of) records of the grand historian]. Xi'an: Sanqin chubanshe.

Skinner, G. William. 1964-65. "Marketing and Social Structure in Rural China." *Journal of Asian Studies* 24 (1): 3-43; (2): 195-228; (3): 363-99.

Smith, Adam. 1976. *The Wealth of Nations.* Vol. 1. Chicago: University of Chicago Press.

Song Ping'an. 1989. "Qingdai Jianghan pingyuan shuizaihai duoyuanhua tezheng pouxi" [Analysis of the multiple features of water calamities in the Jianghan Plain in the Qing]. *Nongye kaogu* 2: 249-54.

Song Xishang, ed. 1954. *Lidai zhishui wenxian* [Historical literature on water control]. Taipei: Zhonghua wenhua chuban shiye weiyuanhui.

Sui Hongming. 2005. *Qingmo minchu minshangshi xiguan diaocha zhi yanjiu* [Studies on the investigation of the customs of civilian and business affairs at the end of the Qing and the early Republic]. Beijing: Falü chubanshe.

Sun Fushi. 1939. *Yangzijiang zhi shuili* [Water conservancy along the Yangzi River]. Shanghai: Shangwu yinshuguan.

Tan Qixiang. 1962. "He yi Huanghe zai Dong Han yi hou hui chuxian yige changqi anliu de jumian: Cong lishi shang lunzheng Huanghe zhongyou de tudi heli liyong shi xiaomi xiayou shuihai de jueding xing yinsu" [Why the Yellow River had a long stable period after the eastern Han: On the rational use of land in the middle Yellow River valley as the decisive factor in preventing floods in the lower reaches]. *Xueshu yuekan* [Academic monthly] 2: 23-35.

—. 1987. "Yunmeng yu Yunmeng ze" [Yunmeng and Yunmeng marsh]. In *Changshui ji, II* [Collection of Tan Qixiang, II], 105-25. Beijing: Renmin chubanshe.

—. 1996 [1987]. *Zhongguo lishi dituji: Qing shiqi* [The historical atlas of China: The Qing dynasty period]. Beijing: Zhongguo ditu chubanshe.

Tan Tianxing. 1987. "Qing qianqi lianghu diqu liangshi chanliang wenti tantao" [On the yields of food grains in Hunan-Hubei in the early Qing]. *Zhongguo nongshi* 2: 29-37.

—. 1988. "Jian lun Qing qianqi lianghu diqu de liangshi shangpinhua" [Brief discussion of the commercialization of food grains in Hunan-Hubei in the early Qing]. *Zhongguo nongshi* 3: 60-68.

—. 1992. "Qing qianqi lianghu nongcun de zudian guanxi yu minfeng" [Tenancy relationships and local customs in the Hunan-Hubei countryside in the early Qing]. *Zhongguo nongshi* 3: 30-37.

Tan Zuogang. 1985. "Qingdai huguang yuantian de lan xing weiken ji qing zhengfu de duice" [The over-reclamation of *yuan* in Hunan and Hubei in the Qing and the governmental policies to deal with it]. *Zhongguo nongshi* 4: 41-47.

Tudi weiyuanhui, ed. 1937. *Quanguo tudi diaocha baogao gangyao* [Outline of the report on the Chinese land survey]. N.p.

Vermeer, Eduard B. 1988. *Economic Development in Provincial China: The Central Shaanxi since 1930*. Cambridge, UK: Cambridge University Press.

Wang Fengsheng. 1832. *Chubei Jianghan xuanfang beilan* [Guidelines for the diversion and protection of the Yangzi River and the Han River in Hubei]. N.p.

Wang Jialun, and Zhang Fang, eds. 1990. *Zhongguo nongtian shuili shi* [A history of farmland water conservancy in China]. Beijing: Nongye chubanshe.

Wang Jian'ge. 2009. *Chuantong shehui moqi Huabei de shengtai yu shehui* [Ecology and society in North China at the end of traditional society]. Beijing: Sanlian shudian.

Wang Lihua. 2000. *Zhonggu huabei yinshi wenhua de bianqian* [Changes in dietetic culture in medieval North China]. Beijing: Zhongguo shehui kexue chubanshe.

—. 2006. "Zhongguo shengtai shixue de sixiang kuangjia he yanjiu silu" [Theoretical frameworks and research methods of Chinese ecological historiography]. *Nankai xuebao* [Nankai journal (philosophy, literature and social science edition)] 2: 22-32.

—. ed. 2007. *Zhongguo lishi shang de huanjing yu shehui* [Environment and society in Chinese history]. Beijing: Sanlian shudian.

Wang Minfu, ed. 1989. *Hubei sheng Jingzhou diqu zonghe nongye quhua* [The comprehensive agricultural divisions of Jingzhou District, Hubei]. Wuhan: Hubei kexue jishu chubanshe.

Wang Pingsheng, ed. 2004. *Dongxihu shihua* [History of Dongxihu]. Wuhan: Wuhan chubanshe.

Wang Xingguang. 2004. *Shengtai huanjing bianqian yu Xiadai de xingqi tansuo* [Exploration of eco-environmental change and the rise of the Xia dynasty]. Beijing: Kexue chubanshe.

Wang Yeh-chien. 1973. *Land Taxation in Imperial China, 1750-1911*. Cambridge, MA: Harvard University Press.

Wang Yuhu. 1981. "Zhongguo nongye fazhan zhong de shui he lishi shang de nongtian shuili wenti" [Water in the development of Chinese agriculture and irrigation and water conservancy in history]. *Zhongguo nongshi* 1: 42-52.

Wen Huanran. 1995. *Zhongguo lishi shiqi zhiwu yu dongwu bianqian yanjiu* [Studies on historical changes of vegetation and animals in China]. Chongqing: Chongqing chubanshe.

Will, Pierre-Etienne. 1985. "State Intervention in the Administration of a Hydraulic Infrastructure: The Example of Hubei Province in Late Imperial Times." In *The Scope of State Power in China*, ed. Stuart Schram, 295-347. London: School of Oriental and African Studies.

Wittfogel, Karl August. 1957. *Oriental Despotism: A Comparative Study of Total Power*. New Haven, CT: Yale University Press.

Wong, R. Bin. 1997. *China Transformed: Historical Change and the Limits of European Experience*. Ithaca, NY: Cornell University Press.

World Commission on Environment and Development. 1987. *Our Common Future*. Oxford: Oxford University Press.

Wu Chen, ed. 1992. *Huabei pingyuan si wan nian lai ziran huanjing yanbian* [The evolution of the physical environment of the North China Plain in the past forty thousand years]. Beijing: Zhongguo kexue jishu chubanshe.

Wu Chuanren, Liu Hui, and Zhao Zhijun. 2010. "Cong Xiaogan Yejiamiao yizhi fuxuan jieguo tan Jianghan pingyuan shiqian nongye" [Discussion of prehistoric agriculture of Jianghan Plain from flotation results of Yejia Temple site in Xiaogan]. *Nanfang wenwu* [Relics from South] 4: 65-69 [64].

Wu Liangkai, ed. 1995. *Qingdai Hubei nongye jingji yanjiu* [Studies on the agrarian economy of Hubei in the Qing dynasty]. Wuhan: Huazhong ligong daxue chubanshe.

Wu Miao. 2007. *Juelie: Xin nongcun de guojia jian'gou – Jianghan pingyuan zhongxing zhen de shijian biaoda 1949-1978* [Rupture: Nation making in the new countryside: Its practical expression in Zhongxing Township in the Jianghan Plain, 1949-1978]. Beijing: Zhongguo shehui kexue chubanshe.

Wu Qi. 1988. "Qingdai Huguang cao e bianxi" [Discussion of the amount of the grain tribute of Hubei and Hunan in the Qing]. *Zhongguo nongshi* 3: 40-44.

–. 2008. "Qingdai Hubei jindu jiqi yunying guanli" [The ferries of Hubei and their operation and management in the Qing]. *Jianghan luntan* [Jianghan tribune] 1: 83-89.

Wu Xianming. 1982. "Tianhu yuan yi an shimo ji" [The whole story of the case of Tianhu yuan]. *Hubei wenshi ziliao* 6: 171-79.

Wu Zhongbi, ed. 1982. *Jiangling Fenghuangshan 168 hao mu xihan gushi yanjiu* [Studies on an ancient corpse in no.168 tomb of the western Han dynasty, Fenghuang Mountain, Jiangling]. Beijing: Wenwu chubanshe.

Wuchang xian. 1938. *Hubei sheng nongcun diaocha baogao 1* [Report of a rural survey of Hubei. Vol. 1]. Compiled and published by the Department of Statistics, Office of Secretariat, Government of Hubei.

Xia Mingfang. 2000. *Minguo shiqi ziran zaihai yu xiangcun shehui* [Natural disasters and rural society in the Republican era]. Beijing: Zhonghua shuju.

–. 2001. "Dui ziran zaihai yu jiu Zhongguo nongcun diquan fenpei zhidu xianghu guanxi de zai sikao" [Rethinking the relationship between natural calamities and the distribution of landownership rights in Republican China]. In *Ziran zaihai yu Zhongguo shehui lishi jiegou* [Natural calamities and the structure of Chinese society and history], ed. Fudan daxue lishi dili yanjiu zhongxin, 295-336. Shanghai: Fudan daxue chubanshe.

Xiangdi cheng'an [Records on the Han River dikes]. 1969 [Qing]. Reprint. Taipei: Wenhai chubanshe.

Xiong Daorui, ed. N.d. *Hubei tianfu gaiyao* [Outline of the land tax of Hubei]. Hankou: Xinchang yinshuguan.

Xu Daofu, ed. 1983. *Zhongguo jindai nongye shengchan ji maoyi tongji ziliao* [Statistical data on agricultural production and trade in modern China]. Shanghai: Shanghai renmin chubanshe.

Xu Dixin and Wu Chengming, eds. 2000. *Chinese Capitalism, 1522-1840.* Trans. Li Zhengde, Liang Miaoru, and Li Siping. New York: St. Martin's Press.

Xu Kaixi. 1990. "Jindai Jing-Sha diqu zhimianye de fazhan he yanbian" [The development and change in cotton farming in the area of Jingzhou and Shashi in modern times]. *Jingzhou shizhuan xuebao* [Journal of Jingzhou Normal College] 3: 70-75.

—. 1991. "Jindai Hubei zhimianye chutan" [Preliminary discussion of cotton production in modern Hubei]. *Zhongguo nongshi* 2: 100-7.

Xu Renzhang, and Yang Mingli. 1989. "Jianghan pingyuan huqu shengtai nongye tidu kaifa moshi chutan" [Preliminary study of the developmental model of ecological agriculture in the lake area of the Jianghan Plain]. *Zhongnan caijing daxue xuebao* [Journal of Zhongnan University of Finance and Economics] 6: 71-74 [50].

Xu xingshui jinjian [The sequel of the golden guidance of inland navigation]. 1937 [1831]. Shanghai: Shangwu yinshuguan.

Yang Guo, and Chen Xi. 2008. *Jingji kaifa yu huanjing bianqian yanjiu: Song Yuan Ming Qing shiqi de Jianghan pingyuan* [Studies on economic development and environmental change: The Jianghan Plain in the Song-Yuan-Ming-Qing period]. Wuhan: Wuhan daxue chubanshe.

Yao Hanyuan. 1987. *Zhongguo shuili shi gangyao* [Essentials of the history of water conservancy in China]. Beijing: Shuili dianli chubanshe.

Yin Lingling. 2000. "Mingdai Dongting hu diqu de yuye jingji" [The fishing economy of the Lake Dongting area in the Ming]. *Zhongguo nongshi* 1: 48-56.

—. 2001a. "Mingdai Hubei diqu de yuye jingji: Yi Jingzhou, Mianyang, Anlu diqu weili" [The fishing economy of Hubei in the Ming: Focus on areas of Jingzhou, Mianyang and Anlu]. *Nongye kaogu* 1: 252-59.

—. 2001b. "Shehui jingji jiegou de zhuanhuan yu honglao zaihai: Yi Ming Qing shiqi lianghu pingyuan wei zhongxin" [The transformation of the socio-economic structure and floods: The Hubei-Hunan Plain in the Ming-Qing era]. In Fudan daxue lishi dili yanjiu zhongxin, ed., *Ziran zaihai yu Zhongguo shehui lishi jiegou* [Natural Calamities and the Structure of Chinese Society and History], 400-20. Shanghai: Fudan daxue chubanshe.

—. 2004. *Ming Qing Changjiang zhongxiayou yuye jingji yanjiu* [Studies of the fishing economy of the middle and lower Yangzi valley in the Ming and Qing dynasties]. Ji'nan: Qilu shushe.

—. 2008. *Ming Qing lianghu pingyuan de huanjing bianqian yu shehui yingdui* [Environmental change and social response in the Hubei-Hunan Plain in the Ming and Qing dynasties]. Shanghai: Shanghai renmin chubanshe.

Yingcheng xian. 1938. *Hubei sheng nongcun diaocha baogao* 4 [Report of a rural survey of Hubei. Vol. 4]. Compiled and published by the Department of Statistics, Office of the Secretariat, Government of Hubei.

Yongzheng zhupi yuzhi [The Youngzheng emperor's vermilion endorsements and edicts]. 1965 (reprint). Taipei: Wenhai chubanshe.

You Xiuling. 1995. *Zhongguo daozuo shi* [The history of rice cultivation in China]. Beijing: Zhongguo nongye chubanshe.

Yu Changlie. 1999 [1840]. *Chubei shuili difang jiyao* [Important notes on water conservancy and dike systems in Hubei]. Wuhan: Hubei renmin chubanshe.

Yuan Zhiqun. 1978. *Zai lun Jianghan pingyuan ji Dongting huqu da gaizao* [Further arguments on the great transformation of the Jianghan Plain and the Lake Dongting Plain]. N.p.

Yunmeng xian. 1938. *Hubei sheng nongcun diaocha baogao 2* [Report of a rural survey of Hubei. Vol. 2]. Compiled and published by the Department of Statistics, Office of the Secretariat, Government of Hubei.

Zai xu xingshui jinjian [The second sequel to the golden guidance of inland navigation]. 1970 [1942]. Taipei: Wenhai chubanshe.

Zeng Yuyu. 1898. *Hubei difang wenda* [Questions and answers regarding Hubei's dikes]. N.p.

Zeng Zhaoxiang, ed. 1984-87. *Hubei jindai jingji maoyi ziliao xuanji, 1840-1949, 1-5* [Selected historical sources of economy and trade in modern Hubei, 1840-1949]. N.p.

Zhang Guowang. 2003. "Jinnian lai Zhongguo huanjing shi yanjiu zongshu" [Review of recent studies on Chinese environmental history]. *Zhongguo shi yanjiu dongtai* [Trends of recent research on the history of China] 3: 12-17.

Zhang Guoxiong. 1989. "Jianghan pingyuan yuantian de tezheng jiqi zai Ming Qing shiqi de fazhan yanbian" [The features of *yuan* in the Jianghan Plain and their development and change in the Ming-Qing era]. *Nongye kaogu* 1: 227-33; 2: 238-48.

–. 1993. "Ming Qing shiqi lianghu waiyun liangshi zhi guocheng, jiegou, diwei kaocha: 'Huguang shu tianxia zu' yanjiu zhi er" [An examination of the process, structure, and position of the export of Hunan-Hubei's food grains in the Ming-Qing era: Studies on 'Huguang shu tianxia zu,' no.2]. *Zhongguo nongshi* 3: 40-46.

–. 1994a. "Ming Qing shiqi lianghu kaifa yu huanjing bianqian chuyi" [A preliminary discussion of the opening of Hunan-Hubei and environmental change in the Ming-Qing period]. *Zhongguo lishi dili luncong* 2: 127-45.

–. 1994b. "'Huguang shu tianxia zu' de neiwai tiaojian fenxi" [An analysis of the internal and external conditions of "Huguang shu tianxia zu"]. *Zhongguo nongshi* 3: 22-30.

–. 1995. *Ming Qing shiqi de lianghu yimin* [Immigration into Hunan and Hubei in Ming and Qing times]. Xi'an: Shaanxi renmin jiaoyu chubanshe.

Zhang Jianmin. 1984. "Qingdai Hubei de honglao zaihai" [Flooding and waterlogging in Hubei in the Qing dynasty]. *Jianghan luntan* 10: 66-72.

–. 1987a. "Qingdai Jianghan-Dongting huqu diyuan nongtian de fazhan jiqi zonghe kaocha" [The development of *yuan* farmland in the Jianghan-Dongting area in the Qing and a comprehensive examination of it]. *Zhongguo nongshi* 2: 72-88.

–. 1987b. "'Huguang shu tianxia zu' shulun – jian ji Ming Qing shiqi Changjiang yan an de miliang liutong" [On "Huguang shu tianxia zu" and a discussion of the circulation of food grains along the Yangzi River in the Ming-Qing era]. *Zhongguo nongshi* 4: 54-61.

–. 1994. "Mingdai Huguang renkou bianqian lun" [On the demographic changes in Hunan and Hubei in the Ming dynasty]. *Jingji pinglun* [Economic review] 2: 82-89.

–. 1998. "Mingdai Hubei de yugong yuke yu yuye" [Fishing tribute, the fishing tax, and fishery in Hubei in the Ming]. *Jianghan luntan* 5: 45-49.

–. 1999. *Hubei tongshi: Ming Qing juan* [A comprehensive history of Hubei: The Ming and Qing]. Wuhan: Huazhong shifan daxue chubanshe.

–. 2001. "Ming Qing shiqi de honglao zaihai yu Jianghan pingyuan nongcun shenghuo" [Rural life and floods and waterloggings in the Jianghan Plain in the Ming-Qing era]. In *Ziran zaihai yu Zhongguo shehui lishi jiegou* [Natural calamities and the structure of Chinese society and history], ed. Fudan daxue lishi dili yanjiu zhongxin, 355-78. Shanghai: Fudan daxue chubanshe.

Zhang Jiayan. 1991. "Qingdai Jianghan pingyuan shuidao shengchan xiangxi" [A detailed analysis of the production of rice in the Jianghan Plain in the Qing dynasty]. *Zhongguo nongshi* 2: 25-33 [17].

–. 1992a. "Ming Qing Jianghan pingyuan de yimin jiqi jieduan xing renkou zengzhang" [Immigration and the periodic increases of population in the Jianghan Plain in Ming-Qing times]. *Zhongguo shehui jingjishi yanjiu* [Journal of Chinese social and economic history] 1: 38-45, 95.

–. 1992b. "Ming Qing Jianghan pingyuan nongye jingji fazhan de diqu tezheng" [The localized features of the development of agricultural economy in the Jianghan Plain, 1368-1911]. *Zhongguo nongshi* 2: 47-59.

–. 1993. "Jianghan pingyuan Qingdai zhonghouqi honglao zaihai yanjiu zhong ruogan wenti chuyi" [Some issues in the study of floods and waterlogging on the Jianghan Plain in the middle and late Qing]. *Zhongguo nongshi* 3: 75-83.

–. 1995. "Ming Qing Jianghan pingyuan de nongye kaifa dui shangren huodong he shizhen fazhan de yingxiang" [The effect of agricultural development in the Jianghan Plain on merchant activities and township development, 1368-1911]. *Zhongguo nongshi* 4: 40-48.

–. 1996. "Ming Qing Changjiang sanjiaozhou diqu yu lianghu pingyuan nongcun jingji jiegou yanbian tanyi: cong 'Su Hu shu, tianxia zu' dao 'Huguang shu, tianxia zu'" [Studies of the differences in the changes of the rural economic structure between the Hunan-Hubei Plain and the Yangzi Delta, 1368-1911: From "Su Hu shu, tianxia zu" to "Huguang shu, tianxia zu"]. *Zhongguo nongshi* 3: 62-69, 91.

–. 1997. "Shinian lai lianghu diqu ji Jianghan pingyuan Ming Qing jingjishi yanjiu zongshu" [A review of research in the past ten years on the economic history of Hunan-Hubei and the Jianghan Plain in the Ming-Qing era]. *Zhongguo shi yanjiu dongtai* 1: 2-11.

–. 2001. "Qingdai Jianghan pingyuan yuantian nongye jingji texing fenxi" [Analyzing the features of the agrarian economy of the *yuan* in the Jianghan Plain in the Qing]. *Zhongguo shi yanjiu* [Journal of Chinese historical studies] 1: 133-42.

–. 2009. "Who Owned More Land? Reappraising Landownership in Pre-1949 China: A Case Study of the Jianghan Plain." *Chinese Historical Review* 2: 178-207.

–. 2013. "Organized Violent Conflicts over Water Control in Rural China: the Jianghan Plain, 1839-1979." *Rural China* 10 (1): 129-58.

Zhang Xiaoye. 2005. "Ming Qing shiqi quyu shehui zhong de minshi fa zhixu: Yi Hubei Hanchuan Diaocha Huangshi de hu'an wei zhongxin" [The civil law order in local society during the Ming-Qing period: Centred on the Huang family's "Lake Case," Hanchuan, Hubei], *Zhongguo shehui kexue* [Social sciences in China] 6: 189-201.

Zhang Xiugui, and Zuo Peng. 2001. "Ming Qing shiqi de honglao zaihai yu Jianghan shehui" [Flooding and waterlogging and Jianghan society in the Ming-Qing era]. In *Ziran zaihai yu Zhongguo shehui lishi jiegou* [Natural calamities and the structure of Chinese society and history], ed. Fudan daxue lishi dili yanjiu zhongxin, 379-99. Shanghai: Fudan daxue chubanshe.

Zhang Youyi, ed. 1957. *Zhongguo jindai nongye shi ziliao* 2 [Data on the agricultural history of modern China. Vol. 2]. Beijing: Sanlian shudian.

–. 1988. "Ben shiji er san shi niandai Woguo diquan fenpei de zai guji" [A re-estimation of the distribution of Chinese landownership rights in the 1920s-1930s]. *Zhongguo shehui jingjishi yanjiu* 2: 3-10.

Zhao Gang. 1994. "Shengtai bianqian de tongji fenxi" [Statistical analysis of ecological change]. *Zhongguo nongshi* 4: 22-29 [79].

Zhao Gang, and Chen Zhongyi. 1982. *Zhongguo tudi zhidu shi* [A history of the land system of China]. Taipei: Lianjing chuban shiye gongsi.

Zheng Zhizhang. 1986. "Ming Qing shiqi Jiangnan de dizulü he dixilü" [Rental rates and interest rates of land in the Yangzi delta in the Ming-Qing era]. *Zhongguo shehui jingjishi yanjiu* 3: 42-52.

Zhong Xin. 1936. *Yangzijiang shuili kao* [A survey of water conservancy along the Yangzi River]. Shanghai: Shangwu yinshuguan.

Zhongguo diyi lishi danganguan, and Zhongguo shehui kexueyuan lishi yanjiusuo, eds. 1982. *Qingdai dizu boxue xingtai* [Formation of rent exploitation in the Qing dynasty]. Beijing: Zhonghua shuju.

—. 1988. *Qingdai tudi zhanyou guanxi yu diannong kangzu douzheng* [Landownership and rent resistance in the Qing]. Beijing: Zhonghua shuju.

Zhongguo kexueyuan dili yanjiusuo, changjiang shuili shuidian kexue yanjiuyuan, changjiang hangdaoju guihua sheji yanjiusuo. 1985. *Changjiang zhongxiayou hedao texing jiqi yanbian* [The features and changes of the river course of the middle and lower valley of the Yangzi River]. Beijing: Kexue chubanshe.

Zhongguo nongye baike quanshu: Nongye lishi juan [Agricultural encyclopedia of China: Agricultural history]. 1995. Beijing: Nongye chubanshe.

Zhongguo renmin daxue Qing shi yanjiu suo, dang'an xi Zhongguo zhengzhi zhidu shi jiaoyanshi, eds. 1979. *Kang Yong Qian shiqi chengxiang renmin fankang douzheng ziliao* [I] [Data on people's resistance and struggle in the period 1662 to 1796 (I)]. Beijing: Zhonghua shuju.

Zhongguo shuili shigao 3 [Draft history of water conservancy in China. Vol. 3]. 1989. Beijing: Shuili dianli chubanshe.

Zhongguo tudi renkou zudian zhidu zhi tongji fenxi [Statistics and analysis of the Chinese population, land and tenancy relationships]. 1978 (reprint). Taipei: Huashi chubanshe.

Zhou Fengqin. 1986. "Jingjiang jin 5000 nian lai hongshui wei bianqian de chubu tantao" [A preliminary discussion of the changes in the high water level of the Jing River in the past 5,000 years]. *Lishi dili* [Historical geography] 4: 46-53.

Zhou Qiong. 2007. *Qingdai Yunnan zhangqi yu shengtai bianqian yanjiu* [Studies on miasma and ecological change in Yunnan in the Qing dynasty]. Beijing: Zhongguo shehui kexue chubanshe.

Zhou Qiren. 2000. "Population Pressure on Land in China: The Origins at the Village and Household Level, 1900-1950." PhD diss., University of California, Los Angeles.

Zhu Kezhen. 1972. "Zhongguo jin wu qiannian lai qihou bianqian de chubu yanjiu" [Preliminary investigations into the changes in China's climate during the past five thousand years]. *Kaogu xuebao* [Acta archaeologica sinica] 1: 15-38.

Index

Contemporary Chinese Studies

Emily M. Hill, *Smokeless Sugar: The Death of a Provincial Bureaucrat and the Construction of China's National Economy*

Kimberley Ens Manning and Felix Wemheuer, eds., *Eating Bitterness: New Perspectives on China's Great Leap Forward and Famine*

Helen M. Schneider, *Keeping the Nation's House: Domestic Management and the Making of Modern China*

James A. Flath and Norman Smith, eds., *Beyond Suffering: Recounting War in Modern China*

Elizabeth R. VanderVen, *A School in Every Village: Educational Reform in a Northeast China County, 1904-31*

Norman Smith, *Intoxicating Manchuria: Alcohol, Opium, and Culture in China's Northeast*

Juan Wang, *Merry Laughter and Angry Curses: The Shanghai Tabloid Press, 1897-1911*

Richard King, *Milestones on a Golden Road: Writing for Chinese Socialism, 1945-80*

David Faure and Ho Ts'ui-P'ing, eds., *Chieftains into Ancestors: Imperial Expansion and Indigenous Society in Southwest China*

Yunxiang Gao, *Sporting Gender: Women Athletes and Celebrity-Making during China's National Crisis, 1931-45*

Peipei Qiu, *Chinese Comfort Women: Testimonies from Imperial Japan's Sex Slaves*

Julia Kuehn, Kam Louie, and David M. Pomfret, eds., *Diasporic Chineseness after the Rise of China: Communities and Cultural Production*

Bridie Andrews, *The Making of Modern Chinese Medicine, 1850-1960*

Kelvin E.Y. Low, *Remembering the Samsui Women: Migration and Social Memory in Singapore and China*